W9-CBU-726

ALSO BY JOHN MACK FARAGHER

Women and Men on the Overland Trail

Sugar Creek: Life on the Illinois Prairie

Rereading Frederick Jackson Turner: "The Significance of the Frontier in American History" and Other Essays

DANIEL BOONE

The Life and Legend of an American Pioneer

John Mack Faragher

A HOLT PAPERBACK
Henry Holt and Company New York

Holt Paperbacks
Henry Holt and Company, LLC
Publishers since 1866
175 Fifth Avenue
New York, New York 10010
www.henryholt.com

A Holt Paperback® and ® are registered trademarks
of Henry Holt and Company, LLC.

Copyright © 1992 by John Mack Faragher
All rights reserved.
Distributed in Canada by H. B. Fenn and Company Ltd.

Grateful acknowledgment is made to the following for permission
to reprint previously published material:

"Boone" by Susan Mitchell from *New American Poets of the 80s*,
Jack Myers and Roger Weingarten, eds. (Green Harbor, Mass.:
Wampeter Press, 1984)

"The Grave of Daniel Boone" from *Stories That Could Be True*
by William Stafford (New York: Harper and Row, 1977)

Library of Congress Cataloging-in-Publication Data
Faragher, John Mack.
Daniel Boone: the life and legend of an American pioneer /
John Mack Faragher.—1st ed.
p. cm.
Includes index.
ISBN-13: 978-0-8050-3007-5
ISBN-10: 0-8050-3007-7
1. Boone, Daniel, 1734–1820. 2. Pioneers—Kentucky—Biography.
3. Kentucky—Biography. 4. Frontier and pioneer life—Kentucky.
I. Title.
F454.B66F37 1992
976.9'02'092—dc20 92-21873
[B] CIP

Henry Holt books are available for special promotions and
premiums. For details contact: Director, Special Markets.

Originally published in hardcover in 1992 by Henry Holt and Company

First Holt Paperbacks Edition 1993

Designed by Paula Russell Szafranski
Cartography by Jeffrey L. Ward

Printed in the United States of America
D 40 39 38

To Robert V. Hine and Howard R. Lamar

Contents

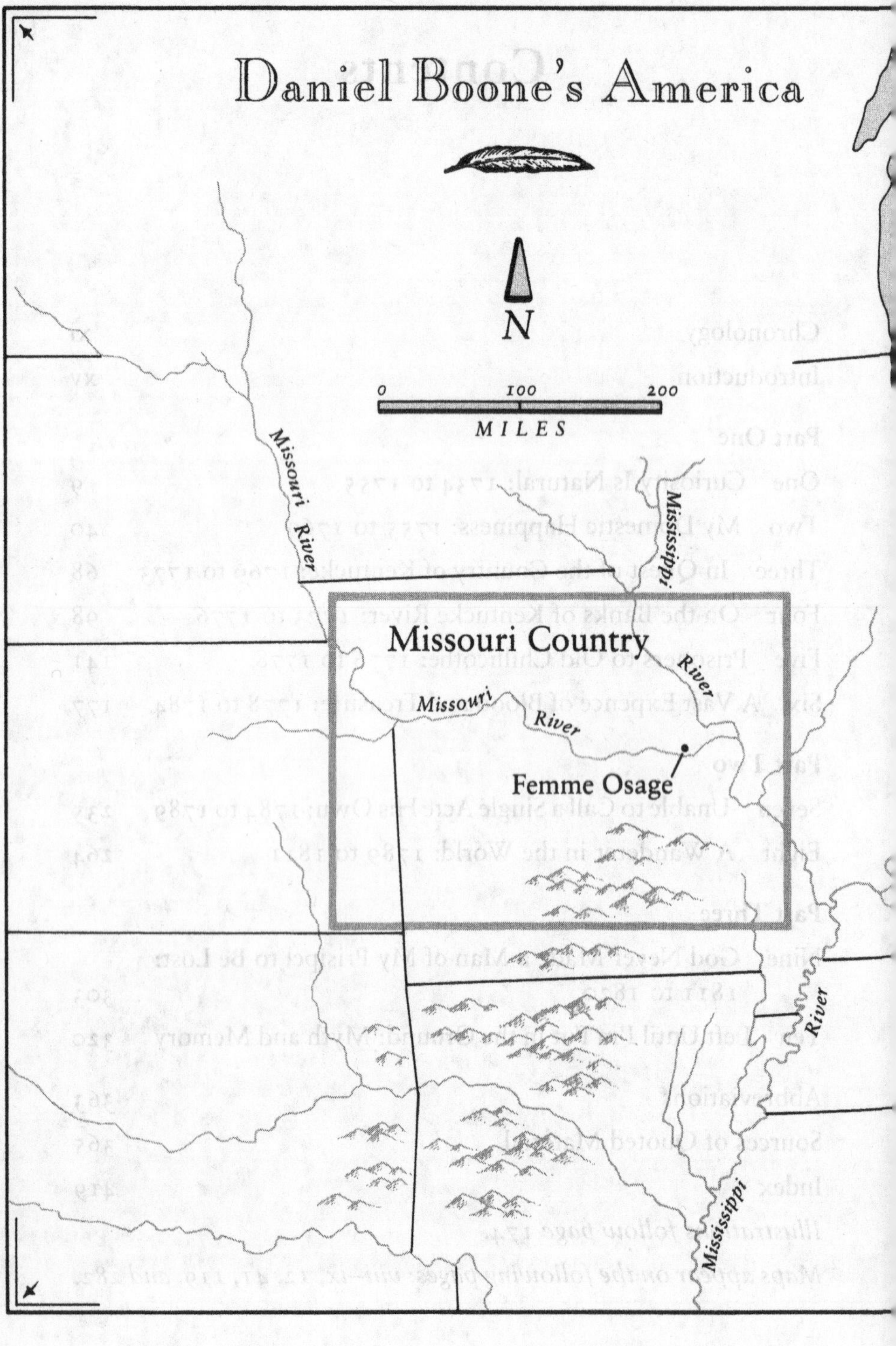

Daniel Boone's America
N
0
100
200
MILES
Missouri River
Mississippi River
Missouri Country
Missouri River
Femme Osage
River
Mississippi

Lake Huron
Lake Ontario
Lake Erie
Detroit
Quaker Homeland
Exeter
Pittsburgh
Kentucke
Ohio River
Ohio River
Richmond
Boonesborough
Yadkin River
Forks of the Yadkin
Backcountry
Atlantic Ocean

Chronology

1713 Boone's father, Squire Boone, arrives in Philadelphia from England.

1720 Squire Boone and Sarah Morgan marry in the Friends' meetinghouse in Gwynedd, Pennsylvania.

1731 Boone's parents relocate to the upper Schuylkill River valley.

1734 Born in Exeter township, near present Reading, on October 22.

1747 Begins hunting with his first gun.

1748 Friends' meeting expels Squire Boone after his son Israel marries a "worldling."

1750 Family leaves Pennsylvania for the western country; Boone engages in his first "long hunt."

1751 Family settles in Rowan County, North Carolina, on the Yadkin River; Boone takes up hunting as his business.

1755 French and Indian War begins; Boone with Braddock's army during the disastrous defeat near Pittsburgh.

1756 Marries Rebecca Bryan on August 14; they soon settle in Rowan County.

1757 James Boone born May 3.

1759 Israel Boone born January 25; during the Cherokee War, family flees to Culpeper County, Virginia.
1760 Susannah Boone born November 2; Boone first crosses the Blue Ridge during his winter hunt.
1761 Participates in the campaigns against Cherokees.
1762 Jemima Boone born October 4; the Boones return to Rowan County.
1765 Father Squire Boone dies; Boone explores the Florida country with an eye to moving there.
1766 Levina Boone born March 23; moves family to a site farther west, near present Wilkesboro, North Carolina.
1767 Reaches Kentucky and hunts along the Big Sandy River.
1768 Rebecca Boone born May 26; Regulator rebellion in North Carolina.
1769 With five others leaves for a long hunt in Kentucky on May 1; captured by Shawnees on December 22; Daniel Morgan Boone born December 23.
1771 Boone returns home after two years in Kentucky.
1773 Jesse Bryan born May 23; Boone leads party of family and friends to Kentucky, but they are turned back at Cumberland Gap by an Indian attack that kills his eldest son, James, on October 9.
1774 Sent by Virginia authorities to warn Kentucky surveyors of pending war with Shawnees; leads defense of Clinch River settlements during Dunmore's War.
1775 For the Transylvania Company, leads party cutting the Wilderness Road to Kentucky in March; founds Boonesborough in the face of Shawnee attacks; brings family to Kentucky in September.
1776 Leads rescue of daughter Jemima and Callaway girls from Shawnees in July; copy of Declaration of Independence reaches Boonesborough in August.
1777 Wounded during a Shawnee attack on Boonesborough in April.
1778 Boone and his men captured by Shawnees while making salt on February 8; he escapes in June; siege of Boonesborough, September 7–18; acquitted of charges of collaboration with British in October; rejoins Rebecca and children, who had returned to North Carolina.

1779 Leads a large party of emigrants to Kentucky in September; settles Boone's Station, north of the Kentucky River.

1780 Robbed of a large sum of money entrusted to him to purchase land warrants in Virginia; Nathan Boone born March 3; participates in attack on Shawnee towns in Ohio; brother Edward killed by Shawnees in October.

1781 Takes elected seat in Virginia assembly in April; captured by invading British forces in June, but soon released; visits family in Pennsylvania in October.

1782 One of the commanding officers at the Kentuckians' defeat by Indians at the Blue Licks, where son Israel is killed, August 19; in command of a company that attacks Shawnee towns in November.

1783 Relocates family to Limestone, on the Ohio River; takes up tavern keeping, surveying, and land speculating.

1784 *The Adventures of Col. Daniel Boon* by John Filson published on Boone's fiftieth birthday.

1785 Retains an attorney to represent him in numerous lawsuits over land.

1786 Commands an attack on Shawnee towns in October.

1787 Helps negotiate prisoner exchange with Shawnees at Limestone in August; takes seat in Virginia assembly in October; visits Pennsylvania relatives over the winter.

1789 With Rebecca and youngest children leaves Limestone and relocates at Point Pleasant, farther up the Ohio River.

1791 Serves once again in the Virginia assembly; wins contract to supply militia companies in western Virginia.

1792 Dispute over supply contracts leads to his abandonment of business and return to full-time hunting; with Rebecca, soon moves to a cabin near present Charleston, West Virginia.

1795 To be nearer family, relocates to a cabin on Brushy Fork in Kentucky.

1797 Son Daniel Morgan Boone scouts land in Spanish Missouri; governor invites Boones to emigrate.

1798 Kentucky assembly names county after Boone; Mason County issues warrant for his arrest for debt; leaves Brushy Fork for a cabin at the mouth of Little Sandy River on the Ohio.

1799 Leads extended family from Kentucky to Femme Osage country in Missouri; appointed "syndic" of district by Spanish governor; daughter Susannah dies of "bilious fever."

1803 Seriously injured in hunting accident; relocates with Rebecca to cabin on the farm of son Nathan; daughter Levina dies; Louisiana Purchase.

1805 Sons open salt works at Boone's Lick in central Missouri; daughter Rebecca dies; Boone nearly killed in fall through the ice of the Missouri River in December.

1806 Appears before the Federal Land Commission, seeking confirmation of his Spanish land grant.

1809 Gets word of rejection of his Spanish land grant; works on petitions to Congress.

1813 Rebecca dies March 18.

1814 Congress grants Boone a tract of Missouri land.

1815 Grandson James Callaway killed in Indian ambush; reportedly goes to Kentucky to settle old debts.

1817 Falls sick during long hunt, his last.

1820 Dies on September 26; buried near Rebecca in the cemetery near Jemima's farm.

1845 A delegation from Kentucky disinters the Boone graves and reburies remains in Frankfort, Kentucky.

Introduction

In the centennial year of Daniel Boone's birth, 1834, old Simon Kenton was asked for his opinion of his late frontier comrade. Lately Boone's reputation had been undergoing harsh criticism. One popular writer of "border history" condemned Boone's leadership during the siege of Boonesborough in 1778, the central episode in claims for his status as the first hero of the American frontier. Acting on Boone's advice, the Kentucky settlers had sent their leaders out to treat with the Shawnees, and at the conclusion of those negotiations there was a confrontation with the Indians that nearly overpowered the Americans. Kenton knew of the complaints, but he would have nothing to do with criticism of Boone. "He acted with wisdom in that matter," declared the old scout. Kenton was a quick-tempered man, but in his last years he resigned himself to the inevitability of revisionist shifts in opinion. He summed up his feelings with a rhetorical shrug of his shoulders: "They may say what they please of Daniel Boone."

Kenton's remark is an appropriate epigraph for the historical materials documenting Daniel Boone's life. They include the public record of the events in which he participated, the accounts of his contemporaries, and several important semiautobiographical narratives of his adventures. There are also letters and accounts written in his own hand in which his distinctive voice comes through loud and clear. But the bulk of the evidence is reminiscence and recollection gathered by nineteenth-century historians and antiquarians. Some people supplied eyewitness accounts, others hearsay information gained at second- or thirdhand. Some recalled relatively recent events, others a past reckoned not in years but in half centuries. Some testimony is clear and is easily corroborated, some is internally inconsistent and contradicted by other documents.

Much of this evidence is what might be called folklore; the facts come inextricably entwined with the legend. Realizing this, Boone's previous biographers sometimes repeated stories that were simply too good to ignore while simultaneously acknowledging problems of suspicious reliability, an understandable strategy, for if Boone's biography required absolute corroboration on all points, it would be thin indeed. I have taken a somewhat different approach, for the folkloric evidence offers more than simply an opportunity to reconstruct the facts of his life. The record of Daniel Boone largely consists of the stories of humble American men and women, written out laboriously with blunt pencils on scraps of paper, or told aloud in backwoods cabins or around campfires and taken down verbatim by antiquarian collectors. The materials for Boone's biography not only document the life of an American frontier hero but reveal the thoughts and feelings of the diverse peoples of the frontier. I have tried to indicate those points at which the evidence is suspect as fact, but I have nevertheless tried to take it seriously as lore. The things people choose to say about Boone provide clues to their own concerns. Backcountry Americans celebrated Boone as one of their own. He was a hero, but a hero of a new, democratic type, a man who did not tower above the people but rather exemplified their longings and, yes, their limitations. People may say what they please, as Simon Kenton put it, but why do they say the things they do?

I accumulated many obligations in the course of researching and writing this book. My greatest debt is to the librarians who provided me with the necessary primary materials and were invariably generous with their time and expertise. I especially want to thank the staffs of the Abingdon Public Library, Abingdon, Virginia; the Filson Club, Louisville, Kentucky; the Hamden Public Library, Hamden, Connecticut; Special Collections, the University of Kentucky Library, Lexington; the Kentucky Historical Society, Frankfort; the Massachusetts Historical Society, Boston; the Missouri Historical Society, Saint Louis; the New York State Library, Albany; the North Carolina Collection, Louis Round Wilson Library, University of North Carolina, Chapel Hill; the Washington University Gallery of Art, St. Louis; the State Historical Society of Wisconsin, Madison; and Sterling Memorial Library, Yale University, New Haven. I also am endebted to the helpful people at the Daniel Boone Homestead, Birdsboro, Pennsylvania; the Daniel Boone Home, Defiance, Missouri; and Blue Licks State Park, Robertson County, Kentucky.

Mount Holyoke College made it possible for me to begin and complete this project with leaves from teaching responsibilities. I especially want to thank former Dean of Faculty Joseph J. Ellis and President Elizabeth Topham Kennan. The good people of Williston Memorial Library were patient with me under the difficult circumstances of a major rebuilding project, and Kuang-Tien Yao was enormously helpful in arranging for the loan of obscure and antique books. I also want to thank my colleagues in the Department of History, especially Robert M. Schwartz, who provided translations of French language documents, and Holly J. Sharac, who kept everything running.

A large number of people provided me with documents, articles, books, clippings, and helpful advice, including: Randall Andrae, Daniel Boone Home, Defiance, Missouri; Tom Appleton, Kentucky Historical Society; Stephen Aron, Princeton University; Charles G. Bowen, San Diego; Donald Eidson, Central Methodist College, Fayette, Missouri; Senator Wendall H. Ford; Etta M. Gheen, city clerk, Point Pleasant, West Virginia; Neal O. Hammon, Shelbyville, Kentucky; Elizabeth Hardy, Jacksonville, Illinois; Charles C. Hay III, Eastern Kentucky University; Ken Kamper, Boone-Durden Historical Society, Hazelwood, Missouri; James Klotter, Kentucky Historical Society; Mrs. J. Milton McGinnis, Shelby County Archives, Kentucky; Susan Neitlich, Hamden, Connecticut; Nancy O'Malley, University of Kentucky; and J. Gray Sweeney, Arizona State University. I owe special thanks to Charles

Grench, for first suggesting the idea of a biography, to Daniel J. Czitrom, for bringing the Draper Collection to my attention, to Gerard McCauley, for making the project possible, and to my editor William Strachan, for believing in this book. Raquel Jaramillo, art director at Henry Holt, arranged for Bryan Leister to paint the portrait of Boone at midlife for the cover. Sandra Dhols, who copyedited the manuscript, saved me from many errors. Stephen Aron, Daniel J. Czitrom, Joseph J. Ellis, Danny O. Faragher, Robert V. Hine, and Howard R. Lamar all read the final manuscript, and I benefited greatly from their insights and suggestions.

From near and afar my children communicated their support, as well as their worry about the number of hours I spent in my study, concerns that touched me deeply. My wife, Michele Hoffnung, accompanied me throughout this fascinating journey, on cold morning trips through narrow mountain valleys as well as long afternoons in stuffy archives. We shared Kentucky hot browns, spoonbread, and the most savory barbeque in the country and learned about a part of America that was new to us both. She listened to the entire manuscript and was, as always, my best critic. Robert V. Hine of the University of California, Riverside, and Howard R. Lamar of Yale University, my mentors in history, have continued to teach me how to look critically and imaginatively at the land and the people. I am honored to be counted among their students and friends, and to them I dedicate this book.

Part One

The dark cloud of war lifted momentarily from Kentucky in 1783, and after nearly ten bloody years the Revolution in the American West came to an inconclusive end. Daniel Boone first got word of the preliminary treaty between Britain and the United States from a messenger who rode over the mountains that spring with a badge on his hat inscribed "Peace." It turned out to be the wrong word, for after a brief respite, warfare along the Ohio River resumed and continued for another ten years as villages of Shawnees, Delawares, Mingos, and Miamis north of the Ohio remained determined to defend their country from invasion. But there was at least an end to major attacks on inland Kentucky stations and settlements, and American energies turned to pursuits other than war. Over the mountains and down the Ohio, pioneer men and women streamed in, adding their number to the twelve thousand who already had settled west of the Appalachians. Men opened the first commercial distilleries for the manufacture and sale of corn whiskey, the trustees of Transylvania Seminary in Lexington met to organize the first institution of higher education in the West, and politicians spoke of the possibility that Kentucky might break away from Virginia to become the fourteenth of the confederated states.

Daniel Boone turned fifty in 1783, and it was a year of transition for him as well. He and his wife, Rebecca Bryan Boone, would move their family to the Ohio River settlement of Limestone, one of the most important ports of entry for settlers, where he would set up as a trader and tavern keeper. Son of a yeoman farmer, Boone had grown up on the frontiers of Pennsylvania and North Carolina; he inherited a share in his father's patrimony but had never owned significant property. Now, as Kentucky moved into its second stage of development, he began to acquire vast sections of virgin real estate.

Boone's fiftieth year also marked the moment when his reputation leaped from local to national, even international, proportions. He had been a leader of the settlers' struggle against the Indian defense of their hunting grounds, and in the last years of the American Revolution the state of Virginia honored him with an appointment as lieutenant colonel of militia and his fellow citizens elected him to the state assembly. He was one of a number of Kentucky military heros, including James Harrod, Benjamin Logan, and George Rogers Clark, but alone among them his name would command world attention.

The man responsible for the sudden ascent of Boone's fame was John Filson, a thirty-year-old schoolmaster from Chester County, Pennsylvania. After spending the war teaching school near Wilmington, Delaware, Filson was caught up in the postwar excitement about the West and set out for Pittsburgh, where he booked passage down the Ohio on a barge and entered Kentucky in 1783. He was an unlikely pioneer, and he comes down to us a folk stereotype, the pedantic schoolmaster, a character perfected in Washington Irving's portrayal of Ichabod Crane. The stories people told about him made him seem the fool—tumbling clumsily off his wagon, being swindled in trade by an old trapper who passed off muskrats as beaver, the butt of crude frontier jokes and pranks.

"When I visited Kentucke," Filson later wrote, "I found it so far to exceed my expectations, although great, that I concluded it was a pity that the world had not adequate information of it. I conceived that a proper description, and map of it, were objects highly interesting to the United States." He loudly disclaimed any "lucrative motives" in this writing project but neglected to mention that before leaving Delaware he had converted his share of his late father's estate into depreciated currency, bought land warrants, and entered claims in Kentucky for more than twelve thousand acres. He possessed no talent for improving these holdings with an ax or plow, but with his pen he hoped to produce a book that would publicize the country and thereby increase the value of his investment. Like nearly everyone else in Kentucky, including Daniel Boone, Filson was speculating in land.

Filson immediately began a tour of the country, traveling from pioneer settlement to station, seeking out prominent men, interviewing them for his book. He was so exceedingly persistent in his inquiries, Kentuckians said, that the only sure way to get rid of him was to tell him all they knew. He could ask more questions and provide fewer answers, they complained, than anyone alive. But these men were happier to talk than they admitted. Filson found them "polite, humane, hospitable, and very complaisant." With the Revolution successfully concluded, the time was right to reflect on the past and anticipate the future. It was also a particularly auspicious time for Filson to meet Boone, attempting to settle into a position earned by years of struggle. Boone lived north of the Kentucky River in a crowded log cabin with his wife, children, and several cousins as well as a married daughter and her family; it was understandable if he looked forward to the opportunity for retreats to Filson's rooms, where he reflected on his Kentucky adventures for a sympathetic listener.

Boone had first crossed the mountains to the fabled land of Kentucky as a man in his mid-thirties. For fifteen years he labored to explore, settle, and defend this land, braving Indian warfare and captivity, suffering the loss of family and friends. It was a terrible struggle, but now he looked forward to prosperity in this land of abundance. Boone rambled, but as Filson accumulated the details, he began to sense dramatic possibilities in these stories that might transform his work into something more than simply the "compleat guide" he had at first envisioned writing. Over the next few months he completed a manuscript divided into two major sections. He first described Kentucky's geography, its rivers, soil, and climate, its flora, fauna, and curiosities, referring the reader to a detailed map he prepared with the close advice of Boone and other experienced surveyors and explorers. Kentucky, he concluded in the swollen prose of the promoter, was "the most extraordinary country that the sun enlightens with his celestial beams." He included a practical discussion of purchasing land and the prospects for trade and commerce. But in the second and more enduring section of the book he attempted something considerably more grand, transforming Boone's stories, taken down "from his mouth," into "The Adventures of Col. Daniel Boon."

Filson structured Boone's narrative to read like an epic. He begins with the perilous journey when Boone leaves home "to wander through the wilderness of America, in quest of the country of Kentucke," his language here recalling medieval legend. After crossing the mountains, Boone and one of his companions are taken prisoner by the Indians; Boone escapes, but the other man is killed. Left alone, Boone is nearly overwhelmed by "dreadful apprehensions." But one day, as he mounts a commanding summit and looks out over the land below, he is struck by the wonder of the landscape: "I surveyed the famous river Ohio that rolled in silent dignity, marking the western boundary of Kentucke with inconceivable grandeur. At a vast distance I beheld the mountains lift their venerable brows, and penetrate the clouds. All things were still. I kindled a fire near a fountain of sweet water, and feasted on the loin of a buck, which a few hours before I had killed." In this moment of epiphany and communion, Boone resolves to make the land his own. He returns to his family "with a determination to bring them as soon as possible to live in Kentucke, which I esteemed a second paradise, at the risk of my life and fortune."

His first attempt at emigration is turned back by an Indian attack that costs the life of his eldest son, but Boone finally succeeds in bringing his kin across the mountains, "my wife and daughter being the first white women that ever stood on the banks of Kentucke river." With other pioneers they establish the wilderness community of Boonesborough, but in the deadly struggle that is the central feature of heroic epic, Boone "passes through a scene of sufferings that exceeds description." Filson related a succession of thrilling episodes in which Boone rescues his daughter and two young girlfriends from Indian kidnappers; is captured by Indians but manages to escape to lead the defense of Boonesborough against savage siege; and suffers during an awful massacre in which more than sixty Kentucky fighters under his command, including his second-born son, are slaughtered in an Indian ambush. Only after General Clark rages across the Ohio with his army, destroying the native towns, are the Indians finally "made sensible of our superiority."

The narrative closes with Boone reflecting in the aftermath of the Revolution. "Now the scene is changed, peace crowns the sylvan shade," he says. "I now live in peace and safety, enjoying the sweets of liberty, and the bounties of Providence, with my once fellow-sufferers, in this delightful country, which I have seen purchased with a vast expence of blood and treasure." Filson emphasized the manner in which Boone's deeds were woven into the fabric of national destiny. The hero's apotheosis is virtuous, not by reaping personal reward but by the promise of Kentucky becoming "one of the most opulent and powerful states on the continent of North-America." "The love and gratitude of my country-men," says Filson's Boone, "I esteem a sufficient reward for all my toil and dangers." Throughout the struggle he has been "an instrument ordained to settle the wilderness."

Filson told Boone's story as romantic myth. In so doing he demonstrated his thorough familiarity with the perennials of colonial American literature—narratives of Indian warfare and captivity and journals of spiritual revelation and growth. Even more obvious is his debt to an ersatz Enlightenment philosophy of "natural man." Filson's Boone declaims: "Thus situated, many hundred miles from our families in the howling wilderness, I believe few would have equally enjoyed the happiness we experienced. I often observed to my brother, You see now how little nature requires to be satisfied. Felicity, the companion of content, is rather found in our own breasts than in the enjoyment of external things: And I firmly believe it requires but a little philosophy to make a man happy in whatsoever state he is."

In May of 1784 Filson left Kentucky to arrange for the publication of his manuscript in the East. The book, with the map attached and folded as the frontispiece, was issued by a printer in Wilmington, Delaware, in an edition of fifteen hundred copies. Filson announced the publication of *The Discovery, Settlement and Present State of Kentucke . . . To which is added An Appendix, Containing The Adventures of Col. Daniel Boon* on October 22, 1784—Boone's fiftieth birthday.

With interest in Kentucky running high, the first printing sold well enough, but Filson found no enthusiasm for a second edition. Eventually he returned to Kentucky, although he had no further connection with Boone, and tried fur trading, school teaching, and more land speculation, before being killed by Indians while working with a surveying party in 1788. But, unbeknownst to Filson, his book became a minor sensation in Europe, where intellectuals celebrated Boone as an American original, the "natural man." Less than a year following its initial American publication, the text was translated into French and published in Paris. Several months later it appeared in Frankfurt, and at least two more German editions soon followed. It was reprinted in England and Ireland in the 1790s. With no copyright laws in effect, neither Filson nor his estate realized anything from the sale of these foreign editions.

Boone thus achieved international fame, and he soon became a national hero as well, though in an abridgment of Filson's narrative that pared it of the philosophizing. In the summer of 1785 the printer John Trumbull, a member of the famous Connecticut family, printed a version that lopped off Filson's asides and conclusions, reducing its length by a third, and revised it to read like a diary of events. Trumbull's version emphasized action over thought, the struggle at the expense of the denouement. The following year Trumbull published his version as a little pamphlet, and it is fair to say that it has rarely been out of print in the more than two centuries since. During Boone's lifetime, when people spoke of reading his narrative, they invariably referred to Trumbull's Boone, not Filson's.

As for the original, critics have subjected it to a torrent of abuse. "Exaggerated and sophomorical," said one nineteenth-century biographer; "minor value as historical material," declared another. "The silly phrases and total disregard for what must have been the rude words of the old hunter," wrote a twentieth-century critic, "serve only, for the most part, to make it a keen disappointment to the interested reader." Although he claimed that the narrative was in the pioneer's own words, it is clear that Filson radically altered Boone's voice. These revisions could become ludicrous, as when the uneducated pioneer compares the rugged passes of the Appalachians to the ruins of the ancient cities of Persepolis and Palmyra. This language, insisted one of the pioneer's sons, was "none of Boone's," a truth readily apparent to anyone who reads the man's letters. A relative suggested that Boone's account had become "adulterated and tangled" in Filson's reworking. "If you had Boone's Naritive as he wrote it himself," he believed, "it would be plain and intillagible. Boone did not pen the errors himself."

Boone himself, however, offered no such apologies or complaints. With his fellow Kentuckians Levi Todd and James Harrod, he signed an endorsement of Filson's book and map, recommending them to the public as "exceeding good performances, containing as accurate a description of our country as we think can possibly be given." Other evidence confirms most of the details of Boone's life in Filson's text. Although Filson's limitations as an amanuensis are clear, *The Adventures of Col. Daniel Boon* is still best understood as a collaboration between the two men. Boone was never reluctant to complain about people who misrepresented his life or deeds, but for Filson's narrative he had nothing but praise. One of Boone's visitors watched "the old man's face brighten up" as he read passages of Filson's text aloud, and he "confirmed all that was there related of him." "All true! Every word true!" Boone reportedly exclaimed following one such reading. "Not a lie in it!"

CHAPTER ONE

Curiosity Is Natural

1734 to 1755

By the time he was fifteen, Daniel Boone had a reputation as one of the best hunters in the Pennsylvania countryside of his birth. An old folktale relates the boy's prowess. Boone and several of his friends are out hunting when suddenly they hear the piercing cry "from the throat of a ferocious panther." Looking up, they see it crouched in the branches above. The other boys flee in terror, but Daniel stands his ground, confidently levels his piece, and shoots the wildcat dead as it is about to spring upon him. Where did young Boone acquire this education in woodcraft? "Curiosity is natural to the soul of man"—with these words John Filson began Boone's narrative of 1784. Boone's was a curiosity that he fulfilled by striking out in new directions; certainly he did not acquire his skills from his emigrant family of English weavers.

Daniel's father, Squire Boone, came to America in 1713 when he was eighteen, with a brother and sister. The three of them were sent to reconnoiter the new American world by their father, George Boone, of the town of Bradninch, near Exeter, England. The Boones were members of the Society of Friends, and the young scouts went immediately to the town of Abington, twelve miles north of Philadelphia, where they had contacts among some of the recently arrived Quakers. Receiving favorable reports from his children, patriarch George Boone emigrated with the rest of the family four years later, and all of the Boones relocated ten miles to the northwest of Abington, where they "joined themselves to Gwynedd Meeting."

A few years later, in 1720, twenty-five-year-old Squire Boone declared his intention of marrying Sarah Morgan, five years his junior. After certifying Squire's "Cleanness from Other Women," an investigating committee of the local meeting approved the match and in September they were married "at a Solemn Assembly of ye People called Quakers." According to a contemporary, Daniel's father was a man of small stature, with a fair complexion, red hair, and blue-gray eyes; his mother was a large woman, strong and active, with dark eyes and black hair. Their firstborn was named for her mother; by the time Sarah Morgan was forty-six she had delivered a total of eleven children. Squire was a weaver, like his father, but with Sarah's help he also worked a tenant farm, raising subsistence crops and livestock.

In 1731 Squire and Sarah Boone moved their family to a location in the upper Schuylkill River valley known as "Oley," an Algonquian word for valley. Other Boones had settled there several years before, and the area had attracted Quakers as well as Swedes, Germans, and Scots-Irish. It was beautiful, gently rolling country covered by hardwood forests that opened to grassy meadows; the loamy soil took a plow gladly. Squire purchased 250 acres several miles south of the stone house of his father and with the assistance of kin and neighbors erected a one-room log cabin directly atop an outcropping of rock with a fresh spring. Eventually he enclosed the spring in a stone arch and laid a fine stone floor in the cellar. In this house, on the banks of Owatin Run, Daniel Boone was born on October 22, 1734.

As an Oley resident later remembered, the Boones were identifiable by their broad Cornish dialect and notable for their clannishness. Squire's farm was bounded on all but one side by the land of three brothers, and three others lived within a mile or two. His two sisters and their husbands were nearby as well. Daniel Boone later remembered how as a child he spent a great deal of time at the home of uncle John Webb, who would "greatly pet him." The Boones were local leaders. Grandfather George served for many years as justice of the peace, and when he became too old and frail to continue, the position passed to his oldest son, George, Jr. The Oley Quakers established a permanent monthly meeting, erecting a brownstone meetinghouse in 1737 on land donated by the Boones, just a mile or two from Daniel's boyhood home. Squire Boone became an overseer of the meetinghouse in 1739 and a few years later assumed responsibility as a trustee of the burying ground. When population growth led to the division of Oley township in 1741, the section in which the Boones resided was renamed Exeter, in honor of their English origins. Family life interpenetrated with civic life.

Like other families, of course, they had their conflicts with the Quaker meeting. Reading the Exeter minutes, nineteenth-century Boone biographer Lyman Draper found records of eighteenth-century Boones reproved for "belligerence" and "self-will," and the old Quaker mistress who showed Draper the manuscripts admitted that "strong drink, so common then, overcame one or more who had to be dealt with." She insisted, however, that "the Boones were active for good" and urged the historian to suppress any "sad stories" that might "annoy the very respectable family of Boones now living in this vicinity." More than a century after Daniel's family had left Exeter, community and family were still woven into a seamless fabric. And so it must have impressed the young boy, growing up amidst this close-knit network of kith and kin.

In his old age Boone repeated tales of his Pennsylvania childhood for the enjoyment of his grandchildren. These anecdotes constitute the first chapter of Boone's unwritten autobiography and offer the best explanation of how this first-generation American became the foremost pioneer of our history. In one tale, which refers to a period earlier than any of the others, Boone told of how his mother confined him to the house during an outbreak of smallpox. (This may have been during the widespread epidemic of 1738–39, which would have made him only four years old.) After a period of intolerable confinement, he and his six-year-old sister, Elizabeth, conspire "to take the smallpox, and when over it, be free to go where they pleased." That night they steal away to a neighbor's and climb into bed with young friends who had the disease. When, after a few days, he begins to show symptoms, his mother confronts him.

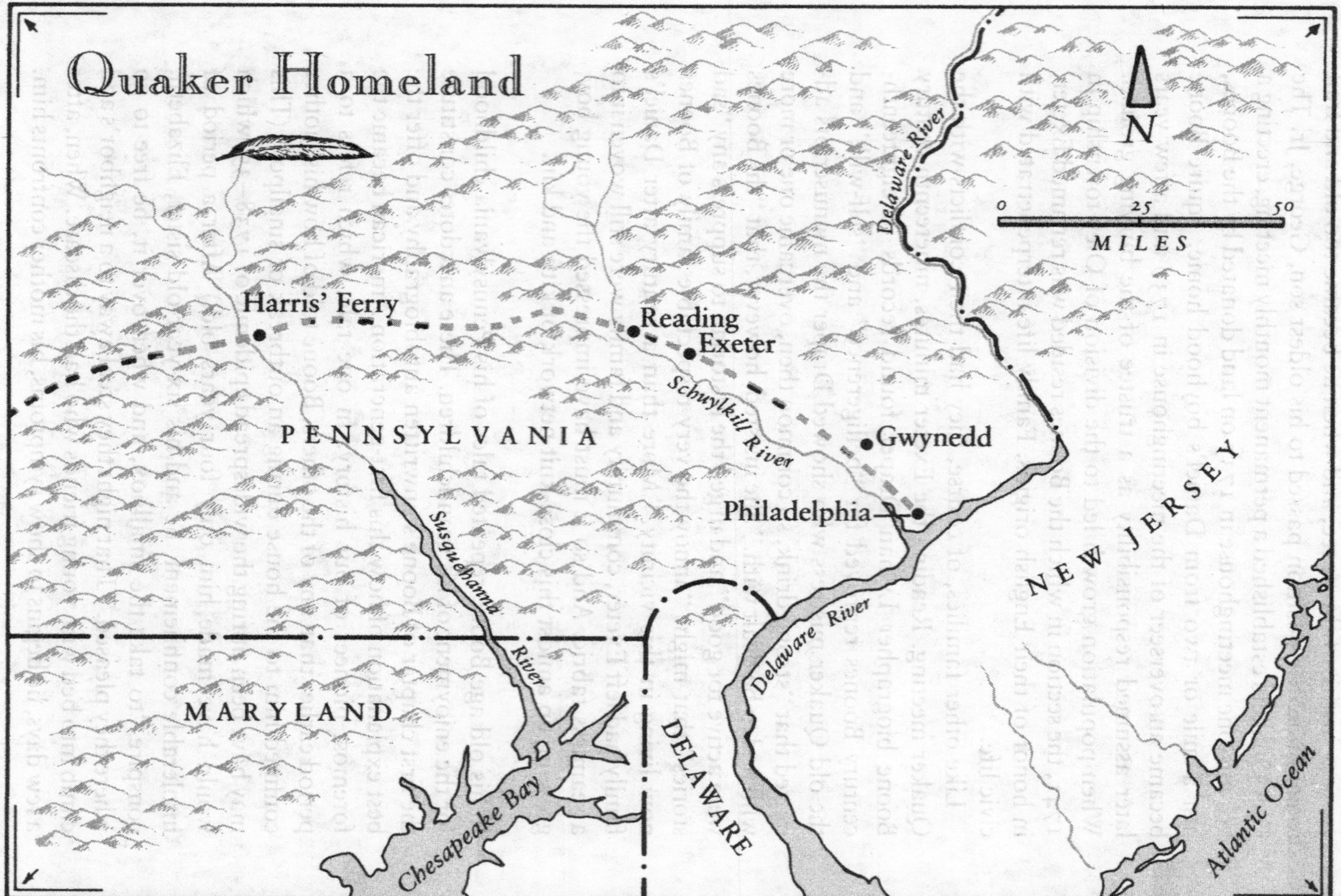

Quaker Homeland
N
0
25
50
MILES
Harris' Ferry
Reading
Exeter
Gwynedd
Philadelphia
Delaware River
Schuylkill River
Susquehanna River
PENNSYLVANIA
NEW JERSEY
MARYLAND
DELAWARE
Chesapeake Bay
Delaware River
Atlantic Ocean

"Now Daniel," says she, "I want thee to tell me the truth." Without hesitation or fear, he confesses the truth. "Thee nasty stinking gorrel!" she cries, "why did thee not tell me, so that I could have had thee better prepared?" Labeling her son the old English equivalent of a lout was about as harsh as she could be with him. In this story, old man Boone counterposed his childish willfulness against Sarah Morgan's maternal indulgence. It was a theme frequently reiterated in his tales. His mother favored him "above all her children," he once told a young hunting companion, and he in turn had been extraordinarily devoted to her.

Another story of his childhood begins with Daniel and his mother on the Schuylkill banks one spring at the annual shad run, she cleaning the catch, he nearby, napping on a flat rock by the river, hat pulled over his face against the afternoon sun. Two girls, caught up in the spirit of rough joking that characterized these festive occasions and tempted by his vulnerability, grab a pail of fish guts and dump them on the sleeping boy. He jumps up and, seeing the culprits, punches them both in the face. The girls run off in tears but are soon back with their mother, who harangues Sarah Morgan about such a son who would bloody girls' noses. Mother looks to Daniel. "They are not girls," he declares. "Girls would not have done such a dirty trick. They are rowdies." Sarah Morgan turns back to the angry woman: "If thee has not brought up thy daughters to better behavior, it was high time they were taught good manners. They got no more than they deserved." Boone smiled at the remembrance of a mother who stood with her son, where others might have stood with their sex.

Other fragments of oral tradition contain important hints about Boone's relationship with his father. When required to discipline his sons, Squire Boone would beat them until they asked for forgiveness, at which point he would put down the rod and reason with them, Quaker fashion. The system worked well with all of his sons but Daniel, who always endured the punishment in silence. A Boone descendant reported that "the father, wishing to gain his point in government, would appeal to Daniel, 'Canst thou not beg?' But he could not beg, leaving his anxious parent to close the matter at his pleasure." This tradition is reminiscent of a tale Boone himself told, in which he and a neighbor boy, one Henry Miller, engage in a verbal standoff that becomes a fistfight. Daniel, who very early in his life established a local reputation as the boy to beat, quickly gets the upper hand and, pinning his opponent to the ground, calls upon him to submit. "I give up, you are the best man," Henry cries out. From that moment the two are fast friends, keeping up a lifetime relationship despite the many miles and years that would separate them. Here the boy imitated his father's style, suggesting his deep paternal identification by embracing and befriending the subdued male. But, unlike Henry, Daniel himself would not submit, missing the opportunity for his father's embrace.

Boone also told of a time when he and Henry, who joined the household as Squire's apprentice, decide to meet their friends in some nighttime revel. Knowing his father would refuse permission to go, the boys wait until the family is asleep, then steal away on Squire's "best nag." Returning double-mounted and in high spirits, they attempt to jump the horse over a cow sleeping on the path, but as they approach at a full gallop the cow starts up and the horse stumbles and breaks its neck. Shaken and horrified, the boys return the saddle and bridle to their place in the barn and creep to bed, leaving the horse lying dead in front of the house. The next day Squire is dumbfounded at how a horse might have escaped from the barn and broken its own neck, but Daniel keeps silent. While he could confess easily and fully to his mother, he held back from his father. Boone would always possess a certain social reticence and maintain a self-imposed isolation that made him seem distant to other men.

Squire Boone had a weaving business in Exeter, with five or six looms, and he also kept a small smith's forge at the house, where he employed apprentice Henry Miller. Besides bearing and raising eleven children, Sarah Morgan managed the garden, henhouse, and dairy. By the time Daniel was ten years old the couple had purchased several dozen acres of grassland a few miles north of the homestead, where they grazed their herd of milk cows. In one of Boone's fondest memories, he and his mother drive the herd to this distant pasture, where there were cow pens and a small dairy house. From his tenth or eleventh year, mother and son spend each "grass season" together there, he tending the stock while she milks and churns during the day, then at night listening to her sing the old Welsh songs before the open fire. He fashions a sharp wooden shaft, which he calls his herdsman's club, and with it becomes expert at killing small game for their supper. The scene has a dreamlike quality—Daniel assuming the role of his mother's provider—and all the markings of an early adolescent fantasy. While it was a Welsh custom for the wife and mother to do her dairy work out at the pasture, she surely would have taken some of her younger children along. It seems scarcely possible that she would leave behind Boone's brother Squire Jr., still a nursing babe in the summer of 1745, or her youngest daughter, Hannah, born in August of 1746.

But this was the way Boone remembered it. As he looked back from the vantage of old age, he recalled those summers as the point when his life's course had been determined. His "love for the wilderness and hunter's life," he reminisced, began with "being a herdsman and thus being so much in the woods." It was Sarah Morgan's pattern to return to Owatin Run weekly, taking home butter and cheese to store in the cool cellar, but young Boone began to remain alone at the pasture, where he grew increasingly fond of solitude. When he was twelve or thirteen his father gave him what he later described as a "short rifle gun," probably a large-caliber European fowling piece. In two or three years of long summers roaming meadow and wood, he developed into an excellent marksman, his growing "love for the chase" frequently resulting in his neglect of the cows. It became common for him to be absent for several days during fall and winter, then suddenly to appear at the door with meat enough to supply the family for a week. Thus did the strapping boy find resolution for adolescent tensions, spending less time at his father's house and more time in the woods, a domain he identified with his beloved mother.

According to Boone family tradition, one consequence of this love for the woods was a neglect of book learning. A nephew related the tale that for a short time Daniel had attended a school taught by a dissipated Irishman who frequently retreated from the classroom to the woods, where he imbibed from a hidden bottle of whiskey. One day Daniel is chasing a squirrel, comes upon the bottle, and as a joke adds to it a powdered herbal emetic. Some hours later the Irishman is in agony and, recognizing the trickster by Daniel's barely suppressed snickers, attempts to cane the boy, but he is knocked to the floor by the robust youth. Daniel runs home, where Sarah Morgan rebukes him but does not force him to return, and so ends his formal education. This is boilerplate American folklore.

A second tale also hinges on Boone's resistance to corporal punishment, but it is somewhat more credible for the inclusion of specific references to members of the family. A bachelor uncle, John Boone, runs a subscription school attended by the neighborhood children, but Daniel intensely dislikes the confinement of the classroom and will not learn. John believes that his nephew's interest in learning can be piqued by a liberal application of the rod, bringing him into open conflict with Sarah Morgan, who knows better. "Dan would learn to spell if Sarah would leave me alone," Uncle John complains to his brother Squire. "It's all right, John," Boone's father reassures him, "let the girls do the spelling and Dan will do the shooting, and between you and me that is what we most need."

Both of these tales locate the roots of Boone's willful adult personality in his childhood resistance to authority. They also make reference yet again to the sympathy and protection of his mother. Most interesting is the polarity they set up between Boone's native accomplishments and the acquirements of civilization. The schoolmaster is tricked by young Daniel's familiarity with the woods, and Squire explicitly raises the contrast between shooting and spelling. Boone's talents, the stories suggest, rendered him ill-suited for school. But with reference to his physical prowess and his developed marksmanship, the tales have Boone already in his teens, leaving unexplained why his parents would have waited so long before initiating his education. Possibly schools were not organized in the district until the late 1740s; a German Lutheran preacher complained of their scarcity as late as 1748: "In Oley sind die Schulen sehr entfernt." But Boone later told his own children that he had never attended school a day in his life. It seems a logical inference that his parents decided quite early that, as the dialogue attributed to Squire implied, what the family needed most was his skills as a shooter, not as a scholar. The tales may have originated as attempts to absolve Squire and Sarah Morgan of any culpability for Boone's lack of formal education.

Actually, by the time Boone reached young manhood he had acquired a level of literacy that was the equal of most men of his times. In 1748, when he was thirteen, his older brother Samuel married a young Quaker woman, Sarah Day. She took young Boone under her wing, taught him to read, to spell a little, and to write in what was known as "a common farmer's hand." "He could at first do little more than rudely write his own name," related Boone's son Nathan, but with practice he gradually "added something to his acquirements as he grew up." During his middle years, when Boone worked as surveyor and trader, he honed his skills with lessons from a son-in-law. Many people have noted Boone's idiosyncratic spelling, but in fact it was no more awkward than that of most literate eighteenth-century Americans. He usually employed a sensible phonetic rendering of his native speech—"clark" for clerk, "sarvis" for service, "Indan" for Indian. His children and grandchildren testified to his lifelong love of reading, and in the company of frontiersmen he was often one of the few who could read or write. Moreover, despite Squire Boone's comment about teaching the girls to spell, most of the women in Boone's life were illiterate. A missionary who once visited Boone's wife, Rebecca, in North Carolina noted in his diary that "she can not read," and judging from their marks inscribed on indentures, deeds, and bills of sale, neither his mother nor his daughters ever learned to write. Within Boone's own household, therefore, his civilized accomplishments were fully acknowledged.

Exeter was at the western edge of European settlement in southeastern Pennsylvania. Before the 1750s this frontier was one of the most peaceful in all of North America, though, to be sure, European colonialism had introduced terrible turmoil into Indian societies. As a result of first Swedish, then Dutch, then subsequently English colonization, the native peoples of the Susquehanna and Delaware river region were devastated by imported diseases, reducing their village populations by as much as 90 percent by the eighteenth century. Commercial trade reoriented native economic life and introduced cutthroat competition among colonists and Indians alike for access to valuable fur-bearing regions and merchant centers.

Unlike other colonies, however, Quaker authorities organized no militia or army, negotiated with Indians over the title to land, and promised natives "the full and free privileges and Immunities of all the Said Laws as any other Inhabitants." A de facto alliance between Pennsylvania and the powerful Iroquois Confederacy of western New York further contributed to a half century of peace. Attracted by this policy, a number of Indian peoples, dislocated from their homelands by the reverberating effects of colonization, relocated in Pennsylvania. In the early century Conoys and Nanticokes from the Chesapeake, Tuscaroras and Tutelos from the piedmont of North Carolina, and Shawnees from southern Ohio joined Susquehannocks and Delawares in the upriver country of southeastern Pennsylvania. Within twenty or thirty miles of the Boone home were numerous Indian settlements, and beyond the Oley Hills, in the Lehigh and Lebanon valleys, were multiethnic Indian communities, including Manangy's Town, later renamed Reading when it was Americanized in midcentury. Down the Schuylkill was Manatawny, later called Pottstown.

The North American frontier was a distinctive milieu, where peoples of different cultural origins made contact and conducted business with one another. This was good for the commonwealth of Pennsylvania, and during the first half of the eighteenth century the Indian trade accounted for nearly a third of the commonwealth's foreign exchange. As merchants, Pennsylvania authorities wanted Indians near at hand. But the colony also operated as a land company, and as real estate agents, authorities sought to gain possession of Indian lands in order to sell tracts to emigrants like the Boones who began pouring into the colony in 1713 at the end of Queen Anne's War. That this was accomplished by what one Iroquois chief described as "Pen-and-Ink work" rather than warfare marked the Pennsylvania frontier as distinct.

Despite the peace, however, even Pennsylvania grew tense with growing Indian resentments and settler fears. At Manatawny in 1728, a party of Shawnees got into a fight with settlers who refused to provide them with food. There was an exchange of gunfire and one Indian was wounded. The Boone neighborhood, just ten miles away, was thrown into panic. Grandfather George Boone, local magistrate, sent a dispatch to the colonial governor pleading for assistance "in order to defend our fronteers." "Our Inhabitants are Generally fled," he wrote, but "there remains about 20 men with me to guard my mill, where I have about 1000 bushels of wheat and flour, and we are resolved to defend ourselves to ye last Extremity." Sometime later a dozen Shawnees, perhaps the same group, extorted food and drink from a few terrorized families in the area. A posse of about twenty local men pursued them, and in a short fight two settlers were wounded. This concluded the only record of Indian warfare at Oley, but it was evidence of increasing settlement and congestion. Under such pressures Shawnees, Delawares, and other Indians began moving west, into the mountains or beyond. A steady stream of Indians, however, continued to pass along the Perkiomen Path, which cut directly through the Boone neighborhood.

Grandfather Boone enjoyed a reputation among the Indians for befriending natives. During the conflict of 1728 he led the rescue of two Indian girls held by a group of settlers who harbored lustful and murderous intentions. Indian hunters and diplomats passing along the path knew they could find food, drink, and a place to sleep at the Boone homestead; when Sassoonan, known as "king" of the Schuylkill Delawares, stopped for a time at the Boone place on his way to Philadelphia, with his retinue of twenty-five men, women, and children in 1736, the visit was important enough to record.

There were other occasions, too, when Indians were an obvious presence in the area. In the winter of 1742, for example, Moravian missionaries held religious services for a large party of Delawares in an Oley barn, and a number of Indians were baptized. As a child, Daniel had numerous opportunities to see and meet the native peoples of many tribes, and discussion of their visits was surely a common subject around the tables of his kinfolk.

When he ventured out of his own neighborhood into the woods surrounding the Schuylkill settlements, the young hunter entered a mixed cultural world. On woodland thoroughfares the hunters of many nations met, and over a smoke of tobacco or kinnikinnick, a pungent mixture of dried bark and leaves, they traded news and information. A pidgin tongue based on Algonquian but employing many English, French, Dutch, and Scandinavian terms served as the lingua franca of the forest, and along the trails trees were often blazed, the bark pulled back and the trunks painted with pictographs that constituted a simple but common written language. There were camping places, sometimes with huts of small logs and bark, where hunters shared meat and sleeping quarters. It was in these circles that young Boone found his forest teachers. There were backwoods hunters descended from European colonists, many of them of Scandinavian background, whom the Delawares called *nittappi*, or friends. There were Indians of many ethnic varieties who also called friend this young hunter carrying the respected name of Boone. These men of the forest frontier instructed Daniel in a way of life that combined elements of both cultures and bridged many of the differences between Indian and European.

This way of life centered on hunting. Hunters from both cultures sought meat and hides to feed and clothe their families, as well as hides and furs for trade. They considered bear the prime game meat but also favored opossum and raccoon. Venison was inferior eating, they thought, but deer provided skins for clothing and footware; there was a steady commercial demand for deerskin and beaver pelts. Firearms were in wide use and included muskets, shotguns, pistols, and rifles. Indians who hunted with bow and arrow did so not from choice but because they lacked European weapons or ammunition. Most desired was the American long rifle, developed during the early eighteenth century by the German gunsmiths of southeastern Pennsylvania to fill the requirements of backwoods hunters for a well-balanced, small-caliber weapon, very accurate at distances of up to two hundred yards. A fine long rifle was a hunter's most valuable possession, and in choosing it, it was said, a man must be "even more particular than in selecting a wife." The tools of the trade were thus European, but its techniques—the calls, disguises, and decoys, the surrounds and fire hunts—were nearly all of Indian origin. Most emigrants to America came without any hunting traditions, for in most European countries hunting had been reserved for the nobility, so the hunting way of life that developed in the backwoods depended on Indian knowledge and skill.

Hunters from both cultures dressed in a composite of European and Indian styles. Moccasins were of deerskin but made and patched with European awls. The hunting shirt was a loose frock that reached halfway down the thighs and overlapped by as much as a foot or more in the front, sometimes fitted with a fringed cape used to cover the head. It was generally made of linsey or linen, sometimes of dressed deerskin, but this material had the disadvantage of being cold and uncomfortable in wet weather. In the front folds of the shirt hunters kept small rations of provisions. From the leather belt that pulled the shirt tight, they hung their powder horns, bullet pouch, knife, and tomahawk. Many Americans wore breeches or drawers, but as they moved further west they took to the Indian breechclout, a length of cloth about a yard long and nine inches wide that passed between the legs, under a cloth belt, with folds hanging front and back. Long leggings stretching to above the knee were supported by garter straps. Beaver hats were de rigueur on the eastern frontier of the eighteenth century, and although west of the Appalachians some men wore fur caps, Boone always despised them and kept his hat. Like Indian men, American hunters let their hair grow long and dressed it with bear grease, plaiting it into braids or knots. In time of war or for ritual occasions, Indian warriors might shave or pluck their scalps, leaving only a lock of hair, which they greased to stand upright or to which they attached deerskin ornaments or feathers. They painted their bodies with vermilion. American backwoodsmen heading into battle frequently adopted a similar style of ornamentation. The frontier American was "proud of his Indian-like dress," wrote a preacher in western Pennsylvania. In breechclout and leggings, their thighs and hips exposed naked to the world, he had seen them strut down village streets and even into churches, which, he added, "did not add much to the devotion of the young ladies." Boone adopted these styles as a youth in Pennsylvania, and they remained his through the whole of his long life.

The woods were a man's world, but American and Indian hunters returned to settlements and villages where women practiced similar forms of cultivation, raising corn, beans, and garden vegetables, nearly all of their primary crops native to the Americas. The farther west Americans moved, the more they incorporated hunting techniques to supplement farming. But as hunting yields declined with the increasing density of population, Indians in turn adopted European livestock, such as poultry, horses, hogs, and, less frequently, cattle. Over time the two economies converged. The Indians as well as British colonists adopted the simple form of log construction introduced during the seventeenth century by Swedish and Finnish colonists in the Delaware Valley. Obtaining iron woodworking tools through trade, Indians learned to build log homes and stockades, at villages with names like Logstown on the Ohio River. These Indian towns were somewhat more concentrated and centralized than those of the Americans, who tended to disperse themselves on individual farmsteads across the face of the country.

The Americans and Indians who lived in these backwoods hunting communities also shared a set of general social values. Both groups were geographically mobile, in part because hunting constantly led them farther into less exploited territory, in part because growing coastal populations pressed on them from the East, in part because that was the way they liked it. Both emphasized personal freedom and independence while at the same time adhering to the loyalties of family and clan. Both were localistic in their attachments, valuing their primary groups over tribes or nations—theirs was a village world. Both were warlike and violent, believers in honor and vengeance, adherents to the ancient law of blood, and for both cultures the bloodshed was made worse by alcohol. By the eighteenth century these two groups were fully acculturated to each other's ways. The noted American anthropologist Alfred Kroeber once described the Indians of the eighteenth-century frontier as "a new, assimilated, hybrid-Caucasian culture." American frontiersmen, in turn, were often characterized by their contemporaries as hybrid Indians. Indeed, many colonial observers commented disparagingly on their "half-Indian appearance," and one missionary described them as "generally white Savages, [who] subsist by hunting, and live like the Indians."

The two peoples also shared a number of cultural traits, such as common dietary conventions, medicinal practices, a belief in the power of omens and the foreshadowing of dreams, but at deeper levels they understood the world in essentially different ways. Europeans and their American descendants tended to make a radical separation between the material and spiritual realms, and whatever their sectarian Christian beliefs, for the most part they were practical instrumentalists, interested in what worked. Indians, by contrast, tended to believe in the inseparability of matter and spirit, and their recorded history is punctuated with frequent and divisive cultural debates about the meaning or consequences of new approaches to the world. Americans were monotheists, lured by the simplicity of grand designs and single causes, while Indians were pantheists, describing a universe with a multiplicity of powers, sometimes in harmony, more frequently in conflict among themselves. Holding to a hierarchical model of reality, Americans favored clear lines of authority and power; Indians, believing in a more complicated and perhaps ultimately unfathomable universe, lived in societies with a diversity of overlapping roles and authorities, all of which seemed perfectly natural to them, but to most Americans seemed a trackless maze and cacophonous din. These descriptions, of course, are at opposite ends of a spectrum, and there were Americans, Boone among them, who moved quite far in the Indian direction of seeing things.

Boone's basic loyalty always remained with Anglo-American culture. His strong and affectionate attachments to his family and community, developed during his childhood in Exeter, were at the heart of his identity, and the private ownership of property, the basis of this way of life, marked a fundamental difference with the communal holdings of the Indians. A number of times during his life he returned to Pennsylvania to renew ties with his kinfolk and refresh the memories of his youth. But during that youth he also grew in his knowledge of the ways of the American woods and of the culture of the Indians. Over the course of his life, despite living through a generation of warfare and suffering the loss of sons and brothers, he practiced the Quaker tolerance he learned on the Pennsylvania frontier. Unlike so many of his peers, he never became an Indian hater. Daniel Boone would always view the central struggles of his life through the lens of his early experiences in Penn's woods.

In the late 1740s, because of the conduct of their family affairs, Boone's parents became subjects of controversy within the Exeter meeting of Friends. The outcome of this controversy had a great impact on the adolescent boy, first because it resulted in the family's moving from Pennsylvania and second because it suggested important lessons about the balance between individual will and communal demands. The dispute had its origins in 1742, when he was seven years old. Early that summer, the family's eldest child, eighteen-year-old Sarah, married a young German, John Wilcoxen. Wilcoxen was not a Quaker but a "worldling," and the wedding was held outside the circle of the Friends. In July, Squire and Sarah Morgan Boone were roundly criticized by "sundry persons" shocked that they had "countenanced" the match despite the fact that Wilcoxen was "not joined to our society." An all-make committee was appointed to meet with Squire about the matter and another committee of women was appointed to meet with Sarah Morgan. A month later both parents stood humbly before the Friends. "He was no ways Countenancing or Consenting to the said Marriage," Squire declared, "but confesseth himself in a Fault in keeping them in his House after he knew of their keeping company." He "was somewhat Sensible that they had been too Conversant," he told the meeting, but "he was in a great streight in not knowing what to do." He "hopeth to be more careful for the future." Without excuses, Sarah Morgan also accepted blame, "and signified that if it were to do again she would not do the like." Squire's reference about his daughter being "too Conversant before" was made considerably more explicit by the report of the women's committee on Sarah Morgan: "Some also suppose her daughter to be with child, which time may make appear." A year later the minutes recorded that the women "had found the truth of a former suspicion viz, that Sarah Wilcoxen, daughter of Squire Boone, was with child before she was married." The offending young wife was required to make a written confession and read it before the meeting.

The promise of Squire and Sarah Morgan "to be more careful for the future" could not have been made idly, for they had many more children to marry off, and those were difficult times for parents. A revival of religious fervor, known as the Great Awakening, was sweeping across the country, stirring Protestants to strengthen their faith. The revival often had the ironic effect, however, of shattering the former discipline of congregations, including Quaker meetings. The emphasis on personal revelation and the emotional process of religious commitment often undercut communal and parental authority. Simply put, it became increasingly difficult for parents to supervise the behavior of their older children. The Boones certainly had a great deal of company in their embarrassment. Throughout the colonies a significant increase in premarital conception signaled a decline in the ability of parents to determine the choices of their children.

The next child to marry was Israel, the Boones' eldest son, who reached the age of majority in 1747, the year Squire gave Daniel his first rifle. Even the most diligent of Boone genealogists have been unable to unearth the name of Israel's bride, but we know that she too was a worldling. In its minutes for October the meeting recorded the appointment of a committee "to speak with Squire Boone for countenancing his Son's disorderly Marriage." But now, five years after his first public humiliation over his daughter's marriage, the committee found a father unwilling to submit further to communal discipline. The difference may have been simply the prospect of having to repeat this same demeaning process again and again with his many children. Perhaps the independent spirit of the times had affected Squire as well.

It also may have been significant that George Boone, Sr., the patriarch of the family, had died during the intervening years, in 1744. During the initial incident in 1742, when the meeting required Squire to submit, George surely recalled public confessions he had been required to make in his own Quaker history. In 1716, before leaving England, he had endured the harsh criticism of his fellow Friends and had made an emotional confession of "my transgressions and sins against God," admitting to "keeping wild company and drinking by which I sometimes became guilty of drunkenness" and owned to a "gross sin by which the honour due unto marriage was lost, for the marriage bed was defiled." Then in 1720, in Gwynedd, after being taken to task for not seeking the permission of the meeting before allowing one of his daughters to keep company with a young man, he humbly acknowledged his "forwardness." The strategy of grandfather George, and the course he undoubtedly urged on his sons and daughters, was submission to the discipline of the meeting—but now George was dead.

The minutes of the Exeter meeting show that in 1747 Squire refused to accept any fault or blame. "The Friends which were appointed to speak to Squire Boone report that they spoke with him and that he could not see that he had transgressed, and therefore was not willing to condemn it until he saw it to be a transgression." Even after repeated discussions with him, fellow Friends could not bring him "to a Sense of his Error," and so "he was not willing to give any satisfaction to the Meeting." On the contrary, they reported, he argued back, "giving Room to a reflecting Spirit even against his Friends who sought his everlasting Peace and Welfare, and against the Orders and Discipline of Friends in general." He even penned an angry letter to the meeting, which the secretary deemed too impertinent to copy into the minutes. Finally, in March of 1748, the Exeter Friends were driven to invoke their ultimate sanction. Although Squire Boone had "been a Professor among us for many Years," the meeting took "Public Testimony against him as not being a Member with us until such time as we may be sensible of his coming to a Godly Sorrow in himself." His wife, Sarah Morgan, remained in good standing and continued to bring the children with her to the monthly meeting, but Squire Boone was finished with the Quakers.

The expulsion of his father from the central institution of communal life was surely a cause of conflict for thirteen-year-old Daniel. His mother and his extended family continued their association with the meeting, but, especially in light of the boy's adolescent struggles, his father's defiance of the meeting's demand—"Canst thou not beg?"—called for admiration, for strengthened identification. Moreover, these events took place at a significant juncture in Daniel's life, as he acted for the first time on his own, first learned the culture of the woods, first began to articulate to himself personal ambitions. The impact of the expulsion must have been heightened when Squire began to express interest in moving the family southwest to the new frontiers of settlement, to places then being much discussed in young Boone's circle of woodsmen.

Squire did not immediately decide to emigrate. Nine months after his expulsion he took out a warrant for an additional 250 acres adjoining his farm. But during the spring of 1749 dozens of settler families passed through Exeter on their way from coastal Pennsylvania to the frontier. Squire's brother-in-law Joseph Stover and his sister Sarah, with whom he had emigrated to America nearly forty years before, had recently moved to the headwaters of the South Fork of the Shenandoah River in the great interior valley of Virginia, from where they sent back encouraging news about the country. Good land, for far less than prevailing Pennsylvania prices, was available as near as Maryland, and in the valley of Virginia or further south, in backcountry North Carolina, land was practically being given away. The decision to move must have been made during the winter of 1749–50. In January of 1750 the minutes of the Women's Meeting of the Exeter Quakers recorded Sarah Morgan's request for a letter of transfer addressed "to Friends in Virginia, Carolina or elsewhere." In April, Squire and his wife sold their Exeter homestead for £300 to William Mogridge, a cousin. When the family began their trek, about the first of May, they were not yet sure where they would resettle, only that it would be on the frontier.

Young Boone's namesake, his mother's older brother, was a traveling Quaker minister, "noted as a man of great bodily strength fearlessly encountering the perils of the wilderness," as one of his descendants proudly put it. Like his uncle Daniel Morgan, Boone now guided his family toward the unknown country to the southwest. Unlike him, Daniel Boone had nothing more to do with the Quakers. Boone later told his family and friends that his ancestors had all been Quakers, and that he too had been "brought up with those Religious views," but when he emigrated from Pennsylvania, he said, he left the Society of Friends forever. His father left them too, but Squire later helped to organize and lead a nondenominational congregation in their new community. Though Boone always considered himself a Christian, he remained unchurched until he died. "I never knew any good to come of religious disputes," he once told a hunting companion. The pattern of attitudes and values formed amid a Quaker family and community, however, characterized Boone for the rest of his life.

The emigration party, guided by fifteen-year-old Daniel, was led by Squire Boone and included his wife, their eight unmarried children, ranging in age from nineteen to three years, their two married sons and daughters-in-law, and their married daughter with her husband and baby, possibly including some members of his extended family. One of Squire's grown nephews joined them, as did the apprentice Henry Miller, Daniel's best friend. A group this large required three or four big Conestoga wagons, with their distinctive bowed beds, huge wheels, and canvas tops, each hauled by a team of five or more horses. The first stage of their journey took them due west over what soon would become known as the Allegheny Trail. At fifteen miles per day, a rate of travel possible only with the benefit of good roads and dry weather, they could have ferried across the Schuylkill by the end of the first day and traveled as far as the settlement of Conrad Weiser, Pennsylvania's Indian agent, by the second. From there it was at least three days' travel through the Lebanon Valley to Harris's Ferry on the Susquehanna River, soon to be renamed Harrisburg. (Their approximate route can be traced today by following U.S. highways 422 and 322.)

From the crossing of the Susquehanna the trail shifted to the southwest, following the great curve of the Appalachian Mountains. Known then as the Virginia Road (today as U.S. 11), this had been the principal artery of communication between Indian peoples of north and south for centuries. By 1750 it was the major route of migration for settlers bound for the southern backcountry. They made up a cultural kaleidoscope. A diarist on the road in the early 1750s noted in his journal that he bought "some hay from a Swiss" and "some kraut from a German," shared a cup of tea with an Englishman, and camped "so as not to be too near the Irish Presbyterians," who had a reputation for contentiousness. Traveling amid this considerable and diverse traffic, with a little luck the Boones might have reached the ford of the Potomac River at Williamsport, Maryland, seven days after leaving Harris's Ferry. It then would take another week to follow the Shenandoah River south down the Great Valley of Virginia to the vicinity of their Stover kin. Since things never went so smoothly, their trip from Exeter probably took them a month.

According to Boone descendants, the family made camp on Linnville Creek, a few miles north of Harrisonburg, Virginia, and remained there for at least one, possibly two, growing seasons. Filled with a spirit of adventure, however, during the summer and fall of 1750 Daniel, accompanied by his friend Henry Miller, started off on his first "long hunt," an extended expedition of several weeks or months, usually undertaken in the fall and early winter. Long hunting was entirely derived from the patterns of woodland Indian culture. Details about Boone's first long hunt came from descendants in the Miller family, who remembered it because Henry later looked back on it as one of the major turning points of his life. The two young men first hunted in the nearby Shenandoah Mountains, but finding the game sparse, took off down the valley, lingering to hunt and trap around Big Lick on the Roanoke River. From there they followed the Roanoke Gap east through the Blue Ridge, then south to the high piedmont country in the vicinity of the Virginia–North Carolina dividing line. Late in the fall the young men returned north, stopping briefly with the family, then continuing north to Philadelphia, where they sold their substantial cache of hides and furs. Years later, with a certain irony, Miller described these profits as "the best spent" of his life.

He and Boone "went on a general jamboree or frolick," he said, that lasted three weeks, until "the money was all spent." Afterward Daniel seemed perfectly content, but Henry was disgusted with himself for wasting his funds. On their way back to Virginia, wrote one Miller descendant, "our grandfather told Boone, if he chose he could go on hunting, trapping, etc., but for his part, he intended to quit, and settle down, make money and keep it." Miller's conclusion to the tale of his long hunt carried a strong moral message for his children. "Boone was very profligate," Henry said to his son. "[He] would spend all of his earnings and never made an effort to accumulate." Such was the memory of a man who had remained in Augusta County, Virginia, where he became a substantial landowner and, building on the apprenticeship spent at Squire Boone's forge, established a noted and profitable ironworks.

Land records indicate that Squire Boone also found his way to North Carolina during the fall of 1750, perhaps traveling in the company of the young hunters. In October he filed a warrant claiming 640 acres in an area called the Forks of the Yadkin River (now in Davie County) "upon Grants Creek alias Lickon Creek including a great Timber Bottom and Paul Garrison's Cabbin." To provide so specific a description Squire must have inspected the ground himself, selecting a settlement site for his family amid the thousands of square miles offered for sale by agents of the Earl of Granville, who owned the entire northern half of the colony. Although the annual quitrents in North Carolina were higher than they had been in Pennsylvania, a square mile of this fine land cost a mere three shillings, which amounted to little more than a filing fee. The Yadkin and its creeks were clear, rapid-flowing mountain streams, offering excellent opportunities for mill sites. There was forest and canebrake along their courses and a good deal of the rolling country was wooded. But the landscape was punctuated by beautiful meadows, perfect for grazing livestock, and well-watered lowlands where the soil was fertile clay, brick-red when plowed and exposed to the sun, a shocking contrast to Pennsylvania's black loam but still fine land for corn and other crops.

Emigrant families usually arrived at their destinations in the fall of the year with provisions sufficient to take them through a first winter on the new land. Some local traditions placed the Boones in a cave on the east side of the Yadkin for their first few months, but it is more likely that they built their first cabin in the Forks when they arrived in late 1751 and moved into it immediately. They certainly had established themselves on their claim by the following February, when a neighbor's plot of land was described as lying "on the E. side of the path that leads from Sandy Creek Ford to Squire Boon's." They were part of a large migration into western North Carolina. "Inhabitants flock in here daily, mostly from Pensilvania and other parts of America," the governor of North Carolina wrote in 1751; "they commonly seat themselves toward the West and have got near the mountains." A Moravian missionary exploring "the back of the colony" for lands suitable for his brethren noted that in 1752 alone "more than four hundred families have come with horse and wagon and cattle." The colonial authorities estimated that the number of adult males in three western counties had jumped from just one hundred in 1746 to at least three thousand by 1753. That was the year Squire Boone completed the purchase of two 640-acre parcels near what later would become the village of Mocksville. At about the time of their arrival, two more of his children were wed, and each of the five young married couples, as well as Squire's nephew, were able to draw from the extensive supply of family land. Over the next decade or so, as the younger children reached maturity, they too were established on land carved from the family estate. The size of these farms and the distances between them were significantly greater than those in Exeter, but otherwise the Boones transplanted to the Yadkin a landscape of kinship very similar to the one they had left behind in Pennsylvania.

Daniel was now the oldest of the Boone children residing at home. Approaching twenty, he was nearly full grown, a man of average height, about five feet eight inches, but of powerful build, with broad shoulders and chest, strong arms, and thick legs. One who knew him described Boone later as "a sort of pony-built man," a bit undersize but built like a horse. During his young manhood he weighed approximately 175 pounds. Boone had pronounced facial features noted by many: a high forehead and heavy brow, prominent cheekbones, a tight, wide mouth, a long and slender nose. He had his father's penetrating blue-gray eyes and fair, ruddy complexion but his mother's dark hair, which he always kept plaited and clubbed in Indian fashion.

His assistance around the homestead was essential to Squire, now a man in his late fifties. Boone cleared land and plowed in the spring, tended the field crops and the livestock in the summer, but he did not enjoy the work. "He never took any delight in farming or stock Raising," his nephew Daniel Boone Bryan remembered, and "was ever unpracticed in the business of farming." Boone himself told his children that working his father's fields during the summers, he would pray for the rains to come, and if they did he would grab his rifle and head for the woods; "and though the rain would cease in an hour, yet he was so fond of gunning, he would be sure to remain out till evening." In fall and winter he could turn his full attention to the woods. "He took great delight in hunting and killing Deer, Bare, etc.," Bryan continued, but "it was not so much a ruling passion of Boone's to hunt, as his means of livelihood, his necessary occupation, from which he could not part." As his son Nathan put it, Boone hunted "not only because he was fond of that roving life, but because it was profitable." After his first long hunt in 1750 he became a professional hunter, and until his last years, when he grew too weak to leave his house, seldom did he ever miss a fall hunt. In North Carolina hunting became, as Boone once put it, his "business of life."

The country of the Upper Yadkin teemed with game. Bears were so numerous, it was said, that a hunter could lay by two or three thousand pounds of bear bacon in a season. The tale was told in the Forks that nearby Bear Creek had taken its name from the season Boone killed ninety-nine bears along its waters. The deer were so plentiful that an ordinary hunter could kill four or five a day, and it was said that Boone and a companion once took thirty between sunup and sundown near the head of the Yadkin. Deer were best when they were "in the red," during summer or early fall, before they acquired their blue winter coats. Beaver, otter, and muskrat were trapped during the winters, when their coats were long and oily.

The deerskin trade was an important part of the regional economy. In 1753 over thirty thousand skins were exported from North Carolina, and thousands more were used within the colony for the manufacture of leggings, breeches, and moccasins. A "buck" was the standard of the trade, and by 1750 the term already had become a synonym in the American colonies for its monetary equivalent, the widely circulating Spanish peso, known by its German name of "thaler," or dollar. By weight, beaver were five times more valuable, so a good winter of trapping could be very lucrative. The deerskins accumulated quickly at the Boone family cabin on Dutchman's Creek during the summer months, and Boone was soon making regular wagon runs to the traders located at Salisbury, the seat of Rowan County, a dusty crossroads town twenty miles south of the Forks, consisting of a few log cabins and a courthouse. A hunter bought his supplies there—powder and lead, traps, tools for gunsmithing, and packhorses—but there was always money besides for gaming and frolicking.

Boone soon acquired a reputation as one of the best marksmen and hunters in the county. In Salisbury he was a frequent competitor at shooting matches, where sometimes the prize was beef but more frequently was whiskey or simply the privilege of collecting all of the lead in and about the target. Boone was always ready to compete and he always scored high. So cocky did he become that he took to perfecting trick shots. He impressed the cronies hanging about the county courthouse by stepping up to the line and firing a winning round with the rifle held in only one of his powerful arms. Then, as one descendant remembered the scene, he would strut proudly before the other riflemen, "pat them on the shoulders, and tell them they couldn't shoot up to Boone."

A Boone family tradition moralized about how such arrogance once got Boone into considerable trouble. An Indian by the name of Saucy Jack, a Catawba with a considerable reputation for both his hunting skill and his bragging, is beaten by Boone in competition. Nursing his injured pride over rum in Salisbury one afternoon, Jack grows loud in his complaints. The more he drinks, the angrier he becomes, until finally he blusters drunkenly that he will eliminate this upstart once and for all. Boone is not present at the time, but word of the threat soon reaches Squire, in town on business. "Well, if it has come to this," the ex-Quaker thunders, "I'll kill first," and seizing a nearby hatchet, he sets out in search of Jack, who, warned by some friends, wisely flees. Boone told John Filson in 1784 that later, when he was a captive among the Indians, "I was careful not to exceed many of them in shooting, for no people are more envious than they in this sport." Saucy Jack's lesson in humility would serve Boone well.

Saucy Jack typified the sentiment and situation of many Indians. Over the previous century the Catawbas had greatly declined in number as a result of European epidemic diseases; they had ceded a great deal of land and pulled back to a small reserved territory on the Catawba River, near the present urban complex of Charlotte, North Carolina. Many of the openings and meadows among the woods were, in fact, old Indian fields. Now the Catawbas were being pressed hard by American settlers, who claimed much of the Indians' former hunting territory for themselves and competed for deerskins and beaver pelts. The Catawbas maintained their friendly alliance with the English, for fear of powerful Indian enemies such as the Cherokees to their west, but the patience of other tribes, under similar pressures, had been stretched to the breaking point by the mid-eighteenth century. In the 1750s these frustrations found expression in the massive intercolonial struggle known to subsequent American generations as the French and Indian War. This conflict, engulfing all of eastern America, became Boone's introduction to Indian warfare.

The war had its beginnings in the country of the upper Ohio River, where most of the Indians of southeastern Pennsylvania had relocated. In the mid-eighteenth century, the Ohio country was thought to begin at the divide between Atlantic and Mississippi watersheds, and by moving west to those waters, the Indians sought to establish the Appalachians as a barrier between themselves and American settlement. To the Pennsylvania authorities in the 1730s, the chiefs of one group of early Shawnee emigrants to the west wrote that "they must starve" had they remained in the east, there being "litle or no Game to be mett with in those parts." American settlements had crowded into the forests, leaving little room for the Indians. These Indians were followed west by Pennsylvania merchants, who continued to trade furs and hides for weapons, ammunition, manufactured goods, and alcohol, products far superior to anything the Indians could obtain from the French.

Yet the Indians were vocal about their grievances with the British. Perhaps the most infamous affront was the so-called "Walking

Purchase," a cession of land from the Delawares of the Lehigh Valley engineered by Pennsylvania in 1737. Under terms negotiated a half century before, the natives had agreed to cede lands vaguely bounded by the distance a man could travel in a day and a half. The Indian understanding was that this was to be a walk taken at the "common" pace, pausing at noon for a midday meal and a pipe. But Pennsylvania authorities prepared a cleared path for a group of specially trained "walkers" who ran to cover more than sixty miles in the specified time, thus succeeding in turning this vague provision into a huge tract of land encompassing the entire upper Delaware and Lehigh valleys and dispossessing a large number of Delawares and Shawnees. It was a clear violation of the spirit of the earlier agreement and displayed an obvious contempt for the Indians.

The Indian perception of events is evident in the tales they told, aimed at explaining how they had lost their land. When the English first arrive they ask for a cession of land only as big as a bull's hide. Reasonable enough, think the Delawares, who wish to be accommodating. But the colonists then soak the hide to expand it, and they cut it into long, thin strips with which they enclose a great quantity of ground. The angry Indians cry out, "You have cheated us, is this the way you are going to treat us always while you remain in this country?" The English respond by asking for just one more piece of land, this one large enough on which to place their chair. Reasonable enough, think the Delawares, who wish to be hospitable. But the English take off the seat of the chair, made from hundreds of small cords, tie them together to make a long string, and with it surround another great piece of land. The Delawares complain, but the English say this is the custom among them. And thus, said the Shawnees, the Delawares are cheated, their lands stolen, and they are forced to move west. Such tales were repeated countless times by the native peoples on the Ohio. "This very ground that is under me," a Delaware chief later declared as he stamped his foot on the ground at one treaty negotiation, "was my Land and Inheritance, and is taken from me by fraud." The Walking Purchase was "not the principal cause that made us Strike our Brethren, the English," he said, "yet it has caused the stroke to come harder than it otherwise would have come."

By the late 1740s Americans had begun to push beyond the

Atlantic piedmont and into the Appalachian highlands of Pennsylvania. Like Boone, these settlers were well versed in the woodland way of life and competed directly with the Indians for forest resources. Indeed, the American conflict with the Indians came not because they were so alien to each other but precisely because they were so much alike. The settlers "interfere much more with the Indians than if they pursued agriculture alone," wrote Sir William Johnson, English agent to the Iroquois. "The Indian hunters already begin to feel the scarcity this has occasioned, which greatly increases their resentment." When in 1752 the British government granted five hundred thousand acres on the upper Ohio to the Ohio Company, a group of prominent Virginian land speculators, and when, two years later, the Iroquois bargained away their right to the Juniata River valley, which penetrated deep within western Pennsylvania, the fears of the interior Indians were further excited. Settler cabins already were being raised on the Juniata, not far from streams that fed the Ohio.

These Indian communities were frequently mixed, with Shawnees, Delawares, and Iroquois migrants living together, often intermarrying. They came to constitute an independent force, allied with neither the British nor the French and free from the control of the Iroquois Confederacy as well. When, in the early 1750s, the French decided to exclude the British from the interior by military force, these independent villagers refused to take part in the campaign, but, supplied by the French, they waged their own independent war against the threatening settlers of the American backcountry. Bands of warriors left their towns on the Ohio and headed south along the Great Warrior's Path, which ran down the west flank of the Appalachians, crossing to the Atlantic side at the Cumberland Gap. They fanned out along the mountains, attacking settlements in the interior valleys. In the summer of 1753 a Shawnee war party struck near the Forks of the Yadkin, destroying a number of isolated cabins before being driven off by a combined force of county militia and Catawba Indians. In this battle several warriors were killed, and on their bodies were found silver crucifixes, beads, looking glasses, tomahawks, and other items of French manufacture. At the time of this incident Boone was a private in the county militia. It is not known if he participated in this encounter, but it was a warning of events soon to follow.

The English and French struggle for the West focused on control of the Forks of the Ohio, the junction of the Monongahela and Allegheny rivers, the site of present-day Pittsburgh. In 1754 Canadians built Fort Duquesne at the Forks, then defeated and turned back a force, led by Col. George Washington, that came to secure the region for Virginia. In response the British sent Gen. Edward Braddock to North America with two regiments of regular troops and orders to drive the French back into Canada. In April 1755 Braddock met with the governors of the British colonies in Alexandria, Virginia, and secured their agreement to a coordinated plan of attack involving colonial militia as well as British troops. In North Carolina the governor's son, Maj. Edward Brice Dobbs, organized a company of frontiersmen to fight with Braddock, and in May it marched north to Fort Cumberland in the mountains of western Maryland, the staging ground for the British attack on Fort Duquesne. Young Boone, the twenty-year-old sharpshooter, joined Dobbs's company as a teamster.

In early June, Braddock's force of nearly two thousand men set off northwest across the mountain divide; the column stretched into a line of march nearly four miles long. Axemen hacked at the old Indian path and the advance party slowly transformed it into a road suitable for the heavy cannon and supply wagons that brought up the rear. A week into the march they had traveled only thirty miles. Frustrated with the pace, Braddock divided his army, leaving much of the baggage behind, and advanced with about half of his troop, who were supported by packhorses and wagons, one of them driven by Boone. This quicker-moving force still required three weeks to cover the one hundred miles to the banks of the Monongahela, where they arrived in early July. To avoid a dangerous narrows in the trail on the right bank, Braddock decided on a double crossing of the river, which would put his army within striking distance of Fort Duquesne.

The column began to ford the Monongahela on the morning of July 9, 1755. It was midday before Boone and the other teamsters finally whipped their teams across, and the sight of the army ahead of him must have impressed Boone. To the sound of fife and drum, red-coated regulars and blue-coated Virginians paraded forward, led by their mounted officers. Following were groups of frontiersmen, cannon, howitzers, and mortars, as well as wagons. The whole maneuver was performed with British spit and polish. Suddenly, however, shots were heard in the distance and gathering clouds of smoke ahead indicated that an attack had begun. Knowing that they could not hold the fort against English bombardment, the French had come forward, desperate to stop the advancing army. While Canadian troops blocked the road, Indians fired down on the British column from the forest cover on both sides.

Had he proceeded with Indian scouts, Braddock might have avoided this battle, but he showed no appreciation of the assistance Indian allies might offer. The Delaware chief Shingas, nephew of Sassoonan, later told of offering the services of his warriors to Braddock, if only the general would reassure him on several important points. What, Shingas asked, did the general intend to do with the Ohio country once he drove the French away? It would then be English land, Braddock replied. But might not the friendly Indians at least "be Permitted to Live and Trade Among the English and have Hunting Grounds sufficient to Support themselves and Familys?" Shingas asked. "No Savage Should Inherit the Land," Braddock responded. Stung by this rejection, Shingas declared that "if they might not have Liberty To Live on the Land they would not Fight for it," and his delegation left to Braddock's shouted taunt "that he did not need their Help and had no doubt of driveing the French and their Indians away." It was Braddock's failure to employ Indian spies and scouts, Boone believed, that cost him the battle.

When the shooting began at the front of the line, American woodsmen charged for the timber to fight in the only way they knew, but the British officers, intent on maintaining discipline, kept their regular troops in suicidal formation. From Boone's position a half mile back, officers hastened their companies forward, leaving a guard for the wagons. As they rushed against the stalled front, the entire army crushed together like an accordion. Chaos soon prevailed amid the rain of fire. In the rear, snipers began to take their toll. The teamsters were ordered not to turn about but to hold their horses at the ready for advance. But with balls whistling past their heads, many of them cut their horses from the wagons and galloped away during the first minutes of the battle. According to

Boone, he remained. Nowhere could the enemy be seen, only the bursts of their rifle fire amid the trees and the men dropping "like Leaves in Autumn," as one British officer later remembered.

The slaughter continued for nearly three hours. Of the nearly fourteen hundred men committed to battle, more than nine hundred were killed or wounded, many by their own fire. Most of the Americans who died probably were shot by regular British troops who mistook them for Indians among the trees. A high proportion of the officers fell. Washington had two horses killed under him, and though balls tore through his uniform, he somehow emerged without a wound. In the rear, two officers, father and son, were shot dead while Boone held his team. Braddock attempted to organize a retreat, but the wagons now blocked passage to the rear. Driven to frenzy, the survivors finally broke for the river when the general himself was hit and fell from his horse, mortally wounded. "The yell of the Indians is fresh on my ear," one soldier later recalled, "and the terrific sound will haunt me until the hour of my dissolution." The Indian cries and the sight of the troops rushing past, death on their faces, finally unnerved Boone. He jumped onto his lead horse, slashed its harness free, and galloped hard for the river. He remained

Until that he saw all attempts were in vain,
From sighs and from tears he could scarcely refrain.
Poor Brittons, poor Brittons, poor Brittons remember,
Although we fought hard, we were forced to surrender.

Members of the Boone family long sang this plaintive backwoods ballad.

Canadians and Indians quickly overran the wagons, but they did not pursue the fleeing men across the ford, for they turned to plundering the rations of rum and other supplies, scalping the dead, and rounding up the wounded, who were lead back to the fort to be tortured and burned at the stake. The Battle of the Monongahela, Boone's initiation into forest warfare, was one of the bloodiest and most disastrous British defeats of the eighteenth century.

After the battle Boone apparently left on foot, heading east to visit his relatives in Exeter, where family traditions placed him before he returned home to the Yadkin. At the crossing of the

Juniata River gorge he suddenly was confronted by a big, half-drunk Indian man standing in the center of the bridge. "He drew his knife on me," old Boone remembered, "flourishing it over his head, boasting that he had killed many a Long Knife, and would kill some more on his way home." Indians on the upper Ohio called Americans "Long Knives" because of the sabers many carried into battle. But here Boone was unarmed—perhaps his weapon had been lost in the debacle on the Monongahela—and he kept his distance. There was no way around the man, however, who repeated his threat. Fresh from the scene of slaughter, Boone thought to himself "that the blood-thirsty red skin had killed his last victim—that it was high time an end should be put to his bloody career." He watched for his opportunity. The drunken man lurched forward, weaving, and quickly Boone dashed at him. Using his low center of gravity to advantage, he drove his shoulder hard under the big man's ribs, lifting him off his feet, throwing him back and off the side of the bridge. He plunged forty feet to the jagged rocks below.

Boone told this story to the sons of his old friend Henry Miller toward the end of his life. Most tales about him "represented him as a wonderful man who had killed a host of Indians," but the truth was, he said, "I never killed but three," and the man lying mangled on the rocks of the Juniata River was the first. Young Boone, shaken, hurried on to his Pennsylvania birthplace. This was nothing to crow about, certainly nothing he could repeat to his Quaker kin in Exeter, and there is no record of Boone ever telling this story to the members of his own family. "Boone had very little of the *war spirit*," one contemporary wrote. "He never liked to take life and always avoided it when he could." It was an aspect of his character that the Indian haters never could understand.

CHAPTER TWO

My Domestic Happiness

1755 to 1769

Daniel Boone returned home from Braddock's defeat during the summer of 1755. The Boones were by that time well established at the Forks of the Yadkin. From the moment of his arrival Squire Boone, speaking for a large extended family and owning several square miles of land, was one of the "big men" of this backcountry section of North Carolina. When rapid population growth led colonial officials to set off this territory as the county of Rowan in 1753, they appointed Boone's father a justice of the peace and in that capacity he sat as a member of the county court, a local governing body exercising not only judicial but administrative powers, overseeing the tax list, poor relief, road repair, and the licensing of mills and taverns. In 1754 Squire presented his fellow justices with a petition that he be allowed to operate a "Publick House at his own Plantation" on Dutchman's Creek, astride what was known as "Squire Boone's Old Mill Road." They issued the license and set his rates at one shilling for a "Dinner of Roasted or Boiled Flesh," six shillings for a gallon of rum, whiskey, or other spirits, and two pence per night for lodging "in a good bed." The Squire Boone establishment was one of the few social centers in the sparsely settled community of the Forks. At about the same time,

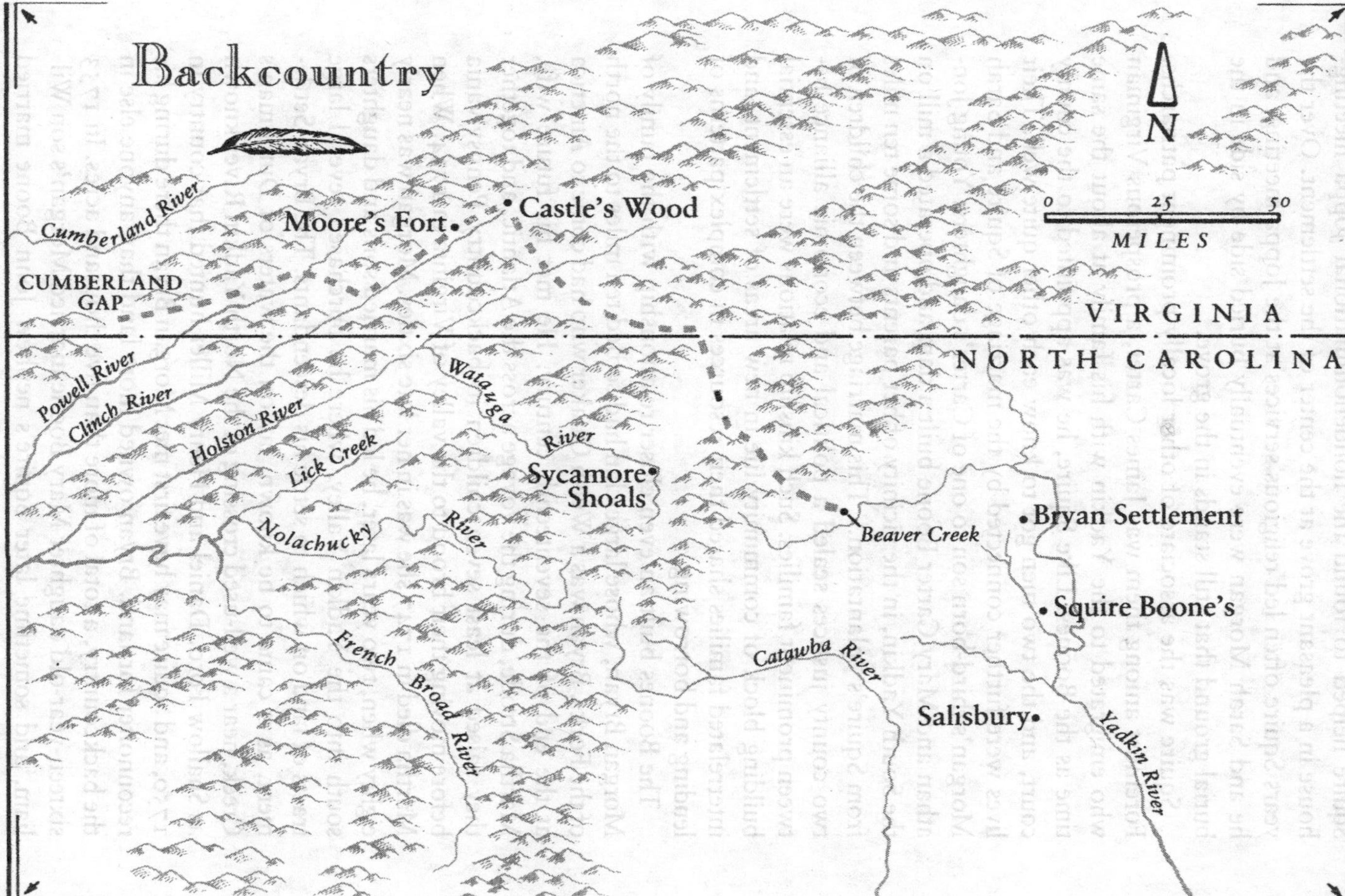

Backcountry
N
0 25 50
MILES
Castle's Wood
Moore's Fort
Cumberland River
CUMBERLAND GAP
VIRGINIA
NORTH CAROLINA
Powell River
Clinch River
Holston River
Lick Creek
Watauga River
Sycamore Shoals
Nolachucky River
Beaver Creek
Bryan Settlement
Squire Boone's
Catawba River
French Broad River
Salisbury
Yadkin River

Squire helped to found the nondenominational Joppa meetinghouse in a pleasant grove at the center of the settlement. Over the years Squire often led religious services at the Joppa meeting, and he and Sarah Morgan were eventually buried side by side in the burial ground that still stands in the grove.

Squire was the associate of other locally prominent patriarchs. Foremost among them was James Carter, a prosperous Virginian who emigrated to the Yadkin with his family at about the same time as the Boones. Like Squire, he was appointed to the county court, and the two men got to know each other quite well. Their lives were further connected by the marriage of Squire and Sarah Morgan's third-born son to one of Carter's daughters. Young Jonathan and Mary Carter Boone built a dam and operated a mill on the South Yadkin, in the vicinity of her parents and some ten miles from Squire's "plantation." This marriage between the children of two county justices sealed a political and economic alliance between prominent families. Such kinship relations were an essential building block of community life in new areas of settlement, and interrelated families shared their resources in complex patterns of lending and borrowing.

The Boones built an even closer relationship with the family of Morgan Bryan, whose large clan had settled ten miles to the north of the Forks. Bryan was a Welsh Quaker who had come to America at the end of the seventeenth century. He met his future wife, Martha Strode, during the voyage across the Atlantic, and together they raised at least seven children in backcountry Pennsylvania before moving their brood to the valley of Virginia in 1734. When Martha died in 1747 she was in her late sixties. Morgan was nearly eighty when, two years later, he led his married sons and daughters south into the Yadkin Valley, where he purchased several large tracts of land on which to settle his descendants. The Bryan Settlement, as it came to be known, lay on the waters of Dutchman's Creek, near a well-used crossing of the North Yadkin River known as Shallow Ford. Daniel and Henry Miller hunted that country in 1750, and Squire may have first met Morgan Bryan there during his reconnoiter for land. Bryan owned more land than anyone else in the backcountry, a total of more than five thousand acres. In 1753 sixteen-year-old daughter Mary Boone married Morgan's son William, and sometime later Squire's nephew John Boone married

Morgan's daughter Rebecca, these unions beginning a family alliance between Boones and Bryans that would continue for generations. For Daniel Boone, this connection would be the marrow of his kinship.

It was at one of these Boone-Bryan weddings of 1753, Daniel and Rebecca Boone told their children, that they first took notice of each other. Daniel hunted frequently with the three oldest sons of Joseph and Aylee Bryan, Rebecca's parents. Along with other Boone and Bryan men these young bachelors would have formed the core of the rowdies who gathered on the wedding morning, passing the jug ("Black Betty") and roaming through the countryside, rousing the farm families for the celebration. As one who excelled in the rough male sports characterizing these occasions, Boone would have been hard to miss by young Rebecca, born in western Virginia on January 9, 1739. Although no likeness of her exists, contemporary descriptions all give her jet-black hair and dark, penetrating eyes. A descendant said Rebecca was "one of the handsomest persons she ever saw." She appears in folktales as "a buxom daughter," and her nephew Daniel Boone Bryan called her "a rather over common sized woman." In middle age, in fact, she would stand nearly as tall and broad as her husband. Bryan recalled her "very mild and pleasant speech and kind behaviour," and one of her granddaughters remembered that she was "one of the neatest and best of house keepers, proverbial for the tidiness and Quaker-like simplicity and propriety of all her domestic arrangements." She was quoted as saying that "folks ought always to keep their things and houses in good order." These comments are akin to descriptions of Boone's mother, Sarah Morgan, and it may have been just such a deep affinity that first caught young Boone's eye. Throughout their marriage he always called Rebecca "my little girl," reflecting back, perhaps, on his first sight of her, when she was scarcely fifteen.

Frontier legend related a different tale of their meeting. On a summer's eve, when the deer congregated at the creeks to avoid the swarms of bothersome mosquitoes and feast on the tender water mosses, young Boone would oftentimes pursue the "firehunt," a companion holding a firebrand aloft while he stalked the creek, rifle at the ready. Starting from their feeding and gazing upon the approaching fire, the deer would stand frozen, seemingly hypnotized by the light, the reflected glow cast by their eyes a target for his rifle. On one such occasion, so the tale was told, Rebecca, whose task it was to herd her father's cows, is out searching for strays when she is overtaken by sudden nightfall. Losing her way in the dark, she strikes a course for home by wading through the shallows of the creek. Suddenly ahead she sees the glow of an approaching torch and the reflection of a rifle barrel. At the same moment, Boone levels his piece at the blaze of her eyes but, sensing that these shining orbs are unlike those of any deer he had seen, holds his fire for a crucial second, long enough for Rebecca to bound away in terror through the woods. Boone pursues and finds her trail leading to the Bryan homestead. There he meets the panting maiden. Thunderstruck at how near he had come to destroying this woman, whom he immediately knows will become the object of his love, he thereafter gives up firehunting.

Variants of this folktale circulated widely in the backcountry settlements of frontier America. The story of the hunter who falls in love with his prey is, in fact, common in the folklore of many hunting peoples; the sexual union of hunter and deer-woman was a recurrent motif in the oral culture of American Indians. Its appropriation in the Boone firehunt tale is another example of frontier borrowing and suggests some of the close affinities between American and Indian cultures. It also hints at important tensions between frontier men and women. Rebecca is placed in deadly peril by Boone's pursuit of his occupation. She is saved by the restraint of his passion, and his transformation from hunter to husband is achieved through the renunciation of an aspect of his livelihood. Thus the tale addresses in metaphor certain discontinuities of gender and suggests that men must forsake certain freedoms to achieve union with women. However, while the tale may contain an important cultural truth, Boone descendants protested its biographical inaccuracy. "Without foundation," a nephew complained; "As fabulous as it is absurd," a niece wrote, correctly pointing out that human eyes do not shine like the eyes of forest creatures. If there had ever been any "shining of eyes," Boone's daughter-in-law Olive Vanbibber Boone cleverly suggested, it took place at the moment Daniel and Rebecca first looked into each other's.

Boone first began to court his future bride in the summer of

1756, the year following his return from the war in Pennsylvania. Family traditions of their courtship placed less emphasis on romance than on the process of mutual testing that took place. Both remembered first being together at a cherry picking, a common occasion for wooing. As they told the tale, the young couple sits together under the trees, he in his ordinary hunting shirt, the costume of the frontier provider, she in her fine white cambric apron, a token of her domestic talents. Daniel is uncomfortable, his conversation halting and stuttered, and in his adolescent embarrassment he draws out his knife and absentmindedly begins to toss it, mumblety-peg, into the turf. Suddenly there are several large gashes in Rebecca's apron. Boone offers no apology, she no reproach. Neither, in fact, say anything at all about it, allowing the incident to pass. He had mangled the apron deliberately, Boone told his children, "*to try her temper*—thinking if it was firey, she would fly into a passion." When she did not, he knew she was the woman for him. If this sounds a bit like an afterthought, it is nevertheless a good example of Boone's wit as well as an accurate assessment of Rebecca's character. "Boone was sometimes odd enough to ordinary appearance," said his son Nathan, "but, as in this case, he had a purpose in his singular ways." Rebecca's life with Boone would present her with many hardships, and more than once her characteristic steadiness and constancy would hold the family together.

A second family tradition had Boone demonstrating his prowess as a hunter and provider by bringing a deer to Rebecca's house. While he dresses the carcass outdoors, she cooks a first meal for him at the hearth. Finishing his bloody task, he comes inside for his dinner. The Bryans were well-to-do folk who, in the judgment of a passing frontier missionary, seemed "to have much of this world's goods." Their manners were probably somewhat more refined than those of the Boones. Daniel's old hunting shirt is still messy with the gore of his butchering and he has not thought to bring a change of clothing. Expecting admiration for his obvious skills with rifle and knife, he finds himself instead the object of the scornful giggles of Rebecca and her sisters, who think it amusing, if not appalling, that this suitor would dare to sit at the Bryan family table in such a state. Throughout his life Boone was overly sensitive to criticism; such teasing during the ordeal of courtship must have stung him with a special sharpness. He sits down to Rebecca's meal and lifts a wooden noggin to drink, but stops abruptly, staring into his cup. "You, like my hunting shirt," he quips, "have missed many a good washing." As one Boone kinsman declared, women were proud and "needed kind subduing." At the wedding of one of Boone's sisters, an old man toasted the groom: "Well, Billy, Betsy will make you a good wife if you will take her down at the first loaf." In the sporting between the sexes Daniel's comment was thought to have evened the contest.

Justice Squire Boone officiated at the marriage of Daniel Boone and Rebecca Bryan on August 14, 1756. The groom was twenty-one, the bride seventeen. They remembered it to their children as a triple wedding, an occasion shared with two other couples from the extended Boone and Bryan clans. After the ceremony the brides' sisters prepared a feast for the guests, with plenty to eat and jugs of cider, rum, and whiskey to drink. In midevening, as part of the traditional events, the bride and groom's attendants escorted the couple to the loft and tucked them into bed. As Daniel and Rebecca lay together for the first time, from beneath the floorboards they could hear the bawdy jokes traditionally told at the expense of the newlyweds as the frolic continued late into the night. "Where is Black Betty?" the men would call out for the jug, "I want to kiss her sweet lips," and then they would offer toasts: "Here's health to the groom, not forgetting myself, and here's to the bride, thumping luck and big children!" Traditionally this party would have been held in the newlyweds' first home, a cabin on Squire Boone's home lot where Daniel and Rebecca lived during the first few months of their marriage. It also was traditional for the bride's patrimonial goods to be displayed for the guests to examine. Coming from a prosperous household, Rebecca brought into the marriage a considerable dowry of linens, furniture, and cooking equipment.

For Rebecca Bryan Boone there was no honeymoon. She immediately became mistress of a household that included the two young sons of Daniel's brother Israel, who had died two months earlier. Israel's wife had predeceased him, a victim of consumption, or tuberculosis; soon after her death, the widower too came down with the disease. With his four children, he had lived in the household of his parents, and his two boys had grown close to their Uncle Daniel. In August of 1755 Sarah Morgan appeared with her consumptive son at the Moravian colony, twenty-five miles northeast of the Forks of the Yadkin at Salem, appealing for treatment from the resident doctor. There Israel remained, hospitalized for several weeks, and when he left, the record noted that there was "small hope of his recovery." Sometime after his death, his two daughters also expired from the disease. The boys, Jesse and Jonathan, however, continued to live with Rebecca and Daniel in North Carolina until the family left for Kentucky in 1773.

Rebecca's own first child, James, was born nine months after the wedding, on May 3, 1757. A second son, Israel, followed twenty months later, on January 25, 1759. Not yet twenty, Rebecca was mothering four children. Over the first twenty-five years of her marriage she delivered a total of ten children—six sons and four daughters—their births separated by an average of only two and a half years. This was not unusual for a woman of her time and place. Hers was a world in which little effort was made to limit conception, and that pattern, which had characterized the women of previous generations, would persist in those that followed. Rebecca's mother, Aylee Bryan, bore ten children and Daniel's mother, Sarah Morgan Boone, eleven. Rebecca's four daughters had thirty-three children between them, and the wives of her three married sons bore another thirty-five. Because her children married young and frequently resided in her household with their spouses, Rebecca often had grandbabies alongside her own. As if all this were not enough, when she was in her early forties she adopted and raised the six motherless nieces and nephews of a widowed brother. Such crowded quarters were commonplace on the American side of the frontier. In 1771 a traveling preacher passing through the Forks of the Yadkin noted twenty-three persons living in the one-room cabin of William and Mary Boone Grant.

Before the birth of James, Boone and Rebecca moved from the cabin on his father's place to a small farm in the Bryan Settlement, nearer her kin, on a stream called Sugartree, a tributary of Dutchman's Creek, a site about two miles east of the present village of Farmington, North Carolina. Here they made their home for nearly ten years, their longest stretch in any single location. With the help of the Bryans, Boone hewed logs and raised a substantial one-story house, measuring eighteen feet by twenty-two feet. A single door opened to the south, and inside was a massive fireplace with a deep hearth, its huge exterior chimney built of soapstone and wood. Nearby was a separate small summer kitchen. This was not a log cabin but a log house—an important distinction—a place meant to raise a family. Over the years Boone laid a floor of oak puncheons over the bare earth and sided the exterior with clapboards fastened with wooden pegs. With the exception of eighteen cast-iron nails in the front door, not another could be found in the construction of the building, a local resident testified in the 1880s.

Slaves were present in a number of the Bryan and Boone households at the Forks. Jonathan Boone purchased a Negro man and girl from his father-in-law, James Carter, in the mid-1750s, Rebecca's uncle Billy Bryan had a number of slaves working as herdsmen for him, and given the prosperity of her grandfather and father, they too probably owned slaves. In the back of the colony, however, slavery was not very important economically. The majority of settlers had come south from Pennsylvania, and very few brought slaves. By official estimate there were only sixty slaves in the three westernmost counties in 1754, and even fifteen years later, when African-Americans had grown to number about 20 percent of the backcountry population, slaves were present in fewer than 10 percent of households. There is no record of Daniel and Rebecca owning slaves in North Carolina, but if they did not, it was simply because they could not afford to.

A slave woman might have provided Rebecca with some useful assistance, but in the domestic economy of the young couple, slave labor would not have been very efficient, because farming and stockraising were only subsistence activities for the family. Boone earned money by doing some blacksmithing in the neighborhood and by "wagoning" back and forth to Salisbury with supplies and goods, but mostly by hunting and trapping. During summer deer hunts he carried home his catch Indian fashion, securing the carcass to his shoulders with "hoppus" strings of sinew. After the harvest was in, however, with leaves falling and frosts killing the undergrowth, Boone, like all hunters, grew restless for the forest. "I have often seen them get up early in the morning at this season," wrote a lifelong resident of the Western country, "walk hastily out, look anxiously to the woods, and snuff the autumnal winds with the highest rapture." Fur animals, it was said, could be trapped in any month spelled with an *r*, but coats were best after October and before March. Fall deer hunting and winter beaver trapping might keep him away from home for weeks, and as the Yadkin filled in with settlement, he was forced farther into the foothills of the Appalachians in search of game and was absent for increasingly long periods.

The farms of the Bryan Settlement were dispersed across the countryside at intervals of a mile or more. Families lived in relative isolation from one another, and when Boone was away on his long hunts, Rebecca was alone with the children. How did these women survive? wondered one Moravian missionary who encountered them in lonely and isolated cabins. "A woman is ill, has a high fever—where is the nurse, medicine, proper food? The wife of the nearest neighbor lives half a mile, perhaps several miles away, and she has her own children, her cattle, her own household to care for, and can give only a couple of hours, or at most one day or one night." This man recommended settlements with clusters of six or seven families, but Americans were much too individualistic to tolerate the Moravian standards of communal discipline, and even in wartime, when collective security offered more incentive for working together, there were always men who insisted on settling their families miles away, in the midst of the wilderness.

A Boone family tale of an incident that occurred during the years in the Bryan Settlement illustrates the contemporary awareness of these problems. Returning from one of his hunts and finding the family grain supply low, Boone sets out for his father-in-law's to thrash out some rye. In the Bryan Settlement there lives an old hunter, Samuel Tate, a frequent hunting companion of Boone's. As he passes Tate's cabin Boone discovers the family in distress because of the husband's prolonged absence, so on his way back he kindly drops off a supply of rye. A few days later, an angry Tate appears at Boone's door. What business did you have at my place? he demands. I was only being neighborly, Boone replies; I would be grateful to any man who looked out for my folks. Well, growls Tate, stay away from my woman! Outraged at Tate's insinuation, Boone gives him "a severe flogging, and said he would do it again should Tate ever throw out any more jealous intimations."

The work performed by backcountry women like Rebecca was staggering. It was the labor of women, in fact, that made possible men's hunting. With men so frequently away from the homestead, many women became the sole support for their families. There was, of course, the cooking and cleaning, spinning and weaving, and washing and sewing, but then there was also water to be fetched each day from the spring, wood to be chopped, gardens to be tended, and cows to be milked. There were fields to be cultivated and crops to be harvested as well. Needing fresh meat for the stew pot, many was the time that Rebecca herself hunted for small game in the woods near the house. In the nineteenth century men along the Yadkin still told of the time she rode north to a salt lick on Deep Creek, her gun loaded with buckshot, and "fired a gun from nearly the top of a tree and killed 7 deer and her mare that she rode there." It was an improbable tale, and coupled with a male barb about the dead horse, yet the story testified to the strength and determination of an able and intelligent woman, the center of an affectionate and close family.

From the middle of the 1750s to the early 1760s, the war between England and France, fought by their colonial subjects and their Indian allies, brought high anxiety to the frontier. During the summer of 1755 reports of attacks westward encouraged people on the Yadkin to build protective blockhouses. The summer Boone and Rebecca were married, several bands of Cherokees extorted food and supplies from farmers in the Forks, and fearful families fled from their cabins into their neighborhood forts. It did not help matters that those were years of drought, poor crops, and shortages of game, for scarcity heightened tensions between Indians and Americans and set everyone on edge. Indian alarms occurred regularly each spring and summer in the Bryan Settlement. According to Boone family tradition, Daniel and Rebecca "forted up" with their neighbors three times before 1760. Shawnees, reportedly armed by the French, raided down from the Ohio in 1758, attacking and killing a number of settlers along the border between Virginia and North Carolina. In the spring of the next year the Cherokees raided a number of farms on the Catawba and Yadkin rivers, burned cabins and fields, and carried off supplies. Unconfirmed rumors of kidnappings and murder swept through the backcountry, and the people of Bryan Settlement abandoned their farms and forted up again.

Not all of the depredations of those years were the result of

Indians. Highwaymen and outlaws also overran the country, taking advantage of the unsettled conditions. Not far from Sugartree Creek, a farmer left his wife and children alone while he searched for some stray horses. It grew late in the evening, and as the woman anxiously awaited his return, her dogs grew restless, howling and running back and forth in front of the cabin. Opening the door to see what was the matter, she was met with a barrage of stones that came flying at her from out of the darkness. Fearing an Indian attack, she quickly gathered up her children and fled into the woods, but looking back saw three white men spring into her house. They were bandits, and they robbed the family of all of its clothing and valuables. Another woman reported that a man came riding up to her cabin, warned of Indians in the neighborhood, and urged her to run with her children to the nearest stockade. After she left, he returned and plundered her place.

One particularly bold gang of house robbers and horse thieves plagued the Boone neighborhood from a hideout on the upper Yadkin. During one raid on the settlement they kidnapped a young girl; her distraught father organized a posse of forty men, and Boone volunteered to guide them along the trails he knew so well from his hunts. He led the vigilantes toward the mountains, where they found the girl running back along the trail toward the settlements. Her captors had gotten drunk and fallen to fighting over which of them would "use" her first, and in the confusion she managed to escape. She led the posse to the hideout, where the vigilantes overpowered the bandits, capturing three men, five women, and eleven children, but the ringleaders got away. The prisoners were taken to the Salisbury gaol and the men soon swung from the county gallows. The group of them, it was said, had planned to lead the French enemy into the back settlements, a report that surely said more about the popular state of mind than the probable motives of the outlaws. Some time later, Boone said, a farmer in the Bryan Settlement was discovered with a cache of the stolen goods. A confession was "sweated" out of him, a torture in which he was suspended by his arms, pinioned behind his back. The angry settlers then forced him to guide a posse, again including Boone, to the outlaw hideout. The leaders were captured and arrested. In retaliation for his act of betrayal this farmer was later assassinated by parties unknown. It was a rough business. When a missionary on the Yadkin wrote that "the people about here are wild," he was not referring to the Indians.

In the fall of 1759, however, the focus shifted back to Indian war. Attakullakulla, a principal chief of the Cherokees, had worked hard to maintain the alliance with the English, but growing numbers of his people favored the French. After several Cherokee women were brutally raped by English soldiers and a band of warriors were murdered and scalped by settlers, the young braves, lead by Chief Oconostota, went to war against the colonists. Boone first heard of the Cherokee uprising while he was in Salisbury serving as a juror of the Rowan County Court. Within days the county militia had mustered, and fifty men under the command of Maj. Hugh Waddell were on their way to reinforce Fort Dobbs at the headwaters of the South Yadkin River in the western hills. Boone may have been among this number, for he later spoke of serving under Waddell at Fort Dobbs.

Cherokee warriors attacked the fort in February of 1760. Attempting to draw the Americans out, small groups revealed themselves at the edge of the woods. Major Waddell was in command of a force pursuing these decoys when he was ambushed by sixty or seventy warriors. Somehow he succeeded in getting most of his men back within the walls, and his militia repulsed the Cherokee attack. Suspecting, however, that the main force of Indians were headed for the settlements on the Yadkin, Boone and a number of his neighbors struck out for home. Arriving, they found evidence confirming their worst fears—the mangled bodies of a farmer and his son, whom they buried before hurrying on to their local stockades. This time, as Cherokees swept down on the Forks, at least a dozen Yadkin men and women met their deaths. With the war now come to their own yards, the Boones, like many others, decided it was time to fall back into Virginia.

In this exodus they were joined by Daniel's parents and the three youngest of his siblings, who yet remained at home—brothers Squire and Edward (always called Ned or Neddy by the family) and sister Hannah—in addition to his older sister Elizabeth, with her husband and children, and possibly others of his grown siblings and their families. The group traveled more than two hundred miles northeast to accommodations among friends in Culpeper County, Virginia. Rebecca was pregnant, and for the next several months Boone remained with her in Virginia, working as a teamster, hauling tobacco to market, while awaiting the arrival of his first daughter, Susannah, who was born on November 2, 1760. Immediately thereafter he returned alone to the Carolina backcountry for his winter hunt.

How much action Boone saw in the campaigns of 1761 is not known. If he returned to serve under Hugh Waddell he would have spent much of that year ranging across the countryside with the militia. The settlements along the Yadkin were pretty much abandoned, and in August, Waddell added his men to the Virginia forces and invaded the towns of the Cherokee on the Little Tennessee, killing and burning and driving the survivors into the mountains. By all accounts the fighting was particularly brutal, with much slaughter of women and children as well as warriors. "We have now the pleasure, Sir," one soldier wrote after one battle, "to fatten our dogs with their carcasses and to display their scalps neatly ornamented on the top of our bastions." Late in the year the Cherokees sued for peace. Although the larger war would not be concluded until 1763, and Pontiac's Rebellion would keep conflicts with the northern Indians active until late in 1764, this treaty with the Cherokees marked the end of the violence in the southern backcountry for some years.

With the Yadkin farm out of service, Boone intensified his hunting. While working the Brushy Mountains between the upper reaches of the Yadkin and Catawba rivers with fellow hunter Nicholas Gist during December 1760, Boone met a man named Burrell, a slave serving as a cowherd for a backcountry settler, who told him of a rich hunting ground at the crest of the Blue Ridge that could be reached by following an old buffalo trace. He led Boone and Gist to a log shelter used by herders on a beautiful high meadow. Here, within a few square miles, were the headwaters of the Yadkin, flowing east to the Atlantic, and those of the New and Watauga rivers, both of which eventually found their roundabout way to the Ohio. It was Boone's first venture across the divide between Atlantic and Gulf waters. The hunters followed an old Indian path leading northwest to Whitetop Mountain in southern Virginia; from the summit they commanded an unobstructed and awe-inspiring view of the Appalachian highlands and valleys. They spent that winter hunting and trapping in what are now the national forests of western North Carolina, eastern Tennessee, and southwestern Virginia. In subsequent seasons Boone frequently used the herders' cabin as a base for his long hunts. It stood for many years, and early in the twentieth century, chimney stones from its ruins were incorporated into a monument to Boone on the site, now the campus of Appalachian State University, in the resort town of Boone, North Carolina.

The abundant game of this region made the area a favorite of Boone's, and during the 1760s he came to know intimately these mountains and gaps, springs and salt licks, and eventually pushed as far west as the valleys of the Holston and Clinch rivers. He certainly was not the first American there, for in addition to herdsmen like Burrell, other hunters had preceded him. Yet because of his prowess with rifle and trap, Boone became identified as the best of the Blue Ridge hunters, and as one early Kentucky settler put it, to be "a great hunter was the greatest honor to which any man could attain." Not only did he require a practical wisdom of animal habits, but he had to be an expert at interpreting the landscape, noting patterns of flora, and reading various kinds of "sign." So accurate an observer and quick a learner was Boone, old Carolinians said of him "that he never crossed a route he had once traversed without at once recognizing the place and knowing that he was crossing one of his former trails." When game was scarce Boone would turn to collecting ginseng roots, valued as an aphrodisiac, and when his sack was filled with "sang," he would deposit his collection at various sites, later returning "strait to them all with unerring accuracy." During the nineteenth century, in the local parlance of the Tennessee mountains, "a Boone" was another name for a good hunter.

Boone was often in the company of other Yadkin men, some of whom would join him later in his explorations of Kentucky. With their horses and dogs they packed large quantities of lead, powder, traps, and smithing tools into the mountains but otherwise expected to live "on their guns and on the range." For long winter hunts they established a base camp as center of operations. Up early, each man would set out independently, usually without breakfast, depending on nuts and other forage to fend off hunger. All day he hunted or set and checked his trap lines. Returning with his catch to camp before dark, each would roast his favorite cut of meat before the fire. Many men loved beaver tail, but Boone disliked its oily taste and preferred elk's liver. He was an acclaimed expert at roasting a wild turkey, tying a piece of bark around its neck and hanging it over an open fire, keeping it turning while basting it with its own juices. "And at supper," wrote a fellow hunter, "it appeared that he not only knew how to cook a turkey but to eat it as well." While they cooked and ate, the men shared news of the day's hunt and spent the long evenings telling stories.

Many a tale was told about Boone, the best of them. One related the time he shared camp with that troublesome old hunter Samuel Tate, a character who appeared frequently as the villain in the Boone lore of North Carolina. Each morning when they awake, the two men divide the range between them, and in deference to Tate's age, Boone allows him to claim the better ground. But each day Tate infringes on Boone's territory, poaching his game, then brags of his greater hunting skill. Finally Boone can take it no more. "Tate," says he, "you boast so much, but I believe I could whip you," and the two men fall to fighting. Tate is powerfully built, and several of his roundhouse swings send Boone reeling. But Boone is the better boxer, and he gives Tate such a whipping that the older man is "glad to cry for quarter." The next morning Tate's face is so badly swollen from the blows that he cannot open his eyes, "and Boone had the whole range to hunt by himself."

By himself, so the tales suggested, was the way Boone preferred it. He might spend several weeks hunting and trapping with no companions save his dog and horse. He would construct a little "half-faced camp," a three-sided shanty covered with brush, the open end facing the fire, and there he would take his evening meals. He had fallen in love with solitude during his youth as a herdsman, and now he developed further his "habit of contemplation." In the nineteenth century his love of isolation was criticized by many as an indication of an antisocial nature, and Boone's family responded defensively. "His wanderings were from duty," declared one niece, arguing that "no man loved society better, nor was more ardently attached to his family." Yet Boone actually relished these opportunities to be alone during his annual hunts, and given the increasingly crowded quarters at home, who could blame him? He frequently carried along a copy of the Bible, or a book of history, which he loved, or *Gulliver's Travels*, his favorite book, to read by the light of the campfire. Then, leaving the fire burning, he would bed down on a cushion of hemlock or dried leaves, head to the backlog, feet to the fire to prevent the rheumatism that was the constant complaint of old hunters, moccasins tied to his gun, standing primed and ready should Indians or outlaws attack.

He was alone, as Boone later told the tale, in the mountains of eastern Tennessee one cold winter night, when Cherokee hunters silently surrounded his camp. "Ah! Wide mouth," one of the Indians exclaimed in English as he lifted the snow-covered blanket from a sleeping Boone, "have I got you now!" He was working in prime Cherokee hunting territory, and the bitter feelings of the recent war remained strong. But betraying no sense of intimidation, he welcomed the hunters as guests to his camp, probably passing his flask among them. His familiarity with the customs of the woods was reinforced by a remarkable ease among its peoples. He never quaked in the presence of Indians but always looked them directly in the eye, speaking with a tone of respect yet determination. Such steadiness was possessed by few Americans, and it marked Boone as an extraordinary man of the forest.

He was released unharmed by these Cherokees, but they took all of his furs. One of his fellow hunters, Benjamin Cutbeard, who was the husband of Boone's niece Elizabeth Wilcoxen, later related that he and Boone were similarly overtaken by another Cherokee hunting party on Roan Creek, a mountain tributary of the Watauga River. "You long hunters are intruding on our hunting grounds and killing too much game," the Indians complained, and they took from the two everything they possessed. About that same time a colonial newspaper printed the report that the Cherokees had complained to the authorities of North Carolinians trapping beaver in their country, in violation of the treaty of 1761.

But Boone's relations with the Cherokees remained generally good, and he seems to have even joined them on an occasional hunt. One tale has him stalking game with a group of Cherokees when they come across what appears to be a buffalo trail. In an earlier time buffalo had trailed over the mountains into the foothills, but with the press of settlement they now remained in trans-Appalachian territory, and at this point in his life, in the mid-1760s, Boone had not yet seen or hunted them. The

Cherokees puzzle over the sign. "No buffala," one of them concludes, "Tawbers." The Catawbas were known to manufacture buffalo sign in order to lure the Cherokees, their traditional enemies, into ambush. Boone and the Indians follow the trail a bit further to a large pile of animal droppings, and Boone breaks down in laughter—"Tawber no make so!" Boone's friendship with the Cherokees was among the reasons he later would be selected to help obtain their permission for a settlement colony in Kentucky.

Perhaps the most famous aspects of these early Appalachian hunting trips of the 1760s was a carving, first discovered in the 1770s, on the bark of a beech tree that stood on the banks of a small tributary of the Watauga River:

D. Boon
CillED A. BAr on
tree
in the
YEAR
1760

It was the first, and surely the most famous, of a great number of Boone carvings found in this region and elsewhere in Tennessee, Kentucky, and Missouri in the more than two centuries since. Next to a spring near the Clinch River, for instance, was found another inscription:

Daniel Boone
Come on boys
heres good water

American hunters were notorious graffiti artists. One party of hunters, robbed by Indians of the product of their winter's work, left their frustrations carved in bark: "Fifteen hundred skins gone to ruination." Some of the Boone carvings may be genuine, but Boone inscriptions have been found in the most unlikely of places, including the rocks and cliffs along the overland trail in the Far West and on an aspen near the continental divide in Idaho, reading "D. Boon 1776." Boone, in fact, always spelled his name with a final *e*, and the use of the semiliterate "Boon" is a tip-off of bogus inscriptions. This caveat applies to that first Boone inscription of 1760 as well, although at least it enjoys a provenance dating to an era before Boone's fame made his name the currency of pranksters.

Boone rejoined Rebecca and the children in Virginia sometime in 1762. The Cherokee war had separated the young couple for nearly two years. Family traditions suggest that before returning, Boone went to their Sugartree farm, put in a crop, and got the house back into shape. If so, he would have ridden north in the fall, after the harvest. In November of 1762 the Boones migrated back to the Forks by packhorse, accompanied by a number of Virginians emigrating to the new country, now seemingly secure from Indian troubles.

In her arms Rebecca carried a new baby, Jemima, born on October 4. If these dates are correct, she was conceived in Boone's absence. James Norman, one of the young Virginians who accompanied the Boones on this remove, afterward one of Boone's hunting companions, told his son years later that "the child was born while Daniel Boone was in the Alleghany war." Other tales of an illegitimate birth in the Boone household were whispered for years in the settlements of North Carolina and Kentucky. When Boone returned home, so the story goes, Rebecca meets him, weeping. What's the matter? asks Boone. You were gone so long, says she, we had supposed you dead. In her sorrow she had found company with another man, and now there was a new baby in the house. "Oh well," sighs Boone after a considerable pause, "the race will be continued." Whose is it? Why, says she, lowering her head in shame, it's your brother's.

James Norman told his son that "the child was layed to his brother Ned Boone." Neddy, Rebecca offered, "looked so much like Daniel, she couldn't help it." But in each of the many versions of the story, Boone takes this thunderclap in stride, acting as if nothing unusual had happened, tossing the child about playfully as though she were his own. "Daniel didn't seem to care much," Norman marveled, and other renditions of the tale conclude similarly. As Boone puts it in one of them: "So much the better, it's all in the family."

In his pursuit of Boone evidence, nineteenth-century historian Lyman Draper relentlessly sought the truth behind these rumors.

He eventually located an old man who claimed to have heard the tale from Boone himself. According to Stephen Hempstead, Boone's neighbor for a time during the old man's last years in Missouri, one evening they got to talking and Boone told him that after a particularly long absence, one that included a period of Indian captivity, he had returned home to find

> his wife quite lusty and in great distress on account of her peculiar situation. She had supposed him dead etc, etc. He enquired who would be the father of the child when born. She told him a certain Boone. He answered, you need not distress yourself so about it, I do not blame you one bit. I could not get away from the Indians any sooner to come to you. It will be a Boone any how, and besides I have been obliged to be married in Indian fashion a couple of times. Pho'pho! Dry up your tears and welcome me home. And that he said was the last of it.

"Mrs. Boone was present at the time he told me," Hempstead wrote to Draper, and as old Boone spoke, "she made her knitting needles fly very fast I can assure you."

None of these stories, of course, can be taken as gospel. As one nineteenth-century informant put it when questioned by Draper about conflicting details, "It may be a damned lie or a damned fact, I tell it as it was told me." The reference in Hempstead's version to Indian captivity, for example, would place the incident at a point in Rebecca's life when there were no corresponding childbirths to raise suspicions. "The main fact is not new to me—I presume there is some foundation for it," Draper replied to Hempstead, "but not at the time you indicate." Draper collected numerous other variants of what in his notes he referred to as "Boone's surprise." Eventually he reached the conclusion that James Norman's version came closest to approximating the truth.

As with so much of the evidence concerning Daniel Boone, these stories originated in the realm of folklore. Interpreted as folklore, they suggest some interesting things about American frontier culture. They were part of a genre of tales about separated couples. One told of a hunter who outstays his welcome at a friend's cabin. "As a ruse to get him off home," his host arranges to have word sent one evening that his folks fear that he has died and his wife is about to marry another man. The next dawn finds him riding furiously back home. One hunter returns after a long absence to find his wife living with another man, with whom she has had a child. He chases off his competitor but takes "his wife into favor again." In a different version a husband has been gone so long, his wife decides to marry "a much younger and likelier man." As the ceremony is about to begin, the absent partner reappears. "Well, Hugh," the frustrated bride exclaims with bitter disappointment, "are you alive *yet*?" These anecdotes were parables about the problems of frontier marriage. They reflected a conflict between conventional prescriptions, which condemned prolonged male absence from the home, and the actual household division of labor in the backcountry, in which women remained at home to farm, while men left the household for long periods to hunt.

Boone was thus condemned by a number of his contemporaries as a man who "didn't live happily with his family, [and] didn't like to work." Such sentiments were akin to the criticism leveled by cultural outsiders at long hunters for the neglect of their families. In North Carolina backwoodsmen "live with less labor" than anywhere else he knew, said the Virginia aristocrat William Byrd, a man who knew whereof he spoke. They made "their Wives rise out of their Beds early in the morning, at the same time that they Lye and Snoer, till the Sun has run one third of his course, and disperst all the unwholesome Damps." Frontier men did "little of the work" around their farms, complained one missionary in the Yadkin settlements, leaving it all for their wives and children to perform, while they enjoyed themselves hunting. Consequently, the work around the home place was "poorly done," animals had to fend for themselves, even in winter, and Indian corn grew where there should have been good European wheat. It all added up to a pattern of "irregular living." "There are many hunters here who work little," wrote another preacher, but "live like the Indians."

As this last remark suggests, the complaints amounted to the rejection of a way of life and had much in common with the European criticism of American Indians. The French emigrant Michel-Guillaume Jean de Crevecoeur described backwoodsmen as "new made Indians," "half cultivators and half hunters" who lived a "licentious, idle life." In the rush to commercial farming in the nineteenth century these criticisms were transformed into a cant, in which frontier ways were made to seem the very essence of barbarism and backwardness. In this climate of opinion, Boone supporters both inside and outside the family attempted to salvage the reputation of the Boone household by claiming that it had been run on solid Victorian principles. "Boone was not unfeeling or indifferent to the domestic relation," wrote the Baptist minister John Mason Peck, a Boone biographer of the 1840s. He could go on his long hunts because "he had sons large enough to raise a crop and manage the business of the farm, under the supervision of their industrious mother." The most unfortunate thing about such special pleading was its anachronism, its irrelevance to the real conditions and dilemmas of frontier life.

The folklore of Boone's family life, by contrast, did not ignore those dilemmas but sought to resolve them. The raconteurs of these tales of illegitimacy did not blame women for their actions. In one story Rebecca Boone "cries for shame," in a second she is "wonderfully mortified," and in a third she "falls upon her knees" at her husband's approach. Boone, who commands the voice of moral authority, bids her "to get up and do so no more," but there is no pious moralizing about fallen women. In the words of one informant, one never heard "a whisper to the disadvantage of Mrs. Boone" in these tales. Accountability rests squarely on male shoulders. In one variant, Boone and the ubiquitous Samuel Tate return from a long hunt to find that *both* of their wives have conceived and delivered babies in their absence. Boone manfully accepts responsibility for Rebecca's, but his companion makes "his wife put her child away." Hearing this, Boone angrily seeks out Tate and insists that he take the child back or suffer the consequences. "We have acted worse, if possible, than the women had," says Boone, for "if we had stayed at home, nothing of this kind would have happened." In another version of the tale, this one related by a woman, Rebecca herself gets a variation on this line. Says she to Boone when he appears: "You had better have staid at home and got it yourself."

The manner in which these stories handled Boone's role in his own family offers an instruction contrast with biographers who for years suppressed the whole incident for fear it would sully the reputation of an American hero. "I could not well use it in a published biography," Draper wrote about "Boone's surprise," and he pursued the evidence, as he explained to one concerned descendant, only so he "could more carefully and guardedly" avoid the matter in print. The storytellers, on the other hand, by making Boone's principal concern the calming of Rebecca's fears, concluded the tale not by soiling the character of the family but by easing Boone back into its bosom. "And so," the story ends, he "hushed her up," then "gathered up the family, brother and all," and returned home. Boone appears as a man of deliberation, slow to anger, ready to forgive. People from Boone's own cultural background were far more understanding and tolerant of the stresses of frontier life than were the historians who would later write the biographies.

Now in his early thirties, Boone was a man responsible for a household that included his wife and six children, including two young nephews. The family genealogy indicates that Rebecca's fifth child, Levina, was not born until March 23, 1766. While there may have been an intervening unrecorded miscarriage, it is possible that after the birth of Jemima in late 1762 she did not again conceive until the early summer of 1765. Of any continuing difficulty between Daniel and Rebecca, however, the record is otherwise silent.

There was a certain restiveness in the pattern of Boone's life during these years. There were, for example, growing difficulties in the pursuit of his livelihood. With the conclusion of the war and the suspension of Indian conflict, the American communities of the Yadkin Valley once again began to grow, and increased settlement drove out the game. Boone found himself caught in a squeeze between his need for income, what with a growing family to support and taxes to pay, and declining supplies of skins and furs. Like other hunters, he was on occasion unable to meet his obligations and sometimes was taken to court by his creditors. "Daniel Boone was rather 'slow pay,' and not particularly 'thrifty,' " reported one North Carolina lawyer who examined the court dockets in the nineteenth century. "Great hunters and fishermen are frequently an unpractical generation." But the record did not support the contention that, as another Carolina attorney put it, "Daniel Boone had the honor of having more suits entered against him for debt than any other man of his day," a claim that is frequently repeated by

Boone biographers. After carefully checking the records, the clerk of the Rowan County Court reported to Lyman Draper in the 1880s that Boone's name appeared very infrequently, "so I trust you will not write of the great Pioneer as also a great litigant."

But the pressure of mounting debt reached a climax in 1764 when the Rowan County Court issued a judgment against Boone for the substantial sum of £50. It may have been to clear this obligation that he sold a fine tract of land on Bear Creek, part of his father's original claim, conveyed to Daniel in 1759. This was his one piece of Yadkin property; there is no evidence that Boone ever owned the farm on Sugartree Creek, which his descendants always referred to as part of the Bryan place. After the sale of this patrimony, then, Boone no longer owned land in the Forks. About this time, according to family tradition, he proposed to Rebecca that the family move into the Blue Ridge Mountains to pioneer a homestead at the site of the cabin in the high meadows. Such a move would have put them almost directly atop the Proclamation Line of 1763, aimed at restricting American penetration of the western Indian country, but would have allowed Boone much better access to his favorite hunting territory. Rebecca, however, would not consider living in such isolation.

Adding to Boone's disquiet was the death of his father. "Squire Boone departed this life they sixty ninth year of his age," reads the crude stone marker still standing in the Joppa burial ground, "in thay year of our Lord 1765 Geneiary tha 2." In the years following, Boone often dreamed of his father, and he considered these visions to be portents of his fortune. If Squire appeared pleasant, as he usually did, there was nothing to fear, but on several occasions he dreamed of an angry confrontation and lack of reconciliation. Boone told his children that evil invariably followed after each of these nightmares. His dreams underline again the strength of his paternal identification. Boone was learning to live with the loss of his father by resurrecting him in dream life. This incorporation of Squire's values as a part of his own signaled Boone's transition to mature independence. Boone was enabling himself to sever his remaining connection to the home place at a time when the demands of his occupation pressed for a move. Meanwhile, other family matters seemed to resolve themselves. His mother, Sarah Morgan, went to live with her daughter Mary and son-in-law Billy

Bryan, where a traveling Moravian would find her "old and sick" several years before her death in 1777. And each of Boone's three youngest siblings—Neddy, Squire, Jr., and Hannah—all married and set up their own households at about the time of their father's death.

Boone was thus in a mood to consider something new when several friends from Culpeper County, Virginia, arrived at his Sugartree farm in the early fall of 1765. They were on their way south to explore some of the new country added to the British domain by the victory over France and Spain in the late war. The year previous, the authorities had announced a policy of providing free lands for settlement in the panhandle of east Florida. Planning to combine his annual fall hunt with a look at these lands, Boone left with this party, which included the five young Virginians as well as his brother Squire and his brother-in-law John Stewart, Hannah's husband. Their route took them south from Salisbury to the fortified town of Ninety-Six, the largest settlement in the back-country of South Carolina. From there they traveled to Savannah, then over the Old King's Road to Saint Augustine, Florida.

The recollections of Boone associates and descendants include only a few details of this extended tour. There is one notable piece of evidence, however, an accounting of expenses that constitutes the earliest surviving manuscript in Boone's hand. In one of his entries he debited three pounds "to one watsh plade away at dise." While an expert at shooting contests, Boone was always unlucky at games of chance. Other things Boone said about the trip seemed to reinforce the impression conveyed by this entry. He recalled that one of his companions, a man by the name of Slaughter, was an accomplished gambler and that his winnings met nearly all of the party's expenses. Indeed, Boone's memory of the tour made it sound something like an extended bachelor party, featuring a good deal of flirting and cavorting with pretty serving girls and Seminole Indian maidens.

Hunting along the Saint Johns River and across the landscape of east Florida to Pensacola was a discouraging experience. High water, boggy swamps, barren sand hills, and swarms of insects offered little to brag about, and scarce game provided them little to show for their efforts. Boone's brother-in-law Stewart was separated from the rest of the party for several days and almost starved before being found, a premonition of things to come in Kentucky. All of them became hopelessly lost in the tangle of some dark swamp and eventually were rescued by a party of Seminoles, who led them to their camp and succored them with venison and honey. Late in his life Boone was once asked if, in all of his wanderings, he had ever been lost. "No," he replied, "I can't say as ever I was lost, but I was bewildered once for three days." He may never have been more bewildered than he was in this strange Florida country.

The men traded their deerskins in Pensacola, also the seat of government, and inquired there about lands available for settlement. "On the whole," his son Nathan later reported, "Boone was not well satisfied with the country." The return trip took the men over a somewhat more familiar landscape, through the rich land of what would later be called Alabama, the country of the Creeks, then, by way of what was known as the Lower Trading Path, through the piney hills of Georgia, South Carolina, and finally home, a distance of more than 750 miles. He made a point of arriving home on Christmas Day, fulfilling a promise to Rebecca to be home for her holiday dinner. According to Nathan Boone, his father told him that he had purchased a town lot in Pensacola, "and would have moved to it, had not his wife been unwilling to go so far from her connections and friends." Nathan's information was generally excellent and there is little reason to doubt this in particular, except that it makes no sense. Why buy land in a country that offered so few prospects? Was it possible that Boone once again had "a purpose in his singular ways"? Rebecca had now declined two of her husband's proposals to move. Could she resist a third?

After the harvest of 1766 the Boones moved sixty-five miles up the Yadkin River and located in a rough cabin at Holman's Ford, on the edge of the Brushy Mountains of North Carolina (a few miles from where U.S. 421 crosses the river today). The family remained there for the winter while Boone pursued his annual hunt, then in the spring relocated several miles upriver, on Beaver Creek. Discovering, however, that this site was within reach of spring floods, the next year they moved again, to opposite the mouth of Beaver Creek, on the north side of the Yadkin, where they made themselves a farm on a hill overlooking the river. Nothing is known about the deliberations between Daniel and Rebecca that preceded their move to this area where, as one observer put it, the people were "very poor, widely scattered, and the roads bad." But perhaps her objections about isolation and the lack of connections were answered by the number of kinsfolk who joined them. Boone's brother George, husband of one of Rebecca's cousins, sold his farm at the Forks in 1766 and, with his wife's brothers and their families, accompanied the Boones upriver. At about this time, Neddy Boone married Rebecca's sister Martha and they settled nearby, at the site of present-day Wilkesboro. Squire Boone, Jr., sold his farm in the Forks and relocated with his wife and son to the Upper Yadkin sometime before 1769, by which time Hannah Boone and her husband, John Stewart, were also in the neighborhood.

By the time Boone became the hero of the Kentucky struggles, a legend already had developed in North Carolina about this and his subsequent moves. "Boone used to say to me," declared a backwoodsman, an old resident of the Carolina hills who claimed to have been one of Boone's hunting companions in his youth, "that when he could not fall the top of a tree near enough his door for fire-wood, it was time to move to a new place." "Daniel's own boast," said a North Carolina descendant, was that it was time to abandon a place when "he could no longer brush his cabin with the laps of the falling trees." A tale in circulation along the Yadkin tells of the time Boone hears that someone is opening a farm about twelve miles to the west of him. "The place is getting entirely too thickly settled," swears Boone, "when a man can come and cut down trees without permission in your backyard!"

There is a simpler explanation for Boone's move to the Upper Yadkin. By 1765 the population at the Forks was four times greater than it had been when the Boones had arrived fifteen years before. As Boone's nephew Daniel Boone Bryan wrote, "Game began to be scarce and harder to take." In the western hills he could continue "to follow his business of hunting." From his farm at the mouth of Beaver Creek, Boone was not more than a day or two from his favorite hunting grounds high in the Blue Ridge, and this convenient location also permitted him to introduce his sons to "his business." He had begun to take James, his eldest, on local hunts when the boy was no more than five or six, and now, at ten, James accompanied his father into the mountains and beyond. Boone later remembered that on snowy winter nights he would build a hot fire in their camp, and father and son would huddle as close to the flames as possible, yet their backsides froze and the boy would begin to shiver. Boone would then tuck James inside the folds of his blanket coat, "hugging the little fellow closely to his bosom" while they sat up together all night by the fire. By his early teens James was developing into an accomplished woodsman.

In the foothills of the Blue Ridge were born Daniel and Rebecca's sixth and seventh children: Rebecca, on May 26, 1768, and Daniel Morgan, on December 23, 1769, named for his father and great-uncle. Boone was not present for the birth of this son; he had been gone for eight months on his first long hunt and exploration into Kentucky. "It was on the first of May, in the year 1769," Filson quoted Boone, "that I resigned my domestic happiness for a time, and left my family and peaceable habitation on the Yadkin River, in North-Carolina, to wander through the wilderness of America, in quest of the country of Kentucke." The Blue Ridge still offered good hunting, but Kentucky offered good land besides, and with several companions Boone had gone to survey his prospects there. Rebecca would not see him again until the spring of 1771, nearly two years after his departure. In that year a Moravian missionary stopped at her isolated cabin. "She is by nature a quiet soul, and of few words," he wrote in his journal. "She told me of her trouble, and the frequent distress and fear in her heart."

Chapter Three

In Quest of the Country of Kentucke

1769 to 1773

Daniel Boone was not the first American to explore Kentucky. European colonists had known for most of the century that west of the Appalachians and south of the Ohio there lay a fertile country, watered by navigable rivers, streams, and numerous springs, with valuable salt licks and abundant game. By the time of Boone's birth in 1734 they had begun to master the complex river system of the continental interior and explore the passes through the mountains, and Indian traders already were doing business in the Kentucky country.

"Kentucky," a name forever linked with Boone's, first came into use about the middle of the century. One returning trader of 1753 reported to the Pennsylvania authorities his visit to a Shawnee settlement he called "the Blue Lick Town on the south bank of Cantucky River." Although there is disagreement about the origins of the name, *Kanta-ke* was an Iroquois term denoting meadows or fields that diplomats of the Iroquois Confederacy used as their designation for the town the Shawnees called *Skipaki-thiki*, or town of the Blue Lick, their term for a salt spring. The Iroquois name referred to the several hundred cultivated acres surrounding the town where the Indian women grew their crops of corn. The

Americans favored the Iroquois place-name because it rolled so easily off their English tongues. Not so the Shawnee, but translated into English, Blue Lick was a name that would reverberate in Boone's life.

The Shawnees were the southernmost of the Algonquian peoples of the Great Lakes region; indeed, one possible meaning of their tribal name is "people of the south." They identified their ancient homeland, "the center of this Island," as lying between the Ohio and the Cumberland, which they called the Shawnee River. A French map of 1684, incorporating information gained during LaSalle's inland exploration, labeled one of the rivers of this region "Skipakicipi ou la Riviere bleue," a clear variation on the Shawnee term for lick, with its literal translation into French. This may have been the river that American pioneers later called the Licking.

In the 1680s the Iroquois attacked the peoples of the Ohio Valley, seeking to extend their control of the fur trade, and the Shawnees abandoned their homeland, dispersing themselves to a number of far-flung locations. By the early eighteenth century many of them had reassembled in Pennsylvania. But the press of colonial population and advancing American settlements drove them west again, and during the second quarter of the century they built several new villages on the Ohio River. These mixed communities, including Indians from a number of ethnic backgrounds, sought to remain independent of British, French, and Iroquois control alike. Blue Lick Town, on a fertile plain north of the junction of the Red and Kentucky rivers, along the Great Warrior's Path leading southeast, was the most isolated village of them all. It flourished until the 1750s and included at its peak perhaps a thousand residents.

Boone told his children that he first heard of "Kanta-ke" while serving with Braddock's army in 1755. The lands west of the mountains were a frequent topic around evening campfires, for the men understood that the fight in which they were engaged for control of the Ohio forks was but a preliminary round in a much longer struggle over the future of the Ohio and Kentucky countries, the northern and southern banks of the river. Boone's informant was John Findley, another of Braddock's teamsters, who recently had returned from a trading expedition to the Blue Lick Town. Born in Ireland in 1722, Findley came to America with his parents, grew up near Lancaster, Pennsylvania, and, like Boone, learned the language and the customs of the Delawares and Shawnees. He entered the Indian trade and by the late 1740s was operating at the Forks of the Ohio. In the fall of 1752 he and four assistants took a canoe loaded with English goods down the Ohio. Meeting a party of Shawnee hunters who invited them to trade at Blue Lick Town, Findley and his men turned south at the mouth of the Kentucky River and after many days of hard paddling arrived at the community, where they found a number of other Pennsylvania traders already in place. The furs and skins brought in by the Indian hunters were of excellent quality and business was good until midwinter, when an invading party of French and Canadian Indians swept down from the north, killing three of Findley's men and carrying six other traders, along with hundreds of pounds of goods and peltry, off to Montreal. Findley and one assistant managed to escape, and they safely reached the Forks of the Ohio by June. This raid, and the subsequent turmoil between the French and English in the Ohio region preceding the Seven Years War, persuaded the residents of Blue Lick Town to abandon the site, and they joined their strength to the larger Shawnee towns on the Ohio.

Indian trader John Findley was the first of a long line of Kentucky promoters and boosters. *Kanta-ke*, he told Boone, was a land of cane and clover, and in its fertile valleys a man might lay claim to land enough for sons and grandsons, and "a great speck" besides. The wild game was beyond imagining, with great profits for hunters, trappers, and traders. Why, the current at the falls of the Ohio was so strong, he claimed, that fat ducks and geese were swept over and dashed against the rocks, and a man had only to pick up as many as he wanted. These tall tales anticipated John Filson's more grandiloquent "Kentucke," "the land of promise, flowing with milk and honey," where "you shall eat bread without scarceness, and not lack any thing." Exaggeration seemed to come with the country. "No, stranger, there's no place on the universal 'arth like old Kaintuck," a later pioneer would declare; "she whips all 'out-west' in prettiness, and you might bile down cr'ation and not get such another." "What a Buzzel is amongst People about Kentuck," wrote a Virginia minister during the early 1770s; "to hear people speak of it one Would think it was a new found Paradise." The most sublime Edenic comparison came in the sermon of a frontier preacher who, wishing to convey to his congregation the glories of the afterlife, sang: "O my dear honeys, heaven is a Kentucky of a place." Sixty-five years after first stirring to these tales, Findley's descriptions remained vivid for old Boone, who told a friend that the Irishman had painted so "charming a description of Kentucky, the Falls of the Ohio, and wild game, that at once fired his imagination, and so completely promised to fulfill his romantic desires, he resolved to visit the country."

Boone made his first attempt to reach this inland paradise on his long hunt during the fall and winter of 1767–68. Accompanied by his brother Squire and his friend William Hill, he hunted the Clinch River to its sources in present-day Dickenson County, Virginia, then crossed the Appalachian ridge to Russell Fork of the Big Sandy River. They had little notion of where they were but, guessing from the river's northwestern course that it must eventually join the Ohio, set out to follow the river to Kentucky, passing along the rim of spectacular Breaks Canyon on the border of Virginia and Kentucky. They tracked fifty miles along a buffalo trace until they reached a salt lick a few miles west of present-day Prestonsburg, Kentucky. There, wrote Nathan Boone, in his own distinctive voice, "they ware ketched in a snow storm and had to Remain the Winter." In the spring Boone and his companions returned to the Upper Yadkin without having accomplished their mission, although the hunting had been good and he finally had seen and killed buffalo, which congregated at the lick, and for the first time had feasted on raw liver and roast hump. It was also a country thick with bears, and thirty years later Boone would return to hunt there many times, but there was little in those rugged laurel hills to justify Findley's more extravagant claims of a fertile paradise.

Some months after this hunt Boone and Findley met for the first time since the war. Part of the Boone legend is that Findley sought out his old acquaintance to lead a return trip into Kentucky, but that seems improbable. Fifteen years had elapsed since Findley's adventure at the Blue Lick Town, and Boone's reputation did not extend much beyond backcountry North Carolina. More likely, as nephew Moses Boone explained it, Findley, who had become a backcountry peddler and horse trader, found himself in the Boone neighborhood quite by accident and the reunion was entirely fortuitous. The Irishman repeated his Kentucky tales to the avid interest of Boone and his hunting friends. "Thus would Findley work upon their feelings and relate adventures of the West," said Moses Boone, "partly from a love of relating such things, and partly to secure their good services in taking care of his horse." Pressed by the hunters about the path to the fertile lands of Kentucky, Findley admitted that he was no woodsman and could not himself find the route from North Carolina. But surely the Great Warrior's Path, used by the Cherokees when they made war on the northern Indians, must mark a better mountain crossing than the one tried by the Boones the previous winter. Once they found their way through the mountains, Findley could guide them to the salt licks and grazing grounds.

Hearing Findley's tales again must have been an influence on Boone, but as his trek along the Big Sandy suggested, he was primed for an exploration of the interior. Findley merely supplied the spark. The news already had reached North Carolina that in the Treaty of Fort Stanwix the Iroquois nations had, in the words of the *Virginia Gazette*, ceded "a vast extent of country to his majesty" between the Ohio and the Tennessee, then called the Cherokee River. The British applied the rule of conquest to this case, arguing that the Iroquois had won title to the Kentucky country by dint of their victory over the native inhabitants during the wars of the seventeenth century, and that neither the Shawnees nor any other Indians actually residing there held a valid claim. In the Treaty of Hard Labor, also signed in 1768, the British acknowledged a continuing Cherokee claim to the Kentucky country and a land cession from this powerful southern nation had yet to be obtained, but the agreement with the Iroquois altered the way backwoodsmen thought about the interior.

So Kentucky pulled Boone. There was also a good deal of push supplied by developments on the east side of the mountains—farming the thin soils of the Upper Yadkin was none too easy. In the early twentieth century the residents of those hills still eked out a livelihood by what was known locally as "yarbin' it," gathering roots, barks, and herbs and selling them to local merchants. Others used simple tools to make baskets of white oak splints, bartering them to produce a meager living. Boone aspired to more than this for his family. That was why he had traveled to western Florida in

1765, but Kentucky seemed to offer a good deal more. "I thought of Kentucky," said one old pioneer, and "if I never could get but ten acres of land, I determined to move to it. If I could get my children in this rich new country, it might be to their advantage." Another wrote that "the prospect of seeing all his Children settled Comfortably in one Neighborhood, their Arms open at any time to receive and assist," would assure him of "a greater degree of Happiness than any other situation." Boone, too, headed an expanding household of sons, daughters, and nephews, and Rebecca could be expected to be pregnant again. His descendants would require land. And it was an auspicious time in Boone's life. He was a vigorous young man in his mid-thirties. His father had recently died, freeing him to pursue distant opportunities, just as Squire had been enabled to leave Pennsylvania after his own father's death. And just as Squire had become leader of the Boone clan on the Yadkin after leading the family south, so, with the family migration to Kentucky, Boone would become the most prominent among the kinsmen of his generation. In the context of a life enmeshed in relationships of extended family, considerations such as these must have had a powerful effect on Boone.

Social developments in North Carolina also played a role in Boone's thinking. Farmers of the backcountry shared a growing anger at their underrepresentation in the provincial assembly, their lack of control over local affairs, and the fees and taxes levied without their consent, and during the 1760s a series of local protests and uprisings shook the colony. By 1768 angry men calling themselves "Regulators" were condemning merchants and "damned lawyers who practiced numberless devilish devices to rob you of your livings." In Hillsboro, Regulators stormed the court, beat officials, including Sheriff Thomas Hart, and burned the house and barn of Justice Richard Henderson. The Regulators took over the court and dismissed all charges and suits against their number. The revolt ended at the Battle of Alamance River in May 1771, when forces from the eastern counties defeated the Regulators in a bloody rout, after which six Regulator leaders were hanged. In Rowan County, where the majority of the population supported the Regulators, many Bryan kinsmen were active in the movement, and afterward they were required to take an oath of allegiance. The Boones seem to have steered clear of the controversy, and the

Upper Yadkin valley was far removed from the scene of the disturbances, but Boone could not avoid the implication of the episode—the early phase of development was closing rapidly, with initiative passing from the frontiersmen to the "damned lawyers."

Through his own business and legal affairs, Boone was associated with several of the gentlemen roughed up and deposed during the revolt. Before his appointment to the superior court, Richard Henderson, as an attorney on the circuit, had argued cases before Boone's father at the Rowan County Courthouse and may have become acquainted with Daniel. In association with his law partner John Williams, with Sheriff Thomas Hart and his merchant brother Nathaniel Hart, Henderson pursued business interests and investments, real estate prominent among them. The Harts had a branch store in Salisbury where Boone traded, and in their legal and business relations with Boone and other hunters these gentlemen paid close attention to talk of the western country. The growing population of land-hungry farmers and the rising price of land made real estate the most popular enterprise of the day, one pursued by such notable Americans as George Washington and Patrick Henry. Next to the law, wrote one colonial attorney, "the best branch of business in America is that of adventuring in lands and procuring inhabitants to settle them."

Among biographers there has been a good deal of debate about when Boone entered into a business relationship with Richard Henderson; there have been suspicions that Henderson and his associates financed Boone's extended hunting expeditions across the mountains in exchange for intelligence. This was the practice of other speculators, such as George Washington, for example, who wrote his agent in the Ohio country to proceed "under the guize of hunting game." Because successful speculation depended on inside information, men kept such arrangements quiet, and as a result one would expect supporting evidence for an early relationship between Henderson and Boone to be woefully thin. An old Appalachian hunter once told the story that he had been with a group of hunters in the Tennessee mountains in the year 1764 when they were overtaken by Boone, who told them he "wished to be informed of the geography and locography of these woods, saying that he was employed to explore them by Henderson & Co." But Henderson and Company was not organized until the early 1770s, and Nathan Boone, generally the most reliable informant on his father's life, believed that Boone was not in Henderson's employ until 1774, a point made by other Boone descendants as well. Boone had reasons of his own for going to Kentucky, they argued, and did not act for others on his first explorations. The land schemes of Henderson and Company began in earnest in 1774, yet in 1773 Boone would help to plan and conduct a movement of sixty or seventy settlers, including his own family and kinsmen, across the mountains. Clearly he did have sufficient motive to act on his own.

Those who argue for Boone's employment by Henderson suggest that the relationship between the two may have originated in Henderson's defense of Boone's numerous lawsuits. But the fact is that most of Boone's legal troubles at the time were initiated by Richard Henderson himself. In 1768 Henderson and his partner John Williams filed suit against Boone in Rowan County Court for the collection of a debt for £20. The case was continued a number of times during the next few terms of the court, with the notation "conditions performed," language that generally indicated that the debtor was paying the usurious interest charges if not the principal. But finally, in the spring of 1770, after Boone had left to hunt in Kentucky, the case came to trial, a jury decided in favor of the plaintiffs, and Henderson had a warrant issued for Boone's arrest. This would have been an odd course to pursue had Henderson been the very man who had sent Boone to explore the West.

Still, the suspicion lingers that Boone's two full years in Kentucky were occupied with more than hunting and scouting potential locations for himself and his kinsmen alone. As Kentucky historian Thomas Clark put it, "He wasn't just bird counting." A trip of that length required ample supplies of guns, ammunition, traps, horses, and other supplies, and Henderson and his associates may have supplied credit in the anticipation of information. Filson had Boone "reconnoitering" and stated that after the trip Henderson was "informed of this country by Col. Boon." A financial connection of some sort between the two is certainly plausible, but this would not have made Boone merely Henderson's "land agent." Nathaniel Hart, Jr., descendant of the Hart brothers, said that on Boone's return he "gave a description of the Country to many Gentlemen in North Carolina, my Father Capt. Nathaniel Hart amongst the rest." Boone's account "so delighted" these gentlemen, Hart wrote, that "several of them associated themselves together under the name of Richard Henderson & Co." Rather than Boone playing a part in a drama scripted by Richard Henderson, Hart's account suggests that things happened the other way around. As he put it, "The origin of the Company is to be attributed to Boon's representations."

Boone, John Findley, John Stewart, and three others left the Upper Yadkin for Kentucky on May 1, 1769, their equipment packed on ten or fifteen horses. Each man carried his own rifle, powder horns, bullet pouch, and hunting knife, but they also needed extra stores of flint, steel, tinder, powder, and lead, as well as tools for casting bullets, traps, blankets, camp kettles, salt, and other provisions. "Boone was the only woodsman," said nephew Daniel Boone Bryan, "tho' Stewart was pretty good with a gun." In fact, Stewart, married to Boone's sister Hannah and ten years his junior, had been west of the Appalachians the year before with a party of hunters led by another of Boone's companions, Benjamin Cutbeard. The Cutbeard party hunted and trapped for several months in Tennessee and successfully sold their catch in New Orleans, although they were robbed by Indians on their return. Stewart thus had valuable experience, and Nathan Boone said that his father "had all the confidence in him that one man could have in another." Stewart possessed that most essential requisite of a hunting companion, said Boone: you could count on him to always be in the right spot at the right time. Little is known about the other three—James Mooney, Joseph Holden, and William Cooley—except that they were neighbors from the Upper Yadkin and were to act as "camp keepers," preparing the skins and assembling them in packs.

The men ascended the mountains along Elk Creek through the present village of Darby, North Carolina, crossed the Blue Ridge, then descended into the high meadow. They continued north and west through a series of gaps, over Stone Mountain and Iron Mountain, leading them to the Holston River. (One can trace this route today by taking the county road from Ferguson up the Blue Ridge to U.S. Highway 421, through Boone, and on into Tennessee and Virginia.) There the hunters connected with the Great Warrior's Path, and their direction shifted due west, crossing a series of

Appalachian ridges and valleys, formed by the waters of the Upper Tennessee River (a route followed today by U.S. 58, known as the Boone Heritage Trail). By 1769 this trail had been worn by the passing of an increasing number of hunters. It took them across Moccasin Gap to the Clinch River valley, then over Powell's Mountain and Wallen's Ridge to the valley of Powell River, where they encountered a group of twenty men under the leadership of Joseph Martin, clearing land for a crop of corn. This was the westernmost settlement yet attempted, and, outraged at this movement into their territory, the Cherokees would break up Martin's settlement before the corn was ripe. From there Boone's men traveled south along the river to the tall cliffs of the Cumberland Mountains known as White Rocks, traditional markers for the Cumberland Gap, the most famous pass in all of North America.

This great V-shaped notch in the mountain wall was long the primary gateway to the West. "Stand at Cumberland Gap," wrote Frederick Jackson Turner in his famous essay on the significance of the frontier in American history, "and watch the procession of civilization, marching single file—the buffalo following the trail to the salt springs, the Indian, the fur-trader and hunter, the cattle-raiser, the farmer—and the frontier has passed by." Boone was by no means first to pass through this narrow defile; travelers on the Great Warrior's Path had used the gap for hundreds of years. In the late seventeenth century Gabriel Arthur, a young Virginian captured by Ohio Indians, returned home via the gap, and he may have been the first Englishman to cross. Dr. Thomas Walker, exploring for the Loyal Land Company in Virginia in 1750, had been through and supplied the name, in honor of the Duke of Cumberland's victory over the Scots at Culloden. Walker found signs of earlier English explorers—the inevitable graffiti chopped into trees and carved onto rock. But it was the effort of Daniel Boone that would bring the pass to popular attention, and eventually more than three hundred thousand settlers would follow this route to Kentucky and beyond.

West of the gap the trail shifted northward to the crossing of the Cumberland River, then northwest to an old Indian camping ground at Flat Lick. From this point the Great Warrior's Path veered north (leaving modern U.S. 25E behind, heading through the rough terrain of the Daniel Boone National Forest; one may form an idea of the route by following Kentucky Highway 11 north to the town of Manchester, then taking U.S. 421 northwest). Today the entire trip from the Yadkin to the Bluegrass occupies no more than a couple of leisurely days of driving, but these men had been traveling hard for more than five weeks and must have begun to wonder if Findley's promised land actually existed. But passing through Sand Gap, a slight depression in the ridge separating the waters of the Cumberland and Kentucky rivers, they soon glimpsed the end of the mountains and began a gradual descent into the region known as the Knobs, where conical hills provide views of the rolling hill country beyond. Knowing that they had reached Kentucky at last, they picked a site for their base camp. Station Camp, as it was called, was a location the Shawnee knew as *Ah-wah-nee* (deep grassy place), two or three miles south of the present-day town of Irvine. Nearby, the towering formation now called Pilot Knob provided a commanding view of the rolling country that lay to the northwest. It was covered with forest, but cane, a variety of bamboo indigenous to North America, grew in wide swaths along the watercourses, and there were extensive grassy meadows.

While Stewart supervised the construction of the camp, Boone and Findley followed the Warrior's Path further north in search of Blue Lick Town. Crossing the Kentucky and Red rivers, less than twenty miles from Station Camp, they found it, abandoned and mostly burned. In the fields, however, the two men found bluegrass growing in abundance. Bluegrass is not native to America but is an English import, sometimes known as timothy. Yet the first Americans to reach central Kentucky found it growing in the rich limestone soils at a number of locations, and the region soon came to be known as the Bluegrass. Boone's nephew Daniel Boone Bryan suggested that the grass was first introduced to the West by John Findley, who packed his trade goods in English hay at Lancaster, Pennsylvania; throwing the packing aside after reaching his destination, the seed sprouted and grew. Other traders surely did the same. The action of buffalo, deer, and other grazing animals then spread the seed to other clearings and licks. At the site of Blue Lick Town, Findley recovered his bearings and was able to provide Boone with a mental map of the land. Moving up the creek that watered Blue Lick Town, they climbed to a spot known locally as

Pilot View, and, in the words of Filson's Boone, "from the top of an eminence, we saw with pleasure the beautiful level of Kentucke. We found everywhere abundance of wild beasts of every sort, through this vast forest. The buffalo were more frequent than I have seen cattle in the settlements, browsing on the leaves of the cane, or cropping the herbage on those extensive plains." Recounting a family tradition, one of Boone's grandchildren later wrote that as Boone looked out over this scene, he exclaimed to Findley, "We are as rich as Boaz of old, having the cattle of a thousand hills."

For the next six months Boone and his companions hunted and trapped. The abundance of animals amazed them. There were plenty of buffalo and elk, which were worthless on the market but were hunted for their meat and their leather, used for tugs or straps, and their heavy coats, which kept the hunters warm. Deer skins, however, promised profit. If hunting was difficult work, so was the preparation of these skins, which kept the camp keepers busy. After skinning, the hair and outer grain had to be scraped off with a knife, then, after the skin had dried, vigorously rubbed across a staking-board until it became soft and pliant. At this point the skins were "half dressed" and ready for packing. Laid in stacks across poles and covered with elk or buffalo skins to protect them from the weather, they were elevated on scaffolds to keep them out of the reach of bears and wolves. When about fifty skins lay piled, they were folded and compressed into a tight bale, making a pack. Two of these packs, swung astride a horse, weighed about 250 pounds and were valued at one hundred dollars or more. At Station Camp and a number of surrounding caches, the men accumulated packs worth several hundred dollars.

Through the fall no one saw any Indians or any sign of them either. Boone's first inkling of trouble came to him in a vision. In the early-morning hours of December 22, 1769, he dreamed he saw his father walking toward him. Boone extended his hand in greeting, but the old man pushed it away with an angry and disapproving look. Boone awoke greatly troubled, and that day, as he hunted with Stewart, nursed a sense of foreboding. Thus far the expedition had been a great success, but here, says Filson's Boone, "fortune changed the scene." As the two men headed back to camp in the late afternoon, a group of Indians suddenly rushed out from a canebrake and surrounded them. "The time of our sorrow was now arrived."

The Indians were Shawnees, led by a war leader from the town of Chillicothe north of the Ohio whose English name was Will Emery and was known as Captain Will. He and his men were returning home from a long hunt when they discovered signs of the Americans. Boone undoubtedly attempted to humor them in his characteristic way, but they were in an angry mood. The Kentucky country was not only their ancient homeland but their most important hunting ground. These Shawnees rejected the right of the Iroquois to cede lands they considered their own south of the Ohio, and ever since learning about the Treaty of Fort Stanwix, they had been patrolling warily for signs of penetration by American hunters, land speculators, or settlers. They had attacked two separate parties of hunters from Virginia and Pennsylvania the year before and recently had taken some two thousand skins from another base camp in the western country of Green River. To the Shawnees, Americans like Boone were poachers. The American method of hunting, moreover, threatened to deplete the game, for it was shamefully wasteful; since only the skins had monetary value, most of the venison was left to rot. This waste angered Indians in much the same way that American farmers resented Indian claims of large territories that they kept as hunting preserves but did not develop and use intensively as farmland. "Show me your camps!" Captain Will demanded as his warriors surrounded Boone and Stewart, waving war clubs threateningly above their heads.

Hoping to warn their companions of what was taking place, so that they might secure the horses, supplies, and skins, Boone and Stewart first led the Shawnees to a number of small caches, attempting to make as much noise as they possibly could. But the Indians quickly realized their stratagem and insisted on being taken to the base camp. Arriving at Station Camp, much to his dismay, Boone found it undisturbed. The camp keepers had indeed been forewarned by the noise, but they had fled in terror. Captain Will had his men load all of the goods and peltry onto Boone's horses and made preparations to leave. But the Shawnee chief did not harm Boone or Stewart or take them into captivity. "In the most friendly manner," Boone told his children, the Indians provided the two Americans with two pairs of moccasins apiece, doe skin for patch leather, a little French trade gun, and a few loads of powder and lead so that they could supply themselves with meat on their journey back across the mountains. Compared to the magistrates who enforced the game laws of England, the Shawnees treated these poachers with amazing restraint. "Now, brothers," declared Captain Will, "go home and stay there. Don't come here any more, for this is the Indians' hunting ground, and all the animals, skins and furs are ours. And if you are so foolish as to venture here again, you may be sure the wasps and yellow-jackets will sting you severely." Then the Indians rode off, leaving Boone and Stewart amid the ruins of eight months of hard work.

If Captain Will thought Boone would return to the settlements with news of the Shawnee determination to keep the Americans from their homeland, he was badly mistaken. Without attempting to locate their four companions, Boone and Stewart immediately began the pursuit of the Shawnees on foot. That night, as the Indians slept, the two Americans crept in among the horses and reclaimed their own, silently walked them out several hundred yards, then mounted and rode furiously south. They planned to locate Findley and the camp keepers and send back to the settlements for supplies, in hopes that they might yet recoup their losses with additional hunting. After riding through the night and thinking themselves secure, they stopped to rest the horses on the sunny slope of a hill. Stewart crouched to tie his moccasin, and Boone tumbled onto the grass, flat on his back, soaking up the morning sun. Suddenly he became aware of a rumbling through the earth and, tilting his head forward, saw the flash of the rising sun on the steel of the Shawnees' guns. The crisp memory of these seconds would remain etched in Boone's mind as he told the story to his children fifty years later. The Indians were upon them before either could rise.

The Shawnees galloped up, whooping and laughing, making sport of these undeniably bold Americans who were fools enough to be captured twice in as many days. "Steal horse, ha?" one of the Shawnees cried out derisively in broken English, and, fastening a horse collar decorated with little bells around Boone's neck, forced him to dance for their amusement. This time Boone and Stewart were tied together with a leather tug and marched north with the Indians. On the evening of the seventh day, they reached the Ohio.

You will be released when we have all passed over, said Captain Will, for then Shawnee horses will be safe from your thievery. Planning a morning crossing, the Indians scattered to make their camp. To himself Boone resolved that this was one river he would not be forced to cross.

Straining at their tugs, Boone and Stewart managed to break loose, and, snatching up guns and ammunition, they dodged into a nearby canebrake. While some of the Indians guarded the horses, others surrounded the brake, but none made an attempt to go in after the fugitives. The next morning the Shawnees crossed the river, leaving the Americans behind. From the beginning their intention had been merely to warn the hunters, and they were anxious to return home with their plunder. It required several days of hard travel before Boone and Stewart reached Station Camp, and they found no sign of their companions. Continuing south another two days, they finally located the men, who already were heading home. With the disheartened camp keepers, however, Boone also found his brother Squire and a companion, Alexander Neeley, who had come over with horses and additional supplies. He had come "in Search of the Western world," Squire said years later, as well as "my Brother Daniel Boone."

As the Boones headed back to the northwest, Findley and the camp keepers continued back across the mountains. At the Holston Valley they parted company, Findley taking the left fork north, the others following the south road back to the Yadkin. The camp keepers "never went west again," said Daniel Boone Bryan, as it was "too disastrous a trip for them." As for John Findley, on his return to Pennsylvania he undertook another trading expedition, but once again he was robbed by Indians of all goods. He outfitted and went west a final time in 1772, and, according to a family tradition, it was the last anyone heard of him.

The Boone brothers, Stewart, and Neeley returned to Station Camp, salvaged what they could, then relocated their base near the site of Blue Lick Town. They spent the winter months trapping beaver and hunting the buffalo that congregated at the nearby salt lick. They reconnoitered the country, "giving names to the different waters" like Adam bestowing names on the beasts of the field. Asked once why he had christened a certain spot Plum Lick, "as there are no plum trees about it," Boone answered that it was because he and John Stewart had "brought plums near a mile in our hats, and ate them while we watched this lick." Some names were descriptive, others purely whimsical. "We had with us for our amusement," Boone later recalled, "the History of Samuel Gulliver's Travels," which he would read aloud to the others in the evenings. The day after reading an installment in which Gulliver encountered the giant race of Brobdingnags at their capital city of Lorbrulgrud, Neeley returned from his hunting joking that "he been that Day to Lulbegrud [as he pronounced and others would spell it] and had killed two Brobdernags in their Capital." It took some time before the men deciphered his code: he had been to the salt lick and killed two large buffalo. Neeley's riddle was memorialized in the name of the creek called Lulbegrud. Hundreds of people have since believed that this strange-sounding place-name must have come from some Indian tongue, never guessing that it was a corrupted name from a satire by Jonathan Swift.

The men worked in pairs—Squire with Neeley, Boone with Stewart—and sometimes were away from the base camp for several days. On one of these trips in the late winter of 1770, Boone and Stewart divided on either side of the Kentucky River to check their trap lines. Boone returned to their temporary camp that evening, but Stewart failed to appear. A heavy rain had swollen the river, so Boone assumed that his brother-in-law was merely having difficulty crossing. After several days the river fell, but Stewart did not show up. Fearing the worst, Boone crossed. He found the remains of a fire and Stewart's initials carved on the bark of a tree, but no trace of the man himself. It was not until 1775, during the expedition to cut the Wilderness Road, that one of Boone's men found a skeleton and powder horn with Stewart's initials wedged into the hollow of a sycamore tree.

Stewart was not only a brother-in-law but a good friend, and Boone was badly shaken by his disappearance. He returned to the base camp and reported the bad news to his companions. Neeley was thoroughly spooked and proposed returning to the settlements immediately. Boone was against it. The beaver catch had been good, yet he was anxious to make up for the lost deer skins and wanted to remain in Kentucky awhile longer. The brothers gave Neeley leave to return alone. He made the journey back across the mountains in safety, but the following year, with another group of long hunters, he somehow got separated from his party without a gun. Alone in the wilderness, desperate for food, he succeeded in capturing and killing a stray Indian dog for meat, which he packed on his back in its own skin. By the strangest of circumstances, it was the Boone brothers who found him wandering through the woods, half crazed, the dog meat "alive with maggots." Rescued, he returned again to North Carolina. In the 1780s, Neeley moved to Kentucky with his wife and large family, and one day in the 1790s he was killed by Indians as he drew water from a spring near his house.

Boone and Squire were thus alone in the Kentucky wilderness. "We were then in a dangerous, helpless, situation," Boone told Filson, "exposed daily to perils and death amongst savages and wild beasts, not a white man in the country but ourselves." The readers of the abridged version of Filson's narrative missed Boone's reflections, which occur immediately following this passage. "I often observed to my brother, You see how little nature requires to be satisfied. Felicity, the companion of content, is rather found in our own breasts than in the enjoyment of external things: And I firmly believe it requires but a little philosophy to make a man happy in whatsoever state he is." While these words were Filson's, not Boone's, the sentiments were true to Boone's character and are found in a number of folktales concerning this period of his life. In one Boone and Squire are confined to their riverbank camp during a heavy rain, huddled together under a horse blanket, which "incommoded Squire very much." Moaning about the wet, the cold, the hunger, and everything else that had gone wrong, Squire erupts angrily at his brother's stoicism. "I believe you would be satisfied to remain here forever," he complains. "You would do better not to fret about it," returns Boone, "but try to content yourself with what we can not help." After the rains cease, they move on and soon come upon a camp that the Indians had abandoned because of the rising water. "See what fretted you so much was really the means of Providence for our salvation," says Boone. "But for the storm we should have run into the very jaws of our enemies."

In the spring of 1770, running short on ammunition, the brothers decided that Squire should return to the settlements with the horses and furs, then bring back fresh supplies. Boone was alone in Kentucky for nearly three months. After Squire sold the furs, he returned with horses and supplies. When the brothers rendezvoused in July, Boone learned that he had become the father of another son, Daniel Morgan, whom Rebecca had named in honor of her absent husband. The brothers now began a sustained hunt through the summer months for deer, and in the fall Squire made a second round-trip to the settlements. It has never been clear why Boone insisted on staying in Kentucky; the two could have better protected their catch if they had ridden back to the settlements together. It may be, as historian Thomas D. Clark suggested, that Boone was "imbued more with wanderlust than love for agricultural labors and domestic tranquility." During his periods alone, however, he "explored a considerable part of the country," committing to memory the lay of the land, the run of the streams and rivers, the springs and licks. Boone would be the reigning expert on "the geography and locography" of Kentucky during the first years of settlement and would be called on by scores of men to locate the best land for them, in exchange for which he was granted a portion for himself. Boone's isolated explorations may not have been designed to provide him with this edge, but it certainly worked out that way.

At first, according to Filson, Boone's loneliness and concern for his family drove him to melancholy, but soon the "diversities and beauties of nature" revived his enthusiasm. Boone declared, said one old pioneer, "that he never enjoyed himself better in his life" than during this period of isolation in Kentucky. "He had three dogs that kept his camp while he was hunting, and at night he would often lie by his fire and sing every song he could think of, while the dogs would sit round him, and give as much attention as if they understood every word he was saying." When Boone was alone in the woods he often would talk and sing aloud, said Daniel Boone Bryan, "for the sake of the pleasure of hearing a human voice." In 1770 another party of hunters in Kentucky, a group led by Caspar Mansker of Virginia, were moving quietly through the forest when they heard a most unusual noise. Mansker signaled the others to take cover, and slowly he crept forward toward the sound, his gun loaded and primed. There on a deerskin spread on the ground of a clearing was a man "flat upon his back, and singing at the top of his voice!" It was Daniel Boone.

This seems careless for a man who was at constant risk of being stung by Shawnee wasps and yellow jackets. According to other sources, Boone worked hard at keeping out of harm's way. He frequently changed the location of his camp, slept in caves, and, when particularly concerned about discovery, avoided making fires and took his meals cold. Nevertheless, he said to Filson, he found evidence that Indians often visited his camp, "but fortunately for me, in my absence." A fantastic tale of escape was later told about this period. Exploring the cliffs along Dix River, near its junction with the Kentucky, Boone suddenly finds himself surrounded by Indians. With no other means of escape, he is "forced to make a leap down the high bank" into the branches of a tall sugar maple. The leaves break his fall and he manages to catch hold of a branch, then lower himself to the riverbank sixty feet below. This feat sounds unlikely, and to any who have seen the cliffs along these rivers, it looks even more impossible. Such tall tales made good telling and exist in numerous versions, not only for Boone but for other American pioneers as well. Significantly, there is no record of their being repeated by family members.

Within the family a more sinister and believable tale of escape was told. His descendants always disputed claims that Boone was a ferocious fighter who had killed a great number of Indians, so it was all the more believable when they told of violence at Boone's hand. Several, including Nathan Boone, repeated a story that Boone had shot a solitary Indian during this period of lonely exploration in Kentucky. One day he discovers signs of Indians in his vicinity. He tries tracking in a number of directions but each time finds his way blocked. Eventually he is hemmed in against the river, but there he sees an Indian peacefully fishing from a fallen tree projecting out over the water. "While I was looking at him," Boone told his children, "he tumbled into the river and I saw no more of him." According to Nathan, "It was understood from the way in which he spoke of it, that he shot and killed the Indian" but was reluctant to admit it outright. The man's death opened an escape route, and Boone took it. He was one of the few Indians that Boone acknowledged killing during his long life on the frontier.

It was not until March of 1771 that the brothers tied up the last of their packs and headed east, their horses loaded with several hundred dollars' worth of beaver pelts. They had passed through the Cumberland Gap and were camped in Powell's Valley when six or eight warriors silently appeared at their fire. In some accounts they are "Northern Indians," in others Cherokees. The Indians asked for food and sat with the Boones for a time, passing Boone's flask and talking of the hunt. Finally one of them proposed trading their poor trade guns for the Boones' much better Pennsylvania rifles. The brothers firmly refused and the mood suddenly changed; the Indians overpowered them and stole everything. So Boone once again lost several hundred dollars' worth of furs and a number of horses. Squire had returned with two loads, but considering all of the losses, it is hardly likely that the expedition had been profitable. In 1772 Boone told a companion that "all the proceeds" of his two years in Kentucky had been stolen from him by the Indians.

It was May 1771 by the time Boone returned to Beaver Creek on the Upper Yadkin. A delightful tale recounts his reunion with Rebecca. He arrives one evening to find his family at a neighborhood frolic. Standing at the edge of the dancing, watching the fun, he realizes that his hair and beard have grown so long and disheveled that he is unrecognized. Delighting in his disguise, Boone steps boldly up to Rebecca and extends his hand for a dance. Repulsed by the stranger's uncouth appearance, she refuses. "You need not refuse," says Boone, laughing aloud, "for you have danced many a time with me." Now recognizing his voice, she throws her arms around his neck, her eyes filling with tears, while the neighbors gawk in amazement to see Mrs. Boone in the arms of the rough old hunter. All soon realize the truth, and "the dancers now took a rest while Boone related the story of his hardships and adventures in the romantic land of Kentucky, where he had encountered bears, Indians, and wild cats—and had seen a country wonderful in its beauty to behold. Thus passed the night with Boone and his friends."

During Boone's absence a substantial number of American settlers had begun moving beyond the Blue Ridge into the river valleys of the Upper Tennessee: the Watauga and the Nolachucky, the Holston and the Clinch. The disorder and discontent surrounding the Regulator rebellion in North Carolina was one force pushing families west, but this was but a symptom of the larger problem posed by development, in which the diminishing supply and rising price of land squeezed poorer hunters and farmers. The people of the backcountry, wrote Virginia governor Lord Dunmore, in 1772, "finding that grants are not to be obtained, do seat themselves without any formalities wherever they like best." Settlers went far beyond the limits set by treaty with the Indians. The Cherokees agreed, in the Treaty of Lochaber of 1770, to a further cession of land on the Upper Tennessee, but Americans persisted in overrunning the boundaries.

It is possible that the Boones followed this migration soon after his return. In March of 1771, while Boone was still in Kentucky, one of his creditors, arguing in court that he "conceals himself that the Ordinary Process of Law can not be served upon him," obtained an order for the attachment of the family property, a sufficient reason perhaps to move. Nathan Boone later felt certain that the family had spent at least a year during the early 1770s living on the Watauga River, near Sycamore Shoals. His older brothers and sisters told him of visits to their cabin there by Cherokee hunters. At about that same time, Boone's name was recorded purchasing goods at a trader's establishment on the Holston River in quantities that suggest they might have been for his family. Whether with his family or alone, Boone certainly spent the fall and winter of 1771–72 hunting in what would become the state of Tennessee. With a North Carolinian named Joe Robertson, the owner of a notable pack of bear-tracking hounds, he hunted bear, pushing as far west as French Lick (later called Nashville) on the Cumberland River, where he met hunters of some of the numerous French parties that came to those licks each year to hunt buffalo.

During the fall of 1772, however, he was back in Kentucky with five North Carolinians, including Samuel Tate and Benjamin Cutbeard, two of his old companions, and a new one, an impetuous young man named Hugh McGary. Discovering a number of Indian canoes hidden on the Kentucky River, they used them to transport themselves and their peltry along the waterways that winter. They may have located their base camp in a cave on Hickman Creek, near its mouth on the Kentucky, a place now known as Boone's Knob. In the early nineteenth century a local farmer there explored the cave and found the inscription "DB. 1773" on the wall, and below it, McGary's name. On the cave floor he found broken rifle flints and chunks of lead.

It was during this winter of 1772–73 that the first Kentucky excitement began to swell in the seaboard colonies. Noting the press of settlement that was taking place all along the Appalachian frontier, land speculators began dispatching agents to select and survey large parcels south of the Ohio. Believing that Virginia might soon grant patents for the area west of the mountains that fell between her northern and southern boundary lines, George Washington arranged for ten thousand acres to be marked off for him. A man who missed the "present opportunity of hunting out good lands," Washington believed, "will never regain it." Meanwhile, an agent of the Ohio Company wrote from the West that surveyors were so thick that "as soon as a man's back is turned another is on his land. The man that is strong and able to make others afraid of him seems to have the best chance as times go now." Finding surveyors' red flags marking territory throughout their homeland, the Shawnees became greatly alarmed, and Indian agent William Johnson warned that their "young Indian Warriors or Hunters are too often inclined to retaliate." Most of this activity was taking place along the Ohio River, north of Boone's camp, but at least two surveying parties were along the Kentucky in the late winter of 1773. One was led by James and Robert McAfee from Virginia, the other by James Harrod from Pennsylvania, and it seems unlikely that they could have done much exploring without Boone's knowledge. Kentucky had "drawn the attention of many adventurers," Boone told Filson. When he passed back over the mountains that spring he knew that the rush for Kentucky was about to begin.

Boone led an attempt to settle Kentucky in 1773. At the time, however, the movement was not identified with Boone as much as it was with William Russell, a well-known Indian trader, tobacco farmer, landowner, captain of militia, and justice of the peace in southwest Virginia. On Boone's way back to the Yadkin in the spring of 1773, he followed the trace up the Clinch River to Russell's settlement of Castle's Wood. It is not known which of the two men originated the Kentucky emigration plan, but Captain Russell was to head the expedition while Boone was to serve as its logician and guide. Arthur Campbell, another of the big men of southwest Virginia, afterward wrote to the governor that "Captain William Russell with several families and upwards of 30 men set out with an intention to reconnoiter the country towards the Ohio and settle in the limits of the expected new government." Another Virginian wrote of joining "the company going with William Russell to Ohio." Boone's name was not mentioned in contemporary correspondence or reports concerning the migration.

This is hardly surprising, since Boone was still an obscure woodsman from backwoods North Carolina, while Russell was a prominent Virginian. The son of a well-known lawyer from Culpeper County, he had attended the College of William and Mary and married a woman from a wealthy tidewater family; after her death he remarried the widowed sister of Patrick Henry. In the 1760s Russell made a name for himself as one of the first settlers in southwest Virginia, representing the area in the House of Burgesses. Governor Dunmore, who met him in Williamsburg, described him as "a gentleman of some distinction." Born to command, Russell was perfectly situated to be a leader of the country about to be opened west of the mountains. Many historians have interpreted the westward migration of this period as part of a struggle for freedom from the "tidewater aristocracy," but in his move to Kentucky, Boone joined himself to gentlemen of that class. It was still the age of patriarchs, and like others of his time, Capt. William Russell so aspired. His relationship with Boone may be summed up in a word or two. Daniel Boone, he wrote, was one of the "best Hands" he knew.

Boone reached the Upper Yadkin, where his family was again living, in late April, just a few weeks before Rebecca delivered her eighth child, Jesse Bryan, on May 23, 1773. James, sixteen, was now as tall as his father, and with his brother Israel, fourteen, shouldered much of the field work around the farm; Susannah and Jemima, twelve and ten, were a help to their mother; and then there were the little ones—Levina, seven, Rebecca, five, Daniel Morgan, three, and the baby. No family traditions relate the discussion between husband and wife concerning the removal of the family beyond the mountains, but surely Boone's intentions about Kentucky must have been clear for some time. Jesse and Jonathan, the nephews raised in the Boone household, now young men, chose to remain in North Carolina. It is likely that the new baby was named to honor the oldest of the departing nephews. But in their move, the Boones were joined by brother Squire, his wife, Jane, and their three young sons, as well as Benjamin Cutbeard and his wife, Boone's niece, and several other families as well as a number of single men, hunting companions of Boone's. The Boones themselves seem to have left the Upper Yadkin sometime in the early summer for an extended visit with their kin at the Forks, where Boone's talk of Kentucky persuaded a number of Bryan families to join the emigration. The Bryan men would remain until the harvest was in; they would pack winter supplies and join the Boones in Powell's Valley, returning for their families once they had established a base in Kentucky. Meanwhile, the Boones and the others from the Upper Yadkin would travel to Castle's Wood to link up with Russell's people.

The final farewells at the Forks came with the knowledge that this might be the last time folks held one another in their arms. Rebecca said good-bye to her parents, siblings, aunts, and uncles. Boone's mother, Sarah Morgan, could not bear her son's departure, so with daughter Mary and her son-in-law, she accompanied the party for the first half day of the march. "When a halt was called for a Separation," a young neighbor later wrote, "they threw their arms around each other's necks and tears flowed freely from all eyes. Even Daniel, in spite of his brave and manly heart, was seen to lift the lapel of his pouch to dry the tears from his eyes whilst his dear old Mother held him around his neck weeping bitterly." As his mother turned in sadness toward her home, Boone and the men of the party fired a ragged salute. Mother and son had gazed upon each other for the last time.

By mid-August the Boones were with Russell at Castle's Wood, where the McAfee brothers, returning from their exploration of Kentucky, saw them making preparations for the journey. There were no wagons to pack, for the trail to Kentucky was little more than a rough trace over mountains and through forests, wide enough only for the horses to be ridden in single file. Their supplies, clothes, tools, and precious possessions were packed on horses. "They had prepared baskets made of fine hickory withe or splints," wrote an old resident of the Clinch River area, "and fastening two of them together with ropes they put a child in each basket and put it across a pack saddle. They had poultry with them which they carried in the same way." Cattle and hogs were driven along. With the crying of the children, the lowing of the cattle, and the bells on all the livestock, "they made a terrible racket." In addition to the Russell family, including the slaves, were a number of young men who would become friends and associates of Boone's during the Kentucky years, including William Bush and Michael Stoner, said to be the two best shots in southwest Virginia. The group, totaling forty or fifty people, set out on September 25, 1773.

Theirs was the first attempt to plant an American settlement in Kentucky. They began with no formal authorization from colonial authorities, though there was no secret about their plans. They were encroaching upon the territory of the Cherokees, who had thus far refused to give up their claims on this country, as well as the Shawnees, who had quite deliberately warned Boone of the dire consequences that would befall him were he to return. The rapid expansion of American settlement threw the Shawnee towns into turmoil, with arguments between chiefs who counseled patience and negotiation and young warriors who believed that only violence might prevent a repetition of the events that had dispossessed the Indians on the east side of the mountains.

The movement of families by pack train was laborious work. The group soon strung out in a long line of march, and it took nearly two weeks to travel the hundred-odd miles down and across the Clinch River, over Horton's Summit to Little Flat Lick, and over Powell's Mountain at Kane's Gap into the valley, where they met the Bryan men from the Forks. Believing that the slow trip would require a greater supply of provisions than he originally had anticipated, early in the journey Boone sent back his oldest son, James, accompanied by John and Richard Mendinall from North Carolina, to arrange for additional supplies at Castle's Wood, where Captain Russell had remained to wrap up some last-minute business. Russell ordered additional horses, packs, and cattle and sent those forward with his own goods, reinforcing the party with two slaves and a hired man under the guidance of an experienced woodsman, Isaac Crabtree.

On the evening of October 9, 1773, James Boone and the others of the supply party camped for the night on the west bank of Wallen's Creek, near its junction with the river at the eastern edge of Powell's Valley. They were just three miles behind Boone's main column and several miles ahead of Russell, who brought up the rear of the march with several other men. That night, around their campfire, they heard wolves howling. The Mendinalls were little more than boys; this was their first adventure into the wilderness, and they admitted to being frightened by the plaintive sound. But Crabtree laughed at their fears, joking that in Kentucky they would hear not only wolves howling but buffalo bellowing from the treetops. His backwoods humor had the effect of calming the boys, and soon all were asleep. There seems to have been no fear of an Indian attack.

Watching from the cover of the forest was a party of fifteen Delawares, accompanied by two Cherokees and two Shawnees, returning from a mission south to discuss mutual concerns about the rising threat of American movement into trans-Appalachia. Seeing this as an opportunity to send a message of their opposition to settlement, at about dawn the Indians fired down into the sleeping group. The Mendinall brothers died in the first fire. Crabtree and the hired man suffered wounds but fled into the woods. The slave named Charles stood petrified with fear, but his companion, Adam, scurried undetected under some nearby driftwood and became the sole living witness to what followed. James Boone and Henry Russell had taken bullets through their hips and lay conscious but immobilized. Running into the camp, most of the Indians turned to gathering the horses and making preparations to abscond with their loot, but one or two pounced on the wounded boys and began to slash at them with their knives. Attempting to turn the blades with their hands and arms, the boys were horribly mangled. From his hiding place Adam heard James pleading for his life, calling one of the warriors by the name of Big Jim, a sullen Cherokee whom he and his father had met in the woods on several occasions. His high cheekbones, broad face, and distinctive chin made this man instantly recognizable. Ignoring the plea for mercy, Big Jim methodically tore the nails from the hands and feet of young Boone and Russell and soon the boys began to beg for death rather than mercy. Adam heard James call out for his mother, then cry out his fear that his family must have fallen victim as well. With the other Indians impatient to be going, the torturers finally ended the torment with heavy blows to the boys' heads, leaving their bodies shot through with arrows before fleeing into the dawn, forcing the slave Charles along.

The massacre was first discovered by a young thief from Boone's camp who had been severely rebuked the day before by the men of the party for stealing some trifle, and in his shame he resolved to steal something of real value and return home. Arising before dawn and taking a pack of deer skins from Boone's cache, he was riding back up the hills when suddenly he came upon the killing ground. Without stopping to examine the bodies, he galloped back to camp to spread the alarm. The people were just stirring and the man's frightened calls threw them into panic. Not knowing the extent of the disaster, and compelled by the necessity of preparing a defense in case of a second attack, Boone sent Squire and a small group back to the ridge. Fearing the worst, Rebecca dug into her pack, pulled out two linen sheets, and gave them to Squire, asking him to carefully wrap the bodies to protect them from the cold earth.

As Squire and the others rode up they saw Captain Russell and his men bending over the bodies. They had risen early that morning in the hope of overtaking the boys and had ridden unsuspecting upon the dismal spectacle. While some of the men began to round up the scattered cattle, Squire and Russell wrapped the Mendinall brothers together in one sheet, James and Henry in the other, and buried them in a common grave. A few days later Crabtree, whose wound proved not to be serious, arrived back at Castle's Wood. Adam, the eyewitness, wandered through the forest in shock after the Indians left and did not find his way home for eleven days. The body of the slave Charles, his head cleaved open with a hatchet, was found later about forty miles away. The sixth victim, Drake, remained unaccounted for until, twenty years later, bones thought to be his were found wedged between two high ledges of rock about an eighth of a mile from the creek.

Squire brought the terrible news back to Daniel and Rebecca. It took a day or two for the cattle to be gathered and driven forward to the main camp, for the fear of attack to subside, and for people to collect their wits. The men called a council. The deaths "discouraged the whole company," said Boone, and they resolved that it would be too difficult and dangerous to proceed with so small a force. They retreated to Castle's Wood, from where families slowly drifted back to their homes in North Carolina. But the Boones remained on the Clinch River, accepting the offer of David Gass, one of Russell's associates, of the use of a cabin on his farm. It must have been a somber winter.

The first published account of the massacre, in a North Carolina newspaper printed in early December, reported that a group of emigrants from the Yadkin, on their way over the mountains, had been attacked by Indians, killing six men, including the son of Daniel Boone. It was the first time that Boone's name had appeared in print. He was rarely mentioned again in the numerous news reports and official correspondence about the event that followed. Virginia's Governor Dunmore, under the assumption that the attackers had been Cherokees, wrote to the Indian agent for the southern colonies, urging him to demand that the Cherokee chiefs exact swift justice against the perpetrators. "You may assure them," he wrote, "of my taking every step in my power to prevent any encroachments on their Hunting Grounds by the Inhabitants of this Colony." Even as he wrote, however, Dunmore had his own agents surveying land for him in Kentucky.

It was several months before the Indian agent wrote back to inform the governor that only two Cherokees had been involved in the attack. Hoping to remain at peace with the colonies, the chiefs agreed to arrest and punish them. Meanwhile, however, Isaac Crabtree had taken revenge of his own. In the spring of 1774 the Americans at the settlements in the Watauga Valley held a festival near the present town of Jonesborough, Tennessee, and invited the Cherokees in order to placate their concerns. While attending a horse race during the festival, Crabtree spied two Cherokee men and a woman among the crowd, went into a rage, and, before the other spectators could drag him off, killed a man known as Cherokee Billy, the kinsman of a chief. Some people worried about the consequences of this murder of an innocent and prominent man and condemned Crabtree as "illiteral and obscure." Envoys were quickly despatched to the Cherokee towns to disavow the act, and the governor of Virginia offered a reward of £150 for Crabtree's arrest. He was soon informed, however, that "it would be easier to find 200 Men to screen him from the Law, then ten to bring him to Justice." Crabtree soon after emigrated to Kentucky.

"The Murder of Russell, Boones, and Drakes Sons," wrote Arthur Campbell in the spring of 1774, "is in every ones mouth," and it inspired an epidemic of Indian hating. Boone was admired among backwoodsmen and Russell well known among officialdom. "It had been my father's intention to settle in Kentucky," wrote Russell's daughter years later, and "after the death of my brother Henry, he fought intirely against the Indians." On the Ohio, at about the same time as Crabtree's revenge, a group of American ruffians lured into their camp a number of Mingos, Western migrants from the Iroquois Confederacy, plied them with rum, then killed and scalped them all. They strung up the pregnant sister of the Mingo chief Logan by her wrists, sliced open her belly with a tomahawk, and impaled her unborn child on a stake. The Mingos would henceforth be sworn enemies of the Americans.

With no crops to harvest, Boone hunted in the vicinity of the Clinch throughout the late fall and winter to keep the family in meat, and despite the skins and furs he brought into Castle's Wood, he ran up a considerable debt of £45 with the local merchant. A number of families from the Yadkin had settled nearby and Boone hunted with old companions. During that winter, Boone later told his children, one of those, a man named Green, was mauled by a wounded bear while hunting with his brother-in-law. Thinking that Green was about to die anyway, his kinsman abandoned him in a rude shelter and, returning to the Clinch, reported his death. Meanwhile, alone in the cold woods, Green found the strength to hack out a cavity in the dirt floor of the cabin with his hunter's knife, got into the pit, covered himself with turkey feathers, and survived by eating snow and jerked bear meat. Early the next spring Boone was among those accompanying the brother to recover and bury Green's body when they encountered this survivor, limping down the mountain, one side of his face completely destroyed. Boone and the others could "scarcely refrain from laying violent hands" on the villain.

With this example of family inconstancy fresh in his mind, Boone set out a few weeks later, in the early spring of 1774, to visit the grave of his son James. He was met by a party of hunters, one of whom remembered Boone's striking appearance, "dressed in deerskin colored black, his hair plaited and clubbed up" in the Indian manner. He was, Boone told them, on his way to Powell's Valley. Arriving alone at the massacre site, he was upset to find evidence that wolves had been digging at the graves, so he rolled away the logs that had been laid atop for protection, took out a hand spike, and dug down. Thankfully he found the bodies undisturbed. Unwrapping Rebecca's sheet, for the first time he gazed upon the mangled body of his son, the boy he had held close during winter storms in the mountains. It lay compressed tightly against Henry Russell's, and so disfigured were both that Boone could tell them apart only by the difference between Henry's dark and James's fair hair. He carefully rewrapped them in his saddle blankets and reburied them separately, disguising the graves as best he could to deter animals and Indians.

As he completed his work, the late-afternoon sky filled with dark clouds and a violent storm erupted. Boone sat by the side of the graves in the rain and wept. It was an experience he often recalled with his family, and during the telling it would be as if he was returned to the graveside once again. With "the melancholy of his feelings, mingled with the howling of the storm and the gloominess of the place," old Boone would whisper in a voice choked with emotion, "he felt worse than ever in his life." When he could stand the pain no more, he moved a few hundred yards away, hobbled his horse, made a fire, and lay down, but he could not sleep. Thinking he heard the sounds of men approaching through the forest, he quietly saddled his horse and rode off into the night.

CHAPTER FOUR

On the Banks of Kentucke River

1773 to 1776

The attack on the Boones and the others bound for Kentucky in October of 1773 signaled the Indians' intention of holding settlers east of the mountains. Cornstalk, principal chief of the Shawnees, told the British that his people feared that the Americans, by moving into Kentucky, "designed to deprive us of the hunting of the country." Fear likewise spread among American settlers scattered along the river valleys of the Appalachian frontier that spring would bring Indian raids and attacks. In the Clinch Valley, where the Boones were staying, the end of winter brought an exodus of frightened families leaving "in such haste," one observer wrote, "that they left all their stock, and the greatest part of their household furniture." But there was no restraining the press of other Americans for the lands of the West. As soon as the ice on the Ohio began to break, surveying parties descended the river, heading into Kentucky. Some represented private interests, others worked directly for colonial governments with competing plans to use land grants to reward veterans and raise revenues. Men like Governor Dunmore of Virginia unscrupulously pursued both public and private interests simultaneously. For every settler fearfully abandoning the frontier, at least two more expectantly waited to advance, touched with Kentucky fever.

In an attempt to quiet the alarm in his district, William Russell of Castle's Wood, leader of the local militia, sent scouts and rangers westward as advance guards. Information gained by envoys to the Cherokee towns suggested that while the chiefs argued for peace, their angry young warriors might form a league with Shawnees and others against the colonists. "Tho' we are apprehensive that the Cherokees and Northward Indians intend war," Russell instructed his men, "yet should you by accident fall in with any of their parties, you are to avoid acting towards them in a hostile manner." He wanted to do nothing that would "blast our fairest hopes of settling the Ohio country."

Caution, however, was not to be the watchword of the hour. Governor Dunmore acted in the conviction that violence and warfare would best serve his purposes. By 1774 the tensions between the colonies and the British Empire were mounting. In the spring Dunmore dissolved the Virginia House of Burgesses after its expression of sympathy for the struggles against imperial authority taking place in New England. An Indian war, thought Dunmore, might be an effective diversion from these political struggles. Moreover, Virginia was locked in competition with Pennsylvania over jurisdiction of the Ohio country. Dunmore had gone so far as to appoint governing officials for districts in western Pennsylvania, and moving an armed force of Virginians into the region would allow him to reinforce their authority. In April, Dunmore's agents circulated an incendiary proclamation through the settlements on the Upper Ohio declaring that a state of war already existed between Indians and colonists.

Cornstalk and other advocates of peace among the Shawnees protested to the British authorities that they had "prevailed on the foolish People amongst us to sit still and do no harm till we see whether it is the intention of the white people in general to fall on us" and asked that they "present our good Intentions to the Governors of Virginia and Pennsylvania." But warriors could no more be controlled by chiefs than backcountry settlers by elites. It was a time of mutual murder and pillage. Numerous killings by Indian-hating Virginians along the Ohio during April and May turned a critical mass of Indian opinion in favor of war. By mid-May there were reports of attacks taking place on settlers in frontier Fincastle County, Virginia.

In June, Dunmore addressed a circular letter to the captains of militia in Virginia's western counties. "Hopes of a pacification can be no longer entertained," he declared, and he ordered them to erect and garrison forts for the protection of settlers, to post rangers along the trails and streams, and to prepare for a campaign against the Indian towns of the Ohio country. The frontier militia, he wrote, would be required to provide "extraordinary means for an extraordinary occasion." William Russell received Dunmore's letter on June 24, 1774, accompanied by an order to employ two "faithful woodmen" to go to Kentucky to warn the legions of Virginia surveyors working there of the impending war. A muster of the local militia was already scheduled for the following day, and Russell took that opportunity to read the governor's letter to the assembled men. By acclamation they voted to construct two additional forts in the Clinch settlements, which, Russell reported, "we shall begin instantly to erect." Regarding the surveyors, he told the men, "I have engaged to start immediately on the occasion, two of the best Hands I could think of, Daniel Boone, and Michael Stoner, who have Engaged to search the Country, as low as the falls" of the Ohio.

Boone volunteered for this assignment. He had just returned from a trip north to Augusta County in the Shenandoah Valley, where in early June he had made arrangements for some Kentucky surveying business of his own. He had met there with Col. Andrew Lewis of Staunton, who requested that while Boone was in Kentucky he contact and warn the surveyors, and Boone had willingly assented. After talking with Russell, who now made the assignment official, Boone approached Stoner and asked if he would come along. He would be happy to go, Stoner replied, if only he had a decent gun. "Well, Mike," said Boone, "you shall have mine, and I'll get another. You're the man for me."

Boone and Stoner had first met during the aborted emigration of the previous fall. They shared origins in southeastern Pennsylvania, where in 1748 Stoner was born the son of German immigrants. Orphaned at an early age, he had been apprenticed to a saddle maker, but "his nature was sutch," his grandson wrote, "that he could not bare to be tied to a sadlers bench." Dreaming of adventure, Stoner ran away at sixteen and headed for the frontier, where he soon joined the ranks of the most highly acclaimed woodsmen.

By the time he settled at Castle's Wood in the late 1760s, Stoner had been through the interior country, including Kentucky. Nathan Boone remembered him as "an awkward Dutchman, a low, chunky man" who spoke with a heavy German accent, but he was renowned as "truthful and reliable" and he became one of Boone's lifelong friends.

The two men took a day to prepare for their journey, then, bidding farewell to their families, set out for Kentucky on Monday morning, June 27, 1774. Boone kept a journal during the trip, probably because he and Stoner spent a portion of their time locating, surveying, and marking settlement sites for a number of men. "I was employed by Governor Dunmore to give the surveyors notice of the breaking out of the Indian War," and while in Kentucky, "on the Creek that goes by the name of Hickmans Creek," Boone later testified, "I cut the two first letters of said [James] Hickmans name on a large water oak with a large stone grown fast in said tree." His journal, which he turned over to his superiors, has long been lost and only a few details of the expedition survive. Boone recalled that coming to a salt lick on a small stream, Stoner taunted a buffalo and was charged. As Boone told the story, his companion wheeled and ran, yelling, "Schoot her, gabtain!, schoot her," while Boone collapsed in laughter. Stoner's memory was that the two of them were constantly apprehensive about Indian ambush, and whenever stopping to eat or rest would sit back to back so as not to be surprised from the rear. But they saw no warriors, and though they carried out their instructions "to take the Kentucky and meander to its mouth," neither did they come across any of the surveyors, though they found the evidence of their work everywhere. "Finding the surveyors were driven in by the Indians," said Boone, "I returned home."

Several parties of surveyors had in fact been attacked. James Harrod was in command of a group who had returned to the location he had explored the previous summer and laid out a town. Indians fired on several men there on July 8, and two were killed; Harrod and his companions immediately evacuated. Another group came upon this spot a few days later and, seeing the evidence of violence, took to the river in canoes, headed for home. An Indian ambush from the banks killed two of them, including their leader, and the survivors wandered through the forests for some time before finding their way over the mountains. A third party found themselves at Harrod's site on the twenty-forth, where tacked to a tree they found the message: "Alarmed by finding some people killed we are gone down." It took these men sixteen days of forced marching to reach the far-western settlements on the Clinch. By the last week of August, however, all of the surviving surveyors had come in, and "an Express from Mr. Boone" reached Russell announcing his imminent arrival.

His mission to Kentucky brought Boone prominently to the attention of the officers of the Virginia frontier militia. John Floyd, who had led one of the surveying parties, wrote to his patron Col. William Preston of the effort Boone had made to locate the Virginians—"for which reason I love the man"—and reported that he enjoyed a reputation among the settlers that was greater than any other man under arms. Maj. Arthur Campbell similarly wrote to Preston that Boone was "a very popular Officer where he is known." Campbell pressed Boone into service to raise a company to join the Virginia forces assembling at the Levels of Greenbriar, 150 miles north, for an attack on the Shawnees. Professing his "great desire to go on the Expedition," Boone started out with a number of recruits, but in a day or two he was overtaken by a messenger with orders from Russell to return to the Clinch. Boone, his superiors had decided, would be better utilized as a leader of the local defense.

During Boone's absence Shawnee warriors had attacked and killed a number of people north of Castle's Wood, and it would be only a matter of time before they struck the settlements of the Clinch Valley. The settlers had crowded into a series of small forts located every five or ten miles along the length of the valley. Boone's family and a number of others took refuge at Moore's Fort, a few miles south of Castle's Wood. The small farms were dispersed on the hill slopes or in narrow hollows, and it was too dangerous to return to them to work the fields. In the forts ammunition and food ran low and sanitary conditions were abysmal, but worst of all was the infernal waiting, with nothing to do. Discipline was lax and the men assigned to protect the fort often let down their guard. One woman who forted at Moore's remembered that the men "would all go out and play at ball, and those that were not playing would go out and lie down, without their guns." This did not sit well with Rebecca Bryan Boone. She and two or three other wives, as well as her oldest daughters, Susannah and Jemima, loaded a half dozen guns light, in the Indian manner, crept out the fort's back side, and fired a fusillade, then ran back in and slammed both gates. The men outdoors bolted for the gate and, finding it locked, ran about in panic; several even jumped into a nearby pond to hide themselves, while the women laughed derisively from inside. When the joke became clear, the men sputtered with rage and a number threatened to take whips to the women, but this caused more conflict and a number of fistfights broke out among them. It was to remedy such disorder that Boone was made a lieutenant and placed in command of Moore's Fort.

Soon thereafter attacks began to take place on the forts, beginning with those north of Castle's Wood. The colony of Virginia had promised men joining the invasion force that "the plunder of the Country will be valluable," adding that "it is said the Shawnese have a great Stock of Horses." Tempted by this offer, a majority of the able-bodied frontiersmen from the valley had left for the north. Local defenses were thus weakened and arms and ammunition were woefully short. In an attempt to stretch resources, Boone was given charge of a troop of fourteen rangers whose assignment was to move up and down the valley, following up on reports of attacks and depredations, and soon he became a familiar and comforting presence to the settlers the whole length of the Clinch.

The first attack close to home occurred on September 23, when a war party composed of Mingos and Shawnees surrounded Fort Blackmore, some twenty miles downriver from Boone's base at Moore's Fort. They were under the command of Mingo chief Logan, known to his own people as Tahgahjute, who was bent on avenging the death of his kinsfolk on the Ohio the previous spring. Formerly Logan had been an advocate of peace with the Americans, "but when you killed my kin," he wrote in a note left on the body of one of his victims, "I thought I must kill too." At Blackmore he captured two slaves who had been sent out to feed the stock, and while the settlers watched from inside the fort, Logan paraded them back and forth, taunting the men to come out and fight or else lose their "bearskins," as these Indians called the blacks. Failing in this stratagem, the Indians killed a number of horses and cattle before disappearing with their captives into the hills that sloped down to the rear of the fort. "It was a skittish time with the women, you may be sure," an eyewitness reported many years later.

Logan's small guerrilla force was back on the Clinch a week later, this time at Moore's Fort. A little after sunset on the twenty-ninth, after carefully checking and assuring themselves that there was no danger, three men left the stockade to check a pigeon trap they had set up about three hundred yards away. Suddenly there was fire from the timber and one of the men fell dead. Hearing the shots, Boone and several others bolted from the gate, and as they charged ahead they saw a painted warrior tear John Duncan's scalp from his head. Before they reached the body, however, the Indians had dissolved into the twilight. The next day a child from the fort, gone to the spring for water, found an ornamental war club left there as a calling card and ran back with it, screaming for her father. She long remembered her father's reassuring response as she threw herself into his arms: "Well, Kate, you must have had a powerful fight with the Indians to take their war club." Boone reported that the club was "difirent from that left at Blackmores" and thought it possible that southern warriors had joined Logan's party, although in general the Cherokees kept themselves out of this conflict.

The final incident in the Clinch Valley during what became known as Dunmore's War occurred ten days later, when a sentinel outside the gates of Fort Blackmore observed some Indians creeping along the bank of the river toward the fort. "Murder, murder!" he shouted, warning the men inside, who quickly slammed shut the gate, unfortunately leaving the young guard stranded outside, where he was killed. The fort's officer had recently abandoned his post, fearing for his own family on the Holston, and the residents sent a messenger north to Moore's summoning Capt. Daniel Smith, Boone, and a party of thirty rangers. In his report of this expedition Smith wrote that when the rangers arrived late in the evening they corralled their horses in a pen adjoining the fort and put up for the night, but the next morning they suffered the "mortification" of finding that a number of their mounts had been taken by the Indians, probably by the same party who had arrived at the fort on foot. Boone "found some footing and Horse tracts not far distant from the Fort," but he was unable to follow the trace beyond the hills.

Boone had earned a reputation among the residents of the Clinch as the best man to call in an emergency. "Mr. Boone is very diligent at Castle's-woods and keeps up good order," Maj. Arthur Campbell reported in September. While he was at Fort Blackmore, Captain Smith was presented with a petition signed by the men of the community requesting that Boone be promoted to the rank of captain and placed in charge of the valley's defenses. "I believe it contains the sense of the majority of the inhabitants in this settlement," Smith wrote to Colonel Preston, "Boone is an excellent woodsman. If that only would qualify him for the Office, no man would be more proper. I do not know of any Objection that could be made to his character which would make you think him an improper person for that office." Boone may have come from lowly origins but he seemed officer material nonetheless. Major Campbell, who already had written glowingly of Boone, endorsed the promotion, noting that the settlers were highly dissatisfied with the leadership of many local officers. "It is men, not particular Officers," he wrote to Preston, "that they are mowst in need of."

Preston immediately promoted Boone, using blank commissions signed by Dunmore left for precisely this purpose. Like all men on the frontier Boone had served in militia companies since he had come of age. Now nearing his fortieth birthday, he was receiving the acclaim of his fellow citizens, frontiersmen and gentlemen alike. One of the distinctive features about life in the American backcountry was what one historian has called its "semi-civil" character, where every man bore arms and might at any time be called to battle. Within this quasi-military world, titles of rank were never forgotten, and Boone would be Captain Boone until promoted again during the Revolution. He treasured this commission and always kept it with him, folded and tucked into his "budget," the little leather purse that both Americans and Indians carried over their shoulders. It symbolized a moment of triumph following on the heels of his most bitter experience, the death of his eldest son just a year before. Twenty years after Boone's death, his descendants submitted this commission as supporting evidence with a congressional petition for remuneration. It fell into the bowels of the federal bureaucracy, along with several other important documents of Boone's life and service, to be forever lost.

After his promotion, Boone told Filson, "I was ordered to take command of three garrisons," Fort Blackmore, Moore's Fort, and Fort Russell at Castle's Wood, but by this time the war had already ended. On October 10 at Point Pleasant on the Ohio River, an inconclusive battle was fought between three hundred Shawnee and Delaware warriors, led by Chief Cornstalk, and one thousand men in the army of Virginia, under the command of Col. Andrew Lewis. The army suffered over 80 killed and nearly 150 wounded, but with a much greater force they were able to follow the battle with a march to the Shawnee towns on the Scioto River. Surrounded, the Indians sued for peace. In the subsequent Treaty of Camp Charlotte, Cornstalk and other chiefs agreed to yield the Shawnees' hunting rights in Kentucky in exchange for Dunmore's promise to keep colonists south of the Ohio, but the treaty was denounced and disowned by other chiefs and warriors. The question of how to deal with the American threat divided and fragmented the Shawnees.

With the American forces returning home by November, the local militia disbanded, with Boone released on November 20. His last official act was to complete the paperwork required of the officer in charge. "Rachel Duncin, one horse in the Sarvis 28 Days," he noted in one of a series of receipts submitted for reimbursement; "Rachel Duncin, one Beef Cowe prased at 3.0.0." The widow of John Duncan, whose scalping Boone had witnessed at Moore's Fort, would have her mite. "I do hereby certify that William Poage acted as Ensign twenty Seven Days under my Command on Clinch River," read the discharge of one of his soldiers, who within a year would be with Boone in Kentucky. Boone, Poage, and hundreds of others now turned their thoughts to the land that lay beyond the mountains.

Americans established a number of permanent settlements in Kentucky in 1775, Boonesborough among them. But although Boone was leader of the men and women who planted the community named in his honor, he once again attached his emigration to the enterprise of a prominent gentleman, this time Richard Henderson of North Carolina. There is no evidence of a relationship between Boone and Henderson following Boone's removal to Virginia in 1773. Indeed, documents of the Rowan County Court in North

Carolina show that Henderson was still trying to secure Boone's arrest for debt. Henderson had lost his house and barn in the Regulator rebellion and may have suffered other financial losses as well in the early 1770s. Moreover, he was preoccupied with his duties as a justice of the superior court until the end of his term in 1773. With this relief from responsibility, however, he turned his full attention to a grandiose Kentucky land scheme. To the original group of investors that composed Henderson and Company, he added other partners, until the company's capital resources were sufficient to consider the "rent or purchase" of a large tract of land in the West from the Cherokees, for the purpose of "settling the country."

Following the defeat of the Shawnees in Dunmore's War and the agreement of at least part of the tribe to cede their right to Kentucky, the Cherokees seemed to be the last remaining Indian claimants. Late in the fall Henderson and Nathaniel Hart, probably accompanied by others more experienced in Indian negotiations, went to the Cherokee chiefs in their mountain towns to discuss the possibility of a purchase of land north of the Tennessee River. Henderson had no authority to enter into such an arrangement; the laws of both North Carolina and Virginia, as well as the British Proclamation of 1763, specifically enjoined private citizens from treating with Indian nations, especially concerning the purchase of land. On their part, the Cherokees, though they occasionally used the Kentucky country as a hunting territory, had no usufruct tradition to this land. Nevertheless, Henderson offered the Cherokees ten thousand pounds' worth of merchandise for their quitclaim, and the Indians offered Henderson a piece of parchment that, he gambled, would provide a sufficient appearance of legality to attract settlers willing to purchase land and pay quitrents. It was a case of mutual complicity in a process both parties knew to be fraudulent.

Reaching a preliminary agreement, Henderson returned with Attakullakulla, the chief called Little Carpenter by the English, and a half dozen other Cherokees, including a number of young warriors and at least one clan matron, who were to examine and select the goods proposed for payment in the interests of their various constituencies. The woman, especially, examined the wares with a shrewd eye, and once they completed the process of haggling over the quality and quantity of the merchandise, the Indians returned to their towns with the understanding that a formal negotiation would take place the following March. It was still more than three months before the completion of the sale, but in order to drum up interest, in December of 1774 Henderson published a broadside enumerating his "Proposals for the Encouragement of settling the Lands purchased by Rich'd Henderson & Co." In this and subsequent advertisements he announced that land would be available at twenty shillings per hundred acres to each emigrant raising a crop of corn before September 1, 1775. "All the Emigrants or Adventurers would settle in a Town or Township, for this year at least, on some convenient part of the land to be chosen for that purpose, [and] during the year every man may be looking out for such land as he may choose to settle on when safe to disperse."

The authorities reacted immediately. To the leaders of Virginia, who had just prosecuted a war of dubious justice in order to secure the Kentucky country for themselves, Henderson's plans posed an immediate threat. "Henderson talks with great freedom & indecency of the Governor of Virginia," reported William Preston, "and says if he once had five hundred good fellows settled in that country he would not value Virginia, that the officers and who have lands surveyed there must hold under him." According to Virginia's Governor Dunmore, Henderson was an "evill disposed and disorderly Person," and his plans could not be tolerated. In North Carolina, Governor Josiah Martin proclaimed the proposed negotiations "contrary to Law and Justice and pregnant with ill consequences," declared that any sale would be "null and void," and threatened Henderson with "the severest Penalties." "Pray," inquired one North Carolina official in a letter to another, "is Dick Henderson out of his head?" Preoccupied with the turmoil of a threatening colonial rebellion, however, the authorities found themselves powerless to prevent Henderson from moving ahead with his plans.

Boone was to play an important role in those plans. Sometime toward the end of 1774 Henderson asked Boone for his assistance in making arrangements with the Cherokees, and by early the next year he was circulating through the Tennessee mountains, passing word of the upcoming negotiation and persuading Indians to assemble at Sycamore Shoals on the Watauga River at the beginning of March. "I was solicited by a number of North-Carolina gentlemen that were about purchasing the lands lying on the S. side of Kentucke

River from the Cherokee Indians," Filson quoted Boone, "to attend their treaty at Wataga, in March 1775, to negotiate with them, and mention the boundaries of the purchase." In addition Boone was "to mark out a road in the best passage from the settlement through the wilderness to Kentucke, with such assistance as I thought necessary to employ for such an important undertaking," then select and fortify a town site in Kentucky. In exchange for these services Henderson promised Boone his choice of two thousand prime acres of Kentucky land from within the company's domain.

Early in February, Boone returned from Tennessee to his family on the Clinch to prepare for the adventure. The emigration of 1773 had been conceived in the traditions of a folk migration. The attempt of 1775 would be considerably different. It would include quasi-legal formalities that promised to eliminate some of the Indian danger, an armed expedition of woodsmen to prepare the route, and the construction of a fort for the protection and defense of emigrating families. Offering wages of more than ten pounds for what would be about a month of hard work in road making, in addition to an opportunity to be among the first on the ground to claim lands that were fabled to be among the best in America, Boone was able to recruit more than a score of men from the Clinch. "Mikel Stoner Entered, feberry the 5, 1775," Boone wrote in his account book; others included William Bush and David Gass, who had been with Boone during his previous try at settling Kentucky.

William Hays was a special case. A twenty-year-old Irishman who had found his way to the Clinch settlements just before Dunmore's War, Hays was hard drinking and hot tempered, but he was also a reasonably well-educated man with the manners of a gentleman. He and Boone came to know each other during the period the family forted at Moore's, and when it came time for Captain Boone to write his final militia reports, a task that Boone always found difficult, Hays offered his assistance. He helped Boone to improve his writing and calculating skills and became one of his closest associates. The truth was, he also was courting the Boones' oldest daughter, Susannah. Although she was barely more than fourteen, she was, in the words of one man, "a pretty good looking woman, medium sized, and rather slim." All of the Boone daughters would marry young, but Susy Boone also had a reputation for "frolicking" with the boys, a concern to her parents, but something they found themselves powerless to control in the disordered conditions of family and social life prevailing in the fort.

Susannah Boone became the subject of a number of ribald tales, and as late as the mid-nineteenth century antiquarians collecting material about the Boone family could expect winks and elbows when her name came up in the conversation. One tale of the 1840s dealt with Susannah's marriage to Hays. The prospective groom comes to Boone to ask for his daughter's hand. She will not suit you, my friend, says Boone, she will cheat on you. But Will loves the beautiful backwoods daughter, waves aside Boone's caution, and the couple is married. Then, in the words of the storyteller, "the thing was realized." Hays comes again to Boone, this time complaining. "Didn't I tell you," says Boone, "trot father, trot mother, how could you expect a pacing colt?" John Dabney Shane, the Presbyterian minister who collected this tale, found it difficult to believe that Boone could have said such a thing. You must remember, his informant responded, that "Boone was raised in the backwoods of Carolina," and "those times were very different from these, and such things then were not what they now would be." One man who claimed to have known Susannah labeled her "a notorious prostitute," but another old Kentucky settler declared that he had never seen any evidence of lewd behavior, and that when he knew her at Boonesborough, she seemed "a clever, pretty, well behaved woman." What seems clear is that Susy was a high-spirited girl, the feminine counterpart of the freewheeling backwoodsman, and such women came in for their share of gossip.

The wedding of Will Hays and Susannah Boone took place at Moore's Fort in early March of 1775. A day or two later Boone rode out of the Clinch settlements headed for Sycamore Shoals, approximately seventy-five miles south. He left owing a substantial debt, and his creditor obtained a judgment against Boone's property and an order for his arrest. "Gone to Kentucky," the sheriff scrawled across the back of the warrant. In addition to his Clinch River friends, Boone was accompanied by Will Hays and his bride Susannah. Her honeymoon would be spent working as a camp keeper for the thirty woodsmen hacking out the road to Kentucky.

By the second week of March, upward of a thousand Cherokee men and women were gathered at Sycamore Shoals, a traditional rendezvous on the south side of the Watauga River a few miles west of present Elizabethton, Tennessee, then the center of the American settlements in the area. The Indians camping on the grounds surrounding the stockade were fed by settler women hired by the company, which recently had adopted the name Transylvania for its intended inland empire. With Boone providing the geographic details, Carolina Dick, as Henderson was known to the Indians, led the delegation of proprietors negotiating with several notable Cherokee chiefs, including Little Carpenter, his son Dragging Canoe, and the old war leader Oconostota. Each side employed a number of "Indian Half-Breeds," wrote one observer, "who understood both Languages, as a check upon the Chief Interpreter, lest he should mistranslate, or leave out, through Forgetfulness any Part of what either Party should speak." Six wagonloads of merchandise were laid on blankets in tents nearby for the Indians to inspect and as a lure to an agreement, although one observer on the treaty grounds disparagingly described them as nothing more than "cheap goods, such as coarse woolens, trinkets, some firearms, and spirituous liquors." Later, when the chiefs who had signed the agreement were criticized by tribal militants for exchanging the tribe's estate for little more than a mess of potage, they argued that "when the young men saw the goods, they insisted on having them on any terms, which their great men were obliged to comply with, otherwise lose their authority in the nation." Besides, they pointed out, they never pretended that they owned the lands being bargained for, and thus gave nothing away.

There was a good deal of self-justification in their explanation, but contemporary accounts of the negotiations suggest that the Cherokees were deeply divided about the wisdom of the sale and there was some candid speech making about lack of Cherokee proprietary rights in Kentucky. "You, Carolina Dick, have deceived your people," one witness remembered old Oconostota saying. "We told you that those lands were not ours, that our claim extended not beyond the Cumberland Mountains." Young Dragging Canoe echoed the old chief but protested the entire proceeding, arguing that the Cherokees should oppose any cession of land west of the mountains, regardless of tribal ownership. Otherwise, he warned, the "encroaching spirit" of the Americans would soon lead them to lay claim to the lands of the Cherokees as well. "New cessions would be applied for, and finally the country which the Cherokees and their forefathers had so long occupied would be called for; and a small remnant which may then exist of this nation, once so great and formidable, will be compelled to seek a retreat in some far distant wilderness." These were prophetic words. But in the end Little Carpenter, whose name signaled his craft at cobbling together disparate views in the Indian process of consensus making, was able to persuade clan and village leaders to authorize the sale of two hundred thousand acres lying between the Kentucky and Cumberland rivers on the west side of the mountains.

With things going his way, Henderson told the chiefs that he also wanted a cession of what he called a "Path Grant," allowing the company to cut a road through the mountains of southwest Virginia leading to the Cumberland Gap. "He did not love to walk upon their land," he declared, and besides, "he had more Goods, Guns and Ammunition which they had not yet seen." Dragging Canoe responded with barely restrained rage. "We give you from this place," he intoned, stamping his foot on the ground and pointing toward Kentucky. While his own countrymen would not molest the settlers, he believed that the northern Indians would. "There was a dark cloud over that Country," he warned in words that would ring through the next two decades of Kentucky history. The sale, including the path grant, finally was agreed to, and on March 17, 1775, the Cherokees signed what amounted to a deed of sale. Before Boone left the treaty grounds to begin marking the path later known as the Wilderness Road, Chief Oconostota took him by the hand and gave him a parting warning. Boone said that these words often came back to him during the ensuing struggles. "Brother," said the old chief, "we have given you a fine land, but I believe you will have much trouble in settling it."

The company of men assigned to hack out the road to Kentucky assembled at the Blockhouse, a stockade near the Long Island of Holston (present-day Kingsport), Tennessee, some fifty miles northwest of Sycamore Shoals. Boone left the treaty ground several days before the final signing ceremonies and on about the tenth of March arrived at the Blockhouse, where thirty or thirty-five men awaited him. Brother Squire had come from the Yadkin with kinsman Benjamin Cutbeard, old Samuel Tate and his son, and a number of others. Capt. William Twitty, "an active and enterprising woodsman," led another group of eight or ten men from Rutherford County, North Carolina, and there were at least ten more men from the Clinch. Felix Walker, a young axman who later wrote an engaging account of his adventure as a road maker, said that by general agreement the men submitted themselves to the "management and control" of Boone, "who was to be our pilot and conductor through the wilderness to the promised land." Boone's daughter Susannah and a slave woman were to do the cooking and keep camp for the men.

The slave woman was owned by Richard Callaway, a man destined to play an important role in Boone's life during the next few years. Callaway had joined Henderson's enterprise at about the same time as Boone and was in charge of hauling the goods and supplies to the treaty grounds. The youngest son of a powerful landowning family in the Shenandoah Valley of Virginia, Callaway was ten years Boone's senior and his superior in the pecking order of frontier militia, having served as a colonel during the French and Indian War. Callaway was officious, bad tempered, and a bit of a blue blood, and it was clear from the beginning that he resented serving under Boone's command of the road-making party.

Despite years of use the Warrior's Path remained a rough trace through the mountains, and the job of the men was to widen and level it sufficiently for the passage of wagons. Blazing the way through the forest was difficult work, chopping saplings, vines, and overhanging branches, removing fallen timber, throwing logs across sinkholes and creeks, burning through dead brush, cutting through canebrakes. The season did not make it any easier, with the late snows and freezing rain in the mountains, the wet and mud of winter's thaw in the valleys. Boone took the lead, marking the way and hunting game for the evening meal. When the party reached the Cumberland Gap it became clear that while wagons might with difficulty be driven to that point, they could not make the passage into Kentucky. It would be another twenty years before "Boone's Old Trace" was transformed into a wagon road. West of the mountains Boone diverged from the main track of the Warrior's Path, directing the road makers in a northwesterly direction across the mountain plateau. Here they occasionally were able to take advantage of "buffalo roads," wide swaths cut by the movement of animals. "Buffaloes made the road," one old pioneer later testified, "Boone marked it." Rather than moving in a beeline toward their destination, the road makers thus cut a path from meadow to lick, meandering with the water courses and the elevation of the land in the manner of animal traces. It was "pretty difficult to follow," one road maker remembered, and there were numerous complaints about creeks "that we crost about 50 times [over] Some very Bad foards." For Henderson, leading the main force about two weeks to Boone's rear, "no part of the road [was] tolerable, most of it either hilly, stony, slippery, miry, or bushy."

After they reached the Rockcastle River, the road makers had to cut their way through many miles of dead brush, followed by another comparable distance of thick cane and reeds. Finally, after two weeks of hard and continuous labor, they began to descend the hills and on March 22 caught their first glimpse of the rolling country ahead, "the pleasing and rapturous appearance of the plains of Kentucky." As Felix Walker remembered it, "A new sky and strange earth seemed to be presented to our view." They pushed ahead another ten or fifteen miles and made camp at the headwaters of a creek, near a "boiling spring," a site a few miles south of present-day Richmond, Kentucky. Delighted and exhausted and feeling that they had all but accomplished their goal, the road makers slept soundly the night of the twenty-fourth.

As Boone and his men neared the end of their journey, the main contingent with Henderson was just beginning theirs. This party included two dozen mounted riflemen, a substantial group of slaves, and some of the partners of the Transylvania Company, including several men of the Henderson and Hart families. There were no women. In addition to forty packhorses and a herd of cattle, a number of wagons were loaded with provisions, ammunition, seed corn and seed for garden crops, and the merchandise to outfit a trader's store to meet the initial needs of an isolated settlement. The group arrived in Powell's Valley on March 30, where John Martin, now in Henderson's employ, had reestablished his pioneer station with an advance guard of several men. In a freezing rain Henderson directed the wagons under rough log shelters to protect the goods, then sent men ahead to scout the trail. They returned to report that the wagons could go no farther. All of the supplies had to be unloaded, with much of it placed in storage at

Martin's, and the party spent several days reorganizing. The evening of April 7 the group was still in camp, waiting out a heavy early-spring snow, when a messenger appeared from "Cantuckey," as Henderson wrote in his journal, with "a letter from Daniel Boone that his company was fired upon by Indians."

Boone's letter exists in the form of a copy, its grammar and spelling obviously cleaned up. It is, nevertheless, the earliest surviving Boone letter, the first document to preserve his description of an important event in his own authentic voice. Dated April 1, 1775, the letter begins "Dear Colonel,"

> After my compliments to you, I shall acquaint you of our misfortune. On March the 25 a party of Indians fired on my company about half an hour before day, and killed Mr. Twetty and his negro, and wounded Mr. Walker very deeply but I hope he will recover. On March the 28 as we were hunting for provisions, we found Samuel Tate's son, who gave us an account that the Indians fired on their camp on the 27 day. My brother and I went down and found two men killed and sculped, Thomas McDowell and Jeremiah McPfeeters. I have sent a man down to all the lower companies in order to gather them all to the mouth of Otter Creek.
>
> My advice to you Sir, is, to come or send as soon as possible. Your company is desired greatly, for the people are very uneasy, but are willing to stay and venture their lives with you, and now is the time to flusterate the intentions of the Indians, and keep the country whilst we are in it. If we give way to them now, it will ever be the case. This day we start from the battle ground, for the mouth of Otter Creek, where we shall immediately erect a fort, which will be done before you can come or send—then we can send ten men to meet you, if you send for them.
>
> I am, Sir, your most obedient,
>
> Daniel Boone
>
> N.B.—We stood on the ground and guarded our baggage till day, and lost nothing. We have about fifteen miles to Cantuck, at Otter Creek.

When the shooting began at Boone's camp, men started up in panic while Indians rushed through the camp, swinging their tomahawks. Twitty was shot in both knees and Sam, his slave, was hit and fell face first into the fire, instantly killed. Two warriors rushed up to take Twitty's scalp as he writhed on the ground, but the woodsman's little bulldog prevented them by leaping to the attack; one of the Indians bludgeoned the dog to death. Walker was wounded but managed to flee with the others into the brush. "Although surprised and taken at a disadvantage," Boone told Filson, "we stood our ground." The fight was quickly over, but it was some time before the men dared to return to camp. According to Walker, "Col. Boon, and a few others, appeared to possess firmness and fortitude," but the attack "cast a deep gloom of melancholy over all our prospects." A few of the road makers immediately packed their things and started back for the settlements. Others threw up a rough log shelter for protection that they named "Twitty's Fort," and laid the wounded men inside. Twitty died a few days later without regaining consciousness. "My wounds, pronounced by some to be mortal," Walker remembered, "produced very serious reflections." Boone took charge of his care. "He attended me as his child, cured my wounds by the use of medicines from the woods, and nursed me with paternal affection until I recovered."

Two nights later Indians again fired on the camp of several men who were hunting and separated from the main group. A light snow was falling and the men were drying their moccasins before a large fire—perfect targets against the flames. They ran barefoot into the snowy night, were easily tracked, and two were killed. The survivors, including Samuel Tate and his son, escaped by running down an icy stream, afterward known as Tate's Creek. When Boone and Squire brought back word of the scalpings it spooked the men completely. That evening the slave woman was gathering wood for the fire at the edge of the camp when she saw someone spying at her from behind a tree. She shrieked and raised the Indian alarm and the men were thrown into a panic. But "Colonel Boone instantly caught his rifle, ordered the men to form, take trees, and give battle, and not to run till they saw him fall," said Walker, and the road makers found their courage. There was then a hallowing from the brush not to shoot, and out came one of their own, a man who had run off during the second attack and had been wandering the whole day in shock.

The axmen remained ensconced at Twitty's Fort for several days while Walker recovered his strength. Boone scouted ahead and, taking a group with him, cut a trace down the bank of Otter Creek to a site he had chosen on the Kentucky River, fifteen miles north. On the first of April he dispatched a swift rider south with his letter to Henderson, then, placing Walker in a litter slung between two horses, led the party on its final day of marching. As the men descended the final hill leading to the river, Walker raised his head from the litter and, gazing down, saw two or three hundred buffalo, startled by the approach of the Americans, making off from a salt lick and fording the river, "some walking, others loping slowly and carelessly, with young calves playing, skipping and bounding through the plain. Such a sight some of us never saw before," he would remember later, "nor perhaps may ever again."

The arrival of Boone's letter threw Henderson's party into shock. A number of men immediately turned around, refusing to await even the dawn of another day. Henderson sent a copy back to the partners in North Carolina, enclosing a short message of his own in which he described the "bad effect" the reports of Indian attack had had on his men and "the absolute necessity of our not losing one moment." That morning he pressed the force ahead to the Cumberland Gap, where they met a group of frantic men "returning from the Cantuckey on account of the late murders by the Indians." Henderson's was not the only settlement effort under way. James Harrod, for example, had led a large group from the Monongahela back to the site of Harrodsburg, arriving before Boone and his party reached the Kentucky River. Most of the Americans in Kentucky, however, were in small groups of two or three, and, hearing of Indian attacks, many fled back to the settlements in terror. The fear was contagious, and at the gap several more in Henderson's party found their nerve wavering and joined the flight, among them one of the partners, Thomas Hart, who told Henderson he thought he might be of more use by remaining in Powell's Valley "to make corn for the Cantuckey people."

As they moved ahead, scores of frightened men passed on their way back east. Henderson was almost afraid to look or inquire among the fugitives, "lest Captain Boone or his company was amongst them, or some disastrous account of their defeat." Haunted by a vision of "the ridiculous figure we should cut in the world in case of failure," he determined to get word ahead, urging Boone to hang on until they could arrive with reinforcements. "It was beyond a doubt," Henderson later wrote, "that our right, in effect, depended on Boone's maintaining his ground." When the pack train reached the banks of the Cumberland River, Henderson assembled his men and called for volunteers to ride north. Capt. William Cocke, a veteran of Dunmore's War, stepped forward. "I proposed that if any one would venture with me," he later remembered, "I would go on to join Boone and spirit up the brave men." But no one else was willing to risk his life on a ride through the wilderness. Henderson was beside himself. Weeping, he took Cocke aside and begged him to go alone, "saying that himself and company was ruined if they did not succeed in making a settlement in the Kentuck Country." Softened "by the tears of said Henderson" but also by a promise of ten thousand acres of choice Transylvania land, Cocke agreed. Henderson supplied him with "a good Queen Ann's musket, plenty of ammunition, a tomahawk, a large cuttoe knife, a Dutch blanket, and no small quantity of jerked beef," and the brave woodsman took his leave on April 10.

Cocke arrived safely in Boone's camp on the Kentucky River after four days of travel. Indians had struck again on April 4, killing an isolated member of Boone's party, but since then things had remained quiet. Boone immediately sent Michael Stoner back along the trail to guide in Henderson's column, and they arrived at "Fort Boone" on April 20. "They Come out to meet us," William Calk, one of Henderson's men, wrote in his diary, "and welcome us in with a volley of guns." Henderson felt as if a load had "dropped off my shoulders," but he knew that "it was owing to Boone's confidence in us, and the people's in him, that a stand was ever attempted." Henderson was now in Boone's element, and their relationship transformed. Things were no longer what they had been when creditor took debtor to court, yet it was an exhilarating moment for Henderson. Spying Cocke, Henderson embraced him and, "expressing himself to be much obliged," promised yet

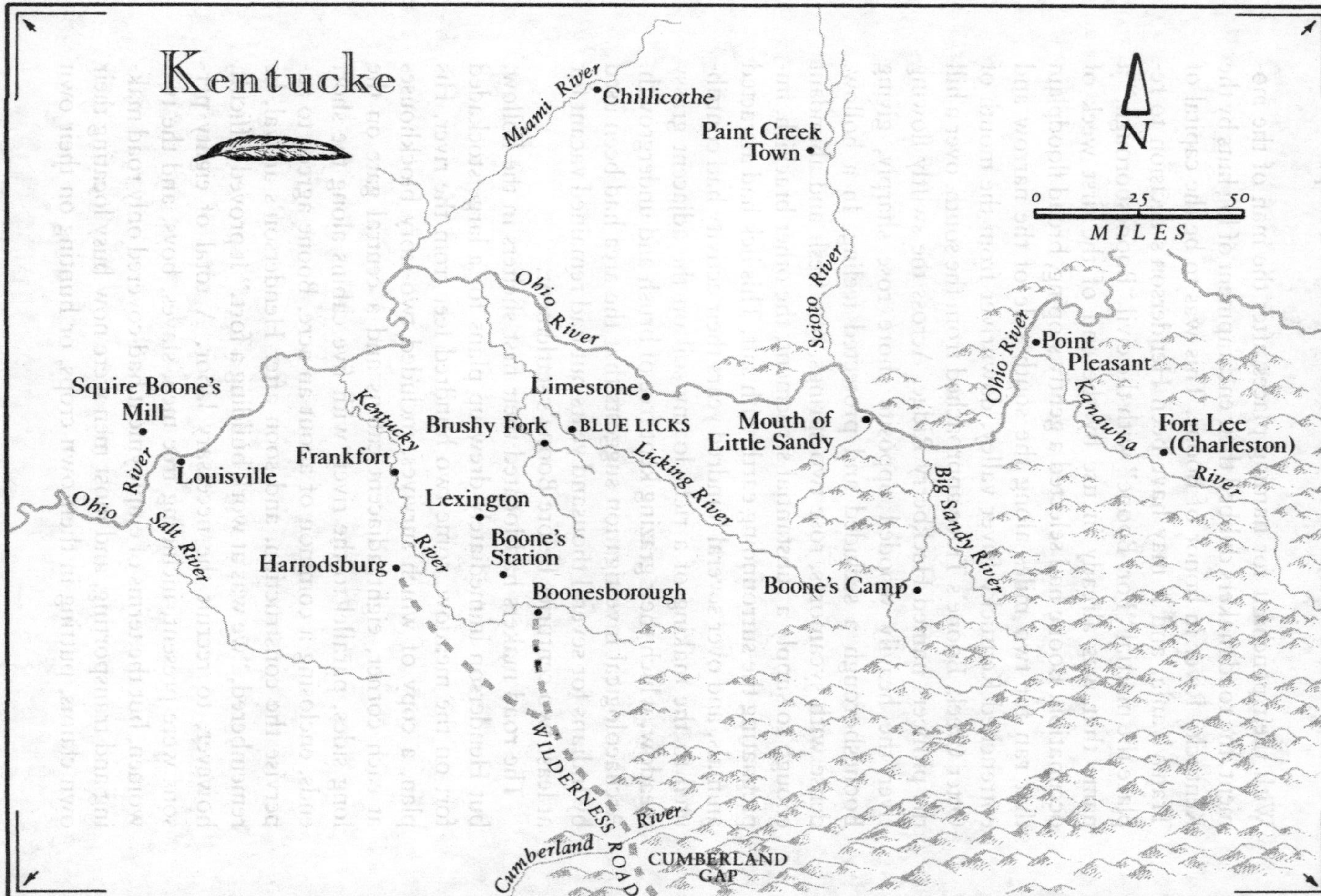
Kentucke
N
0 25 50
MILES
Miami River
Chillicothe
Paint Creek Town
Scioto River
Ohio River
Point Pleasant
Kanawha River
Fort Lee (Charleston)
Squire Boone's Mill
Limestone
Brushy Fork
BLUE LICKS
Mouth of Little Sandy
Kentucky River
Frankfort
Louisville
Licking River
Big Sandy River
Lexington
Boone's Station
Harrodsburg
Salt River
Boonesborough
Boone's Camp
WILDERNESS ROAD
Cumberland River
CUMBERLAND GAP

another five thousand acres for his valiant efforts. Promises came easily at that moment, but they would be harder to keep.

With their penchant for naming places after the man of the moment, the road makers dubbed their encampment of log huts by the Kentucky River in honor of Boone. This was to be the capital of Transylvania, and it may have been Henderson's decision to replace the martial "Fort Boone" with the civil "Boonesborough," a name that was already in use by the end of the first week of occupation. Boone had selected a gently sloping, broad floodplain that ran for two miles along the south side of the narrow and entrenched Kentucky River valley, downriver from the mouth of Otter Creek. Boone's Trace approached from the south, over a hill the pioneers named Hackberry Ridge. Across the swiftly flowing river the heavily wooded opposite shore rose sharply, giving Boonesborough a secluded and protected feeling. In a hollow, dense with sycamores, rose two springs, one fresh and abundant enough to supply a substantial settlement, the other brackish, impregnating the surrounding earth with salt. This lick had attracted animals, and over several hundred years their activity had contributed to the making of a rich, loamy soil on the adjacent grassy meadow, which their grazing kept free of brush and undergrowth. Archaeological investigation suggests that the area had been used by Indians for several thousand years but had remained vacant for at least two centuries before Boone's settlement.

The road makers had located their first shelters in the hollow, but Henderson immediately drew up plans for a large stockaded fort on the meadow, some two hundred feet from the river. His plan, a copy of which survives, included two-story blockhouses at each corner, eight adjacent cabins and a central gate on the long sides, parallel to the river, with five cabins along the short ends, enclosing a common of about an acre. Boone agreed to supervise the construction, and soon after Henderson's arrival, he remembered, "we was at work building a fort." It proved difficult, however, to recruit the necessary labor. A total of eighty persons were present, including free men, slaves, boys, and the two women, but the terms of employment had covered only road making and transporting, and most men were now busy locating their own claims, putting in their own crops, or hunting on their own hook for skins and meat. Before summer Boone managed to get a small powder magazine built, and possibly one or two of the corner blockhouses, but the rest of the fort went up piecemeal over the next two or three years. Agreement was difficult to come by even among the partners. Dissatisfied with Henderson's plans, Nathaniel Hart settled at a separate location upriver. "Should any successful attack be made on us," Henderson noted caustically, "Captain Hart, I suppose, will be able to render sufficient reasons for withdrawing from our camp and refusing to join in building a fort for our mutual defense." A settler who arrived several months later reported that "there was only four or six cabbins built along the Bank of the Kentucky river," and they "were not in a row, but scattering," and not picketed. The fort was not finished before 1778, and it is unlikely that it ever assumed the ideal form of Henderson's design.

It was but one aspect of the settlers' unwillingness to adopt collective measures. Despite the Indian attacks of the previous month, only a few days after arriving at the river the men abandoned efforts at a common defense. Boone attempted to organize a militia, but with little effect, and men even refused to stand guard at night for the whole company. Instead the settlers hastened about their individual work "without care of caution," as Henderson put it. The leadership at Boonesborough "was all anarchy and confusion," wrote one visitor of that summer; "you could not discover what person commanded, for in fact no person did actually command anything." Many of the settlers had come west precisely to escape hierarchy and control, and in their radical notions of independent action they resembled no group more than the Indians. Military leaders "could advise, but not command," wrote a lifelong resident of backcountry Virginia. "Those who chose to follow their advice did so, to such an extent as suited their fancy or interest." Henderson found himself half hoping that "the Indians should do us the favor of annoying us, and regularly scalping a man every week," so that discipline might be invoked. Indeed, it was not long before he developed a generally unfavorable view of the men. They were "a set of scoundrels who scarcely believe in God or fear a devil," he wrote, "if we were to judge from most of their looks, words, and actions." Boone, coming from the same culture as the men, had more confidence in them and felt more certain of the settlement's security. "I feel pleased with the work we have done here," he wrote toward the end of May, and "feel sure we can hold against a huge number of savages."

The Boonesborough settlers were preoccupied with land. This was inevitable, but some of the more disagreeable consequences of their obsession resulted from bad planning by the company. The agreement was that all would reside in a central location for the first year, each working two-acre "tending lots" of their own. When the company was ready to lay off the town, these plots would be combined, part laid off as a commons, and each bona-fide settler given ownership of a town lot. By the time Henderson arrived the road makers had selected their tending lots, and before the men in the main party had even unloaded their horses, they too were scurrying about, trying to locate lots of their own. Naturally, most men staked claims on the rich meadow, precisely where Henderson thought it best to place the fort. Thus Boonesborough's history began with a confrontation between company and settlers, with demands for the immediate survey of the prospective town and the location and distribution of lots so that men might know in advance the stake they had in the future of the enterprise. Henderson ordered the survey begun the very next day. On Sunday, April 23, with the dogwood and redbud in bloom, all hands turned out for a drawing of lots, and the men spent the next two days pacing them off and haggling about locations. There were so many complaints about this distribution that Henderson organized a second lottery, "at the end of which every body seemed well satisfied."

Company rules specified that only those raising a crop of corn in 1775 would be entitled to locate tracts of five hundred acres within the Transylvania domain at the advertised rate of twenty shillings per hundred acres. Thus a great deal of effort went into breaking ground and planting crops on the tending lots. In the abstract this seemed like a good idea, for it put the provision of a food supply as the first order of business. But by the end of the summer the number of settlers had dwindled to fewer than twenty, and ultimately much of the individual effort was wasted. Henderson made some effort to channel energies into common agricultural work, and a number of men agreed to assemble together for work each morning at the blast of a trumpet, but because this had not been specified in the initial agreement, it was not required, and for the most part the strong commitment to individual property prevailed. As a result the fall harvest was very skimpy.

The food supply, in fact, quickly became a critical problem. The plan had been to live through the summer on the abundant game of the countryside, but that very abundance led to enormous waste during the first few weeks. For most of the men these were the first buffalo they had seen, and, as always seemed to be the case, there was an initial orgy of killing, with most of the flesh left to rot as men gorged themselves on choice hump and tongue. "Many a man killed a buffalo just for the sake of saying so," one pioneer remembered. By the middle of May the game had been driven so far from Boonesborough that hunters were forced to travel fifteen or twenty miles to find meat. Stores of flour and meal quickly ran short. On April 25, William Calk noted in his diary, "this day we Begin to live with out Bread." The company partners and men like Callaway, who had slaves, set them to work clearing and tending gardens for themselves. Henderson's man Dan, for example, raised vegetables, kept a milk cow, and took catfish from the river, thus managing on most days to set a decent meal before his master, but the majority of settlers were not so lucky.

In addition to the eighty Americans at Boonesborough, there were an estimated two hundred or more settlers at other locations in Kentucky who had come on their own and did not recognize the authority of the Transylvania Company. Disputes over land claims began immediately and threatened to escalate into violence. With the need for order as his pretext, Henderson called for a convention at Boonesborough to draw up a temporary government. In late May, Boone was elected by the Boonesborough men to serve as one of their representatives, along with his brother Squire, William Cocke, and Richard Callaway. Among the dozen from other settlements were James Harrod of Harrodsburg and John Floyd, in Kentucky representing the interests of William Preston, one of the wealthiest and most powerful men in the backcountry and the official surveyor of Fincastle County, Virginia. The convention met under the branches of a huge elm near the uncompleted Boonesborough stockade. Henderson used the occasion to attempt to validate the Transylvania Company's proprietary claim and its governing authority. "All power is originally in the people," he announced in his opening address, but the government he outlined provided for extraordinary powers of appointment and veto by the company proprietors. If collected, annual quitrents of two shillings per hundred acres would have amounted to a fortune in revenues. In an attempt to awe the assembled delegates, Henderson staged a ceremony of "livery and seisin," in which he took possession of a bit of Kentucky turf in a moment of feudal pageantry.

The delegates proposed and passed a series of bills, creating a system of courts, providing for the punishment of criminals and the collection of debt, and establishing a militia. Boone introduced two measures, both approved, one to preserve game through restrictions on hunting, the other to encourage horse breeding, thus inaugurating one of Kentucky's most celebrated traditions. Squire Boone proposed a bill to preserve the range, and together these measures clearly suggested the concerns of the Boone brothers. The delegates passed legislation requiring that the surveyor general of the country be financially independent of the company, that a land office be established as quickly as possible, and that it remain open year-round. They appointed Boone, Harrod, and Cocke to meet with Henderson to clarify the company's terms for the sale of land and to make known the delegates' hope that grants would be available only to men who actually participated in the settlement of the country. The selection of these three for this important task was a good indication of the men the delegates considered to be their most respected leaders. Among the interesting footnotes to the convention, the Reverend John Lythe, a minister of the Church of England who acted as chaplain for the meeting, presented a bill to outlaw the profane swearing that must have burned his ears, and Dick Callaway, in an action that suggested the cut of the man, insisted on bringing young John Gass before the convention to be reprimanded for insulting him in some unspecified manner. Overall, however, the concerns of the delegates were entirely practical, and it is likely that they spent little time worrying over the trappings of Henderson's proposed system of government.

Henderson lost the support of the settlers in September, when the Transylvania partners doubled the price of land while simultaneously selling a number of large tracts to friends at low prices and reserving for the proprietors all of the land adjacent to the Falls of the Ohio. These actions "roused the attention of a number of people of note," wrote one of the partners, and settlers declared themselves unwilling to "hold lands on any other terms than those of the first year." The new terms for land sales eliminated any possibility that the company might claim the loyalty of the majority. By this action, said George Rogers Clark, recently arrived at Harrodsburg from Virginia, the partners "work their own Ruin."

The opposition of the leaders of North Carolina and Virginia also dashed Henderson's hopes for a proprietory colony in Kentucky. On May 29, the day after the close of the Boonesborough convention, news finally arrived of the battles of Lexington and Concord, fought more than a month before. Could Henderson have realized, as he noted the news in his journal, that the coming Revolution would insure the failure of his scheme? Denounced by British authorities such as Governor Josiah Martin, who labeled Henderson and his associates "an infamous Company of land Pyrates," the company now appealed to the authority of the Continental Congress for recognition of Transylvania as a separate western province. It found little support, for many congressmen were men whose own financial interests in western lands were threatened by Henderson's claims.

Their public objections, however, rested on the ground of principle. Thomas Jefferson argued that "quit-rents is a mark of vassalage"; John Adams noted that the Transylvania claim lay "within the limits of Virginia and North Carolina, by their charters," and the company was told to lay their case before the respective revolutionary governments of these states. It was a foregone conclusion that Virginia and North Carolina would invalidate the purchase of Sycamore Shoals, although they did eventually award Henderson large grants of land elsewhere for his trouble. The Transylvania Company had voted "that a present of two thousand acres of land be made to Col. Daniel Boone, with the thanks of the Proprietors, for the signal services he has rendered," but with the failure of their claims to Kentucky, Boone's grant was forgotten and he never received any compensation. The same thing happened to Michael Stoner and William Cocke, both of whom spent many years locked in litigation with Henderson's estate. But that was not Boone's way. According to his son Nathan, once Henderson passed out of Boone's life, he "troubled himself no further about it."

"Boone set off for his family," Henderson noted in his journal for June 13, "and the young men went with him for salt." Most of the salt originally intended for Kentucky had been left at Martin's Station when the wagons were unloaded, and although there had been a hope that the sulphur spring at Boonesborough could be worked, its salt content proved too weak. Leaving his companions at Martin's to await his return with the family, Boone continued on a distance in the company of Dick Callaway, then they parted ways, Boone heading up the valley of the Clinch, Callaway across Moccasin Gap and then north to Bedford County, Virginia. Both planned to recruit emigrants for Boonesborough. Boone found Rebecca in the final stages of her ninth and most difficult pregnancy. She did not deliver until sometime in late July, and the baby, William, died soon thereafter. Rebecca was not fit for travel for several more weeks, so Boone sent word back to the waiting men to go on without him, but they refused to move without their captain. "Our salt is exhausted, and the men who went with Col. Boone for that article are not returned," Henderson wrote in disgust on July 18. "We are informed that Mrs. Boone was not delivered the other day, and therefore do not know when to look for him, and until he comes, the devil himself can't drive the others this way."

Meanwhile, Boone put together a company of emigrants. Seventeen young men signed on, but fears of Indian attack kept most families back. Three finally decided to go with the Boones, including Hugh McGary, with his wife and children. McGary, one of Boone's hunting companions from the Yadkin who had accompanied him on his Kentucky long hunt of 1772–73, was known as "a headstrong man, of fierce passions." His wife was an equally strong-minded widow woman who, it was said, "could manage McGary where a whole army couldn't." The entire party of some fifty persons, including twenty-one riflemen, left with their goods loaded on packhorses about mid-August. Fifty miles south of Boonesborough, about half of them, including the families, left the Boones and took the left fork of the trail, headed for Harrodsburg. With Mrs. James Harrod that made four adult women at that settlement, "just enough for two four handed reels," one old settler remembered years later. "Part of the men would guard at one time, and part at another, while the rest alternately danced with the women."

Boone, with his family and the bachelors, rode into Boonesborough on September 8, and with the return of the acknowledged leader of the fort, Henderson finally felt free to depart for North Carolina. Boone had now made the ultimate commitment, guiding his wife and children to this outpost in the wilderness. At first his family lived in one of the log huts in the hollow. Heavy rains that winter raised the river, flooding many of the people living there, but by that time the Boones had moved to a cabin in the meadow, part of what would become the fort complex. Boone's accounts, listing payments for the construction of this house, indicate that it was a solid building with wooden floors, doors, glass window panes, and even an interior stall for his horses. Boone also drew on the company store, set up in one of the corner blockhouses, purchasing "4 peecs of Linin" for Rebecca, a total of about a hundred yards of cloth.

Before the end of the month Callaway returned with another group of forty or fifty settlers, including his own family and two others, and soon thereafter Squire Boone arrived with Jane and the children, along with several more men from the Yadkin. By summer's end Boonesborough had regained its strength of the spring and added a number of families to its population, a sign of permanent settlement. "My wife and daughter," says Filson's Boone, were "the first white women that ever stood on the banks of Kentucke river." Actually, Boone's daughter, Susannah Boone Hays, had been in Boonesborough since spring. Susy put a naughty twist on that famous line of her father's: "Every Kentuckian ought to try her gait," men remembered her announcing, "since she was the first white woman in Kentucky."

The beginning of hostilities between the colonies and Great Britain magnified worries about Indian warfare. Chief Cornstalk tried to assure the Americans that Shawnees were not responsible for the attacks in Kentucky, and hunters from Boonesborough several times encountered small parties of Shawnees at the nearby salt licks who protested their friendly intentions. But chiefs like Cornstalk had relatively little power to control angry young warriors. In

October the Shawnee chiefs signed the Treaty of Pittsburg, acknowledging to agents of the Second Continental Congress the outcome of Dunmore's War, formally ceding their rights to Kentucky and setting the Ohio River as the southern boundary of Indian country. But Cornstalk warned the Americans that many of his Shawnee countrymen had sworn to drive them from Kentucky. Some Shawnee chiefs were more responsive to the sentiment of hunters who depended on the Kentucky grounds or had lost kinsmen in fights with the settlers. The chief Blackfish, for example, urged retaliation and put himself forward as a rival for Cornstalk's position as paramount leader. Other Shawnees, fearing the consequences of renewed warfare with the Long Knives, already were beginning to move west to Spanish territory, out of harm's way.

A steady trickle of settlers arrived at Boonesborough and the other stations during the fall of 1775. By the end of the year the Transylvania Company had registered over nine hundred claims for more than a half million acres of land, but in the general uncertainty about the company's authority, few claimants were willing to make payment. Many settlers, like those at Harrodsburg, disputed the company's authority altogether, defending their right of "getting land for taking it up." Many probably agreed with Hermon Husband, a leader of the North Carolina Regulators, who argued that the people had "a Kind of Right" to "move out, from the interior parts to the back Lands with their Families and find a Spot, whereon they built a Hut and made some improvements." "The people in general," John Floyd wrote to William Preston, "choose to settle as they have done on Holston," that is, by squatter's rights, according to what they called "the ancient cultivation law." Relying on the provisions of the Virginia code that protected the preemption claims of those who resided on vacant land and raised a crop of corn, these settlers cleared a patch of ground or simply killed the trees by girdling them, used their tomahawks to chop in corn seed amid the stumps, and erected pens, half-faced shelters, or crude log cabins. They became known as "cabiners." Some of these were honest settlers, others petty speculators who returned home and sold their claims to others for a few dollars. "Many have come down here and not stayed more than three week," Floyd complained, "and have returned home with 20 cabins apiece." It seems that while Floyd thought it perfectly appropriate for his wealthy patrons to engross the lands of Kentucky, it was an entirely different matter for these "miserable wretches" to get their small piece of the action. Since the cabiners employed no real system of surveying, their claims made up a crazy quilt of conflicts. "I am afraid to lose sight of my house," one settler wrote, "lest some invader should take possession." Floyd feared that disputes over land would result in "a civil war among the people" and predicted "there'll be bloodshed soon."

Boone was one of the first to locate and file a claim with the Transylvania Company, for one thousand acres on Tate's Creek, southwest of Boonesborough. The "surveys" for such claims were terribly imprecise. In a deposition taken later during a land dispute, Boone provided an example of the way these claims were made. In the fall of 1775, "in the time Bucks were rutting," he left Boonesborough, accompanied by the Hart brothers and several other men, to hunt and explore the lands westward, toward the Falls of the Ohio. "Having traveled a great distance through a broken Beechey country," they arrived "upon the top of a ridge where the land changed suddenly," and here "the company concluded to Stop, noon it, and dry their cloths, which was wet by a rain that fell the over night." They were on the waters of Guist Creek, in what is today southeastern Shelby County, Kentucky. Thomas Hart and Boone separated from the others and together located "a beautiful rich piece of ground" about a half mile down Jeptha Creek. "Whilst they were looking at the land," said Boone, he spied and killed two deer, and as he set to work skinning them, Hart carved his initials and the date in a large beech tree, claiming the site as his own. The two of them then paced off lines enclosing several hundred acres, noting the corners by notching distinctive trees, and on their return Hart filed this claim with the Transylvania Company office, and later with the state of Virginia. But other settlers and speculators claimed the same site, and the question arose of whose had been staked first. Boone and the attorneys in this dispute traveled to the site, and twenty years after he and Hart had notched the trees, he guided them to the beech with the carving, "which said marks appears to be as old as the date thereof." Because of Boone's outstanding woodcraft this dispute was resolved happily for Hart—not all of Boone's legal affairs would end so well.

A few days before Christmas, 1775, the Virginian Arthur Campbell, assisted by two young men, ferried across the river at Boonesborough to locate a tract of land. A few minutes later people heard a shot and cries of distress. A few men jumped into the lone canoe tied up at the river landing and anxiously paddled across, where they found Campbell, frightened but safe. Two Indians had fired on him but missed, he told them excitedly; he did not know the fate of the boys, for they had run off in another direction. Boone raised a posse and went out in search, but they returned late in the day having found only a few indistinct moccasin tracks and no sign of the young men. A dozen men were away from the settlement hunting or scouting for land and there was naturally a good deal of concern for their safety. The hunters returning over the next couple of days had no report of Indian sightings. People had begun to doubt Campbell's story when scouts brought in the body of one of the boys, who had been found lying facedown in a cornfield on the north side of the river about three miles from Boonesborough. His friend may have been taken into captivity, for he was never heard from again.

Following this incident many people packed their things and left Boonesborough; it was the first of many violent confrontations. Although no raids were mounted against the settlement itself during the next few months, throughout the spring of 1776 small mixed parties including Mingos, Shawnees, and Cherokees terrorized cabiners and hunters. "The Indians," Filson quoted Boone, "seemed determined to persecute us for erecting this fortification." So persistent did the attacks become that William Russell, writing from Castle's Wood, urged the complete evacuation of Kentucky. Men and families who had outlying claims pulled back to the central forts, and some followed Russell's advice and left altogether. After a trip filled with terror, one party arrived at Fort Blackmore on the Clinch, where they found other refugees "sporting, dancing, and drinking whiskey," in an attempt to forget their fears. "Imagination had painted Indians as thick in the wilderness as Bees in a buckwheat patch," wrote one settler. By late spring of 1776 no more than two hundred Americans remained in Kentucky, most of them forted up in the settlements south of the Kentucky River at Harrodsburg, Logan's Station, or Boonesborough. Things could get pretty rancid after a long period of confinement in "a row or two of Smoky cabins, among dirty women and men with greasy hunting shirts," one pioneer remembered. In the words of another, by the early summer the people were "dirty, lousy, ragged, and half starved."

On the afternoon of Sunday, July 14, 1776, Jemima Boone and Elizabeth and Frances Callaway, daughters of Richard Callaway, "tired of the confinement of the fort," took a canoe out onto the Kentucky River. Jemima had hurt her foot a few days before, and she wanted to soak it in the cool river. She "was so fond of playing in the water," her cousin recalled, "her common name was Duck." The other girls went along to gather flowers and wild grapes along the riverbank. Jemima and Fanny were thirteen and fourteen, respectively, Betsy was sixteen and already engaged to marry Samuel Henderson, nephew of Richard Henderson. Jemima would say later that her father had warned her to stay close to the cabins and never to cross to the opposite shore. The Callaway girls teased her caution: "Perhaps she was more afraid of the yellow boys than she was of disobeying her father." Betsy guided the canoe through the eddies near the sycamore hollow, but suddenly it was caught up by the swift flow of the river. "Mother was an expert hand in managing a canoe," wrote Betsy's daughter, but "the current proved too strong" and the girls found themselves quickly carried downriver, toward the north bank.

A small war party of two Cherokees and three Shawnees, five men in all, were watching the settlement from the timber across the river. They had been in the area for a week or more and already had murdered an isolated farmer some miles away. Now they trailed the progress of the canoe downstream, and when the girls got within a few feet of the north shore, one of the warriors jumped into the river and grabbed the buffalo tug dangling from its bow. Little Fanny Callaway was sitting up front, and seeing the Indian dive in the water, she jumped up; but thinking he was a familiar Indian man who lived among the settlers at Boonesborough, she cried, "Law! Simon, how you scared me!" At almost the same instant she realized her mistake and laid into the warrior's head with the paddle. All three girls began to scream. "Grandmother said she screamed as loud as she could," wrote one of Jemima's descendants, "so her father would pursue them." But silently and swiftly the Indians drew the canoe to shore, where a warrior grabbed the hair of one of the girls, making signs with his knife that indicated clearly what would happen if they did not shut up. Then the Indians pulled them into the woods.

This kidnapping, and the subsequent rescue, was to become one of the most famous incidents of Boone's life. Among Boone's Kentucky contemporaries, his leadership during the crisis marked the summum bonum of his reputation, and the episode was a lodestone for drawing together an enormous amount of Boone lore. A number of the participants in the rescue contributed firsthand accounts, and many other people, including each of the kidnapped girls, passed versions of the story on to their descendants. "When I was a small boy, I heard my mother relate the incidents of the captivity and rescue," said Betsy Callaway's son, and when she finished, "I thought the yard was full of Indians and I was afraid to go out of doors." "How well I remember," wrote one of Jemima's granddaughters, "my Grandmother relate to me from the time I was 5 years old up to the age of 12, again and again about her being captured by the Indians. I have saw it in print, but not as she told me." Lyman Draper collected accounts from forty persons, providing a more detailed portrait of Boone during these few days than during any other period of his life.

As was the custom, Boonesborough's residents kept the Sabbath, some worshiping but most simply visiting and relaxing. Women put on fancy dresses and men wore their best bib and tucker, with pantaloons rather than their everyday breechclout, leggings, and hunting shirt. Nathan Reid remembered that he and his friend John Floyd, both young bachelors, were dressed to the nines that day, but without young women to court they took a stroll together through the hollow, where they lost themselves in reveries about the future, "giving free rein to our heated imaginations, constructing many a glorious castle in the air." Samuel Henderson, Betsy's sweetheart, was in the midst of his weekly routine of shaving. Boone himself had discarded his Sabbath clothes and was stretched out on his bed, taking his Sunday afternoon nap.

The alarm was raised by those who heard the girls' cries. One of Callaway's boys came running up to Reid and Floyd, screaming, "The savages have the girls." Within seconds men and women were shouting and running about the settlement. At the sound of the commotion, Boone jumped out of bed, snatched his pantaloons, and hopped into them as he ran along barefoot to the riverbank by the hollow, calling all the while for the men to join him. Samuel Henderson followed, sobbing in terror, his face half covered with shaving soap. Dick Callaway loaded his gun as he ran. Reaching the river, the men saw the canoe, swamped and useless on the opposite shore. Callaway, with his nephew Flanders Callaway, John Holder, the Harts, and a number of others, mounted horses and galloped for the ford of the river about a mile below. As the others stood helpless, twelve-year-old John Gass stripped, courageously dove into the swift-flowing current, and, while the men shouted encouragement, swam to the other shore. Righting the canoe, he paddled it back across. Boone, Floyd, Reid, Samuel Henderson, and William Bailey Smith jumped in and quickly recrossed. A number of men remained behind, to protect the settlement against a possible attack. About an hour of daylight remained as the rescuers ascended the steep bluff on the north side to the trail at the crest of the hill. There "Boone directed us to divide," said Reid, "in order to discover, as soon as possible, the course they had gone." With Floyd and Smith, he went upstream, while Boone and the others went down, where they soon met the horsemen. Here Boone once again counseled a division of forces. Believing that the Indians would be heading north with their captives for the towns in the Ohio country, he urged Callaway and the others to ride hard for the crossing of the Licking River in an attempt to cut them off.

The men upstream already had found the Indians' trail and, losing no time, had forged ahead. They had gone five miles and it was growing dark when Boone hollered and came up with his group on their left. Moving several hundred yards more, they heard the barking of a dog; thinking it might be the Indians' camp, they crept forward. It was a party of cabiners, including among their number Boone's friend William Bush, and here the rescuers decided to make camp. Boone sent young John Gass to Boonesborough for ammunition, provisions, breechclouts, and moccasins. The uncomfortable pantaloons "impeded our movement," said Reid, and Boone was still barefoot. Gass now performed his second heroic duty of the day, making the round-trip in the dark and returning with supplies before daylight. At first light the men took off, joined by three of the cabiners, including Bush, but they sent the boy back to the settlement with acclaim for a job well done.

After their capture, the crying and shrieking girls made every attempt to slow the march of their captors, who pushed and pulled them northward through the woods. Jemima's injured foot caused her to fall, and she then made a point of tripping and sprawling at every opportunity, screaming in mock pain. When it grew dark the Indians made a cold camp and "held a little chat." Then, assembling the girls, they "cut their clothes off to the knees, took off their shoes and stockings, and put on moccasins." The girls too had been clothed in their Sunday best, fancy little dresses, bonnets, and wooden-heeled shoes. This preparation was a sure sign that the Indians planned further travel. One of the men was a Cherokee named Scolacutta, known to Americans as Hanging Maw. He knew Boone and his family from their days on the Upper Yadkin or in Tennessee and could speak a little English. Recognizing Jemima by her long black hair, he asked if these were her sisters. Yes, she told him, believing that the Indians might think twice before harming Daniel Boone's daughters. "We have done pretty well for Old Boone this time," Hanging Maw laughed. That they were headed for the Shawnee towns in the Ohio country, he confirmed. The Indians all across the frontier were rising up against the Americans, he told her, and it would not be long before Boonesborough fell. Tying the girls together with rawhide tugs, the Indians retired with neither food nor water. While they slept, the girls strained uselessly at their cords. Jemima remembered a little penknife in her pocket and spent a frustrating night trying in vain to reach it.

The Indians were up before dawn and set a hard pace, refusing now to be held back. When they could the girls broke brush, pulled up vines, anything to leave a track, and when discovered, the Indians threatened them with clubs or knives. There was no pause for rest or drink, and by afternoon they had put twenty-five miles between themselves and Boonesborough. Distraught and exhausted, the girls could hardly move another step, but they had not lost their ingenuity. When they finally paused to rest, one of the Indians went out to scout and came back with a haggard old horse he had found abandoned in the wild. Harnessing it with a piece of tug, they tried to force the girls onto its back. These three had been practically reared on horseback, but in these circumstances they acted as if they had never before seen a horse. They kept falling off, and by pinching and kicking the poor animal got it to fight back, bucking and threatening with its teeth, which caused the Indians to "laugh and halloo," Jemima would recall later. It was her first indication that they were beginning to relax about being overtaken. She never wavered in her conviction that her father was on their trail, but these signs of Indian self-confidence were disheartening. Abandoning the horse, they pushed on several miles more before it grew dark. The Indians again went without fire, but they did draw water from a stream, and everyone drank; the girls, however, could not force themselves to eat the jerked buffalo tongue the Indians offered to share.

Boone and his men were perhaps ten miles behind the kidnappers at the beginning of the second morning, but the trail was difficult to follow and they made little progress. After some miles, Boone stopped. This would never do, he declared, for the Indians "were making tracks faster than we were." From their general direction he now was certain that the captors were heading for the crossing of the Licking at the Upper Blue Licks, and, according to Reid, "paying no further attention to the trail, he now took a strait course through the woods, with increased speed, followed by the men in perfect silence." Breaking from the tracks made the men uncomfortable, but they could only rely on Boone's woodcraft. Later in the day they crossed the trail of the kidnappers once again, and, finding a sign left by the girls, their spirits revived and their confidence in Boone strengthened.

Both pursuer and pursued were pushing ahead at first light the third day. The Indians forded Hinkston Creek, thirteen miles from the crossing of the Licking, in midmorning. Boone and his men crossed the same creek about an hour later. "Here Boone paused a moment," said Reid, "and remarked that from the course [the Indians] had travelled, he was confident that they had crossed the stream a short distance below." He shifted them northwest, "and strange to say, we had not gone down more than 200 yards before we struck the trail again." The Indians were traveling along a buffalo trace paralleling the Warrior's Path leading to the Upper Blue Licks. Boone set a jogging pace, which the men kept up for three-quarters of an hour. Now the rescuers began to encounter convincing evidence that they were closing in—muddied water at the crossing of a stream, a dead snake along the trail, and finally the carcass of a buffalo calf, recently butchered, blood still oozing from its hump. "The Indians would stop to cook at the first water," said Boone. Then at a branch now known as Bald Eagle Creek, just east of the present town of Sharpsburg, the trail disappeared. Boone divided the party, four men going in each direction. Their aim, wrote Floyd, was "to get the prisoners without giving the Indians time to murder them." They proceeded without speaking, "no man to touch a trigger until he had received the sign from Boone." Reid had moved twenty or thirty yards downstream and, finding nothing, had turned around when he saw Billy Smith upstream "waving his hand for us to come on."

The Indians had grown confident. Their rear scout saw no evidence of a party approaching from behind, and they were soon to cross the Licking, where they expected to link up with other war parties. They had paused to kill and butcher game and now had made camp, where they were roasting their meat on a spit. In a fine mood, one of them playfully pulled at Betsy's hair while she knelt at the fire warming herself, and she defiantly scooped up a load of hot coals with a piece of bark and dumped them on his moccasins. He hopped around in pain, much to the amusement of the other men, and Hanging Maw, admiring Betsy's spunk, called her "a fine young squaw."

As the spirits of the Indians rose, Betsy's fell. She had tried to buoy up the two younger girls and had maintained her own courage by telling herself that her father would soon appear, but now, as the Indians enjoyed a laugh, she "gave herself up to dispair." Like her sister Fanny and Jemima, Betsy would remember in detail everything that happened during the next few moments. She collapsed on a log about ten steps from the fire, and the two others settled themselves at her feet, resting their heads on her lap. Betsy fell into a routine that must have been commonplace in the crowded conditions of the fort: "She unconsciously was opening their hair, lousing their heads, and shedding a torrent of tears." One or two Indians left the fire to gather fuel, one knelt tending the meat, and another reclined on the ground nearby. Off to the side the sentinel leaned his gun casually against a tree, walked back to the fire to light his pipe, and stood rummaging through his budget, looking for something.

Jemima heard a sound in the brush and saw the Indian at the fire suddenly look up, stare into the woods, then return to his work. The camp was in a small glen, and, glancing up along the ridge, she suddenly caught sight of her father "creeping upon his breast like a snake." At a distance of a hundred yards their eyes met, and with the implicit language of father and daughter, he signed her to keep still. The other men were assembling on the ridge and were to fire down together, but in the excitement of seeing the camp below, one of them fired prematurely. Fanny had her eyes on the Indian at the campfire. Suddenly "she saw blood burst out of his breast before she heard the gun." He fell head first into the flames, then jumped up, holding his gut, and hobbled off into the brush. "That's Daddy!" Jemima cried. As Boone, Floyd, and another rescuer hurriedly got off their shots, Jemima and Fanny hit the ground, but Betsy leapt to her feet, and one of the Indians aimed his war club at her. "She sensibly felt it touch her head as it passed by," she would tell her children. Raising the war whoop, Boone and the others came charging down the slope while the Indians fled into the cane, as Floyd wrote, "almost naked, some without their mockisons, and no one of them so much as a knife or tomahawk." Betsy ran toward her rescuers. Dressed in the rough woolen matchcoat of one of the Indians, with her dress cut short and her legs exposed, her dark hair loose and disheveled, she was mistaken by one of the Americans for an Indian rushing to engage him, and he clubbed his gun, preparing to bash out her brains. "For God's sake," Boone bawled out, "don't kill her when we've travelled so far to save her."

Boone hollered at Betsy to get down, lest the Indians take to the trees and fire back, but their Indian captors had fled. The men rushed to the other girls and took them in their arms. They looked awful, their clothes torn to shreds, their legs scratched and bleeding, their eyes swollen from tears and lack of sleep. Boone took blankets from the packs and covered them. As the excitement of the moment began to subside, the man who had nearly made the fatal mistake collapsed in sobs. "Thank Almighty Providence, boys," said Boone, "for we have the girls safe. Let's all sit down by them now and have a hearty cry." As Jemima would remember it, "There was not a dry eye in the company."

Concerned that the Indians might join with comrades north of the Licking, Boone made no attempt to follow them. Before the men turned toward Boonesborough, however, they ate heartily from the buffalo roasting on the spit. Along the way home they found the same tired old horse, and this time Fanny and Jemima had no trouble mounting and riding him in. Betsy, the most worn out and exhausted of the three, rode home on the back of her fiancé, Samuel Henderson. When the party reached the Kentucky, Boone called over and they were ferried across. Her mother's relief was beyond expression, Jemima would remember. "She both laughed and cried, as she always did when she was over joyed." Later the same day Callaway's party of horsemen returned to the fort. They had not encountered the Indians at the crossing of the Licking and, tracking back, had found evidence of the Indians' flight and hurried home, praying that there had been a rescue.

Floyd was certain that he had hit his mark during the encounter, but Boone was less sure he had scored with his. Chief Cornstalk, still working to achieve an accommodation with the Americans, later told American officials at Point Pleasant, however, that two Shawnees were mortally wounded during the rescue, one of them the son of Chief Blackfish. Among his own people, Cornstalk blamed the deaths on those who had kept the pot boiling "and not the white people," but the younger Shawnee warriors increasingly scorned the old chief's words. Hanging Maw survived the attack and returned to the Cherokee towns in the south. He later became a friend of the Americans, and when he died in 1796 he was eulogized as "a man distinguished for his love of peace."

The kidnapping marked the beginning of an intensified guerrilla war against the Kentucky settlers. While the rescuers were gone, another war party attacked the homestead of Nathaniel Hart, about a half mile from Boonesborough, burning his cabin and destroying his crops, including several hundred young apple trees he had set out in an orchard. Settlers again evacuated their outlying farms and fled to Boonesborough, Harrodsburg, or Logan's Station. Once again the migratory tide ebbed back to Virginia. "Ten at least, I understand, of our own people are going to join them," wrote Floyd, "which will leave us with less than 30 men at this fort." But under the threat of continual attack, Boonesborough was gradually taking the shape of a real fort. Boone and the others set to work stockading the spaces between the cabins and securing the settlement's defenses during the remaining weeks of the summer. In September more of the fort's defenders, including Floyd and Reid, went east to participate in a campaign being planned against Dragging Canoe's Cherokees, leaving Boonesborough more vulnerable.

Yet life went on. In the months following the kidnapping, all three of the young victims were married. Elizabeth Callaway and Samuel Henderson had returned to the fort looking quite a sight, she dressed like a poor Indian, he with his face half bearded, but now she wore a dress of plain Irish linen, he a fancy embroidered hunting shirt that he borrowed from Nathan Reid to replace the Sunday clothes ruined during the rescue. Boone officiated in his capacity as magistrate of Transylvania, although Dick Callaway required Henderson to post a bond that he would have the marriage solemnized by less dubious authority at his earliest opportunity. The next spring Callaway, who held a Virginia appointment as justice of the peace, officiated at a double wedding, his daughter Frances taking John Holder and Jemima Boone marrying Flanders Callaway, both young men rescuers who had been with the riders. These three were among the very few women at Boonesborough, and quite a number of the settlement's single men had been "smitten with them," as one unsuccessful suitor later admitted.

Many tales of the girls' captivity and rescue suggested that one of the Indians had fondled or raped one of the captives. This fate was one of the persistent nightmares of settlers, and throughout the ordeal Dick Callaway was tormented by the fear, as one man put it, that "the Indians should violate his daughters." But Boone descendants were quite emphatic that, in the words of one, "no attempt was made on the part of the Indians to make love to the girls." This "was not characteristic of the Indians," wrote Daniel's nephew Moses Boone, and on this point he spoke with a real understanding of woodland Indian ways.

Jemima's own account did, however, detail a strange intimacy between herself and Hanging Maw. In numerous versions of the captivity tale told by her descendants, the Indian compliments her as a "pretty squaw" while he pats her on the head. Her contemporaries described Jemima as "real handsome," and "a fine woman." Hanging Maw was especially attracted to her hair, which takes on special significance in a number of tales. He asks for permission to take out her combs so that he can see her tresses fall; she had long black hair that hung nearly to her knees. Then he carefully winds her hair and puts the combs back in again. On the last morning, Hanging Maw asks Jemima to dress his hair and "look over his head." Ugh! cried Jemima's young niece when she heard her aunt tell this story during the 1820s. "I woudn't have done it, look a lousy Indian's head, not I." "O yes, you would," the elderly woman replied. "Every such thing tended to delay their progress, and that was what we studied every art to effect." Yet there seemed more to it than that. Jemima emphasized the Indians' "honorable conduct to her and her fellow captives." Despite the kidnapping, she refused to hate them, and her views were remarkably sympathetic. "The Indians were really kind to us," she told her niece, "as much so as they well could have been, or their circumstances permitted." In this opinion she sounded ever so much like her father. And besides, she was so tired and upset that as she inspected Hanging Maw's head, she added, laughing, she "could not have found a louse, had it been as large as her thumb."

During her captivity, Jemima swore to herself that if she "ever laid eyes" on her father again, she would never disobey him or disregard his warnings. When it was over, "so glad she was to be under his care and counsel she would not let him leave her one minute." It is not unusual for people to make these innocent promises under such desperate circumstances, but the fact was, through the years that stretched ahead, Jemima was the child most frequently at her father's side. When he later was captured by the Shawnees and the rest of the family retreated to the safety of the settlements, it was Jemima who remained waiting for him at Boonesborough. And it was in Jemima's house that Boone lived for most of his last years. Her captivity and deliverance, her memory of that sudden moment when she saw him crawling through the woods to her rescue, bonded her to him in a way unlike any of her siblings. Jemima died in 1829, just nine years after her father. After having spent so many years with him, it is perhaps not surprising that her attitudes so reflected his own.

CHAPTER FIVE

Prisoners to Old Chillicothe

1776 to 1778

The news of American independence first reached Kentucky in August 1776. A settler arrived with a copy of the Declaration of Independence, it was read aloud to the assembled residents of Boonesborough, and that night they lit a bonfire and held a celebration. Many supporters of independence, Whigs in the label of the day, could be counted among the settlers there, but the center of revolutionary activity was Harrodsburg, where a Committee of Safety had been elected in June. Although Kentuckians lived "remote from the Seat of Government," the Harrodsburg committee wrote to the newly formed state government of Virginia, they were "desirious of contributing to the utmost of their power to the support of the present laudable cause of American Freedom." Patriotic fervor, however, was not their only motivation. As the petition made clear, the first item on their agenda was convincing Virginia to "claim this country" and immediately confirm the titles of men who "by Preoccupancy, agreeable to the Entry laws of Virginia," had established homesteads "to provide a subsistence for themselves and their Posterity." The settlers of Harrodsburg had been opposed to Richard Henderson's claims from the beginning. But Boonesborough was the western seat of the Transylvania

Company, and its relationship to the revolutionary authorities in both Virginia and North Carolina was somewhat more ambiguous.

In the West there was, in fact, considerable Loyalist and neutralist sentiment. In one of the Revolution's many ironies, the leadership of the independence movement in the South was drawn from the very tidewater elite that had opposed the Regulators, and consequently many backcountry populists tended toward Loyalism. Communities, churches, even families were torn by partisan division. When the Baptist meeting at the Forks of the Yadkin, which included Boones, Bryans, and Cutbeards, took up the question of the coming Revolution in late 1775, there was a distinct lack of enthusiasm "conserning the American Cause." The congregation allowed that "if any of the brethren sees cause to joyn in it they had the leberty to do it without being called to an acount by the church for it. But wheather joyn or not joyn they should be used with brotherly love and freedom for the futer." In this revolutionary situation, however, political divisions led almost invariably to conflict and violence, and following the crushing defeat of a North Carolina Loyalist army by patriot forces at the Battle of Moore's Creek Bridge in February of 1776, many Crown supporters, as well as others who simply wished to steer clear of conflict, moved west. Whigs and revolutionaries in Kentucky found this migration alarming. Immediate measures needed to be taken, proclaimed the Harrodsburg Committee of Safety in June, to prevent "this immense and fertile country" from becoming "an asylum to those whose principles are inimical to American Liberty."

Rebecca's kinfolk, the Bryans, many of whom had been Regulators, were among the best-known Loyalist migrants to Kentucky. In the spring of 1776 John Floyd noted the founding of a settlement on the headwaters of the North Fork of the Elkhorn "by Bryans and other Tories." Two of Rebecca's uncles became officers of the Loyalist militia in North Carolina, and before the war was over, one had been killed in battle, the other sentenced to hang as a traitor, although later he was freed as part of a prisoner exchange. Other Bryans actively fought for the Whigs, and, like many families, they were divided among themselves on the issues of the Revolution. But it was Bryan Loyalism that was remembered most. "There was no finer Family than the Bryans," Boone's niece Rebecca Boone Lamond wrote of her collateral kin, "but some of them erred gravely in their opinion of liberty." Despite efforts by Boone descendants to dissociate the family's revolutionary reputation from the Bryan stain of Toryism, some of it rubbed off on Boone. "He married a Bryan, and the Bryans were all loyal to the English," one North Carolina lady later wrote. "Boone had no desire to join in with the rebels." A Tennessean reported that Boone "was rather unpopular in this section owing to the fact that he stuck to the King during the Revolutionary war."

This is mistaken. Boone was no Tory, but neither was he an avid partisan of independence. He had been honored, for example, to accept the captain's commission from Lord Dunmore in 1774, even after the governor had acted to dissolve the House of Burgesses, an act that outraged Whigs such as William Cocke, Henderson's heroic messenger on the Wilderness Road, who refused point-blank to accept a similar royal appointment because it compromised his political scruples. According to Rebecca's father, Joseph Bryan, Boone "always acted with the Whigs" but nonetheless kept his British commission close at hand, "ready to exhibit in emergencies," a practice, Bryan said, that became "a subject of conversation," which is to say a subject of controversy. In Filson's narrative Boone gives no expression to revolutionary sentiments and goes to some length to portray his British opponents as honorable gentlemen. On the other hand, as a descendant testified, he found the Loyalist sympathies of the Bryans "one of the most trying things he ever met with, to see some of his best friends so carried away in so bad a cause." In short, while Boone would fight to defend the security and interests of his own community during the Revolution, he aligned himself with neither ideological camp, a neutrality that became increasingly difficult to maintain as the conflict sharpened and grew bitter. After the Revolution people were loath to admit it, but Boone's stance was representative of a great deal of popular ambivalence. He was a moderate and cautious man whose deepest loyalties were those of clan and community.

In the West, the Revolution continued the conflict between settlers and Indians for control of the Ohio Valley. That struggle had begun in earnest with Dunmore's War in 1774 and did not reach its concluding phase in Kentucky until the defeat of Indian forces at the Battle of Fallen Timbers twenty years later. Over this period at least two thousand Americans and Indians in countless hundreds lost their lives in what was the bloodiest phase of the three-century campaign for the conquest of North America. From 1775 to 1782, 860 Kentuckians met a violent death, the greatest loss relative to population suffered by any section of the country during the Revolution. While in the thirteen coastal colonies there were about ten war-related deaths for every one thousand persons in the population, in Kentucky there were better than seventy.

Years after those battles had been fought and won, when he was an old man, Boone characterized the origins of the settler-Indian conflict with considerable candor. "We Virginians had for some time been waging a war of intrusion upon them," he was quoted as saying, "and I, amongst the rest, rambled through the woods in pursuit of their race, as I now would follow the tracks of ravenous animal." But Boone's description to Filson of the struggle in the immediate aftermath of the Revolution placed the Americans in the role of the pursued rather than the pursuer. Speaking of the Indians, Filson's Boone says that "they evidently saw the approaching hour when the Long Knife would dispossess them of their desirable habitations; and anxiously concerned for futurity, determined utterly to extirpate the whites out of Kentucke." While the use of the term *dispossess* here matches the honesty of *intrusion* in the later passage, otherwise Filson's Boone better fit his views to the common sentiments of the day. He did not, however, go quite so far as others in portraying the Americans simply as victims. The Harrodsburg Committee of Safety, in their petition to the state of Virginia, for example, begged for arms to prevent what they described as "the inroads of the Savages" and "the effusion of innocent blood," an altogether disingenuous formulation, for surely there was little that was innocent about the American invasion of Indian country.

In a passage from the Declaration of Independence intended to appeal directly to western settlers, Thomas Jefferson argued that the British had "endeavoured to bring on the inhabitants of our frontiers, the merciless Indian Savages, whose known rule of warfare, is an undistinguished destruction of all ages, sexes and conditions." To be sure, the Indians of the Ohio country were a formidable threat to the western settlers; the Delawares, Miamis, Shawnees, and other tribes counted no fewer than three thousand fighting men. But at the time those words were written, in June 1776, the British were urging restraint on their western Indian allies. It was the Indians themselves, with reasons of their own, who chose war against the Kentuckians. Fearful that American independence would mean the loss of their Ohio homes, many warriors and their families clamored for battle. A substantial portion of the Shawnees, for example, rejected the counsel of peace chiefs such as Cornstalk. Encouraged by a renewed supply of trade goods flowing from Canada, the Shawnee leader Blackfish, one of Cornstalk's rivals, argued for a sustained attack on the Kentucky settlements. But like the Americans, the Shawnees were divided among themselves, and during the final months of 1776 their council houses were the setting for many acrimonious and divisive meetings. One faction was absolutely convinced of the impossibility of any final accommodation with the Americans, and these clans began to leave the Ohio country and migrate to the West. Ironically, the Shawnees who remained were committed to finding a way of living with the Americans as neighbors. They had concluded, however, that war was their only immediately viable course.

American military leaders believed that it would take a massive attack against British-Indian centers like Detroit to end the threat in the West, but, lacking the resources and manpower to implement such a strategy, for the most part the western settlers fought a defensive war. Even as the Shawnees decided to launch a sustained campaign in Kentucky, the Americans, their supplies of ammunition nearly depleted, were abandoning the last remaining stations north of the Kentucky River and pulling back to fortified positions. To relieve Boonesborough through the fall hunting season, Boone was able to obtain a little powder and lead from the stores of the Fincastle County militia, but it was not until the winter of 1776, when Virginia created Kentucky County, that the state authorized the shipment west of several hundred pounds of gunpowder and lead. So preoccupied was the state government with preparations for war along the seaboard that it was unable to do more than legitimize the existing military organization in the West, appointing George Rogers Clark major in command of the Kentucky militia, with John Todd, James Harrod, Benjamin Logan, and Daniel Boone captains at the American strongholds south of Harrodsburg, Logan's Station, and Boonesborough. On March 5,

1777, the Kentucky County militia held its first muster at those three locations. A total of 121 men were available to take up arms in defense of 280 settlers. Harrodsburg, with forty families and eighty-four men, had the largest component, Logan's Station, with a force of fifteen, the smallest. At Boonesborough twenty-two men defended ten to fifteen families, including about a dozen adult women, thirty children, and ten to fifteen slaves of all ages.

By the time this muster took place, Blackfish already was leading an army of two hundred or more armed Shawnees south across the Ohio. As they marched single file down the Warrior's Path, they sang their war song.

> My brothers! The Enemy is at hand.
> We must fight. Retreat would be disgraceful.
> We shall conquer if we are brave.
> The water will wash them away,
> The wind will blow them down,
> Darkness will come upon them,
> And the earth will cover them.
> Let us go forward together and we shall succeed.

The Indians established their base camp near the crossing of the Licking River, while Blackfish went ahead with several small advance groups to test the strength of the settlements.

The first incident of this campaign took place at Boonesborough on March 7, 1777. Shots rang out from the sycamore hollow and a black man working in the field before the fort was killed and his master wounded. The sentry sounded the horn and the settlers, who had dispersed to their farm lots to prepare for the planting, quickly reassembled in the fort, but the Indians failed to show themselves. Boone divided the men into two companies to alternate as guards and farmers. Despite the threat of war, it was essential that the farming continue if the settlement was to survive. Several days later word came from Harrodsburg that almost simultaneous with this ambush, Indians had attacked a group of sugar makers there. When those men failed to return from their work in the evening, Boone's associate Hugh McGary rode out with a search party and, coming upon the horribly mutilated body of his stepson, he swooned and nearly fell from his mount. When McGary's wife, the strong and capable widow Ray, heard the news, she was overcome and took to her bed, and though surviving for a year or two more, she remained in a helpless stupor. The following morning the Harrodsburg guards saw Indians setting fire to the cabins outside the fort walls. McGary rushed out with several men, and in a sharp fight he and another man were wounded, but they killed a Shawnee found to be wearing the hunting shirt of McGary's dead stepson. In a mad rage, McGary hacked the Indian's body to pieces and fed them to his dogs. Harrodsburg women gossiped that while McGary's wife was yet alive, he sought solace with other women but, returning to his own cabin, his dead stepson would "appear to him as a spectre, wrapped up in sheets, and talk to him of it." The deeply troubled McGary would later be the instrument of great tragedy in Boone's life.

The attacks against Harrodsburg continued through March, but for a time the Shawnees left Boonesborough alone. Communications between the settlements depended on the scouts Thomas Brooks and Simon Kenton at Boonesborough, both men in their early twenties but hardened to life on the border, "men with the bark on," as people then put it. Brooks, who later married a Boone woman, was one of three equally irascible brothers. He so loved a fight, it was said, that after going a spell without one, he offered a big stranger a guinea to go a round or two in a local tavern. The man accepted and proceeded to beat him up badly; Brooks left the tavern hurting but happy. Kenton, who hid under an alias, had fled from his home in backcountry Virginia after a violent altercation in which, he feared (mistakenly, as it turned out), that he had killed his opponent. An experienced hunter and superb marksman with a reputation for fearlessness, Kenton had been in Kentucky since before Dunmore's War but was newly arrived at Boonesborough.

As it happened, the scouts were at Boonesborough on the morning of April 24, and thus failed to discover the approach of Blackfish's Shawnee army. The first sign of trouble came when the cows refused to go out to pasture and milled around the gate. Boone sent out two men to investigate but they saw nothing unusual. As they were returning, suddenly a small group of Shawnees burst from the sycamore hollow and fired on them. This hollow would prove to be Boonesborough's Achilles' heel. The two men ran for the open gate seventy yards away, but one was hit and a small group of Indians immediately engulfed him and quickly set to work lifting his scalp. Kenton, standing at the gate with his gun loaded, impulsively broke from the fort, and as a warrior rose from the crowd screaming the war cry as he waved his bloody trophy, Kenton stopped short, aimed, and shot him dead. The other Shawnees scattered.

In an instant Kenton was joined on the plain before the fort by Boone, Brooks, Michael Stoner, William Bush, and about ten or twelve others, and they fanned out in pursuit. Stoner, a few yards ahead of the rest, saw a warrior dodging along a rail fence to the west. He fired and hit his mark, but before he could reload he was struck by return fire, one ball passing through his wrist, another lodging in his hip. As the Americans assembled around Stoner they heard a rush of footsteps to their rear and, looking back, saw the lane to the fort filling with several dozen Shawnees who had been hiding in the hollow. It was a deadly trap. "Boys, we have to fight!" Boone cried out. "Sell your lives as dear as possible!"

Desperately they charged toward the Indians who blocked their path to the fort, individuals stopping to fire at will, then dashing forward with guns swinging, raising the blood-chilling war cry. The Americans "made right at them," a witness reported, coming "near enough to see the white of many an eye," but "the Indians would always give way." The Indians took a more cautious approach to combat, watching for their best opportunity and attempting to avoid hand-to-hand combat. The Americans managed to break through in the chaos, but not before a number were wounded, Boone among the first. As he ran, a bullet crashed into his ankle and threw him to the ground, where he lay semiconscious. Tomahawk raised, an Indian jumped astraddle his body, but from close quarters Kenton fired and the man collapsed by Boone's side. Another Shawnee ran up, his knife drawn, but Kenton lunged forward, swinging the breech of his gun, and crushed the man's skull. Hoisting Boone to his shoulders, Kenton ran toward the fort as bullets sang by his head and smashed into the stockade wall.

Bush and Stoner were the last to come up. Bush already had fired twice and "had put the powder in the gun, and was holding the bullet in his mouth" to load for a third shot when he saw Stoner faltering from loss of blood. He threw his arm around his friend and began to pull him along, but Stoner shook him off. "Tem gottam yellow rascals vill schoot us," he cried in protest, "ve are too pig a mark, Pilly Push." Stoner hobbled ahead as Bush held the Indians, leveling his unloaded gun at them as if he was about to fire, slowly backing toward the gate. Suddenly looking around, he saw that his comrades had all reached the safety of the fort, and he thought "what a fool he was to be standing there alone." He spun around and began to run, saw the Indians level their guns, heard the discharge, and saw the balls crashing into the ground all around him. Miraculously he was not hit, but by the time he passed through the gate, his legs were cut to shreds from the gravel and stone kicked up by the shots.

The Indians kept up an intermittent fire, but they soon left, carrying their dead and wounded with them. Kenton reported to George Rogers Clark at Harrodsburg that "40 or 50 Indians attacked Boonesborough, killed and scalped Danl. Goodman, wounded Capt. Boone, Capt. Todd, Mr. Hite, and M. Stoner. Indians 'tis thought sustained much damage." There were no physicians in Kentucky to treat the wounded, but plenty of men were skilled in the extraction of bullets and the application of poultices. The ball in Boone's ankle had smashed a good deal of bone, and he was confined with his leg in a sling for the next five or six weeks; for the rest of his life he suffered acute pain in this ankle after strenuous exertion or with sudden changes in the weather. But his life had been saved by Kenton's decisive action, and after the fight Boone called the young scout to his bedside. "Simon," he said in his understated manner, "you have behaved like a man today. Indeed, you are a fine fellow."

"Boone was badly wounded," read the report to the Virginia authorities in June. Brother Squire also suffered in the attacks that summer. While he was at Harrodsburg the fort came under sniper fire, and with a small company Squire went out "to hunt Indians." As he stooped to examine some tracks in the dust he heard someone holler, "Boone, come up!" He turned in the direction of the voice, then heard another cry of "Boone!" from the opposite direction and, shifting back, was hit by a shot that shattered one of his ribs. He had not fully recovered from this wound when he was with a small group ambushed in a cornfield. As he squatted in the grass to return fire, the man by his side fell over dead upon him. Not seeing

Squire beneath the body, the Indian who had fired the fatal shot rushed up to claim the scalp, and when he was only a few feet away Squire jumped up with his sword drawn. Caught by surprise, the Indian swung his club but missed his mark, succeeding only in cutting a deep gash across Squire's forehead. Seizing the Indian's belt with one hand, with the other Squire rammed his sword through the man's abdomen and completely through his body. The Indian grappled for the knife in Squire's strap, but the blood gushing from both of their wounds kept him from getting a firm grip on the handle. Locked together in deadly embrace, the two spun wildly until finally the Indian collapsed backward, falling on the point of the sword and snapping it. It was "the best little Indian fight he ever was in," Squire declared, "both men stood and fought so well." He later claimed that during the Indian wars he had suffered a total of eight wounds in seventeen separate engagements, and one man who once saw his scars testified that he was "literally riddled by rifle balls."

Boone was still abed with his own wound when Blackfish launched a second series of coordinated attacks on all of the forts in late May. At Logan's Station sustained rifle fire kept the settlers pinned down for several days, and at Harrodsburg a number of people were killed. At Boonesborough the men were at work in the cornfields on May 23 when a guard noticed a glint of sunlight on a gun barrel in the woods on Hackberry Ridge. He sounded the alarm, and all fled into the fort, where they were besieged for two days by the Shawnee army. Three men were wounded, but perhaps most serious was the loss of many cattle, butchered by the departing warriors. A third concerted attack began on July 4, when two hundred warriors thronged over the riverbank and hid amid the tall corn growing in front of the fort. By this time Boone was up and around on a crutch, directing his men in a cautious defense from behind the stockade wall. The Indians again kept up their fire for two days, killing one American and wounding two more, but the most devastating effect was the destruction of the cornfields, which the Indians burned along with the outlying cabins in the hollow.

This attack proved to be the last of Blackfish's 1777 campaign, although the settlers remained in a state of anxious watching through the fall. In July, Blackfish led his army back across the Ohio to the Shawnee towns. He had failed to dislodge the Americans from their forts but had kept them tied down, prevented from farming and hunting, and he returned with the knowledge that there would be hunger and misery in Kentucky over the subsequent winter. Perhaps this would put the settlers in a mind to reach an accommodation with the Indians. For their part, the settlers' calls for relief from Virginia finally were answered in early August when Col. John Bowman arrived at Boonesborough with an additional one hundred men and took charge of the Kentucky militia. Over the next two months all three forts were bolstered by additional companies. To Boonesborough came William Bailey Smith with fifty men from Boone's old neighborhoods on the Clinch and the Yadkin, and Capt. Charles Gwatkin with another fifty volunteers from Bedford County, Virginia. A further appearance of stability was the convening of the Kentucky County Court for the first time in September. Along with Clark, Harrod, Callaway, and several others, Boone was named a county justice of the peace, assuming the position his father had held on the Yadkin twenty-five years before.

Impressed by the raids, the British now made the decision to engage the Indians in a strategy designed to demoralize the American settlements on the border. Lieutenant Governor Henry Hamilton in Detroit was directed to employ them "in making a Diversion and exciting an alarm upon the frontiers of Virginia and Pennsylvania." He sent scores of small parties into Kentucky and directed several large campaigns against Wheeling on the Ohio, forcing the Continental forces stationed at Fort Pitt onto the defensive. Because of the bounty the British paid Indians for scalps and prisoners, Hamilton became known as the "hair buyer." Had it not been for the outrage of Americans over these payments, Hamilton's offer of full pardon and grants of land to any who came over to the British might have been more attractive. The spirits of the Kentucky settlers were buoyed by the news of mid-November that the British advance from Canada had been stopped at Saratoga, but American officers took no chances, destroying copies of Hamilton's proclamation, fearing the effect it might have on the people.

There was reason to fear demoralization. Although the Kentucky settlements were now in their third year, because of the ferocity of the Indian war they were barely holding on. At

Boonesborough, once Henderson closed his store there was no way to obtain manufactured goods or cloth without going back to the settlements for them. "My wife and I had neither spoon, dish, knife, or anything to do with," a pioneer later recalled. Their wares were made by a Boonesborough artisan who "turned dishes and bowles and being no hunter exchanged them for meat and tallow to us hunters." Decades later this man looked back on these conditions with nostalgia, writing that "a parcel of those dishes out of buckeye, new and shining and set on some clap-boards in the corner of the cabin, I felt prouder of than I could be of any dishes to be had now," but it seemed considerably less romantic at the time. Clothing wore thin and tore. A man who came out with two changes of clothes in the spring was walking around in rags by the fall, and many people returned to the settlements simply because of their humiliation at their state of undress. Others adopted buckskins, but there was always a premium placed on textiles—the women of Boonesborough devised a way to weave the fibers of wild nettles with buffalo hair to make a serviceable, if coarse, cloth.

In this and many other ways the men were dependent on the few women of the fort. "The women could read the character of a man with invariable certainty," one man recalled. "If he lacked courage, they seemed to be able to discover it, at a glance, and if a man was found to be a coward, he stood a poor chance to get his washing, or mending, or anything done." The young single men, like those who came in with Bowman's company in the fall, were in an especially hard way. "If we was only now in Old Virginia," one ranger sighed, "so many perty Girles their. If I was their I could go with some of them and eat a good Dinur, have something good to Drink. But hear we are."

Slaves were another important component of Boonesborough society. There were a number of slave families who should be counted among the settlers, although few found their way into the historical record. One who did was a man known as Uncle Monk, owned by James Estill, who arrived with his family in 1775. Monk was one of the most valued men at Boonesborough, a superior hunter and marksman, an accomplished musician who played at all of the dances and frolics, and a blacksmith who knew how to manufacture gunpowder from sulphur, saltpeter, and charcoal, an art he taught to Boone, who recorded it in his account book: "Boyle your Brimstone till all the gaus is oute, then Way your pruportions, put them in a pott, Stur them togather till the Sulphur Melts and all unites With the Niter." Monk's son Jerry was the first black child born at Boonesborough. Slaves made up 10 percent of Kentucky's American population and were concentrated among the best-fixed families, like the Callaways, who owned several. By the late 1770s the Boones probably owned one or two as well.

To feed this population the people of Boonesborough harvested little food in the autumn of 1777. The share of corn for his family, according to one man, was only two bushels, "and that had to do us." One of the rangers in Bowman's company later testified that "he was allowed but one single pint of Corn per day, and that he had to grind himself of a hand mill. The balance of the time he had nothing furnished him but meat, [for] there was nothing else." With most of the cattle destroyed and few dairy products to supplement the meager supply of corn, game became a staple for many. Families offered room and board to experienced hunters in exchange for supplying meat. Young William Cradlebaugh hunted for the Boones. In 1775 a drove of hogs had been brought in by Henderson's party, and, as was the common practice, these had been allowed to forage in the woods. Their feral offspring became so ferocious that even the wolves dared not attack them, but Boonesborough's gourmands considered them a prime delicacy and Boone had Cradlebaugh bring in a supply, which he salted and placed in storage for emergencies. In their destructive rounds the Indians had missed the potatoes and turnips; there were wild papaws and grapes at the edge of the woods, and all fall the people worked to collect great quantities of forest nuts.

Yet by year's end Boonesborough's food supply was so low that some of the women followed the cattle around, watching to see what they ate, then boiled the same greens with a piece of salt pork for their families. Because "the Indians have burned all our corn they could find the past summer," Colonel Bowman wrote his superiors at Fort Pitt, "many of the families are left desolate." "We have no more than two months bread," he warned, and he begged for a shipment of corn. The people were surviving on provisions taken from the woods, he said, but it was "difficult to keep the garrisons plenty in meat." The problem, as Boone and his fellow settlers pointed out in a letter to the Virginia authorities, was that they were "almost destitute of the necessary article of salt." Without salt, the diet of cornmeal and greens was intolerably bland. Even more important, salt was required "for curing the provisions of the garrison." An inability to preserve the catch necessitated nearly constant hunting and resulted in a diminished supply of game, wasted ammunition, and increased exposure to attack. Although "bountiful Nature hath plentifully furnished this country with salt springs," they wrote, "by reason of the incursions of the different nations of Indians this year past, we have been prevented from making what quantities would be necessary for ourselves and families." The situation had nearly reached the point of crisis when, during the first week of January 1778, Boone agreed to lead a party of men to the lower salt springs on the Licking River to make salt for the Kentucky settlements.

His medicine had no effect on the Americans, an Ohio Indian mystic once complained to a Moravian missionary, "because they use so much salt in their victuals." The abundant salt springs and licks of Kentucky not only attracted throngs of wild game and the backcountry men who hunted them but promised to supply the American taste for highly salted food. The Bluegrass region of Kentucky is underlain with surface layers of limestone, and at numerous locations waters seeping upward through fissures absorb a high content of calciferous salts. Near Boonesborough the licks of most importance lay along the Licking and were both known as the Blue Licks. Of the two, the one furthest downriver, the Lower Blue Licks, had a higher salt content and heavier flow and attracted not only animals, whose insatiable appetite after consuming the salty soil kept the surrounding area entirely free of underbrush, but hunters and salt makers as well. In the nineteenth century an entrepreneur built a spa for health seekers on the site, and later there would be a bottling plant marketing its product under the Blue Lick label, but during the Revolution the Blue Licks were a site of conflict and tragedy.

Colonel Bowman had carried a number of large iron kettles to assist the Kentuckians in the manufacture of salt. Packing these and additional supplies by horseback, Boone and about thirty men left Boonesborough on January 8, 1778, for the Lower Blue Licks and made their camp on the south bank of the river there. The spring discharged approximately ten thousand gallons of brine each day, and it took five or six hundred gallons to make a fifty-pound bushel of salt. Working at an exhausting pace in miserable January weather, the men were able to produce about ten bushels a day, some collecting brine, others chopping wood, hauling fuel, tending the fires, or scraping the salt residue from the sides of the kettles. Boone immediately sent the first small sack back to Boonesborough to relieve the people. After four weeks the men had produced several hundred bushels and dispatched about half of it to the settlements. The river had risen, submerging the spring, and with no work possible the salt makers had little to do but await the arrival of the relief company, which was scheduled to come from Boonesborough under Captain Gwatkin once the first shipment had arrived there.

Boone, his son-in-law Flanders Callaway, and Thomas Brooks were working as scouts and hunters. It was necessary to cut a wide circuit to find sufficient game to feed the large company of men, and on the morning of February 7 all three left camp to hunt, Boone heading southwest to Hinkston Creek, where he had set a trap line, the other two upstream to see what they could find at the upper lick. It was a cold day and snow was falling, but after checking his traps Boone succeeded in killing and butchering a buffalo and packed three or four hundred pounds of meat onto his horse. He was slowly leading his mount along a narrow defile by the creek when, sensing something, he looked back and through the snow made out several Shawnee warriors coming up on foot perhaps thirty paces behind. Thinking to mount and escape, he pulled at the tugs of fresh buffalo hide with which he had tied the meat, but they were frozen hard. He reached for the knife in its sheath on his belt, but, having put it away greasy and bloody, it too was frozen in place. He looked back again and saw that the Indians were quickly closing on him. Abandoning his horse, Boone darted off on foot.

The four Shawnees in pursuit were part of a large war party of more than one hundred men under the command of Chief Blackfish, who had returned to Kentucky to attack the settlements once again. Winter campaigns were highly unusual, but there were special circumstances that demanded immediate attention. In November the Shawnee chief Cornstalk had gone to the American commander at Point Pleasant on the Ohio to talk of ways to avoid further bloodshed between their people. He was taken hostage, however, along with his son and entourage, and several days later a group of frontiersmen, in a mad rage over the killing of an American by the Indians, broke into the dungeon that held them. Hearing their approach, Cornstalk's son began to quake. Do not be afraid, his father told him, "for the Great Spirit above had sent them there to be killed." The imprisoned Shawnees were shot and mutilated in their cell. Everyone among the Shawnees knew that Cornstalk had been the tireless advocate of accommodation and peace, and their outrage was immeasurable. The young warriors pressed for revenge, and to mollify them Blackfish had organized this small army. Point Pleasant was heavily fortified, so instead he pointed them south to Boonesborough, the nearest of the Kentucky settlements. They were camped on Hinkston Creek and these four scouts were returning from the Licking, where they already had spied Boone's men at work.

The Indians quickly overtook Boone's horse, and while one began to cut the tugs and throw off the meat, the others continued on foot after him. They were all young warriors and quickly gained on Boone, who was in excellent shape but was a man in his mid-forties. He had run about half a mile when he looked back and saw one of the Indians coming up on the horse and the others leveling their guns at him. Two bullets knocked up the snow on either side of him, then another hit his powder horn. Tiring, and concluding that escape was impossible, Boone dodged behind a tree and leaned his gun against the trunk, a sign of surrender. Then the Indians came up, whooping and laughing. Thus it was, as Boone would put it later, that "I was taken prisoner by a party of Shaney Indians."

The scouts took him without delay to Blackfish's encampment about three miles away. They arrived to general clamor, and Boone was astounded to see so many Indians, painted for war, in the midst of winter. There were 120 warriors, accompanied by two French Canadian traders, both in the service of the British, and a black man named Pompey who as a child had been taken from his master in Virginia, had been raised among the Shawnees, and now worked for Blackfish as a translator. As the Indians crowded around to see the captive, Boone recognized among them the face of Will Emery, the man who had taken him prisoner on his first exploration beyond the Appalachians. "Howdydo, Captain Will," he called out. Startled by the greeting, Captain Will squinted at the captive and asked him in halting English where they had met before. "Do you not recollect taking two men prisoners eight years ago on Kentucky River?" Boone replied. For a moment Will looked puzzled, then suddenly his eyes brightened and he broke into a wide smile, grasping Boone by the hand. "Howdydo, howdydo," he echoed and, laughing, said it appeared that Boone had forgotten his warning about Shawnee wasps and yellow jackets. That was long ago, Boone declared; now he was in command at Boonesborough. Other Indians pressed up to shake the hand of the American chief, and there was a round of introductions and greetings. It struck him as an incongruous scene, Boone said afterward, but he "bore it with all the grace and politeness of which he was master."

The Indians ushered Boone before Blackfish, the man who had directed the Shawnee raids of the previous summer. In his late forties, not much older than Boone himself, Blackfish was short and slight but carried himself with the gravity and authority of a great commander. Shunning the mock formalities of his men, he immediately got down to business, speaking to Boone through Pompey. Whose men were those his scouts had seen at the lick? he demanded. They are my men, Boone replied. Well, we have come to destroy your town on the Kentucky, to avenge the death of Cornstalk, Blackfish told him, but before we do, we will go back to the lick and kill your men. The Shawnees outnumbered the salt makers by more than four to one, and Boone worried that the appearance of an Indian army at Boonesborough would come as a complete surprise and that there would be a bloody rout. Quickly he devised a stratagem he thought might be the only way to save the settlement, a stratagem that forever after would be the subject of controversy.

His men surely would resist, he told Blackfish, and many on both sides would die, but if the chiefs would pledge not to mistreat them, he would convince his men to surrender as prisoners of war. The Shawnees already had subjected the Americans to punishment all the previous summer, he told him, and because the settlers at Boonesborough had been unable to raise corn, they were poor and ready to join the British. But if the Shawnees took the fort now, the badly weakened women and children would perish in the cold march to the Indian towns. Instead why not let him lead the Shawnees back to Boonesborough when the spring came? He would negotiate the capitulation of the fort on the Kentucky and they could all return together. The Shawnee leaders listened carefully to Boone's offer. There was much to recommend it. It was difficult to wage war in the winter, when there was little to forage and hunt, and their corn was already running dangerously low. The American women and children would further deplete that supply, and it would be much easier to force their surrender in the spring. What if Boone was lying? If he was, they would soon know it. He offered them more than two dozen captives, all able men who could better withstand the march to the Ohio country. They would have prisoners to burn or adopt, and the British would pay a handsome ransom for the rest. What, then, was to be lost by taking Boone back to the lick? There was a short and hushed consultation, then Blackfish told Boone that they would leave for Blue Licks in the morning. Boone "used duplicity," he later told his daughter-in-law, to forestall the attack on Boonesborough, but he knew that he would have a difficult time the next day convincing his men to surrender.

Although the snow lay a half foot deep, the next morning dawned sunny. Boone and the Shawnees set off immediately and arrived at Blue Licks at about noon. Blackfish told Boone to march directly into the camp, warning that if there was a sign of the slightest resistance, he would be the first to die. When the men, who were sunning themselves on their blankets, looked up to see Boone leading in a column of men, many at first believed that it was Captain Gwatkin and the relief party. But someone quickly raised the Indian alarm, and the men were up and at their arms. "Don't fire!" Boone called out. "If you do, all will be massacred." They were completely surrounded by a large party of Shawnees, he shouted, and resistance was useless. Their only option was to surrender with the promise of good treatment. Asking his men to trust him, he told them to disarm. "We were ordered by Colonel Boone to stack our guns and surrender," one of the men later wrote, "and we did so." The last to give up their weapons were William and Samuel Brooks, brothers of Boone's scout Thomas

Brooks, but finally they too added theirs to the cache. Immediately the Indians came in from every side and encircled the men, ordering them to sit down together.

It appeared that the Shawnees had been right to trust Boone, for now before them were twenty-seven American prisoners, taken without firing a shot. But many of the warriors protested to Blackfish that Cornstalk's murder could not be avenged without the shedding of blood, and they argued for killing the Americans and marching on Boonesborough immediately. The power of Shawnee leaders, even tribal chiefs like Blackfish, depended on consensus, and he called for a council of all of the warriors to decide the matter. Blackfish invited Boone to join in their circle, while the rest of the captive Americans sat huddled together to the side, under guard. As one of them would remember the scene, Pompey sat next to Boone, providing a translation of the proceedings in a low whisper, but none of the salt makers could make out what he said, and, not speaking Algonquian, they understood nothing of the debate. One after another, in a process that went on for several hours, Indians stood to deliver impassioned speeches in favor of killing or sparing the Americans. Finally Blackfish offered Boone the opportunity to make a closing argument. He spoke in English, with pauses for translation, and his men realized for the first time that their lives hung in the balance.

> Brothers! What I have promised you, I can much better fulfill in the spring than now. Then the weather will be warm, and the women and children can travel from Boonesborough to the Indian towns, and all live with you as one people. You have got all the young men. To kill them, as has been suggested, would displease the Great Spirit, and you could not then expect future success in hunting nor war. If you spare them, they will make you fine warriors, and excellent hunters to kill game for your squaws and children. These young men have done you no harm. They unresistingly surrendered upon my assurance that such a step was the only safe one. I consented to their capitulation on the express condition that they should be made prisoners of war and treated well. Spare them, and the Great Spirit will smile upon you.

The vote was taken and the result announced: fifty-nine for death, sixty-one for life. Boone believed that Blackfish had allowed him to speak because he and the other chiefs did not want to break their agreement.

The decision made, the Shawnees made preparations to return north with their captives. They took some of the precious salt and dumped the rest. An angry warrior who had been on the losing side of the debate came up to Boone and thrust one of the heavy kettles at him, but Boone pushed it back violently and knocked the man backward. As the warrior arose, violence in his eyes, Blackfish stepped between them and the man sulked off. The Indians marched their captives a few miles north that afternoon, then a little before nightfall began to set up camp. Boone noticed that some of them were clearing a ground, as if in preparation for a gauntlet, a traditional ordeal for captives providing the Indians with a chance to vent their anger. Grabbing Pompey, he went to Blackfish to protest that the chiefs had promised not to harm his men. "This is not for your men but for yourself," Blackfish responded, "you made no bargain for yourself." He gave Boone the choice of running here or waiting until they arrived at Chillicothe, Blackfish's town on the Little Miami River. "I'm a man, and no squaw," Boone answered, "and not afraid to run. If I must, I prefer to do so here, in the presence of men and warriors, and not before mere women and children." Women and children, in fact, often inflicted the most severe and humiliating torture on captives. The warriors formed into two lines with sticks and clubs in hand, a number swinging their weapons in the air as if they intended to bash out Boone's brains.

Stripped to his breechclout and leggings and placed at the head of the lines, Boone awaited the blow on his backside that would signal the start of the run. He knew that a man could expect no mercy, and that if he fell, he might be pummeled to death. The only thing to do was to run fast and keep running, no matter what happened. The first powerful kick nearly knocked him over, but "I set out full speed," he would later tell a grandson, "first running so near one line that they could not do me much damage, and when they give back, crossed over to the other side, and by that means was likely to pass through without much hurt." Many of the warriors went lightly on him but others came down ferociously, staggering him with their blows and opening a large cut on the crown of his head that flooded his eyes with blood and clouded his vision. As he neared the end, "a wily fellow broke the lines for the purpose of giving me a home lick. The only way I had to avoid his intention was to run over him by springing at him with my head bent forward, taking him full in the breast, and prostrating him flat on his back, passing over him unhurt." With this final bold move, a cheer went up from the Americans and the Indians as well, who crowded around him, "giving me their hand saying, 'velly good sojer,' " and adding expressions of scorn for the fellow sprawled on the ground, condemning him as a "damn squaw."

The next morning the Americans were forced to carry salt, kettles, and other equipment. "It was a heavy load," the captive Ansel Goodman would remember. "He was packed heavily from the time he was taken until he arrived at the Town." A number of the men resisted. William Brooks threw off his load and would not pick it up until Boone persuaded him that otherwise he would be killed and lightened the pack by taking some of it on his own back. One warrior, perhaps the same one who had tried to assign the kettle to Boone the day before, now demanded that it be carried by James Callaway, the obstinate nephew of Dick Callaway. He adamantly refused, and when the Indian drew his tomahawk and raised it, Callaway bent forward, took off his hat, and patted his head, saying, "Here, strike! I would as lief lie here as go along, and I won't tote your kettle." With a dry smile the warrior turned away, put up his tomahawk, and found a more compliant bearer.

"We proceeded with them as prisoners to old Chelicothe," Boone told Filson, "the principal Indian town on Little Miami." The journey of more than a hundred miles through cold and snow took ten days. At the Ohio River they ferried across in a wide boat of buffalo hide that held twenty persons. The Indians had little food and the weather was so severe that the hunters failed to find game. The warriors killed and ate their dogs, and although they offered to share this meal with the Americans, many preferred going hungry. Most of the Americans were young men who had signed into the Virginia militia in a burst of revolutionary patriotism, with little or no experience in the western wilderness, and they suffered greatly. Others were hardened woodsmen, like

Boone, who had experienced similar periods of winter fasting. "It was all habit in eating so much," Boone believed. "He would buckle his belt tighter and get along very comfortably." He told his men to chew the bark of the slippery elm and eat the ooze from white oak in order to keep their digestive systems operating. The hunters finally brought in a deer and were willing to share it with the captives, but before allowing any to eat, they insisted that the men consume a portion of a jelly made from the entrails. Boone tried some but threw it up, much to the amusement of the Indians, and it required repeated efforts before he or any of his men could keep it down. Only then, however, would the Indians allow them to eat the venison, saying that otherwise it surely would have killed them.

On the eighteenth of February, 1778, the Shawnees and their captives arrived at Chillicothe, sixty or seventy miles up the Little Miami River, a place now called Oldtown, to the east of Dayton, Ohio. "Before they got in sight of the town," said Ansel Goodman, "he was compelled to strip himself (cold as it was) entirely naked" and "made to sing as loud as he could holler. The object of that, he afterwards learnt, was to give notice of their approach." Hearing the cries of captives, people came out from the village to greet the returning warriors. In the summer Chillicothe was home to as many as a thousand Shawnees, but now it was midwinter, and most of the families were dispersed to hunting camps. Only a few dozen old people and children were present to witness the arrival of one of the largest groups of American captives ever taken by the Shawnees.

The town Americans called Chillicothe was named for the Chlahgawtha clan, who were its principal residents and who, in the traditional order of the Shawnee nation, were responsible for providing political leadership. Each time the Shawnees relocated, the pattern was for each clan to build a separate town within a common cluster, so there had been previous Chillicothes and there would be more before their collective movements ended on the reservation lands of Oklahoma. "All these Chillicothys are elegant situations," wrote the American general Josiah Harmar, sent to destroy one of them several years later. "The savages know how to take a handsome position, as well as any people on earth." Chillicothe was considerably larger and more impressive than any of the settlements Americans had planted in Kentucky. Built on a hard ridge near the river, in the midst of a fertile prairie, it commanded easy access to a fine spring, extensive cornfields, grazing for horses and cattle, excellent fishing, and abundant hunting in the surrounding wooded hills. As the captives entered the town from the southwest they passed down lanes along which stood several hundred Shawnee homes. Some were constructed in the traditional manner, bark over bent saplings, but most were simple one-room log cabins, replicas of the settlers' own structures but without windows and chimneys. Indeed, as John Filson put it, the town was "built in the form of a Kentucky station," with the outer walls of cabins forming a protective enclosure. In the center stood a big council house, sixty feet square, made of notched hickory logs, open at the gable ends, and there the warriors repaired to engage in a set of rituals designed to remove the stains of warfare and prepare them again for the civil life of the village.

The few Shawnee villagers insisted on setting up a gauntlet for the Americans to run, most of whom got through with little difficulty under the circumstances. Samuel Brooks, however, rather than running through quickly, stood and fought each of his tormentors and as a result suffered a badly broken arm. That evening the Shawnee warriors stripped nearly naked and held a great war dance, during which the captives "were ordered to dance like the whites" for the amusement of the villagers. Afterward the Americans were dispersed to cabins and tied down, but few could sleep because of the sounds of dancing and singing that went on late into the night. They now had ample opportunity to consider their fate, and many suffered from bitter reflections. "Some of them thought they could have defended themselves" at the Blue Licks. Others had doubts that they could have survived a struggle but "regretted they had not fought and resisted till they died." Few placed much faith in Blackfish's promise to Boone that they would be treated well. They might be tortured and burned in the morning to avenge Cornstalk's murder, or they might be permitted to live, only to suffer lives as miserable slaves to the Indians.

Had the men been destined for torture, the women would have painted them black upon their arrival in the village. There would be no burnings this time, but slavery remained a possibility, although the Shawnees were generally more interested in candidates for adoption into the families who had lost husbands and sons in battle. From the perspective of Americans, who tended to divide the world into immutable forces of "us" and "them," this custom was inexplicable, but the Shawnees, like other Indians, believed in transmutation. With the application of the correct rituals an admired enemy might be made over into a beloved brother, actually thought to assume the identity of a deceased kinsman. During the eighteenth century hundreds of Europeans and Americans were captured and adopted into Indian tribes. Typically the induction ceremony included ceremonial washings that symbolized an end to old roles, as well as body painting, hair plucking, and dressing, to mark the assumption of new identities. "We have taken as much care of these prisoners as if they were our own Flesh and Blood," the Shawnees told the British when returning several dozen captives after the Seven Years War. "They have been all tied to us by adoption, and we will always look upon them as our relations."

Young adoptees often became so well adjusted to their new lives that they elected to remain with the Indians, and many of those who returned to their former lives continued to be attached to their adoptive families. Many returned captives later escaped back to their Indian families, and one Shawnee man reported that "Shawnee women used to steal into Kentucky to visit their former adopted children." But the successful assimilation of adult captives was rare, and most adopted American men eventually tried to escape. This did not prevent the Shawnees from continuing the practice. Perhaps nothing else so suggested the differences between the Indian and American worlds as this custom of adopting enemies in the midst of bitter warfare.

Word circulated among the towns that there were captives at Chillicothe, and Shawnee men and women looking for adoptees soon began to arrive to survey their prospects. The Shawnees adopted at least ten captive salt makers, dispersing them to various camps and towns. Boone and two others remained at Chillicothe. William Hancock joined the household of Will Emery, to replace one of his fallen sons; the other man, Andrew Johnson, was physically unimpressive but actually one of the toughest and most experienced woodsmen among the group. From the beginning of his captivity he had been playing the fool for the Indians. When asked about this curious behavior, Boone went along with the deception, saying that Johnson "was mad, and of no sort of account anyhow." This actually endeared Johnson to the Shawnees, who believed that people touched with madness were specially blessed and that good fortune came to those who were kind to them. Given the name Pequolly, "Little Duck," Johnson's adoptive parents allowed him a good deal of latitude.

Most of the salt makers thought of their adoption as an expedient, and the majority succeeded in escaping to the Kentucky settlements within a year or two of their capture. At least two, however, established more lasting ties. Joseph Jackson, renamed Fish, remained among the Shawnees until 1799, when he made a brief attempt to return to live with his American brother in Kentucky, then moved to Missouri and spent his last years with his Shawnee friends and relations who had removed there. Jack Dunn, one of the first Americans to escape, was never able to resolve the conflict he felt about his identity, and he later returned to Chillicothe to warn his Shawnee family of an impending American attack. Captured by Kentucky rangers soon afterward, he was tortured to death as a turncoat.

In Boone the Shawnees saw great qualities of leadership, and it thus was appropriate that the family of Blackfish himself considered him for adoption. Soon after arriving at Chillicothe, Boone remembered, he was questioned about the death of Blackfish's son, one of the Shawnees killed at the rescue of Jemima and the Callaway girls. Had he not been in command of that company? one of the Shawnees asked Boone. Yes, he had been, he answered candidly, and he had fired on the kidnappers. His might have been one of the mortal shots, although it was impossible to know whose gun had actually done the killing. But "many things happen in war," he concluded, "that were best forgotten." For a moment there was silence as his interrogator pondered this reply, and Boone wondered if he might not be murdered on the spot. Suddenly the tension broke as the Shawnee burst into a smile and slapped Boone on the shoulder. "Brave man! All right!" he declared. "When we in war you kill me, I kill you. All right!" His adoption into Blackfish's family, Boone thought, "must have been to replace that slain son." Taken to the river, clan matrons dunked and vigorously scrubbed him, then plucked his hair, leaving only a tuft on the top of his head for the scalp lock, which they decorated with ribbon and feathers.

Then, at the council house, he was inducted by Blackfish in a long ceremony that included much smoking and feasting. His new name was Sheltowee, "Big Turtle," a reference to his strong, compact frame.

Flanders Callaway and Thomas Brooks, whose two brothers were among the salt makers, returned to Blue Licks from their hunt the day after the Shawnees had departed with their prisoners and, finding the camp abandoned, soon guessed at what had happened. The relief company arrived shortly, and while men attempted to salvage what salt they could, and cached the remaining kettles, Simon Kenton followed the Indians' trail. It led across the Ohio, he confirmed, and they all hastened back to Boonesborough with the melancholy news that Daniel Boone and twenty-six men had been taken "prisoners from the Salt licks on licking Creek, without Shedding one drop of blood."

Rebecca was "much Dejected at the loss of her Husband," said her cousin Daniel Boone Bryan, but the worst of it was the uncertainty, "not knowing whether he was murdered or made prisoner or whether he would return." In Boone's absence, rival officers from Virginia vied with one another for command of the fort, and the vacuum of leadership led to serious problems of discipline among the unattached men. Living conditions in the fort were at low ebb. A visitor to Kentucky left a vivid description of life in the confinement of a pioneer station: "The whole dirt and filth of the Fort, putrified flesh, dead dogs, horse, cow, hog excrement and human odour," combined "with the Ashes and sweepings of filthy Cabbins, the dirtiness of the people, steeping skins to dress and washing every sort of dirty rags and cloths, will certainly contribute to render the inhabitants of this place sickly." Arriving at Boonesborough with a militia company in March, one ranger "found a poor, distressed, half-naked, half-starved people." "It was hard times," wrote another arriving emigrant. "No bred, no salt, no vegetables, no fruit of any kind, no Ardent sperrets, indeed nothing but meet."

But with the people so terrorized by the Indians that "hunters were afraid to go out to get Buffaloe," soon even meat was in short supply. Desperately hungry troops finally took things into their own hands, stealing hogs and killing and butchering one of Dick

Callaway's largest steers. Callaway came up with his rifle loaded, swearing that "if any man killed another head of his stock, he would shoot him." David Gass defused the explosive confrontation when he invited the rangers to go up to Otter Creek and hunt his hogs, and after a few hours they returned with five fat ones, which they barbecued for the company.

Word of Boone's capture reached Virginia in March. Governor Patrick Henry refused to believe that "all of Boone's party are lost," but reports of their deaths continued to circulate. Daniel Boone Bryan, returning to Boonesborough with several of his kinsmen after wintering in North Carolina, heard the news from a group of Kentuckians at Moccasin Gap. Boone and his men, they were told, "were captured at the Blue lick while making salt and caried off and murdered by the Indians." In shock, the Bryans turned back to carry the sad tidings home to the Yadkin. Rebecca and the children, with William Hays and Susannah, followed about the first of May, traveling in the company of rangers who had mutinied and were abandoning Kentucky. She had waited for Boone for two months, but finally, "supposing her husband dead," she said, "she thought best to leave the troubles of Kentucky and try to get to her friends in Carolina." Only Jemima remained at Boonesborough, with her husband, Flanders Callaway, refusing to give up hope of her father's return.

It is likely that suspicions of Boone circulating at Boonesborough encouraged Rebecca to leave. To some, like Boone's brother Squire, the absence of any sign of a battle raised hopes that the men were alive, but to others, like Richard Callaway, it suggested treachery. On the Upper Ohio that spring a number of prominent frontiersmen went over to the British side, most notably Simon Girty, his brothers James and George, and Alexander McKee, all of whom became notorious Tory agents among the Indians. Boone had Loyalist kin, and his disappearance was interpreted by some in the context of considerable anxiety about frontier loyalties.

On March 10 Blackfish and forty Shawnees left for Detroit to deliver the remaining unadopted salt makers to the British in exchange for a bounty of twenty pounds for each man. These captives included the obviously recalcitrant, men like James Callaway and Samuel Brooks. A measure of manly resistance was thought to be a positive trait, and one family decided to take a chance on Brooks's brother William, who was admired for his courage. But when the women attempted to wash him in the river, Brooks pulled them into the water and held them under until they were rescued by several warriors. Some of the Shawnees laughed and called Brooks "Big Sturgeon," but after that, his daughter said, "they were glad to leave him alone" and he was sent to Detroit along with his brother. Compared to the captives remaining with the Shawnees, this group endured far more suffering, some toiling at forced labor, others rotting in damp dungeons. "We were much better treated by the Indians than by the British," one salt maker taken to Detroit told his son. Samuel Brooks died in confinement because of his untended arm and four other men disappeared, their fates unknown. About half of the British prisoners eventually escaped, but the rest remained in custody until the end of the Revolution.

Indians "conducted me to Detright" with the other captives, Boone testified afterward, so that Governor Hamilton, who already had been informed of his capture, could interrogate him. "They had the good fortune to make Prisoners," Hamilton wrote in his report of the Shawnee raid, "Captain Daniel Boone with 26 of his men, whom they brought off with their arms without killing or losing a man." Boone emphasized to Hamilton the weak and defenseless position of the settlers in Kentucky and hinted that they were ready to abandon the American cause and accept a British offer of pardon. Hamilton wrote in his report of the interview,

> By Boone's account, the people on the frontiers have been incessantly harassed by parties of Indians. They have not been able to sow grain and at Kentucky will not have a morsel of bread by the middle of June. Cloathing is not to be had, nor do they expect relief from the Congress. Their dilemma will probably induce them to trust to the Savages who have shewn so much humanity to their prisoners, and come to this place before winter.

Hamilton asked Boone whether he had heard any news of Burgoyne's march south from Canada. Yes, Boone replied, he had learned of the surrender at Saratoga before his capture. The governor's face fell. "The report of Burgoyne's disaster, I fear, is too true," he called out to his secretary in the next room. "Captain Boone says it was well known in Kentucky before he was taken." He asked that Boone keep from the Shawnees the importance of this defeat.

Hamilton treated him "with great humanity," Filson quoted Boone as saying, and the governor even attempted to ransom him from the Indians and "give me a parole to go home." But Hamilton's offer surely had more to do with politics, for Boone seems to have been completely convincing about his Loyalist sympathies and his potential usefulness to the British cause. According to Rebecca's father, Joseph Bryan, Boone displayed his captain's commission from Dunmore, and that was "the true reason why he was treated so well at Detroit and ransomed from the Indians." Blackfish and the Shawnees refused Hamilton's ransom offer, said Boone, because "their affection for me was so great, that they utterly refused to leave me there with the others." But in his report Hamilton suggested that something more than affection was at stake. The Indians "took Boone with them," he wrote, "expecting by his means to effect something." To Blackfish, Boone was now Sheltowee and had incurred all of the obligations that adoption implied. Boone had succeeded in convincing Blackfish, as he had convinced Hamilton, that he would return with them to Boonesborough in the spring to negotiate the surrender of the fort and would lead the settlers across the Ohio into Indian and British territory, where they would "all live with you as one people."

After collecting the bounties for the American captives, paid in trade goods and supplies, Blackfish, Boone, and the Shawnees made a round of the Mingo and Shawnee towns on the Scioto River. Blackfish spread the notice to assemble in the spring for a grand expedition against the settlements in Kentucky. When they returned to Chillicothe at the end of April they learned that Pequolly, the "fool," had escaped. One night, as the warriors danced celebrating a successful raid into Kentucky for horses, Andy Johnson stole a knife, gun, ammunition, and blanket coat, and fled down the Little Miami on foot. Missing him in the morning, the Indians went out in pursuit, but he so expertly hid his tracks that soon they were trailing in circles. That was because Pequolly "was no woodsman," Boone told them. "He had probably wandered off and got lost." But in fact, Johnson had reached the Ohio, rafted across, and after a week or more of travel, arrived in Harrodsburg.

Johnson's report confirmed the worst suspicions about Boone's capture. According to Johnson, "Boone was a Tory, and had surrendered them all up to the British, and taken the oath of allegiance to the British at Detroit." Boone's deception had convinced Johnson as well as it had the Shawnees and the British. He was playing a dangerous game that put him at risk on every front. William Hancock, who saw a great deal of Boone at Chillicothe during the spring of 1778, was at a loss to understand "how Boone could be whistling and contented among the dirty Indians while he was so melancholy." This was all part of his plan, Boone later explained to Filson, "always appearing as chearful and satisfied as possible." Like the great hunter he was, Boone's greatest talent was his ability to blend in with his surroundings.

The stories that Boone told his family, however, suggest that his relationship with the Shawnees was more than simply artifice. He seemed to feel very much at home among them and became particularly attached to Blackfish and his family. His Indian parents, he told one of his granddaughters, were always "friendly and sociable and kind to him." Blackfish addressed Boone as "my son," and Boone later described his Indian father as "one of Nature's noblemen." Although Boone expressed a distaste for "the housewifery of his Indian mother," who "allowed her chickens to roost on the lubber pole from which the kettles were hung to boil over the fire," he nevertheless referred to her affectionately as his "old mamma" and spoke of her "with the greatest kindness," as one nephew remembered. Boone also grew attached to Blackfish's two little daughters, and he frequently indulged them with presents. Many years after Boone's death, one of his granddaughters encountered an old Shawnee woman in Kansas who, upon learning of her ancestry, showered her with affection. The old woman, it turned out, was one of Sheltowee's adoptive Shawnee sisters.

Some biographers have fixed on vague suggestions in the evidence that Boone may have lived with a Shawnee woman at Chillicothe. "I have been obliged to be married in Indian fashion a couple of times," a friend quoted him as admitting to Rebecca. "Grandfather Boone said he had a squaw that claimed him as her Buck," a descendant wrote. "He said she mended and dried his leggins [and] patched his mocksins." But lest these remarks conjure up a romantic image of love in an Indian lodge, this same descendant described Boone's Shawnee woman as an "Old Squaw" who "made him help her do all her drudgery work" and "would do Every thing to Punish him," like forcing him to stand in a tub of hot hominy corn, tramping off the husks with his bare feet, laughing and beating him back with a club as he tried to run off.

This is but one of a number of stories Boone told about his initiation into Shawnee life: After the adoption ceremony Blackfish takes him to the cornfields and assigns him to work with his mother and the other women. "Never much on raising corn," however, Sheltowee recklessly hoes up about as much as he clears. Angered, the women chase him away with their hoes. Seeing Blackfish, he complains, "I'm a chief at home, and I won't be made a squaw of here." "Good warrior," says Blackfish, patting his new son on the shoulder, "you should not be required to do any drudgery," and Sheltowee is freed from the tyranny of the squaws. Blackfish then leads him into the woods and, providing an ax, tells him to make him a trough to use for feeding the horses. Sheltowee begins to chop but, unaccustomed to handling an ax, blisters his hands and lays down to rest. "You haven't done much," says Blackfish, returning. "When I am at home I don't do this kind of work," Sheltowee replies, "I have Niggers to work for me. But here you make a Negro of me. You and your Squaw calls me your Son, but this don't look like you love me." Whether Kentuckian or Shawnee, men were hunters and warriors, not laborers, and in the end the tales suggest Boone's discovery of the similarity between the two cultures in the realm of gender. "My son," Blackfish concludes, "if you don't like to do it, don't work any more," and from then on Sheltowee associates only with the men.

The Shawnees watched him closely, Boone remembered, but he pretended not to notice and attempted to win their confidence. "I often went a hunting with them," says Filson's Boone, "and frequently gained their applause for my activity at our shooting-matches." But his Indian mother, wise in "the habits and customs of the young braves," advised him "to let the young Indians beat him sometimes" in their shooting matches. It was a lesson he recalled from his experience with Saucy Jack in his youth. But still the warriors were wary. After a day of hunting, two of them would lay their blankets close on either side of him, aware of his every movement during the night. According to one tale Boone told, one day he decides to confront the suspicions of the warriors directly. Arising early one morning as the Shawnees still sleep, he uses a bullet screw to remove the balls from every loaded gun in camp, then makes noise enough to wake the men. "I'm going home," Sheltowee announces to the startled Blackfish. "No you ain't," says the chief, "if you attempt it, I'll shoot you." "Shoot then," says he, and walks off unconcerned. The Shawnees grab their guns and fire, to no effect, and as they stand stunned, Sheltowee walks back, laughing, the balls in his hand. "Here take your bullets, Boone ain't going away." Gradually their confidence in him increased to the point where he was allowed to hunt alone. Powder and ball were measured out to him, but gradually he was able to secrete a small cache of ammunition in the fold of his hunting shirt. Boone felt he had "completely deceived Blackfish and his simple-hearted people."

"I now began to mediate an escape," says Filson's Boone. But he explained to his family that "I felt it to be my duty to remain till all my men within my reach had, by one means or another, got off." Michajah Callaway, who was living with a Shawnee family in a nearby town, testified that although Boone "could have escaped much earlier," he awaited an opportunity to get away together with his men. Boone whispered to one of the salt makers that he was making plans for an escape and would take him along. Two events, however, forced Boone to take independent action and flee on his own.

Just before dawn one day in late May, a hunting party on the outskirts of Chillicothe that included Blackfish suddenly found themselves under fire. The Indian towns of the Miami Valley had never before been attacked by American settlers from Kentucky, and Blackfish believed that these raiders must be Indians from another village. "Huy! Huy!" he called out. "We are Shawnees!" But the fire kept up, two of his warriors died from gunshot wounds, and he lost a number of horses. Blackfish returned to Chillicothe the next morning and was telling his son Sheltowee about the encounter when another group of Shawnees rode in with the news that they had seen the raiding party passing south across the Ohio with the stolen horses. The raiders were not Indians at all, they reported, but Americans, and leading them was Pequolly, the escaped captive Andy Johnson. With his knowledge of the lay of the land and the pattern of Indian settlement north of the river, Johnson had organized an expedition of Harrodsburg men "to go to there towns for horses." "Painted like and drest like Indians," one of these raiders wrote, they crossed the Ohio on rafts and rode up the Little Miami Trail to spy out the towns. But finding the Indian "number too great to attack them upon Equal Footing," they decided to ambush an outlying hunter's camp and succeeded in stealing "seven Horses, and them of a good Quallity." Pequolly had turned out to be no fool, the angry Shawnees declared to Boone, "but a great rogue."

This raid opened the way to further American attacks on the Shawnee villages of the Miami region. "The worst act the Indians ever did," said Boone, "was their taking the salt boilers, and learning them the way to their towns and the geography of the Indians country." The Shawnees understood this larger meaning all too well, and it encouraged them to accelerate their planning for a renewed campaign against the American settlements. For Boone, it must have been clear that more aggressive incursions such as Johnson's were likely, and that these would dash the credibility of his claims of American demoralization and the likelihood of surrender at Boonesborough.

A few days later, on about the first of June, Blackfish, with Boone, his family, and several others, left Chillicothe for the Shawnee and Mingo communities on the Scioto River to the east, where he planned to recruit warriors for his Boonesborough expedition while his family made salt at a nearby spring. During his stay there, a large mixed company of warriors returned from a series of unsuccessful attacks at Point Pleasant on the Ohio and other American strongholds in the Kanawha River country south of the river. Blackfish encouraged them to turn their frustrated energies toward the poorly defended Kentucky settlements. As part of their preparations for this campaign, the Indians gave Boone a number of guns to repair, and from the supply of parts he was able to hide an unstocked rifle barrel and a lock among his belongings. Boone told his family that "as soon as he found out that they had determined to make the march, he resolved to make his escape, and warn the settlement of their danger."

Boone provided Filson with a characteristically terse description of this escape. "On the sixteenth [of June], before sun-rise, I departed in the most secret manner, and arrived at Boonesborough on the twentieth, after a journey of one hundred and sixty miles; during which, I had but one meal." A number of tales, however, provide additional details. After two weeks of manufacturing salt and making plans for the spring, Blackfish and his party began their return to Chillicothe on the Little Miami. They had not traveled far when, seeing in the distance a flock of fat turkeys, the men galloped off and scattered to hunt, leaving the women behind with Sheltowee, who was leading a horse loaded with the salt kettles. Thinking that this would be his best opportunity, "Boone cut the tugs," according to the captive Joseph Jackson, who heard the story from the Shawnees, "and said to the squaws that he wanted to go see his squaw and children, and dashed off."

In most versions of the escape, the Shawnee women "shreek" a warning to the men who come back to pursue Boone, but in a tale Boone told to his Bryan nephews, Sheltowee engages in a final departing conversation with his Indian mother. "She tried to persuade him not to attempt it," for "the Indians would certainly overtake and kill him, or he would get lost in the vast wilderness and starve to death." She and his sisters "layed hold of him and beged him go back with them." But when his mother "found that she could not prevail on him to remain, she went to work to prepare him something to eat to take with him." As Sheltowee rides off, "they cried heartily." There is more than a touch of improbability about this version, especially considering the desperation with which Boone must have made his break while the Shawnee hunters remained so close. Rather than an accurate depiction of the women's reactions, this is more likely a reflection of Boone's nostalgia as he looked back on a relationship that meant a great deal to him. As he galloped away from his Indian mother and his Shawnee life, he told the Bryan boys, "he really felt sory."

Boone rode furiously until his horse gave out, then continued on foot, disguising his trail as best he could by running down streams, over rocks and fallen trees, finally reaching the Ohio River. The Shawnees pursued, but eventually they missed his trail. "Boone is lost," one of the captives overheard the report of the returning trackers. "Went so—so," they said, signing a zigzag route in the air

Chester Harding's oil sketch of *Daniel Boone* (1820). Painted at the home of Jemima Boone Callaway, this is the only life portrait of Boone. Although he looks gaunt in his eighty-fourth year, the artist catches the dignity of his direct gaze and the determination of his hard-set mouth. Boone's son Nathan pronounced this an accurate likeness, "except that it did not exhibit the plump cheer, and hence the broad face he used to exhibit in his robust days." *Courtesy Massachusetts Historical Society, Boston.*

James Otto Lewis's engraving of *Col. Daniel Boon* (1820) is a copy of a full-length portrait by Chester Harding that no longer survives, and thus is the only image that suggests Boone's figure. It was the first published print to feature the authentic costume of the American frontiersman. Boone leans on his long rifle, dressed in fringed hunting shirt, leggings, and moccasins, a hunting knife tucked in his belt, his beaver hat in hand. *Courtesy Missouri Historical Society, St. Louis.*

Thomas Cole's oil painting, *Daniel Boone at His Cabin at Great Osage Lake* (1826). Boone was often celebrated as the "natural man" of the woods, but others condemned his wanderlust. Here Cole depicts him as an unhappy hermit in the midst of an inaccessible and overpowering wilderness. After spending his lifetime searching for "elbow room," he sits silent and dejected, finally realizing the cost of his social disaffection. "Alone! Alone!—How drear it is always to be alone," he laments. *Courtesy Mead Art Museum, Amherst College, museum purchase.*

Engravings from Timothy Flint's biography of Boone (1833). Boone despised coonskin caps, but they became symbolic of the fighting frontiersman of nineteenth-century popular culture. Boone descendants scorned Flint's best-selling biography because of his fanciful stories, as when he had Boone escape from the Indians by swinging through the forest. "I suppose it was this vine," complained one of Boone's nephews, "that Mr. Flint swong so often from the truth." *Reproduced from Timothy Flint,* The First White Man of the West; or, The Life Exploits of Col. Daniel Boone *(Cincinnati, Ohio: Anderson, Gates & Wright, 1858).*

Horatio Greenough's marble statue, *The Rescue Group* (1852), stood on the east front steps of the Capitol in Washington, D.C., for over a century, but officials who found it embarrassing finally had it removed in 1958. *Photograph courtesy the Library of Congress.*

The lithograph *Daniel Boone Protects His Family* (1874). Greenough intended his work as a general statement on "the superiority of the white-man," but most viewers of the nineteenth century took it to represent Boone, an association made explicit in this popular print. *Courtesy Missouri Historical Society, St. Louis.*

George Caleb Bingham's oil painting, *Daniel Boone Escorting Settlers through the Cumberland Gap* (1851–52), rises above the images of Indian hating so prominent in nineteenth-century perceptions of the frontiersman. Although considerably younger and heavier, and with a cleft chin, this Boone shares the dignity of the original Harding portrait. Bingham also copies the costume of the Lewis engraving, and like Boone himself, disdains the uncouth coonskin cap, choosing instead the Quaker-style beaver. *Courtesy Washington University Gallery of Art, St. Louis, gift of Nathaniel Phillips.*

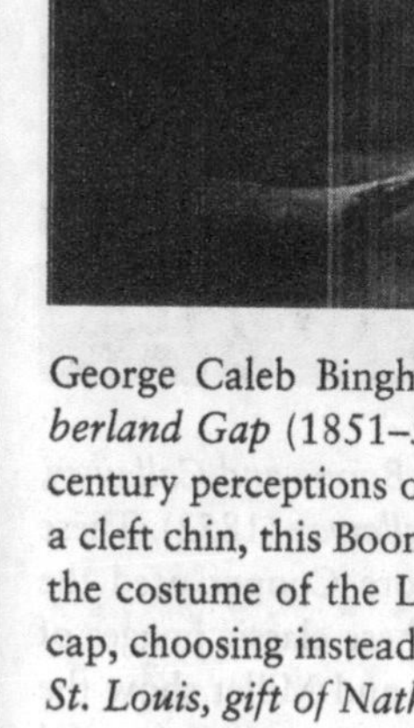

Drawings by Daniel C. Beard and James Daugherty from the early twentieth century make the connection between Boone and the American boy. Beard's drawing of the regulation outfit was inspired by the Lewis engraving. *Reprinted with the permission of Charles Scribner's Sons, an imprint of Macmillan Publishing Company from* The Boy Pioneers: Sons of Daniel Boone *by D. C. Beard. Copyright 1909 Charles Scribner's Sons; copyright renewed 1937. Sketch reproduced from* Daniel Boone: Wilderness Scout *by Stewart Edward White (Garden City, New York: Garden City Publishing Company, 1922).*

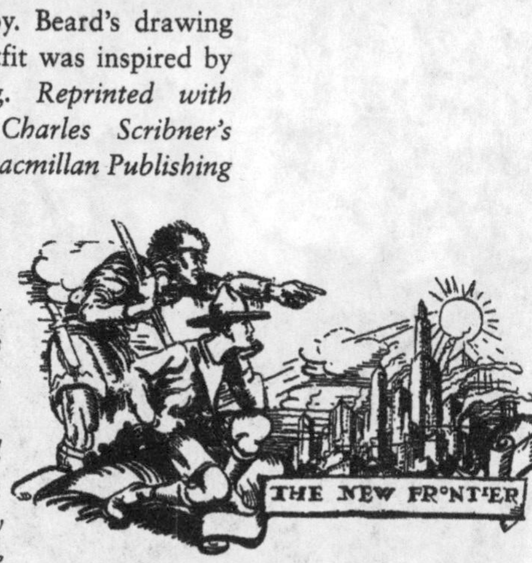

Lithographs by Jean-François Millet, *The Abduction of the Daughters of Boone and Callaway*, and Karl Bodmer, *The Deliverance of the Daughters of D. Boone and Callaway* (1852). These scenes became a popular theme for writers and artists. James Fenimore Cooper used the incident as the basis for the kidnapping in *The Last of the Mohicans*. These classic images of captivity were intended to illustrate life in the American West. Bodmer and Millet show the moment of capture with some accuracy, although their version of the rescue is a fanciful composite. *Courtesy Washington University Gallery of Art; gift of Mrs. Charles W. Bryan, Jr.*

Boone's discharge certificate for one of his men (1774) is the earliest surviving example of Boone's handwriting and signature. He was as literate as most ordinary men of his times, writing in what was known as a "common farmer's hand, " and was said to love reading, often carrying a book with him into the woods. A missionary who visited his wife Rebecca noted, however, that "she can not read," and judging from their marks on indentures, deeds, and bills of sale, none of the Boone women were literate. *Courtesy The Filson Club, Louisville, Kentucky.*

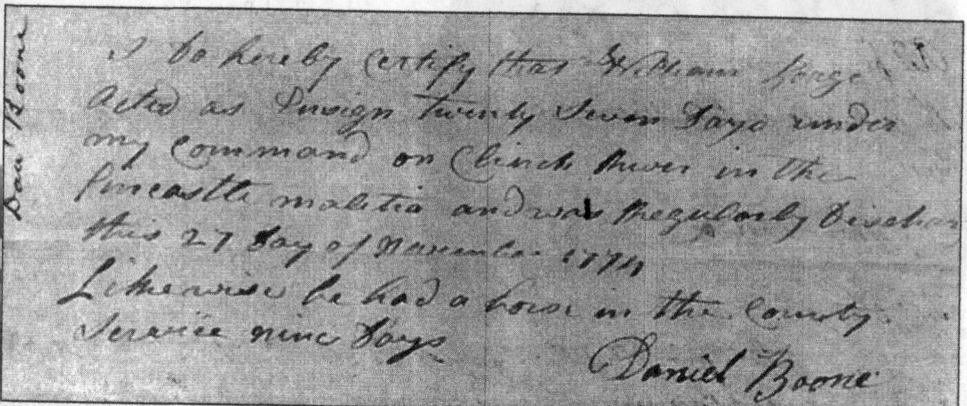
Dan'l Boone

I do hereby certify that William Poage Acted as Ensign twenty seven Days under my Command on Clinch River in the Fincastle malitia and was Regularly Discharged this 27 Day of November 1774 Likewise he had a horse in the County Service nine Days

Daniel Boone

An arrest warrant for Boone (1775). As the terse notation on the reverse indicated, the sheriff was unable to serve this warrant because Boone had already taken his family to Kentucky. Boone was occasionally taken to court by his creditors, but a court reporter who checked the North Carolina record wrote to Lyman Draper that Boone's name appeared very infrequently, "so I trust you will not write of the great Pioneer as also a great litigant." *Courtesy Archibald Henderson Papers, North Carolina Collection, University of North Carolina Library at Chapel Hill.*

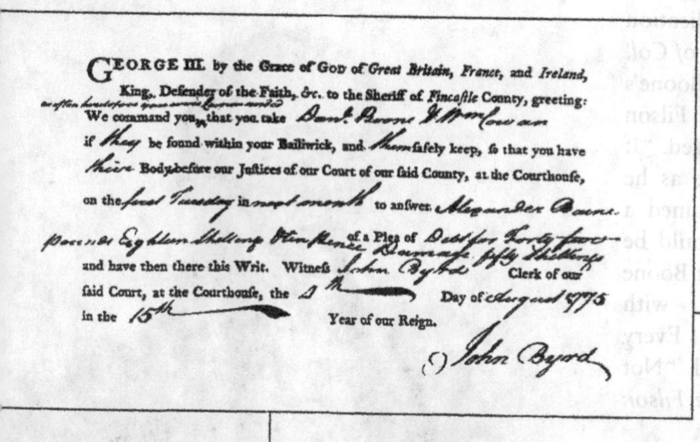
GEORGE III. by the Grace of God of *Great Britain, France,* and *Ireland,* King, Defender of the Faith, *&c.* to the Sheriff of *Fincastle* County, greeting: We command you, that you take Danl. Boone & Wm. Cowan if they be found within your Bailiwick, and them safely keep, so that you have their Body before our Justices of our Court of our said County, at the Courthouse, on the first Tuesday in next month to answer Alexander Boane of a Plea of Debt for Forty two pounds Eighteen Shillings & ten Pence Damage fifty Shillings and have then there this Writ. Witness John Byrd Clerk of our said Court, at the Courthouse, the 2th Day of August 1775 in the 15th Year of our Reign.

John Byrd

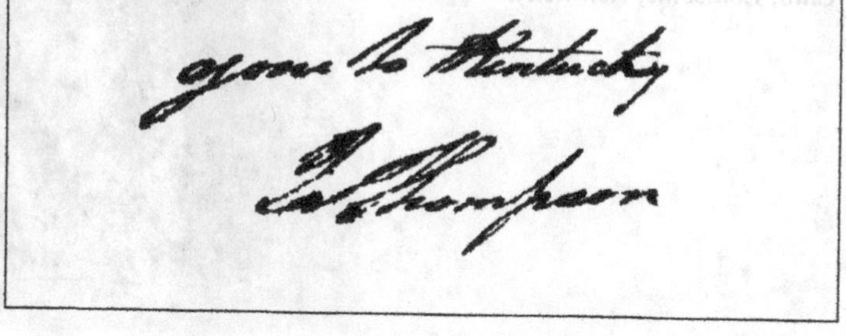
gone to Kentucky

J. Thompson

An anonymous oil painting of Nathan Boone, dating from about 1850, when he retired as a lieutenant colonel from the United States Dragoons. A fellow officer described Boone's youngest son as "a remarkable woodsman who could climb like a bear and swim like a duck." He and his wife Olive were the most important informants about Boone's life for the historian Lyman Copeland Draper. As Draper prepared to leave their Missouri log cabin after a stay of several weeks, the couple handed him the few surviving papers of Boone, "carefully rolled up in the pieces of deer skin in which he left them." *Courtesy Missouri Historical Society, St. Louis.*

John Filson's unflattering self-portrait in pencil (1785), done about the time of the publication of Filson's *The Adventures of Col. Daniel Boon.* For telling Boone's story as romantic myth, Filson has frequently been criticized. "If you had Boone's Naritive as he wrote it himself," complained a Boone descendant, "it would be plain and intillagible." But Boone himself was delighted with Filson's version. "All true! Every word true!" he exclaimed. "Not a lie in it." *Courtesy The Filson Club, Louisville, Kentucky.*

A daguerreotype of Lyman Copeland Draper from about 1855. Draper devoted his career to preserving pioneer history, in fifty years traveling more than fifty thousand miles collecting materials and interviewing hundreds of people. Infamous in the border states as "the man who stole all our documents," Draper built the most important historical archive of the mid-American frontier at the State Historical Society of Wisconsin, where he became director in his early forties, at about the time this was taken. *Courtesy State Historical Society of Wisconsin.*

A Boone carving along Boone's Creek in Carter County, Tennessee, dated 1760 and photographed about 1875, was apparently known as early as the 1770s and is the most famous of a great number of Boone carvings found in the most unlikely of places, including the Far West. Boone, in fact, always spelled his name with the final *e*, and the semiliterate "Boon" is a tip-off of bogus inscriptions. This caveat applies to this inscription as well, although at least it boasts a provenance dating to an era before Boone's fame made his name the currency of pranksters. *Courtesy Draper Papers, State Historical Society of Wisconsin.*

John Filson's *Map of Kentucke* (1784) was folded inside his guidebook and illustrates the pioneer perception of the West as a series of watercourses. It shows all the important sites of Boone's Kentucky adventures, including Boone's Trace (Virginia to Kentucke"), "Boonsburo," his residence on Marble Creek ("Col. Boon's"), the road to the Blue Licks, and the Indian towns across the Ohio. *Photograph courtesy The Filson Club, Louisville, Kentucky.*

View Along the Kentucky River, photographed circa 1910. At the top of such a cliff, Boone is said to have found himself surrounded by Indians during his first exploration of Kentucky. With no other means of escape, he makes a leap into the branches of a tall sugar maple. Such tales made good telling, and exist in numerous versions, not only for Boone, but for many other American pioneers as well. *Reproduced from* Artwork of the Bluegrass, *courtesy Special Collections University of Kentucky, Lexington.*

An early drawing of Boonesborough. One settler arriving there in 1775 found a few cabins along the bank of the Kentucky River, "not in a row, but scattering." The stockade and the corner blockhouses were not completed until 1778, and in its final form the fort was probably a good deal more irregular than it is depicted here. The woods in front of the fort were cut down to make way for cornfields, leaving a litter of stumps like those seen on the river side. *Reproduced from Lewis Collins and Richard H. Collins,* History of Kentucky *(Covington, Kentucky: Collins and Co., 1878). Courtesy The Filson Club, Louisville, Kentucky.*

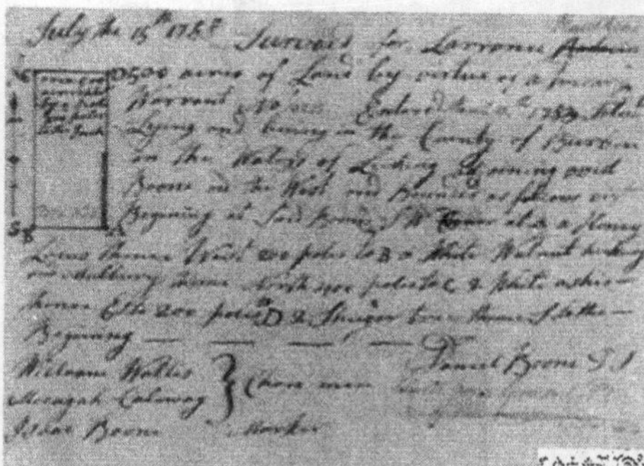

Boone's survey plat (1788) is typical of the many he executed in his own hand. Nathan Boone admitted that his father's "knowledge of surveying was limited," and that while he "could survey square or oblong bodies," he frequently got into trouble with anything much more complicated. *Courtesy Special Collections, University of Kentucky, Lexington.*

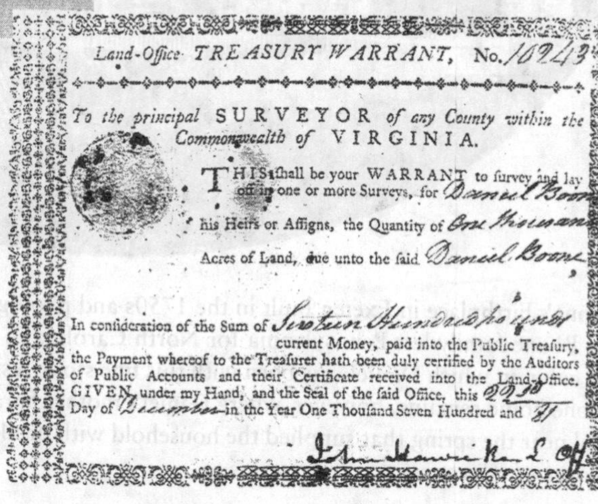

Land-Office TREASURY WARRANT, No. 10243

To the principal SURVEYOR *of any County within the Commonwealth of* VIRGINIA.

THIS shall be your WARRANT to survey and lay off in one or more Surveys, for Daniel Boone his Heirs or Assigns, the Quantity of One thousand Acres of Land, due unto the said Daniel Boone,

In consideration of the Sum of Sixteen Hundred pounds current Money, paid into the Public Treasury, the Payment whereof to the Treasurer hath been duly certified by the Auditors of Public Accounts and their Certificate received into the Land-Office. GIVEN under my Hand, and the Seal of the said Office, this 22nd Day of December in the Year One Thousand Seven Hundred and 81

"Treasury Warrant No. 10243" (1781), one of the Virginia warrants entitling the bearer to enter claims on Kentucky lands, in which Boone invested when he became a land speculator in the 1780s. Buying warrants was a lot like gambling, because if other claimants demonstrated prior rights, the claim was lost, and with it the entire investment. *Courtesy The Filson Club, Louisville, Kentucky.*

The home of George Boone in Exeter, Pennsylvania, built in the 1730s and photographed about 1890. George Boone was a local justice of the peace, and his stone house became the center of the neighborhood. He had a reputation for befriending passing Indians, offering them food and a place to rest, and here his grandson Daniel had his first opportunity to meet and talk to native Americans. *Courtesy Archibald Henderson Papers, North Carolina Collection, University of North Carolina at Chapel Hill.*

Boone's birthplace in Exeter, built in the 1750s and photographed about 1860. Sometime after the Boone family left Pennsylvania for North Carolina in 1750, the new owners replaced the log cabin in which Daniel was born with this fine stone residence. The original basement of the Boone home remains, however, where Daniel's mother Sarah Morgan kept her milk and butter cool near the spring that supplied the household with drinking water. *Courtesy State Historical Society of Wisconsin.*

The Boone cabin on Brushy Creek, Nicholas County, Kentucky, built in 1795 and photographed about 1935. Salvagers discovered this, the last of Boone's Kentucky homes, when they removed the clapboard siding from an abandoned house. Workers later dismantled and reconstructed it on private land east of U.S. 68, near where a state historical marker stands today. *Courtesy Special Collections, University of Kentucky, Lexington.*

The *First Stone Dwelling in Missouri*, in Femme Osage, Missouri, built in the 1810s and photographed about 1890. In 1820, Boone died in the small front bedroom on the right of the entrance of this house, built by his son Nathan. It evokes the stone dwellings of Boone's Pennsylvania birthplace. *Courtesy The Filson Club, Lexington, Kentucky.*

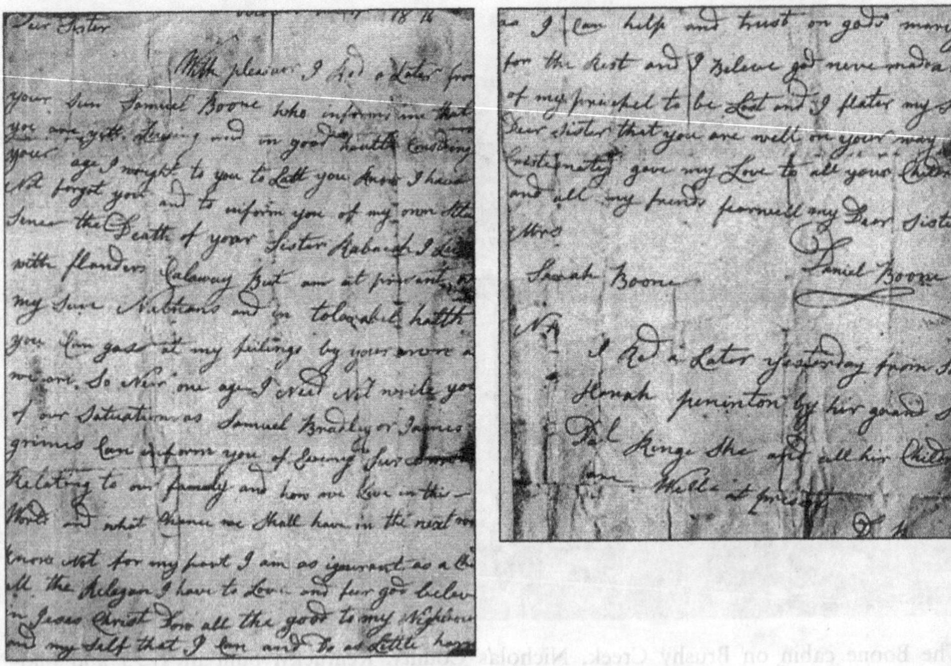

Deer Sister 1816

With pleasur I Red a Later from
your Son Samuel Boone who informs me that
you are yett Living and in good health Considring
your age I wright to you to Latt you know I have
Not forgot you and to inform you of my own Sta
Sence the Death of your Sister Rabacah I Liv
with flanders Calaway But am at present
my Sun Nathans and in tolarabel hallth
you Can gass at my feelings by your owne a
we are So Near one age I Need Not write yo
of our Satuation as Samuel Bradly or James
grimes Can inform you of Every thing
Relating to our family and how we Live in this
World and what Chance we Shall have in the next we
know Not for my part I am as ignerent as a Chi
all the Relegan I have to Love and fear god beleve
in Jesas Christ Don all the good to my Neighbour
and my Self that I Can and Do as Little harm
as I Can help and trust on gods marcy
for the Rest and I Beleve god neve made a
of my prisipel to be Lost and I flater my Se
Deer Sister that you are well on your way
Cristianaty gave my Love to all your Childre
and all my frends farwell my Dear Sister
Mrs
Sarah Boone Daniel Boone
NB
I Red a Later yesterday from Sa
Hanah peninton by hir grand So
Dal Ringe She and all hir Children
are Well at presant

Boone's letter to his sister-in-law Sarah Day Boone, October 19, 1816, in which he makes an expression of his religious views, is the final surviving piece of correspondence in Boone's own hand. Raised as a Quaker, Boone remained unchurched for the whole of his adult life. "I never knew any good to come of religious disputes," he once told a companion. But when questioned by a preacher about his faith, he replied that "I always loved God ever since I could recollect." *Courtesy Draper Collection, State Historical Society of Wisconsin.*

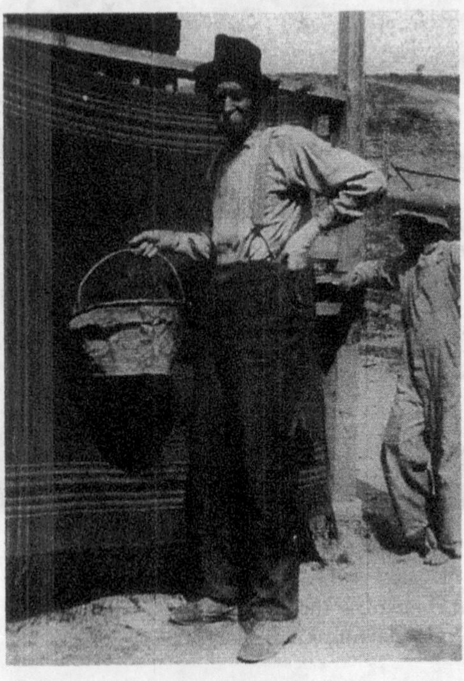

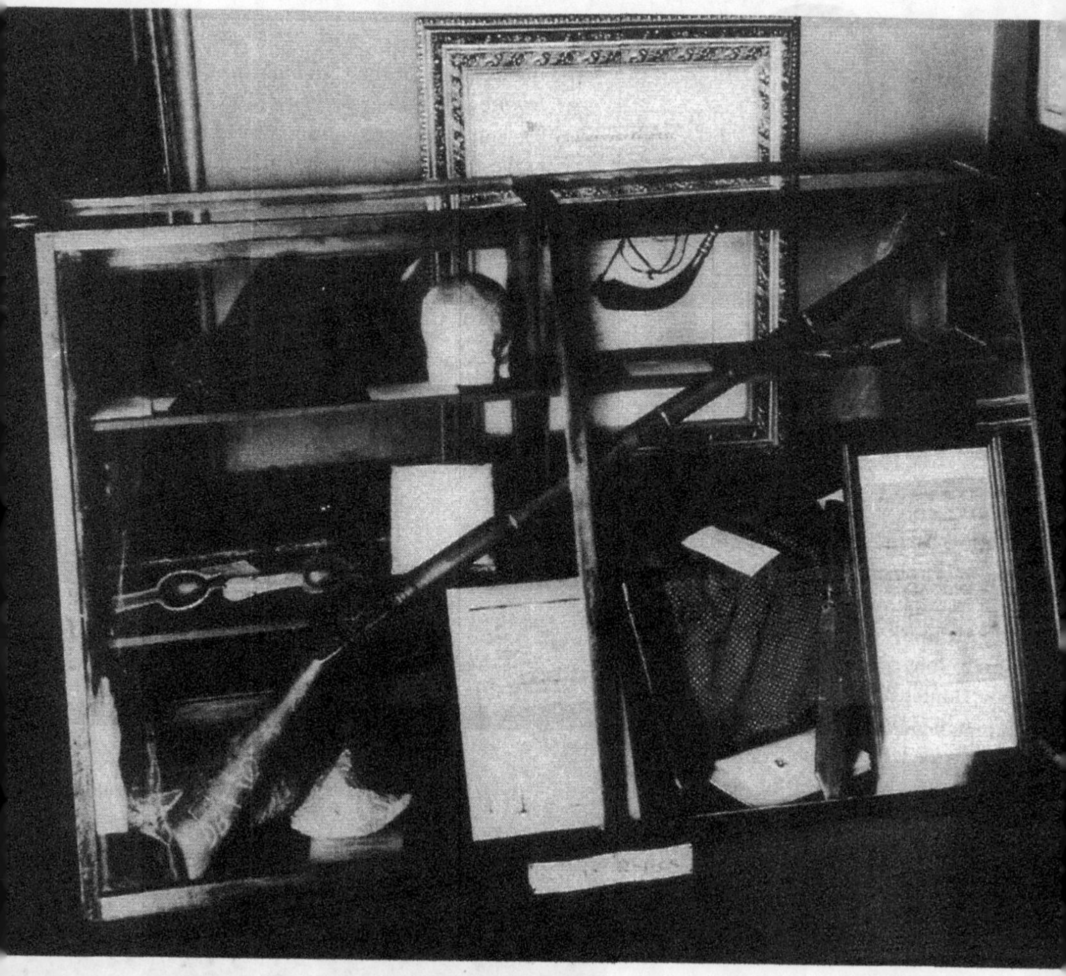

The *Display of Boone Relics in the Old Capitol* in Frankfort, Kentucky, photographed about 1930. In the case are what were reputed to be Boone's rifle (with carved notches), powder horn, and other artifacts and documents, including the plaster cast of his skull, made at the time of the Kentucky reburial in 1745. In their eagerness for a piece of the true cross, curators abandoned good sense, displaying artifacts of dubious origin and provenance. "If all the so called relicts of Boone were collected together it would take several rooms to hold them," wrote one level-headed researcher, "whereas, bear in mind, that Boone lived in a one-room cabin." *Courtesy Kentucky Historical Society Library, Frankfort.*

Opposite page: Residents of Tennessee proudly display their Boone relics for photographers about 1910. The kettle, unearthed by this farmer in Carter County, Tennessee, was inscribed with Boone's name. The willow basket, purchased from Boone descendants, was said to have been used during the emigration to Kentucky. The fascination with Boone relics was part of a new kind of historical commemoration of a vernacular past, contrasting with the formality of grand statues and monuments. *Courtesy Archibald Henderson Papers, North Carolina Collection, University of North Carolina at Chapel Hill.*

Ink sketches of the *Original Burial Stones of Daniel Boone and Rebecca Boone* (1955). After their bodies were disinterred and removed to Kentucky, these gravestones were left lying broken on the ground. Eventually they were saved by a descendant, who donated them to the museum at Central Methodist College in Fayette, Missouri, where Merril E. Gaddis of the history department made these sketches. *Courtesy Missouri Historical Society, St. Louis.*

The Boone-Bryan burying ground on Tuque Creek, Missouri, photographed about 1900, contains many unmarked graves, and controversy continues over whether it might include the remains of Daniel Boone as well. The lonely hillside overlooks land once farmed by Boone's children and his slaves, as well as the nearby village of Charette, where, during Boone's day, there lived a mixed population of Indians, French, and Americans. *Courtesy Missouri Historical Society, St. Louis.*

Daniel Boone's Grave, Frankfort Cemetery, photographed about 1950. This fifteen-foot monument was completed about 1860, just in time to be defaced by Union soldiers during the Civil War. Over the next fifty years souvenir seekers picked and chipped away at it until it was practically mutilated. After restoration in 1910, cemetery officials surrounded the monument with a substantial fence to protect it from Boone's adoring public. Beyond the grave can be seen the inspiring vista of the wooded hills and the Kentucky River gorge, with the state capital below. *Courtesy Kentucky Historical Society Library, Frankfort.*

with their fingers. Years later one of Boone's Shawnee friends told him of the Indians' reaction after he fled. "They all said let you go," he remembered, "that you would never get home, you would Starve to death." "But I told them," he asserted, "that you would get home, for you went as Straight as a leather String." According to tradition, Boone followed the Bullskin Trail, which led due south from the Scioto towns.

At the river he placed his precious store of ammunition and the broken gun atop a floating log, paddled into the current, and was carried a considerable distance downstream before collapsing in exhaustion on the Kentucky side. This late evening of the seventeenth of June marked the end of his four months in Shawnee captivity. He awoke the next morning with his feet throbbing, "scalded" by the desperate run he had made. But now feeling himself safe, he made a poultice of oak ooze to relieve the swelling, ate some of the venison jerky he had in his blanket pack, and rested for several hours more, putting the time to advantage by cutting down and shaping a small sapling with his knife and attaching it firmly to the rifle barrel with the hoppus strings of his pack. Rested, he began trotting downriver toward the trails that lead south to Boonesborough. It was "on June 19, 1778," he later testified, "being on run from the Indians who had me lately before in captivity, I came to a large open space of ground at the forks of three branches, waters of Johnson's Fork." Here his makeshift gun stock passed the test when he shot and butchered a buffalo. "You may depend upon it," he told a friend, "I felt proud of my rifle." After roasting some meat, he cut out the buffalo tongue and smoked it, intending it as a gift for his eight-year-old son, Daniel Morgan.

It was not until late the next day, June 20, that he crossed the Kentucky at the ford above Boonesborough and hailed the settlers from several hundred feet away. He had to be cautious, for with his head plucked he could not be distinguished easily from an Indian. "Bless your soul," pronounced one of the men as Boone came up, and others stood in stunned silence. The Boonesborough settlers gathered at the gate but offered no uproarious greeting. Quite the contrary, Boone found them sullen and suspicious; Andy Johnson's report of treachery had spread from Harrodsburg and infected Boonesborough. Looking about for a friendly face, Boone inquired after Rebecca and the family. "She put into the settlements long ago," someone answered, "packed up and was off to the old man's in Carolina." Boone went to the family cabin, which stood empty and hollow, to nurse his bitter disappointment. As he sat, the family cat, left behind when Rebecca moved back to North Carolina, suddenly reappeared and settled itself in his lap. Not long after, Boone's spirits lifted when Jemima, hearing of his return, burst into the cabin.

CHAPTER SIX

A Vast Expence of Blood and Treasure

1778 to 1784

"Capt. Boone has runaway from the Shawnese and arrived with abundance of news," a Kentuckian wrote home to Virginia. He had come to warn the settlement of impending attack, and despite the distrust and hostility with which his fellow settlers greeted him, Boone leapt to his assignment. He went to William Bailey Smith and the other leading men of Boonesborough to make his case. In order to save the settlement he had played an elaborate game of deception with the Shawnees and the British, he told them, and "he was now come home to help his own people fight." Let them think what they would, but "they must make what preperration they could," for "the indeans would certainly be their in a few Days." Boone's explanation did not resolve the doubts many had about him, but his argument was unassailable, and Smith placed the experienced frontiersman in charge of Boonesborough's preparations for battle. Boone organized the shoring up of defenses, had the men replace sections of the stockade that had rotted, strengthen the gate, and reinforce the two existing corner bastions and finally complete the other two, providing the fort's riflemen with a clear view of all of the walls. He had the women pool their provisions for the common subsistence of the fort, mold bullets, and prepare bandages. He ordered the area around the fort cleared of brush and continued the work in the cornfields, despite the fears that the Shawnees might appear at any minute and destroy the growing crops.

Smith sent messengers to Harrodsburg and Logan's for reinforcements, and soon ten or fifteen men arrived to reinforce the fort. "Arms and amunition were given to the Negro men," wrote a settler, and they were "stationed by the commanding officer in such a manner so as to make the best defense possible." Any "well-grown boy was furnished with a small rifle and shot pouch," another man remembered, "became a fort soldier, and had his port-hole assigned him." Black and white, young and old, Boonesborough could count a total of about sixty men at arms, defending perhaps another dozen adult women and twenty children. The Callaways and Boones were the two largest clans. William Hays had come back to Boonesborough after leaving Susannah with her mother in North Carolina, and soon afterward Squire Boone came back from Harrodsburg with his family, joining Jemima and her husband, Flanders Callaway, and Boone's nephew Daniel Wilcoxen and his wife, Sally. Dick and Elizabeth Callaway headed a group that included his grown sons Caleb and John and their wives, and married daughters Betsy and Fanny with their husbands, John Holder and Samuel Henderson. There were perhaps another ten families, some including uncles or half-grown boys who bore arms in the fort's defense, in addition to a large number of unattached men.

On July 17 some of the settlers heard the faint cry of a man calling for help from across the Kentucky River. Going over in the canoe, the sentries found the salt maker William Hancock, naked and bruised. He had escaped from Chillicothe and was so exhausted after his flight that he could not walk on his own power. It took a week of nursing before he was back on his feet, but he reported his news immediately. After Boone's escape, knowing that Boonesborough would now be preparing for their arrival, Blackfish and the Shawnees had sent a runner to Hamilton, asking for additional support. The governor dispatched Antoine Dagneaux de Quindre, a French Canadian lieutenant from Detroit leading a troop of militia, with arms and ammunition sufficient for an army of four hundred. Hancock had heard a rumor that the British had supplied the Indians with four swivel guns, small artillery pieces, "to batter down our fort." Hancock's Indian father, Captain Will, told him that Blackfish would still give the settlers a chance to surrender and join the British, but if the offer was rejected the Shawnees "intend to lie around our fort, and live on our stock, till they starve us out," then "kill all the men and take the women prisoners." Hancock became agitated when Captain Will told him of these plans and challenged the Shawnee right to plunder the American settlements. Pointing to Captain Will's mare in exasperation, he exclaimed, "Why you stole her from Boonesborough." But my son, Will responded with determination, "all the men and all the horses at Boonesborough belong to me." His answer echoed the comment he had directed to Boone in 1769, that all the animals in Kentucky belonged to the Shawnee.

So Hancock resolved to escape to warn Boonesborough, but, forewarned by his son's belligerence, Captain Will began to guard him more closely. At night he demanded Hancock's clothes and laid his own mat against the jamb of the cabin door to prevent any sneaking out. One night not long after, Will returned late from a war council, having drunk a little too much rum. "Wil-lum, Wil-lum," he called to his son in a loud whisper. Hancock was awake but played possum. "Wil-lum ne-pan," Will mumbled aloud—William's sleeping—and lying down next to the doorway, he too was soon sound asleep. Finally Hancock silently left his mat and, taking three pints of corn he had hidden away, succeeded in squeezing by his Indian father and fled stark naked into the spring night. He ran south down the Little Miami Trail and on the second day entered the swiftly flowing Ohio, clinging to a piece of driftwood, but was carried downstream some twenty miles and washed ashore in unfamiliar territory. He wandered for seven days more in Kentucky, with only the parched corn to sustain him, and finally collapsed of hunger and fatigue, "neaver to arise," he thought. Awakening some hours later, he looked up and, miraculously, saw a nearby tree with the name "Hancock" carved upon it. Realizing that he had been in this very spot hunting with his father and brother the previous fall, he regained his sense of direction. It was not more than four miles more to Boonesborough, and with great difficulty Hancock dragged himself to the Kentucky River.

An Indian army with British advisers and swivel guns! The prospect was daunting, and on July 18 Boone wrote to Virginia, requesting reinforcements. "Both French and Indians [are] coming against us to the number of near 400 which I expect here in 12 days from this," he wrote, and "if men can be sent to us in five or Six Weeks, it would be an infinite Service, as we shall lay up provisions for a Siege." He then hastened to sound a note of optimism in the face of this, the most serious threat yet to the Kentucky settlements. "We are all in fine Spirits, and have good Crops growing, and intends to fight hard in order to secure them." Two weeks later Boone's letter was in the hands of Arthur Campbell, commander of the Fincastle County Militia, and he forwarded it to the Virginia Executive Council, urging them to approve a plan to send a relief company of eighty men under Maj. Daniel Smith, which he could have ready by August 15. Virginia's "attention is too much engross'd with the affairs Eastwardly," Campbell wrote to William Fleming, and "don't feel for the miseries that happens on the Western frontier." Nevertheless, he refused to take action on his own and awaited authorization from his superiors. The council did not act positively on the request until August 12, and Campbell did not have their reply before the end of the month. It was early September by the time Smith and three companies of men left for Kentucky and over two months from the time of Boone's initial request before they arrived at Boonesborough.

Meanwhile, Boone had to prepare his people for the expected siege. He appointed scouts and lookouts and kept the men organized into companies. By August, with the corn harvest coming in, the lofts of the fort's cabins began to fill, but still there was no sign of Indians. From Detroit, British governor Hamilton noted that "the Shawanese have drawn together a considerable number of Warriors, by the last accounts their numbers amount to upwards of 400." But it was considerably more difficult to manage a large armed force than it was to launch war parties, and the Shawnee departure was delayed until the end of August, providing Boonesborough ample time to prepare its defense. The waiting confronted Boone with a different problem, however, for with Hancock's return, suspicions were revived about Boone's loyalty. "Boone when a prisoner promised to give up the fort to the Indians," Hancock muttered angrily, "promised every thing." Who knew what treachery might follow when the Shawnees arrived.

By the third week of August these rumors were threatening to seriously disrupt Boonesborough's defenses, and Boone decided he must take preemptive action. He proposed that they wait no longer, but in advance of the siege should mount a raid on the Shawnees in their own homes. He knew of an undefended village on Paint Creek, a tributary of the Scioto, "not far over the Ohio," he told the men, "and if a few men would go with him he would conduct them to this little Camp, and as these indians was rich in good horses and beaver fur, they could go and make a great speck and Git back in good time to oppose the big army of Indians." Thirty men volunteered for this mission, conceived in the spirit of Andy Johnson's horse raid of earlier in the year. To some of Boonesborough's leading men, however, Boone's plan seemed pure madness. "Richard Calliway apposed the plan with all his might," wrote the settler Daniel Trabue, "but they went." Boone's biographers have been hard pressed to defend his action, which depleted the armed defense of the fort by half. By this raid he sought, they suggest, to further delay the Shawnee expedition, or perhaps to gain additional intelligence of the Indians' plans. But while such goals may have provided some motivation, what most attracted the men was the prospect of "a great speck." Backcountry settlers, much like the Indians, followed "big men," warrior chiefs whose prestige and authority rested on their ability to provide honor, adventure, and plunder for their followers.

They set out on August 30, but the next day while hunting for provisions at the Blue Licks about a third of the men, mostly those with families, had second thoughts about the expedition and turned back. With eighteen young fighters Boone went ahead and crossed to "the Indian Shore" at the mouth of Cabin Creek on the Ohio. They "painted their faces, assumed the disguise of savages," and advanced on the Indian towns of the Scioto Valley. Simon Kenton, scouting in the lead, came unexpectedly upon two Shawnees and brought a whole war party down upon himself. Hearing the shots, the other Americans rode up furiously, and Boone found his opportunity to lead the men in a stiff skirmish, proving his valor and offering a reminder of his loyalties. They drove off the Indians and stole several horses. Kenton again went forward to spy and returned with the news that the village on Paint Creek was vacant of warriors and horses. The Shawnees must be on their way to Boonesborough, Boone concluded, and turned his men back south. The Paint Creek raid had yielded little plunder, but Boone had begun to repair his reputation among the most volatile group of Boonesborough's men. A report of the raid, printed in October in a Virginia newspaper, captured its spirit. "Captain Boone, the famous partisan," it announced, "has lately crossed the Ohio with a small detachment of men, and near the Shawanese towns repulsed a party of the enemy, and brought in one scalp, without any loss on his side." The Paint Creek raid was a dangerous and opportunistic episode in Boone's career.

That danger was soon made obvious, for returning to the Ohio crossing, Boone discovered that Blackfish and the Indian army of four hundred, mostly Shawnees but including warriors from a variety of tribes, and supported by de Quindre and his company of Detroit militia, already had ferried across and now were deployed between the raiders and the fort. The Indians had been unable to obtain artillery from Hamilton but were fully supplied with ammunition and explosives sufficient for a long siege, and they now moved slowly down the Warrior's Path toward Boonesborough. Boone and his men recrossed the Ohio, and by avoiding the main trails, moving through unbroken country where the thick woods made travel almost impossible, they bypassed the Shawnees. On Sunday evening, September 6, Boone and his men rode into the fort with the news that the Shawnee siege of Boonesborough would begin the next day.

Monday, September 7, 1778, dawned clear and warm. People arose anxiously but, finding the plain before the fort empty, women went out to the spring and boys watered the stock at the river as usual. Boone and several men patrolled the periphery of the settlement, watching for the approach of the Indians. The army appeared in midmorning, coming down Hackberry Ridge. Blackfish and the Shawnees had camped the night before on the north side of the Kentucky, then crossed about a half mile below the fort at a place known thereafter as Blackfish Ford. Climbing the steep southern bank, they passed to the rear of the ridge, marched along its base until opposite the fort, then came across the hill and through the cover of trees to just beyond a rifle shot. Boone saw them first and, hustling back to the stockade, yelled a warning to his nephews, Squire's boys Moses and Isaiah, who had been watering some horses. The boys too had seen the Indians, but, thinking they were the expected reinforcements from Virginia, had begun to ride out to meet them. Now they galloped into the fort, followed by Boone and the other scouts, who closed and barred the gate.

As the Americans watched from behind the log walls, the Indians emerged from the timber in what seemed an endless single file and assembled on the meadow, three hundred yards away. The Detroit militia followed them in, their colorful uniforms and flags contrasting with the nakedness of the Indians. The Shawnees quickly constructed a small arbor in a peach orchard where the chiefs established their headquarters. Within thirty minutes a figure was seen coming forward under a flag of truce to within 150 yards of the fort. It was Pompey, the black interpreter. Climbing onto a cornfield fence, he called for Captain Boone. Boone hailed back his presence. Chief Blackfish had come to accept the surrender of the Long Knife fort on the Kentucky, Pompey hollered, and he expected Boone to keep his promise. He had letters from Governor Hamilton promising safe conduct to Detroit for everyone. The leading men of the settlement clustered about Boone. Ask to see the letters, they demanded, but before Boone could answer, another voice was heard from the Indian camp. "Sheltowee, Sheltowee." It was Blackfish calling for his son. Your father wants you, Pompey explained. He would meet Blackfish, Boone yelled back, at a point some sixty yards in front of the gate, well within the range of the fort's riflemen.

Boone boldly walked out, "as freely and readily as I would go to my yard fence," remembered John Gass, a mere boy at the time. Slowly Blackfish and several other leaders, including Moluntha, a chief of all the Shawnees, came from the Indian arbor to meet him. "Howdy, my son," said Blackfish, extending his arm. "Howdy, Father," Boone replied, shaking his hand firmly. They sat together on a blanket while several Indian boys shaded and fanned them with leafy branches. Watching this friendly encounter, Gass recalled, "every one in the fort was then sure that Boon was gone." In the words of another witness, many people "thought very strange of Boons conduct," and rumors flew "that he intended to surrender the fort." Suspicions died hard, and the moment of truth was at hand. Blackfish first turned to personal matters, communicating directly with Boone in Shawnee, without benefit of translation. It was an emotional confrontation. "My son, what made you run away from me?" he asked, his tears flowing freely. "Because I wanted to see my wife and children," Boone offered. "Well, if you'd asked me," his Indian father responded, "I'd have let you come." Before Boone could argue with this, Chief Moluntha, who had always treated him with kindness, intervened angrily in the conversation. "You killed my son the other day over the Ohio river," he accused. Boone was caught off guard. "No, I have not been there," he lied. "It was you," Moluntha declared with icy assurance. "I tracked you here to this place." Sheltowee was being shamed by his elders.

But before much more could be made of this, the discussion turned to official matters and Pompey began to translate. Blackfish reminded Boone of the promises he had made and handed over a letter from Hamilton, addressed to him. This letter has not survived, but it apparently made reference to Boone's agreement to surrender the fort and promised pardon and safe conveyance to Detroit for all of the settlers. The British would honor claims for lost property and maintain officers at rank if they joined the British service. Should the Americans resist, however, the governor could not be held responsible for the resulting bloodshed. Blackfish then passed Boone a wampum belt, a missive from the Shawnees themselves. These are our options, he told Boone, pointing to the belt. At one end was Detroit, at the other end Boonesborough. The rows of colored beads represented the paths connecting them, and it was for Boone to decide which they would walk together. The red, said Blackfish, was the warpath the Indians had come along, the white was the path they could take together back to Detroit, and the black "showed they would be put to death if they did not surrender."

There was much to consider in these papers and his belt, Boone finally replied. But "he had been gone so long, there were other officers in his place," and he must consult with them. Of course, Blackfish said, he understood about such things; in warrior societies leadership shifts with shifting reputations. In the meantime, he said, his people were hungry. Knowing that the Indians would take what they wanted anyway, Boone graciously offered them the use of the settlement's cattle and corn. I have brought a gift for your women, Blackfish responded, and one of his men presented Boone with seven smoked buffalo tongues. Thus doing what they could to honor their relationship, the two men parted after smoking together, and Boone returned to the fort. Some of the settlers feared that the tongues might be poisoned, but Boone scoffed at the notion that the Shawnees would do such a thing, and he pronounced them delicious.

Inside, the men of Boonesborough held a council to consider their choices. Reading the letter from Hamilton, Dick Callaway immediately fixed on it as further evidence of Boone's treason. Boone once again explained that his actions had all been "policy," but he refused to let Callaway's intervention deter the leaders from a careful deliberation of the offer. There was "a powerful army before our walls," Filson quoted Boone as saying, "whose appearance proclaimed inevitable death, fearfully painted, and marking their footsteps with desolation." A struggle against the Shawnees would be difficult, and victory by no means was assured. On the other hand, Boone thought there was a chance that "they could make a good peace." Young John Gass's impression was that uppermost in Boone's mind was making sure he would be "free from blame should they [choose to] hold on and the Indians overcome them." Samuel South, also a boy at the time, testified that there was a great difference of opinion within the fort, "half of the men willing to surrender, and the other half ready to fight and die," but all "were willing to risk the getting of a treaty, and to get it thro' any means, if it could be gotten." Boone asked that those favoring surrender "turn out," or speak up. At this suggestion Callaway "swore he would kill the first man who proposed surrender," effectively ending that discussion. Asked his opinion, Billy Smith, second in command, advised that they "refuse the offer and defend the fort." Then Squire Boone spoke up, saying "he would never give up, but would fight till death." The men then voted unanimously for resistance. "Well, well," Boone said after the vote, "I'll die with the rest."

But it still made sense to stall for time, for every hour of delay, they hoped, brought closer the arrival of reinforcements from

Virginia. The men appointed Boone and Smith to parley again with Blackfish, and Boone called to Pompey from the fort to arrange a meeting for the late afternoon. Smith dressed in his best military uniform, with scarlet coat and plumed macaroni hat, and the two Americans and the Shawnee chiefs sat down together on a panther skin spread on the grass before the fort. What did they think of the letter and belt? Blackfish asked after formal introductions and smoking. It was indeed a kind offer, said Smith graciously, but such a remove would be difficult for their women and children. "I have brought forty horses and mares for the old people and women and children to ride," Blackfish responded. "I am come to take you away easy." That was good, Boone told him, but there were many chiefs in the fort and it would take more time to fully consider the offer. Blackfish agreed to another day of discussions, but Boone thought he saw a cold determination in his Indian father's eyes. Both sides now agreed to rules governing their behavior during the interim. Indians would not come within thirty yards of the fort, and colonists would not inaugurate fire or come out of the gates armed. The women would be allowed to go to the spring for water, and the Indians would use, but not wantonly destroy, the settlers' cattle and crops. Despite the ease with which they agreed to these arrangements, Boone left convinced that this would be the last delay. They had better put this day to good use, Boone told Smith as they returned to the fort, for "they wouldn't be safe to go back any more."

All that day and the next the Americans spent preparing for the siege that was about to begin. Riflemen were posted conspicuously along the fort's parapet, and women dressed in men's hats and coats paraded before the open gate to create the illusion of greater strength. An American captive had falsely reported to Hamilton that the forts in Kentucky had been reinforced with over two hundred Virginia militia; this misinformation caused the Indians to overestimate the strength of Boonesborough's defenses. Some of the men set to work digging a well, long uncompleted, within the stockade, and brave women made numerous trips to the spring in the hollow, filling every vessel they could find with water. The Indians did not interfere with them but watched attentively, some of them calling out that these women looked like "fine squaws."

About midday on Tuesday, Pompey came up with a request: Blackfish and his warriors wished to see Boone's squaws. No, Boone hollered back, since the kidnapping of his daughter they were very much afraid of the Indians. You only need to bring them to the gate, Pompey called back, they all had heard so much of Boone's pretty daughter that they wanted very much to look her over. To humor them and keep up the delay, Boone decided to comply, and, accompanied by several riflemen, Jemima and one or two other women stepped in front of the open gate. From a hundred feet away, Blackfish and Pompey stood with a small group of warriors, looking on. Let down your hair, Pompey called, speaking for the Indians. "They took out their Combs," Jemima's daughter wrote, and "let their hair flow over their Shoulders." The Indians finally departed, nodding to each other with pleasure. None of the Indian conduct during this strange exhibition seemed to cause much of a stir among the men of the fort, but they harbored a great deal of bad feeling about the presence of Pompey. He had an officious manner, which he undoubtedly calculated to infuriate the Americans, who expected and demanded blacks to display a slavish demeanor. When they next saw him near the fort, some of the men yelled at him that if he came any nearer, they'd kill him, and they swore to one another that if he approached again they would shoot him and let the fight commence, agreement be damned.

Finally, toward evening, Pompey called from a distance to say that the time had come for Boone to meet again with Blackfish about the surrender. Boone, Smith, and a number of other leaders left the fort, expecting the worst. "The people have determined to resist surrender as long as there was a man living," Boone declared to the Indians. Blackfish seemed stunned by this reply. For this news he was unprepared, he told Boone after a pause, and now found himself in a tight spot, for in spite of what Hamilton had suggested in his letter, he had ordered the Shawnees to avoid a massacre. Let us negotiate further, Blackfish proposed, in a treaty session that would include the chiefs of all of the Shawnee towns. This offer of continued discussions was "contrary to our expectations," Boone told Filson, but "sounded grateful in our ears; and we agreed to the proposal." Likewise, Boone told Blackfish, they must include all of the chiefs from the fort. The parties separated, agreeing to meet again the following day.

During Boone's captivity, George Rogers Clark, commanding a force of Americans, had undertaken an offensive campaign by setting out for the Illinois country and, in a brilliant maneuver, captured the French towns there in July. It was "hearing that the Indians gladly treated with you at the Illinois," John Bowman explained to Clark following the siege of Boonesborough, that encouraged the settlers "to think the Indians were sincere" in this offer to negotiate. With hindsight, William Bailey Smith later wrote that he had "placed no confidence in the negotiations," and "considered all this a mere deception," and Boone indicated to his children that even after Blackfish's offer of further negotiations, he had continued to believe that the American rejection of the original surrender terms had doomed the chance to avoid conflict. Nevertheless, it seems that the Americans entered into the negotiations with a mixture of hope and skepticism. As for the Shawnees, there were certainly men among them who longed for the opportunity to take scalps and avenge their dead, to burn Boonesborough and drive the Americans from the country. But for most, war was designed not to annihilate, for it was clear to them that they would have to deal with the Americans again, but rather was necessary in order to force an accommodation in which both sides accepted the Ohio as a boundary. Blackfish's principal concern was balancing the views of these factions.

The women of Boonesborough spent the morning of Wednesday, September 9, preparing a meal of venison and buffalo tongue, green corn and garden vegetables, cheese, milk, and bread. The treaty session was to begin with a meal for the Indians, and one of the objects of the settlers was to convince the Shawnees and their British allies that the fort had sufficient supplies to withstand a prolonged siege. The men carried out tables and chairs and set them with their wives' pewter ware. After the Shawnee chiefs and their retinue had consumed the food with relish, everything was taken back inside. Then the Americans walked ceremoniously to the meeting ground, in the shade of the great elm near the sycamore hollow. In addition to Boone the delegation included William Bailey Smith, Richard Callaway, Squire Boone, Flanders Callaway, Isaac Crabtree, William Buchanan, Edward Bradley, and John South, all leading men of the settlement. Boone had stationed riflemen in the bastions, where they had an unobstructed line of fire, and ordered them to take "well directed aim at the enemy," and at the first sign of trouble "to shoot without one moment's delay." Do not hesitate for fear of hurting your own people, Boone instructed them, because "as Indians were more numerous, they were most likely to be hit."

At the conclusion of the formal introductions, Boone objected to the many Indians on the grounds. "These are not chiefs," he said, pointing out a number of warriors, and Blackfish ordered them away, but that still left the Shawnees outnumbering the Americans by two to one. One of the Americans, and perhaps one of the Detroit militiamen as well, kept a record of the proceedings and wrote a summary document at their conclusion, but because the negotiations ended in violence this written record was lost, and only vague hints survive of the substance of these discussions. Blackfish apparently began by putting forth a proposal that he withdraw his army in return for the settlers' agreement to leave Kentucky within six weeks. This the Americans rejected out of hand, and Blackfish grew angry. Boone later recalled a portion of the conversation that followed: Blackfish demanded to know "by what right had the white people taken possession of this country." Boone, who had been at the Sycamore Shoals treaty, responded that "they had purchased by Dick Henderson of the Cherokee Indians." Blackfish turned and consulted with his delegation, which included a Cherokee ambassador. "Did your people sell this country to the whites?" Boone heard him inquire. Yes, the man answered, he thought they had. After further discussions with his chiefs, Blackfish turned back to the Americans. "Well," he declared somewhat disingenuously, "if that was the case, his claim was no better than that of the white man, [and] they must live in peace."

At this point Blackfish made a second proposal, the terms of which have been shrouded in mystery ever since. Smith, as well as a number of other contemporaries, said that the Shawnee chief proposed that both sides agree to recognize the Ohio as a boundary between them, and that after a period of disengagement, both be free to cross the river to hunt and trade. There seems, however, to have been another essential provision that Smith failed to mention. In his conversations with Boone during his last years, the Baptist minister John Mason Peck learned that this understanding was to be secured by the Americans promising "allegiance to the King of Great Britain."

It would have been a tenuous agreement for both sides. Blackfish had led this army south by promising the militant young warriors that they would force an American surrender, taking many scalps and captives. The terms of this proposal meant that these militants would have to settle for a good deal less. Among the Americans there were also grave suspicions of bad faith on the other side. But had they simply been stalling for time, they could have gained a full six weeks by agreeing to Blackfish's first offer of their withdrawal from the country. While doubting that the terms of his second proposal would be kept, the Americans nevertheless seemed to believe that, unlike the first offer, this one contained conditions with which they could live. It is not necessary to believe that the Boonesborough defenders were ready to become Loyalists; they seemed willing to play a shell game with the Indians similar to the one Boone himself had played at Chillicothe. "It was deemed best to carry out the treaty," said Boone's nephew Moses, "hoping it might end well." Although "we could not avoid suspicions of the savages," as Boone told Filson, "the articles were formally agreed to and signed" with a good deal of ceremony. This agreement would be a dead letter practically before the ink was dry on the parchment, but it is important for what it suggests about the things both sides were willing to give up in order to forgo war.

Only one more thing remained, Blackfish told the Americans: he must "give out the big talk, that all his young men around might know that a firm peace was made." Indeed, he had a good deal of explaining to do. Addressing the army of Indians assembled in the distance, in a voice that one observer described as sounding like that of a frontier preacher, Blackfish gave a lengthy formal speech in Shawnee. Boone had difficulty following all of it, but none of what he understood alarmed him. Then Blackfish turned to the Americans and said a few more words, which Pompey translated. "Brothers! We have made a long and lasting treaty, and now we will shake long hands." Extending both arms, he walked toward his son Sheltowee, and the other chiefs in turn each moved toward the Americans.

What happened during the next few moments ended all hope of

an agreement. Each American was surrounded by at least two Shawnees. It suddenly became clear, Boone said, that "their policy was to take us prisoners." According to this view, having failed to win the surrender of the fort, Blackfish now sought to capture its leaders, in order to achieve his goal by extortion. This traditional interpretation, however, fails to adequately explain why the Shawnees had not resorted to violence earlier, when the Americans had first rejected Hamilton's offer, before the complicated negotiations that had just taken so much effort. After the fact, of course, it was easy for the Americans to believe in Indian duplicity, and what happened on the treaty grounds convinced all of the people within the fort, who previously had been divided in their views, that resistance was their only option. But there is little hard evidence to suggest that this assault was premeditated. Both sides were rightly suspicious of the other, and Blackfish had hidden marksmen in the sycamore hollow, just as Boone had placed them in the fort's bastions, all of whom stood ready to fire at the first sign of trouble. That sign may have been given by the highly volatile Richard Callaway, who immediately began to struggle with the chiefs who attempted to embrace him. "Calleway was the first that Jurked away from them," wrote Daniel Trabue, and as that struggle began, American riflemen from the bastion, and perhaps Indian riflemen from the hollow as well, began to fire.

It suddenly made little difference whether there had been a plan to take the Americans captive or not, for with the firing, a general melee erupted. Blackfish grappled with Boone and was thrown to the ground. A nearby warrior who had been carrying the calumet from man to man swung at Boone with the pipe, catching him in the back and opening a large gash. Each of the other Americans, all of them large men, succeeded in breaking free from the Indians' grip. When later asked how it was possible for them to overpower twice their number, Flanders Callaway confessed that the entire event was a blur in his memory and he simply could not explain how they achieved the feat. Boone believed that it was the marksmanship from the fort that saved them; several of the Indians seem to have been hit in the first volley. Moreover, when the Shawnees saw Blackfish on the ground, many believed that he had been shot, and concern for his welfare momentarily stalled their effort to hold the Americans. "They had a dredfull skuffil," in the words of Trabue, "but our men all got to the fort safe." Squire Boone was shot, a ball lodging in his shoulder and knocking him down, but he quickly jumped up and scrambled inside the gate. The siege of Boonesborough now began.

The Americans had escaped amid a hail of fire from both sides. In the bastion, one rifleman had trained his sights on a chief "well ornamented with half-moons and brooches," thinking to himself "what a fine mark he would make." He heard a gun go off, pulled his trigger, and the Indian fell dead. Another American was stretched full length on the upper ledge of the bastion, aiming his rifle, and at the first fire he was peppered with a dozen shots and tumbled down. Surely he was dead, thought his comrades as they ran to him, but though they found "fourteen bullet holes were shot through his clothes," said John Gass, "his skin was not broke," and he returned to the fight. Some of the Shawnees had taken up positions on the hillside across the river and enjoyed an unobstructed line of fire down into the fort.

The children of Boonesborough long remembered the first terrifying moments of battle—the deafening gunfire, the fierce whooping on both sides, the barking and baying of the dogs, and the panic of the cattle, horses, and other livestock as they raced around the interior of the fort in wild abandon, the storm of dust they raised mixing with the acrid smoke of exploded powder. "The women cried and screamed," remembered ten-year-old Moses Boone, "expecting the fort would be stormed." Early in the fight the Shawnees rushed the gate in waves, intent on battering it down, but fire from the marksmen in the bastions forced them back. Most of the women and children huddled in a cabin in the center of the compound, where little Kezia Callaway, a girl of eight or nine, remembered their "utmost confusion." Her mother, Elizabeth Callaway, found a man cowering under the bed and, grabbing a broom, chased him outside, hollering at him to get with the other men. "I was not made for a fighter," he cried in protest and jumped into the half-completed well, where he hid through the first barrage.

After the Americans beat back the Shawnee charge there came a lull in the fighting, and Boone made a round of the positions. He found his brother Squire in agony. Squire's wife had quickly looked over his wound and pronounced it only a graze. "She was always his doctor," said her son Moses, "he never had any other," and as always, he accepted Jane's judgment without question. But the wound continued to burn and upon further examination Boone found the bullet lodged in the bone, and its removal required a deep incision. The wound was serious enough for the men to carry Squire to his bed, where he remained for a day or so. But the crusty fighter insisted that his son bring him an ax, which he kept at his side, saying he would use it should the Indians scale the walls.

Jemima Boone also was wounded early in the fighting. She was among the men, loading guns, carrying ammunition, and running back and forth for food and water, exposing herself to the constant fire from the hill across the river. As she entered a doorway she thought she felt someone slap her backside, but, spinning around, she realized she had been hit. Luckily the bullet was spent and had buried itself superficially in her flesh, not even penetrating the fabric of her linen petticoat. She tugged at her clothes and the ball fell out. It became clear that it was not safe to move about the yard or between the cabins, and the first night of the siege the men chopped openings in the connecting cabin walls so that people could get around without being exposed to fire. Many of the cattle and horses were shot and killed during the siege, however, and men and women were kept busy butchering their carcasses to supply the fort with fresh meat.

The firing ended with nightfall of the first day but began again on Thursday morning, and there was more or less steady firing throughout that second day, with little obvious advantage for either side. This raised the spirits of the Americans, however, for no artillery had appeared and yet they had been able to hold back the Indian charge. The Shawnees needed a way to breach the stockade walls. That evening, under cover of darkness, they set fire to a store of flax that was drying next to the stockade wall. Seeing the blaze, John Holder slipped outside the gate and dashed water on the fire, then scampered back inside with bullets striking all around him. Holder enjoyed renown as a cursing man, one of those "habitual swearers," said historian John Dabney Shane, who "think no sentence smooth and euphonious, which is not filled up in their style." Throughout this episode, as Holder risked his life, he cast forth loud and creative curses at the Indians in his thundering voice, which everyone in the fort heard. When he was finally back inside, panting and still profaning, his mother-in-law, the irrepressible Mrs. Callaway, scolded him for his language, saying, "It would be more becoming to pray than to swear." "I've no time to pray, goddammit," he shot back. It was a moment remembered by many.

On Friday morning Boone cautioned the men to target their fire more carefully, for they could ill afford to waste ammunition. The fire from both sides now slackened, and in the absence of the din of the previous two days the settlers gradually became aware of another sound, of digging and chopping. Looking out, they saw no activity in the Shawnee encampment that could account for the noise. Someone finally noticed a muddy stain in the river issuing from a spot on the bank some sixty yards from the rear wall of the fort. The Kentucky was at low water, exposing steep banks some ten feet high and a pebble beach fifteen or twenty feet wide. Although from the fort no one could actually see what was causing the discharge of mud, it became clear that the Indians were excavating the bank, beginning the construction of a tunnel to undermine the fort. The prospect of the Indians coming in under the walls terrorized the people inside.

That night, the Shawnees set up the most intense barrage of gunfire thus far, intended as a cover for attempts to set fire to the fort. Warriors came running forward by twos and threes, armed with blazing torches made of shell-bark hickory rubbed with black powder, and hurled them into the fort. It was a frightening sight but actually rather ineffective. The runners made excellent targets, the mortality rate among them was high, and most of their torches fell harmlessly into the interior yard. Some did land on the cabin roofs, but, using long poles, the women were able to rip off most of the burning shingles. Squire Boone improvised squirt guns, made from old rifle barrels, that also were effective against the small fires. Squire seems to have been an ingenious inventor; some people also remembered his manufacture of an improbable wooden cannon, two sections of a black gum tree banded together with iron strips from a wagon wheel, which he fired at a group of charging Shawnees. The first blast frightened the Indians considerably, but a second burst the contraption wide open, nearly causing a disastrous explosion. "Why don't you fire your damned cannon again," the Indians jeered.

The Shawnee tactics this night did succeed, however, in claiming the first American fatality of the siege. A small fence that adjoined the back wall of one of the cabins was set afire, and, fearing that it would burn through, several men dug under the cabin floor, and London, a slave whose master was away from the settlement, squeezed out and succeeded in pushing the blazing timbers away with a forked stick. As he lay in the dark outside the fort, London saw a Shawnee warrior hidden nearby behind a tree stump. He whispered to the men behind him to pass up a loaded gun, took aim, and pulled the trigger; the lock snapped, failing to ignite the powder, and the warrior jerked toward the well-known sound, peering into the darkness without making out the shooter. London cocked and pulled again, and this time the powder in the pan flashed, but the gun failed to fire. Now the Indian saw his attacker clearly, illuminated by the burst of powder, and shot him dead. Such failings of weapons were among the common dangers of battle, when haste prevented the necessary precautions in loading and cleaning. Later, appealing for compensation for the loss of "so valuable a slave," London's master wrote the Virginia authorities that "if the said Negro had been suffered to remain within his cabin, he could not have been hurt," but his petition was scornfully rejected.

The Shawnees pressed the siege for another week, each night attempting to fire the fort, each day working at the tunnel. The marksmanship of the riflemen continued to be an effective defense against the first tactic, but the defenders felt powerless against the threat of the mining. Finally Boone set a company to work digging a trench along the interior rear wall of the fort, which at least gave them a sense of taking countermeasures. As the trench deepened, the men could hear the sound of digging gradually growing louder. At least when the Indians break through, said Boone, we'll be ready for them. Frustrated by their inability to fire on the Indian diggers hidden behind the riverbank, a number of men began hurling the stones that they were excavating over the fort wall in a great arc, hoping that some would fall on the heads of the enemy. The Indians were soon heard cursing. "Come out and fight like men," one of them cried up from the river, "and not try to kill with stones, like children." An old woman, carrying water to the diggers in the fort, heard their cry. "For God's sake, don't throw stones," she implored, "it might hurt some of the Indians and they will be mad and take revenge." The men burst out in cynical laughter and began tossing rocks over the wall by the dozens, chanting, "Don't throw stones! Don't throw stones!"

The shooting now became more deliberate and was accompanied by a continual exchange of insults, a practice the Americans called "blackguarding." "What are you doing down there," the riflemen in the bastion yelled to the men toiling at the riverbank. "Digging a hole to blow you all to hell before morning, may be so!" an Indian answered back. "Dig on," the American hollered, "we'll dig and meet you, make a hole to bury you yellow sons of bitches." Vulgar gibes were tossed back and forth, although nineteenth-century decorum kept even the best of collectors from recording much of this language. One salty-tongued Kentuckian informant, reviewing the notes that one antiquarian had taken during his interview, protested the absence of the profanity, arguing that the story simply couldn't be told "without these necessary ornaments." The interviewer, however, defended the expurgation, maintaining that the swearing was "repugnant to good taste, and renders the narrative obnoxious to persons of refined and Christian feeling." For the most part, imagination must supply the language the two sides used in the verbal exchanges during the siege.

One Boonesborough resident told of a young Shawnee warrior, well out of rifle range, who "climbed a tree and showed his prankes," or in the words of another, "turned the insulting part of his body to the besieged and defiantly patted it." Such affronts formed a steady part of the daily routine, but this particular display was so infuriating, so the tale was told, that a rifleman in one of the bastions loaded a large-bore rifle with a heavy charge of powder, steadied his piece on the porthole, and let go with a blast that exploded into the prankster's backside and brought him down, despite a distance said to be about a quarter mile. Although an expert on the American long rifle has written that "at any considerable distance beyond 300 yards" accuracy was "in a great measure a matter of chance," the tale of "the long shot," sometimes attributed to Boone himself, became an essential part of the Boonesborough legend. "In all his best days," wrote one of Boone's more skeptical nineteenth-century biographers, "Leather Stocking never surpassed this."

In the exchange of sniper fire Boone received a glancing shot in the upper shoulder as he ran across the yard of the fort. When Jemima unwound the ever-present stock cloth from her father's neck, blood spurted out and she was badly frightened, but it looked worse than it was, proving to be only a superficial wound. She bandaged Boone and persuaded him to lie quietly for awhile. Missing the well-known voice of the fort's commander directing the defense, the Shawnee marksmen who had seen him hit called out, "We've killed Boone, we've killed Boone." Unable to resist their taunts, Boone rose from his bed and made his way to the parapet. "No you haven't," he yelled back, "I'm here ready for you yellow rascals." This was precisely the purpose of the taunts, to so anger a man that he answered back with voice or fire, thus exposing his position. Waiting until a defender shot through one of the embrasures of the fort, the Shawnees would then take aim at the cloud of white smoke and hope to hit the rifleman who might still be peering through the haze to determine the results of his own fire. The second of the Boonesborough fatalities occurred in this way, a man's forehead smashed by a well-directed bullet. He lived for several hours afterward, hunched against the log wall with his head in his hands, rocking back and forth as his life oozed out of the bloody fissure in his skull, his wife with her arms about him, in a half-crazed prayer thanking God "dat de ball didn't hit 'im in de eye."

Pompey, who took a special pleasure in infuriating the Americans, was one of the most active participants in the blackguarding. He challenged their courage and manhood and dared them to come out and fight or else surrender. But he got carelessly carried away with the game, popping up from the bank of the river to hurl repeated insults and fire his gun toward the fort. The men in the bastions answered in kind with words and fire, while others took aim at different spots along the bank where Pompey might next appear. Unable to resist another retort, he jumped up one time too many and took a shot square in the face. The Americans did not see him after that, and they jeered down at the Shawnees, "Where's Pompey?" "Pompey ne-pan," the Indians at first replied—Pompey's sleeping—but the torment continued until one of them finally put an end to the banter by calling back, "Pompey ne-poo"—Pompey's dead. The marksmanship of the Americans gradually took its toll on the Indian "pranks," and the blackguarding finally ceased.

The settlers had been shut up for eleven days when on the night of Thursday, September 17, the Shawnees launched what proved to be their final assault. The intense firing on both sides brightened the night sky with exploding powder, and "it was so light in the fort," Moses Boone remembered, "that any article could be plainly seen to be picked up, even to a pin." Hidden in the woods of Hackberry Ridge was William Patton, a Boonesborough resident who had returned from a long hunt during the siege. Watching the battle this night, he saw warriors "run up to the fort, a large number of them, with large fire brands or torches and made the Dreadfullest screams and hollowing that could be imagined." This time numerous fires were ignited and defenders had to climb the roofs to put them out, exposing themselves to the Indians' fire. From inside the fort Patton "heard the women and Children and men also screaming." Convinced that he was witness to a disastrous climax, he fled toward Logan's Station, where he announced the terrible news that the Indians had taken Boonesborough by storm.

But the biggest losses that night were suffered by the Shawnee attackers—the fort's riflemen succeeded in killing more Indians in this assault than in all of the previous days of the siege. The fires threatened, but a heavy rain in the late evening put them out and forced the Indians to retire again. On Friday morning the settlers found that the Shawnee camp had been disbanded. Sporadic firing continued through the day, but it gradually became clear that the Indians had given up the siege and were pulling out. On late Friday afternoon the defenders made their first tentative moves outside the gates. At the river they found that the Indian mine reached a full forty yards toward the fort, but the water-soaked earth from the rain had caused a collapse. "They quit on this account," a British official later told Simon Kenton. For the Shawnees it had been a disastrous campaign in which, by Boone's estimate, they lost thirty-seven men. They had thrown enormous resources into the fight, with few results. Around the fort walls people collected spent balls amounting to 125 pounds of lead. The Shawnees now broke into small parties and harassed other settlements and stations, inflicting more loss of life and property with these traditional tactics than they had done during the whole of the siege.

At Logan's Station the settlers prepared for the attack they expected would follow on Boonesborough's defeat. On Sunday, September 20, the sentry saw a party coming slowly toward the fort in single file. "Damn you, come on!" the men hollered out to the approaching column, thinking that the Shawnees finally had arrived. But as the riders came closer someone yelled out, "It is our boys." They were the men from Logan's who had gone to the defense of Boonesborough. "Are you all alive? We heard you was killd." "Yes! Yes!" they called as they rode into the fort. "They was not surprised at Mr. Patton for thinking the fort was took," wrote Daniel Trabue, "for the Indians did rush up to the fort and make the Dredfullest adoos that was ever heard of." But Boonesborough had stood the test. A few days later the reinforcements arrived from Virginia.

Boone wrote to Rebecca soon after the siege was lifted. He included a description of his captivity and escape and spoke of his plans to join the family. He would be delayed, he regretted, because he had to defend himself against a formal charge of treason brought by Richard Callaway and Benjamin Logan. There was to be a court-martial, with officers of the Kentucky militia acting as his judge and jury. Boone made his own views of the British clear to his wife. "God damn them," he declared, "they had set the Indians on us." But except for this sentence, remembered years afterward by Rebecca's cousin Daniel Boone Bryan, this letter of Boone's does not survive. Shocked by her husband's use of profane language, Rebecca destroyed it.

Before she consigned it to oblivion, however, several other Bryans read it, and they were the only members of the family who would later recall the court-martial. In the middle of the nineteenth century Nathan Boone and the descendants of Boone's other children claimed to know nothing at all about it. When he told his life story to Filson, Boone made no mention of the trial. He remained silent because this was the most shameful and humiliating moment of his life. A large number of settlers attended the public trial at Logan's Station, but the official records of the proceeding disappeared, perhaps these also destroyed by some well-meaning friend who found them embarrassing.

The sole piece of evidence is an account written nearly half a century later by a man who attended the proceedings. According to Daniel Trabue, four charges were pressed against Boone: That when captured, in order to save his own skin, he had handed over the salt makers "against their consent," although at the time the Indians were "not going towards these men." That as a prisoner he had consorted with the enemy, and at Detroit "did Bargan with the British Commander that he would give up all the people at Boonesborough." That on his return he had weakened the garrison by persuading a large number of men "to leave the fort to go away over the Ohio River" on a foolish and perhaps treacherously conceived raid. And finally, that he had exposed Boonesborough's leaders to ambush by agreeing "to take all our officers to the Indean camp to make peace out of sight of the fort." It was not the facts that were in dispute but their implication, and Callaway offered the worst possible reading, arguing that Boone's conduct amounted to nothing less than treachery and treason. "Boone was in favour of the British government," he declared to the court. "All his conduct proved it," and "he ought to be broak of his commission."

Boone offered a simple defense, repeating once more what he had been saying since his return from captivity. He had surrendered his men to keep the Indians from going to Boonesborough, where "the fort was in bad order and the Indeans would take it easy." "He thought he would use some stratagem" and had told the Shawnees and the British "tails to fool them." As to the charges regarding his leadership, the outcome of the siege ought to speak for itself. After taking testimony from Callaway, the escaped captives Andrew Johnson and William Hancock, and Boone himself, the officers retired to deliberate and were quickly back with their verdict. "The court Marshal Deseded in Boon's favour," Trabue wrote, "and they at that time advanced Boon to a Major." It was not simply an acquittal but a vindication, for by means of this promotion Boone's fellow officers found a way to applaud his leadership while heaping scorn on Callaway and Logan.

But Boone, who was always hypersensitive to criticism, felt crushed by the mere fact of the accusations. A whispered debate, of which he was painfully aware, continued for years over his conduct. After they returned, the former captives were asked scores of times for their opinion. For the most part, they exonerated Boone of any blame for their ordeal. "It was Boons management that saved our lives at the Blue Licks," Richard Wade told his inquiring son. "It was conceded by all conversant with the circumstances that the course he pursued was the only wise, safe, and prudent course." To be sure, "his men thought very hard about it," Benjamin Kelley admitted when his grandson asked how the men felt about their surrender, but he hastened to add that "it was doubtless a wise thing in Boone, for by it he saved the lives of defenseless women and children." William Brooks, who not only lost his brother Samuel but remained in British irons longer than any of the captives, "always spoke well of Col. Boone's conduct on that occasion," said his daughter. This was gratifying, but for Boone it was painful having these matters aired at all, and he did his best to avoid any discussion of the whole affair for the rest of his life.

At this he did not always succeed. He maintained a close, if feisty, relationship with the former captive William Hancock, who had been with Boone at Chillicothe and had contributed to rumors of Boone's treason. Many a time, said Boone's granddaughter Delinda, she heard Hancock "complain of Boone surrendering the salt boilers," and Boone would respond irritably that if he had not done so, the people at Boonesborough "would all have been killed." Once again they would rehearse the debate, with Hancock always finally admitting that Boone "had done more than any one else would under similar circumstances" and that "he was well satisfied Boone acted from the best of motives."

Others, however, were not so sure. "Col. Calleway and Capt. Ben Logan was not pleased about it," Trabue remembered of the verdict. Callaway did not have long to nurse his bitterness. A year and a half later, just a few miles from Boonesborough, he was murdered by Indians as he worked with his slaves. His body was scalped, mutilated, and rolled in a mud hole, leaving him, in the words of John Gass, "the worst barbecued man I ever saw." But his sentiments about Boone were kept alive by the members of his family who remained at Boonesborough. Years later Richard Callaway, Jr., gave "a long and interesting account of Boons attempted treachery," and his sister Kezia Callaway French, who admitted she could "never bear an Indian's presence," said that the Shawnees surrounding Boonesborough called often for Boone, and he "would rise up, and go out freely to and among the Indians; did so repeatedly." For her and others it was Boone's obvious ease with the Shawnees that made him suspect. "Boone was willing and wished to surrender" the fort, she believed, and she taught her children that "Boone never deserved any thing of the country." Soon after the court-martial Boone left for North Carolina with Flanders, Jemima, and his son-in-law William Hays.

Boone was on the Yadkin by November 9, 1778, where a diarist noted his return: "Mr. Daniel Boone was here. He was seized recently by the English near the Salt Springs in Kentuck, but escaped." Rebecca and the five children were living in a cabin on the property of her uncle Billy Bryan, husband of Boone's sister Mary. After his arrival Boone moved them to a larger cabin on Rebecca's father's place that could accommodate the entire family, including Jemima and Flanders, Susy and Will, both of whom were beginning families of their own. That winter Boone hunted his old grounds in the Blue Ridge.

There are hints that all was not well between Boone and Rebecca. "The history of my going home, and returning with my family," Filson quoted Boone as saying, "forms a series of difficulties, an account of which would swell a volume," but he said no more. His cryptic allusion to "difficulties" has been the source of considerable speculation, much of it focusing on the possibility of "Boone's surprise," misplacing the incident of marital infidelity that occurred during a much earlier period of their married life. It is more likely that he referred to a conflict over their return to Kentucky. Nathan Boone believed that his mother "may have well opposed" moving back to the frightening "dangers and exposures" from which she had fled. Moreover, he thought "the Bryans, some of whom were Tories, might have used their influence to prevail upon Mrs. Boone not to return." Boone had cast his fate with Kentucky and was determined to go back, but he may have had considerable difficulty convincing Rebecca.

The balance in favor of a return was tipped by the coming of revolutionary conflict to the South. The military campaigns of 1778 and 1779 took place in Georgia and South Carolina but their reverberating effects were felt in backcountry North Carolina, and in the subsequent and final years of the war civil violence completely engulfed the Yadkin. Partisan feeling ran high in the Boone and Bryan neighborhoods, where there was growing support for the patriot cause and increasing hostility to Loyalism. The North Carolina Tories "had to run off," one man concluded, they were so hated. A person "could hardly get along the road for them," he wrote, and the emigration to Kentucky in 1779 was "all grand tories, pretty nigh." Although this is an exaggeration, there is little doubt that the party Boone organized for the return to Kentucky included a good many Loyalists. Many of the Bryans who had not previously emigrated decided that despite the Indian terrors in the West, their families would be safer in Kentucky than in North Carolina. Rebecca's uncle Morgan Bryan moved his family across the mountains, then returned to fight with the Loyalists, and was killed in an engagement near the Bryan Settlement in 1781.

During the spring and summer of 1779 Boone recruited emigrants throughout the Yadkin settlements. Adding weight to his arguments was the passage by Virginia of a law that promised to regularize the sale and allocation of western land. At reasonable rates new settlers could purchase Virginia treasury warrants redeemable for land in Kentucky. Men like Boone, who had improved a tract and raised a crop of corn before January 1, 1778, could claim a settlement grant of four hundred acres at the price $2.25 per hundred; such claimants, and others who merely had built a cabin, also were given the opportunity to preempt another thousand acres at forty dollars per hundred. Governor Thomas Jefferson's land commission was scheduled to meet in Kentucky during the winter of 1779–80 to verify and confirm these claims, so it was imperative that Boone return. Pushed by the rising war fever at home and pulled by the promise of land, he recruited a number of Yadkin families long associated with the Boones as well as a large number of Bryans. The company included the families of each of his brothers and sisters, with the exception of Squire and George, who already were living in Kentucky. Their mother, Sarah Morgan Boone, had died in 1777 and now lay beside her husband in the Joppa graveyard.

The company, one hundred strong, left the Yadkin in the middle of September. The weather was glorious and the spirits of the people high: "It was like an army coming out," one of them remembered. At Moccasin Gap they were joined by others from Virginia, including the family of Abraham Lincoln, grandfather of the future president. The 1779 migration to Kentucky was the largest to date and one of the largest ever on Boone's Trace over the Cumberland Gap. "We began our journey all afoot, except the women and small children," one man wrote, but many people, men, women, and children alike, walked the entire way. The husband of one poor young couple walked barefoot, his wife beside him with a baby at her breast, leading a single mule loaded with their meager possessions. The Boones and Bryans were considerably better off. Billy Bryan packed his property on twenty-eight horses, led by slaves; Boone had about a half dozen packhorses, on which he had strapped kettles, tools, and even a butter churn. His wealthy kinsman James Carter, a colonel in the Rowan militia, gave Boone two small swivel guns for the defense of the new settlement he planned, and these were packed on a strong horse. But after struggling over the gap the horse died of the strain. "This misfortune put the wits of Boone to work to devise a way to proceed with his burdens," remembered one friend along with the party, and he built a device he called a "truckle," something like an Indian travois, with which he attempted to haul the swivels, but they proved too heavy and he was forced to cache them along the trace. Boone was never able to retrieve these cannon, but he never forgot them, and as late as 1817 he and his son Jesse were still trying to retrieve them.

At one river crossing the company found the waters running high and fast, and Boone directed them to wait. The next day the women remained anxious about crossing, but impatient with the delay, Jemima cried out that she would lead them across. Riding double with a young girl, she plunged into the water. Her horse had nearly reached the opposite bank when, frightened by some floating driftwood, it threw its two riders. "A loud scream went up from the women," an emigrant later wrote, "but immediately they came to the surface and we seized them and bore them to the shore. The little girl was badly strangled, but Jemima seemed to enjoy the misfortune." She laughed as the men carried her ashore. "A ducking is very disagreeable this chilly day," she declared, "but much less so than capture by the Indians."

The party arrived at Boonesborough in late October of 1779. Little of the damage inflicted during the siege had been repaired and the settlement remained a small, disorderly cluster of stockaded cabins. It was "a dirty place, like every other Station," one settler wrote, and another British traveler that summer compared its stench with the one that arose from the gutters of Edinburgh. The Bryans immediately went on to resettle Bryan's Station on the Elkhorn River. Boone had no intention of remaining at Boonesborough, where he felt scorned, but he had to await the proceedings of the land commission, which arrived there in December. After it had approved his claim, on Christmas Day, Boone and a number of kindred families led their packhorses and dogs across the frozen Kentucky to a site where he had previously raised a cabin and made a crop of corn in anticipation of claiming the land for himself. The watercourse had become known as Boone's Creek, and here, at the intersection of several buffalo traces, six miles northwest of Boonesborough, he planted his new settlement of Boone's Station.

They constructed "half-faced camps made of boards and forked sticks" in which to dwell during the first winter. There was already more than a foot of snow on the ground when they arrived, and the weather, in the words of one of the land commissioners, was as "severely cold as ever I felt it in America." It was the beginning of what was known afterward as the Hard Winter. Livestock froze to death and game starved; wild turkeys, too weak to move, died on their perches and tumbled into the snow, but, according to Daniel Trabue, they "weare too poore to eat." Hunting was difficult, for the cold made it "impossible to load our Guns." Many settlers "like to have starved to death," one settler remembered, and Trabue reported that a number of people "did actuly Die for the want of solid food." It was certainly a hard winter for the families in their huts at Boone's Station, but Boone had brought an ample supply of corn from North Carolina, which he "divided even to his last pone with the newcomers," and brought in an adequate supply of game. There was a sugar grove nearby, and with the coming of spring the women and children hastened to make maple sugar to augment the meager diet. "The poor miserable buffalo would come to drink the sugar water," one of Boone's nieces remembered, and they "could hardly drive them off, they were so poor." Meanwhile, the men "erected cabins and stockaded them, with port holes," as protection from Indian attack. Boone and Rebecca may have lived for a time at the fort, but according to descendants, they soon moved to a cabin several miles southwest on Marble Creek.

His departure from Boonesborough and his relocation in the woods fueled talk that had begun in North Carolina about Boone's antisocial behavior. Years later one old man told a tale of a visit he had made to Boone's Marble Creek farm when he was a boy in the early 1780s. As he and his father ride up to Boone's "hut," they see the "old backwoods hunter" sitting on his porch, "dressed all in leather" and surrounded by his dogs. He hails them to come on, and while the boy plays with Boone's two young sons, the men chat about "how many deer, buffalo, and bear Boone had killed that day." Boone asks the distance to their place. About seventy miles, the man replies. "Old woman," Boone calls to Rebecca, "we must move, they are crowding us." This folk image of the "old backwoods hunter," however, had little in common with the real-life Boone of the early 1780s, the head of a growing and influential clan, an aspiring landowner and businessman, and a respected leader of frontier society.

Boone's Station, a settlement in the heart of the Bluegrass, near what is today the town of Athens in southern Fayette County, was in the early 1780s home to fifteen or twenty families, including Boone's married daughters Jemima and Susannah, his brothers Samuel, Jonathan, and Edward, and his cousins the Scholls. On Marble Creek the Boones lived in a large double cabin with the five children who remained at home: Israel, their oldest, now a young man in his early twenties; Levina and Rebecca, who were reaching marriageable age; and the two boys Daniel Morgan and Jesse Bryan. In the summer of 1780 Rebecca surprised everyone with her tenth pregnancy. She was forty, Boone forty-five, and they were about to enter their twenty-fifth year of marriage. Nathan, the last of their children, was born on March 3, 1781. Also with the Boones were the six motherless children of Rebecca's uncle James Bryan; they would grow up in the Boone household, and their children would think of Boone and Rebecca as grandparents. In addition, Will and Susy Hays, with two or three children of their own, lived with the Boones in the early 1780s. It made for a household of nineteen or twenty persons.

The family grew corn and tobacco and raised cattle and horses;

Boone continued to hunt, but increasingly he concentrated his attention on real estate. His formal acquisition of Kentucky acres began when he filed a petition before the commission meeting at Boonesborough, claiming a settlement and preemption of fourteen hundred acres on Stoner's Creek "lying on the waters of Licking, including a small spring on the northeast side of a small branch, a camp and some bushes cut down at the same, about twenty miles east [actually north] of Boonesborough." With "satisfactory proof being made to the court" of Boone's "settling and raising a crop of corn in the years 1775 and 1776," the commissioners granted his claim. Less than a month later he paid and made final entry for the four hundred–acre tract, and he completed the entry for the preempted thousand acres the following year. He also began the process of obtaining grants to his Marble Creek farm and other lands in the vicinity of Boone's Station.

To raise the capital necessary for these ventures Boone hired out his services to other land speculators. Among the pioneers, Boone possessed the greatest store of knowledge about the lands and waters of Kentucky and was considered the best man in the country for the location of claims. Typical was the arrangement he made with the Virginia merchant Geddes Winston in 1781. Winston held Virginia land warrants good for five thousand acres of Kentucky land, and he hired Boone to locate and enter these for him. "He doth bind him Self and his heirs to Locate the Said Warrants," read Boone's contractual obligation, "for which Consideration the said Geddes Winston doth agree to give to Said Boon Two thousand acres of the aforesaid Lands to be laid off agreably as to Quality and to pay all Expenses that may attend the Surveying and Securing of the Said lands." It was Boone's usual practice to sell these lands in order to raise capital. After completing his work for Winston, for example, Boone wrote to inform the merchant that "the 2000 acres of Land you are to make me a titel to out of your 5000 acres I have Sold to Mr James Parbery and Desire you Would Make him a Deed."

He undertook his first assignments in the fall of 1779, locating claims for a number of men, including Thomas and Nathaniel Hart, his old associates from the Transylvania Company. After Boone had completed the field work, the Harts persuaded him to travel to Virginia for them to purchase land warrants in Williamsburg. On February 12, 1780, Boone gave them a signed receipt for over £2,500 in Virginia money, "to be advanced on warrants at Wmsbg." Several other men joined in the enterprise, including Will Hays, who gave Boone four hundred pounds "for to bring a warrant for a settlement and preemption a laying on the north fork of Licking." When Boone left a week or two later he was carrying twenty thousand dollars in depreciated currency. This trip ended in disaster. Arising from a night's sleep in a backcountry Virginia inn, Boone reached into his pocket to pay the bill and found all of the money stolen. He believed that he had been drugged and robbed by the landlord but had no way to prove it, and he never recovered the money. The Harts, Hays, and some of the others who had retained Boone forgave him the loss. "I will freely grant him a discharge for Whatever Sums of mine he might be possest of at the time," Thomas Hart wrote. But a few men insisted that Boone accept responsibility, and it was several years before he was able to pay them off.

"It was a heavy loss to Boone," said his son Nathan. According to one of his friends, he felt "completely unmaned," not because of his own losses but "from the fact that others were to suffer" on his account. Malicious people floated rumors that Boone had staged the whole affair in order to pocket the money. "I feel for the poor people who perhaps are to loose even their preemptions," Hart wrote to his brother Nathaniel in what amounted to a ringing testimonial for Boone,

> but I must Say I feel more for poor Boone whose Character I am told Suffers by it. Much degenerated must the people of this Age be, when Amonungst them are to be found men to Censure and Blast the Character and Reputation of a person So Just and upright and in whose Breast is a Seat of Virtue too pure to admit of a thought So Base and dishonorable. I have known Boone in times of Old, when Poverty and distress had him fast by the hand, And in these Wretched Sircumstances I ever found him of a Noble and generous Soul, despising every thing mean.

Hart, it turned out, expressed the sentiments of most of Boone's fellow settlers. In November of 1780, when Kentucky was divided into three counties, Virginia officials promoted Boone to the rank of lieutenant colonel in the Fayette County Militia, and soon thereafter his fellow citizens elected him to serve as the county's representative in the Virginia State assembly. The following year he also was chosen county sheriff.

But the Indian war continued, even quickened. In late May of 1779, during Boone's absence in North Carolina, Col. John Bowman led a force of three hundred Kentuckians across the Ohio to attack the Shawnee towns on the Little Miami. The army opened fire on Chillicothe at dawn, wounding Chief Blackfish in their first volley. "Run to the councilhouse," Blackfish called to his warriors, "and fight as long as you live." Because many of the Shawnees had moved to the safety of Spanish territory, not more than forty men and boys were present to defend the town. The Americans made several halfhearted attempts to storm the council house but were considerably more interested in looting property and stealing horses. Bowman had to content himself with the destruction of crops and cabins. The rangers simply could not sustain the kind of organized military campaign necessary to take and hold territory. They withdrew south but along the way suffered casualties because of their insistence on defending their plunder from the counterattacking Shawnees. The militia lost nine men, the Shawnees only two, but one of them was Blackfish, who died of an unchecked infection. After the Americans crossed the Ohio they divided loot amounting to five hundred dollars per man. The military consensus, however, was that Bowman, as Daniel Trabue expressed it, had "made a broken trip of it, got some of our best men killed and killed very few Indians."

The season of war in 1779 ended with a devastating Indian attack on an American convoy on the Ohio loaded with supplies sent from New Orleans. Forty Americans died, others were captured, and the supplies plundered or destroyed. The Hard Winter had the positive consequence of deferring violence, but the fighting season reopened in the spring with the Indians once more on the offensive. A combined British and Indian army, carrying cannon this time, moved into Kentucky and forced the surrender of Ruddle's and Martin's stations, carrying away more than three hundred prisoners. There seems little doubt that these captives included many Loyalists. "I don't believe we have more than two Families really Rebels," reported the British commanding officer, who thought they would "faithfully defend the country that affords them protection." American officials reached similar conclusions. "Should the Enemy approach the frontier and offer protection," an American officer wrote from Fort Pitt, "half the Inhabitants would join them."

After the disastrous attacks of June, General Clark attempted to regain the offensive by recruiting an American volunteer force for an invasion of the Ohio country. Boone was among the few officers who came forward, and he was appointed one of Clark's scouts. When sufficient troops failed to appear, however, Clark impressed an army, sweeping up residents, transients, and visitors alike. On August 1, 1780, an ill-equipped and poorly provisioned force of eleven hundred men crossed the Ohio at the mouth of the Licking River. The Shawnees fled from Chillicothe, leaving it a smoking ruin, and made their stand to the north at their town of Piqua, where the battle was joined on August 7.

There was brutality on both sides. Upon the approach of the army, the Indians murdered most of their American captives. The Americans, with orders to take no prisoners, scalped dead and wounded alike and even collected scalps from Shawnee graves. In a notable act of savagery they killed a woman "by ripping up her Belly and otherwise mangling her." The Shawnees later reported to the British that the Americans fought with a "madness" that they could not withstand. The Shawnee defense, however, was equally impressive to many Americans. "The Indians stood at the Pickaway battle," one man told his daughter, "till they were powder burnt." Finally the Shawnees withdrew and the Americans entered the town, plundering and burning, and destroyed as well the extensive Shawnee cornfields. The Americans returned to their settlements feeling that they had struck a decisive blow, but the Shawnees and their allies moved a little north and west, rebuilt their towns, and suffered relatively little from the attack.

A number of tales dating from this period detail Boone's hairbreadth escapes from the Indians. After a day of hunting or surveying in the woods, while his men conversed before the fire, Boone sits "silent and seemingly unheeding, darning his hunting shirt, mending his leggins, or preparing his rifle-balls for use." Then, suddenly, something unheard or unseen by the others stirs his attention and he disappears into the night. "And now," the men whisper, "we shall know something sure, for old Daniel's on the track." One tale was told of such an occasion, when Boone was surveying for the Harts near the forks of the Kentucky River. In the evening the company sits together, passing around a bottle of "old Monongahela," which Boone had a reputation for supplying to his crews. Suddenly the horses snort and Boone stiffens. "There are Indians near," he whispers. "Be silent." Acting under his instructions, the men build up the fire, arrange their blankets and packs to make it appear as if the whole party lies sleeping, and quietly walk their horses into the night. As they leave, Boone turns to the man still holding the bottle. "We must do something with the whiskey," he declares, "for if the Indians catch us, and get drunk, they will kill us all." Nearby was a distinctive tree with a hollow in its fork, marking the final corner of the survey, and in it Boone places the bottle before escaping. A decade later there occurs a dispute about the boundaries of this piece of property, and as the original surveyor Boone is called to verify the corners. With the attorneys for both sides, he walks the lines until he spies this old tree, which his keen woodsman's eye recognizes despite ten years of growth that has filled in the hollow. "Cut it down," he commands. "If whiskey is found, the question is settled." Inside, of course, they find the bottle.

One of the best known of these tales reportedly was told by Boone himself a few years before his death, at the wedding reception of a granddaughter. At his Marble Creek farm Boone is arranging tobacco leaf for drying in a shed when at the door four Shawnee warriors appear. "Now, Boone, we got you," they laugh. "We carry you off to Chillicothe this time. You no cheat us any more." From his perch on the drying rack above them Boone looks down on their loaded guns. "Ah, old friends, glad to see you!" he exclaims as he gathers up an armful of dried tobacco. Suddenly he dumps it down into their faces, blinding them with the pungent dust, and escapes to his cabin. Sputtering and disoriented, the Shawnees leave, "cursing him for a rogue, and themselves for fools."

A final tale of escape was an elaboration of an actual event. In October of 1780, following the Clark campaign against the towns on the Little Miami, Boone and his brother Edward were returning to Boone's Station, their horses loaded with game taken in the vicinity of the Blue Licks. About halfway home they stop at a grassy creek to graze and cool their horses. "Let's crack some of these nuts," Ned proposes, pointing to an abundant walnut tree nearby. But Boone feels uneasy. "I have an uncommon dread on my mind," he worries aloud, and "this is a very likely place for Indians." "I don't believe there is an Indian in one hundred miles of this place," says Ned, making light of his brother's concerns, and, laying aside his gun, he begins breaking the nuts on a small stone in his lap. Boone turns, sees a bear lumbering off a short distance away, and brings it down with a shot from his rifle. "Keep a good lookout," he calls as he trots toward his catch, forgetting for the moment his fear of ambush. He has not gone far when shots ring out, and, turning, he sees a small war party gathering around Ned's body. "We've killed Daniel Boone," he hears one of the Shawnees exclaim. At this moment Boone recalls the words of Rebecca from so many years before: "He looked so much like Daniel."

Boone himself told Filson a spare version of this story. After shooting Edward, the Indians chase Boone into a canebrake, then send their dog in, following its yelps. This is the only time in his life when he has found himself "wanting a dog to seize him, so he could kill him with his knife, and save the load [in his gun] for the other pursuers." But the dog remains at bay and Boone is forced to shoot him. Without sufficient time to reload, he retreats a few paces, throws himself to the ground, and, looking up through the cane, sees the Shawnees come up, roll over the dog, and let out a frustrated moan. The Indians quickly retreat, content to let this one American go, still believing that they have killed Daniel Boone. He is able to flee on foot down the creek, covering the twenty miles to Boone's Station by morning. Without rest, he leads a party of his kinsmen back to the scene of the murder. As they come up, a wildcat is gnawing on Edward's body, which already has been beheaded by the Indians, who wanted evidence that Daniel Boone has finally been killed.

Intent on vengeance, the men follow the muddy horse tracks of the attackers northwest to the mouth of Cabin Creek on the Ohio, passing along the trace numerous Indian "choppings, blazings, and paintings" on the trees, but the Shawnees have hurried ahead and already crossed. On their return, Boone, with his son Israel and his cousin Peter Scholl, leave the others to hunt and make meat for the widow, Martha Bryan Boone, Rebecca's closest sister and the mother of five children. As they load their horses Boone tells the young men they are near the spot where he rescued Jemima and speaks movingly of the occasion when he nearly lost the girl whose paternity had once been "layed to" his dead brother Edward.

In April Boone left for Virginia to take his elected seat in the legislature. He was in Richmond for the convening of the session on May 7, 1781, but the advance of the British under Cornwallis forced a hasty adjournment and retreat to the town of Charlottesville. Cornwallis dispatched several units of cavalry to sweep west and capture the state government there. The town had only about an hour's warning, and Boone and a young friend from Kentucky were overtaken by a company of British dragoons as they rode down a road on the morning of June 4. Dressed in his hunting shirt and leggings, Boone was not recognizable as a legislator, and they rode for a distance, conversing with the officer. Finally, coming to a fork in the road, Boone's young friend, looking for an excuse to separate, turned to Boone and remarked, "Colonel, this is our road." "A *colonel*, ha?" the officer exclaimed, "you are just such prisoners as we want," and he took Boone into custody.

With a number of other Virginia state officials, Boone was marched to British headquarters, but after several days they released him. "Boone, who was with Lord Cornwallis, is since parolled," William Christian wrote at the end of June, and the records indicate that Boone returned to the assembly, which reconvened in the Shenandoah Valley town of Staunton, at the end of the month. His children believed he had been released on his promise "not to take up arms any more." If so, it was a pledge he did not keep, and there were those in Kentucky who pointed to this as further evidence that oaths meant nothing to Daniel Boone.

He was back in Kentucky during the summer but returned east for the second session of the assembly in the fall. He went by way of the Ohio River, crossing Pennsylvania to visit his relatives in Oley, his first trip to his birthplace since 1755. His cousin James Boone recorded a single terse line in his family Bible: "October 20. then Daniel Came to See us the first time." By November, Boone was sitting again with the assembly, assigned to a committee on frontier affairs. He did not take to the work, however, and was absent a good deal of the time, meeting with old friends or escaping into the woods for short hunts. On December 7 the assembly speaker ordered "that the Sergeant at Arms attending this House take in his custody Daniel Boone."

During Boone's term in the assembly, Cornwallis surrendered the British army at Yorktown, and when Boone returned to Kentucky in February or March of 1782, he carried the hope that there might soon be an end to the war. But while British and American diplomats negotiated in Paris, the bloody conflict continued in the West. The Americans and Indians already had endured eight years of intense fighting. On both sides, wartime conditions evoked qualities in men that stable societies must seek to suppress. The tales of those times are filled with foolhardy risks and dares. A group of Kentuckians is out hunting with a "green" immigrant from Ireland who is desperate to establish his reputation. Observing abundant Indian sign, the party takes refuge in the loft of an abandoned cabin, and as they are about to settle down for the night they hear noises outside. Looking down between the boards, laid loosely over the rafters, they see seven Indians enter the cabin. Excited that the fabled savages of the forest are near, the immigrant cranes his neck to catch a glimpse, and the boards shift and give way. "Come on, by Jesus," exclaims the Irishman as they tumble down on the Indians below. "Come on, boys, by Jesus, we've got them." The panic-struck Indians flee, leaving their arms and possessions, which are grabbed up by the Americans. In another tale, two men are returning to their pioneer station on horseback. One, a wild fellow, keeps galloping ahead, whooping and shouting as if daring the Indians to attack, then sauntering back to ride awhile with his friend before repeating his foolish maneuver. Finally the man behind hears a rifle shot and, coming up, finds his companion sprawled on the road. "Ah," the dying man cries out, "the damned Indians have killed me at last."

"Fool-brave was the instinct of the times," wrote the historian John Dabney Shane after interviewing dozens of veterans. "Its spirit imbued every member, in every class, of all ages and conditions in society." Any expression of caution by a man was likely to raise questions about his manhood. A group of men are moving through the woods, aware that Indians are all about them, when they see a buffalo. One of them suggests that they shoot it for breakfast. "For such boyish conduct," another protests, "their scalps would surely be the forfeit." "We'll see who the *boys* are," comes the scornful reply. A man's expression of caution was likely to brand him a coward. During an Indian fight, one ranger "fouled his pantaloons as a consequence of his extreme fear" and forever after must live with the nickname "dung-breeches." On another occasion one ranger asks another if he is scared, and, overhearing them, their commander dryly remarks that they had nothing to fear, "they wouldn't die until their time came." So accustomed did Kentucky women become to caring for men recklessly sacrificed that one woman wrote, "the most comely sight she beheld" during the wars "was seeing a young man dying in his bed a natural death." The scene was so unusual that "she and the rest of the women sat up all night, gazing upon him as an object of beauty."

It was the imputation of cowardice in the criticisms of his conduct during the episode of captivity and siege that so offended Boone—the notion that he had sought to save himself, that he had wished for surrender. The reckless expedition against the Paint Lick town had been for him a method of reclaiming the status of valor in the eyes of his men. Now, in what Kentuckians came to call "the last battle of the American Revolution," the horror of cowardice and the chimera of bravery propelled Boone toward a tragic confrontation.

In March of 1782 three hundred rangers from the Monongahela country drove north across the Ohio and attacked the Indian villages on the Muskingum River, murdering ninety-six defenseless Delaware Christian converts, two-thirds of them women and children. In June another American force sought to duplicate this dubious accomplishment but were trapped by an angry army of Indians that slaughtered many Americans, took others captive, and burned the commander William Crawford at the stake. In the aftermath of this failed campaign the British utilized Indian outrage to lay plans for what they hoped would be a decisive invasion of American territory in the West.

Numerous Indian raids took place during the summer of 1782.

Indian activity seemed to concentrate south of the Kentucky River. South of Boonesborough, Capt. Samuel Estill and twenty-two of his men were killed in a battle with Wyandots in May. Boone's old associate Nathaniel Hart was killed at his farm near Boonesborough in July. Boone and others pursued these attackers but failed to engage them. By early August there were many signs that "a very formidable army of English and Indians would come Quickly." "We have a few more of the yellow militia to deal with," concluded John Floyd. Indeed, as Floyd wrote, an army of several hundred Indians from various tribes already had crossed the Ohio. One of their leaders was Simon Girty, the American adoptee of the Shawnees who had gone over to the British in 1778. Before they crossed the river, Girty gave an impassioned speech. "Brothers," he declared, "the Long Knives have overrun your country and usurped your hunting grounds. They have destroyed the cane, trodden down the clover, killed the deer and the buffalo, the bear and the raccoon. The beaver has been chased from his dam and forced to leave the country." He called on them to fight in the interests of a ravaged Indian Eden. "Were there a voice in the trees of the forest," he cried, it "would call on you to chase away these ruthless invaders who are laying it to waste."

The army made its way to Bryan's Station, north of the Kentucky on the Elkhorn, confident that the raids south of the river had decoyed the Kentucky forces. Acting under the advice of British officers, the Indians once again besieged an American fort, destroying crops and livestock, burning outlying cabins, and attempting to storm and burn the stockade. Desperate messengers escaped to rouse the militia, and, learning of the attack, Boone and other officers rode north with their men from Boone's Station, Boonesborough, Lexington, Harrodsburg, and other settlements. These various groups, totaling 182 men and including 45 from Fayette County under the command of Lieutenant Colonel Boone, assembled at Bryan's Station on the afternoon of August 17 but found the Indians already gone. Lacking artillery, they had been unable to take the fort.

The officers held a council to decide whether to pursue the retreating Indians immediately or to wait for the arrival of Col. Benjamin Logan, known to be traveling north with a force of several hundred men. In command of the Fayette militia was John

Todd, a patrician lawyer from Virginia and now a leader of the settlement at Lexington, who had served in the Illinois campaign with Clark, where he had gained the rank of colonel. Boone served directly under Todd. The men from Lincoln were led by Col. Stephen Trigg, who had remained in Kentucky after coming west with the Virginia land commission in 1779. Assisting him was Maj. Hugh McGary of Harrodsburg. In the five years since the death of his stepson, McGary had become increasingly unstable. He bickered constantly with his new wife and in a public fight with his brother-in-law had threatened to "shoot his damned gourd." In the meeting of officers at Bryan's Station, however, McGary cautioned against hurrying out, suggesting that they wait for Logan to arrive. Scorning what he characterized as McGary's "timidity," Todd declared that they could ill afford to let the Indians get away. The decision was made to pursue in the morning, hoping that Logan would join them. McGary silently licked his wounds.

On the following day's march the Americans pursued the trail of the Indian army to within a few miles of the Lower Blue Licks. Boone was disturbed by what he saw along the way. The Indians were "concealing their numbers by treading in each others tracks," he observed. "I was with Col. Boone," one Kentuckian later remembered, "when he, by counting the Indian's fires, concluded there were at least 500." But on the other hand, they seemed to be doing everything possible to make their trail easy to follow, littering the trace with their garbage and blazing the trees. It added up to ambush. The American forces arrived on the south bank of the Licking, near the Blue Licks, early the next morning, Monday, August 19, 1782. Here the river makes a sharp loop around a rocky hill that had been laid bare by the sharp appetites of the animals who came to the lick. Hidden from view, the Indian army lay in wait in a series of wooded ravines at the crest of the hill. As the American rangers assembled on the opposite bank of the river below, a number of warriors strolled into view on the hilltop, calmly smoking their pipes, lures for the ambush.

Todd and Trigg called another council of officers that included Boone, McGary, and others, totaling perhaps fifteen men in all. Todd asked Boone, the most experienced woodsman in the group, for his opinion of their options. "Colonel," Boone said, "they intend to fight us." "How do you know?" asked Todd. "They wish to seduce us into an ambush," he declared, presenting the evidence he had noted along the line of march. It had been here at the Blue Licks that he and the salt makers were taken captive, here he had hunted and lounged; he had been over this ground a hundred times and it was not the place to make a stand. Let us not "run heedlessly into the trap so artfully set for us," he argued. "I say not [to] follow, they largely out-number us, and it is not prudent to pursue." Among the officers there seemed to be considerable sentiment for awaiting the arrival of Logan and his Lincoln County militia.

It may have been the mention of prudence or caution that roused McGary, still smarting from Colonel Todd's rebuke of two days before. He heatedly protested any delay, interjecting that "we have force enough to whip all the Indians we will find." McGary's interjection forced a short discussion about the tactics the officers might employ were they to decide on an attack. If you are determined to proceed, Boone advised, divide your force, cross half the men here, the others upstream where there was a good ford, bringing the two together in a pincer movement. For an army of poorly organized Kentucky rangers this would have been a complicated operation requiring good communications and coordination. It risked the destruction of two widely separated and badly outnumbered wings. It was the practice of the Kentuckians to impetuously assume the offensive, and there was a strong desire to inflict punishment and take revenge. "By Godly," McGary shouted in frustration, "what did we come here for?" He turned directly to Boone. "I never saw any signs of cowardice about you before." His words hit with the force of a rifle ball. "No man before," Boone shot back, "has ever dared to call me a coward." One of his nephews, standing nearby, saw Boone "actually burst into tears." "I can go as far in an Indian fight as any other man," he shouted furiously.

All rational discussion ended in these frustrated taunts. Once Boone had lighted his fuse, McGary blew off like a keg of black powder. He rushed for his horse, mounted, and charged into the river, waving his rifle over his head. "Them that ain't cowards follow me," he screamed to the assembled rangers, "and I'll show where the yellow dogs are." The explosion reverberated through the ranks of the Kentuckians. McGary's company from Harrodsburg charged forward to join their officer, and others began to mount and follow. "The contagion was irresistible," said one of

Boone's kinsmen, for "the taunt of cowardice was unpalatable to a Kentuckian and stung them on to recklessness." In a regular army, colonels Todd and Trigg would have ordered McGary shot on the spot. This was no regular force, however, but a highly irregular band of Kentucky warriors, ready to follow the chief who boldly commanded their immediate loyalty. Bowing to the inevitable, Todd and Trigg ordered their men to take up the charge, hoping to bring some order to the chaos once they had crossed the river. Having made this decision, all of the officers became implicated in the blunder, thus saving McGary from a court-martial after the battle. Boone hurried to join his company. "Come on," he cried as he led them into the river, "we are all slaughtered men."

Once they had crossed, the officers organized their men into three ragged formations, Trigg commanding on the right, Todd in the center, and Boone on the left, leading the men from Boonesborough and Boone's Station, including his son Israel; his nephews Thomas, Squire, and Samuel Boone; and his cousins Abraham, Joseph, and Peter Scholl. We "kept near to Boone," wrote Peter Houston, one of the Boonesborough rangers, "having faith in him to get us out of trouble." Some of the officers remained mounted, but most men left their horses standing at the river's edge and, loading their guns, began the half-mile march along the trace to the crest of the hill, following McGary and two dozen rangers in the van. As these first men reached the summit, Houston remembered, "a terrific war whoop was heard, which was caught up all along the ravines on both sides." The Indians suddenly arose from their hiding places and, in a coordinated volley of deadly fire, cut down all of the advance rangers but three. In an odd quirk of fate, McGary was among these survivors. It was said that the others "were shot down like pigeons."

"It fell to my lot," Boone wrote in his report of the battle, "to bring on the attack." He urged his men forward and rushed up the hill. An Indian arose from behind a stump, Boone fired, the warrior fell, and he ran forward, over the body. "He *believed* he had killed Indians on other occasions," said Nathan Boone, "but he was only *positive* of having killed this one." His men followed, and as they advanced together, the Indians fell back. Boone later recalled feeling "elated with success" at the progress of his charge. Suddenly

McGary came galloping up on his right. "Boone, why are you not retreating?" he shouted. "Todd and Trigg's line has given way, and the Indians are all around you." On a ridge on the right the Indian fire had cut Trigg's column to pieces within the first minute. Trigg himself had been shot from his horse and lay bleeding to death. Fighting from rock to stump, these warriors pressed the attack against the American right flank in the center, and the rangers quickly gave way and shifted in behind Boone's advancing column. No one had been left to guard the horses at the river, and as Boone now looked back down the hill he could see Indians rushing for the mounts. "The Enemy was immediately on our Backs," he wrote, "so we were obliged to Retreat."

At this point the battle had been raging for no more than four or five minutes. The firing was constant, the sounds of explosions mixed with wild whooping and agonized screams. The Americans were exposed to Indian fire from the ravines, while other warriors dashed into the fray, making reloading extremely difficult. Much of the fighting was hand to hand, so the Americans, with guns rather than bayonets or knives, were at a great disadvantage. The rising smoke and dust made it impossible to know for sure what was happening. At least forty Americans already lay dead or dying. The mounted officers made particularly good targets, and fifteen of the two dozen had been mortally wounded. Maj. Levi Todd of the Fayette militia was one of the few to survive. He saw his brother, Col. John Todd, take a bullet in his chest and slump over in his saddle as his horse charged off wildly; it was the last he ever saw of him. Pvt. Jacob Stevens was advancing with a group of men and heard the smashing of bullet into bone on his left. He looked to see the man next to him spitting blood, teeth, and rifle ball from his mouth. At the same moment the man on his right exclaimed loudly, "Damned if I didn't shoot one." "Take care," Stevens cautioned him, "and scarce I said it, when he received a shot in the collar bone." "I had fired 3 times and was just priming for the fourth, when the word was given for to retreat." The men turned and ran madly down the hill, directly into the Indians who had filled in their rear and were standing "in a body all in front of us, seeming to be 7 or 8 deep." There was desperate fighting with knives and tomahawks. Somehow Stevens made it through, dived into the river, and began to swim across.

Seeing the growing confusion, Boone called his men about him, ordered them to remain together, and sent them into the woods on their left, from where they could rush under cover for a better river crossing. He remained behind with several others to guard their retreat. Catching a glimpse of his son Israel still fighting at his side, Boone grabbed a riderless horse and ordered him to mount and flee. "Father, I won't leave you," Israel declared. Thinking to find a second horse so they might escape together, Boone turned away. Suddenly he heard a moan and the sound of a struggle on the ground behind him, and he spun around. Israel lay on his back in the dust, his arms outstretched plaintively, his body quaking, blood gushing in a pulsing stream from his open mouth. Boone bent over his son in horror and saw that his eyes had already glazed over. He knew immediately that the wound was mortal. Dazed, operating now only on the shock of adrenaline, Boone wheeled to his left into the timber and rushed down toward the river.

At the river ford some of the men had been able to remount, while others charged into the water on foot. A great many were killed as they struggled across, and the Licking became clogged with floating bodies. One ranger was grazed by seven balls but emerged from the water unwounded. Reaching the south shore, another sat and peeled off his waterlogged buckskin breeches, "bullets all the while showering round me" and one of them slicing through the breeches in his hands. Another man paused momentarily at the water's edge to drink, bullets kicking up the water all about him. A number of brave men stood on the south shore shooting back at the Indians. "Stand and fire," one of them shouted to the others, and "give our men a chance to cross the river." It was on the bank a little downriver from the ford that the men from Boone's Station reassembled. Many were suffering from wounds. Squire, the son of Boone's brother Samuel and his wife, Sarah, who years before had taught young Boone to read, had taken a ball in his hip that would cripple him for life. The men took count and found six of their number missing. Among the dead was Thomas Boone, another of Samuel's sons. Abraham Scholl reported to the panting survivors that he had seen Israel fall, and with Boone himself nowhere to be seen, the men feared that he too must be lying on the hill. Suddenly one of them remembered, "We saw a man plunge into the river some seventy-five yards below." It was Boone, who quickly came running up to them. Yes, Israel was dead, he confirmed, "shot through the neck." He pointed the men south, running with the other Americans down the trace in confused retreat.

Boone hurried his men back to their station, then went immediately to Rebecca with the news of their son's death. Within a day or two he was back at Bryan's Station, helping to organize the sorrowful task of burying the dead who still lay on the ground at the Blue Licks. As they approached the Licking on August 24, flocks of vultures circled above, and, mounting the ridge, they looked down on the horrible spectacle of the birds gorging themselves on the bodies that lay black and bloated after five days in the August heat. Most of the men had been scalped, and their bodies were so mangled and distended that it was difficult to identify them positively. "The smell of a human," one man vividly recalled later, "was the awfullest smell he ever had in his life." Nathan Boone believed that his father found Israel and buried him separately from the others, but other members of the family thought that Israel was interred with the others in the mass grave that is now marked by a monument at the crest of the hill.

George Rogers Clark blamed the disaster on the reprehensible leadership of the officers. Writing from Fincastle County, Arthur Campbell agreed that the defeat had resulted from "a want of proper authority." In Kentucky history, Hugh McGary is the scoundrel who brought on the disaster. "I understand I am much sensured for incouraging the men to fight the Indians when we came up with them," he wrote soon after the battle to his commander Benjamin Logan. But the rumors of "my bad conduct," he asserted, were being spread by officers who had schemed to "gain great applause" by hurrying to the Licks before Logan arrived, and the ambush had been the result. McGary had absolutely no self-reflective capacity, but it was characteristic of Boone that he proved the worth of his character by critically examining and attempting to understand his own behavior. Boone "blamed himself in some degree for the Blue Lick battle," reported his cousin Abraham Scholl, who had fought with the contingent from Boone's Station. "His caution was misconstrued as cowardice, and he let his zeal get the better of his judgment." With reasons of his own to be sensitive to criticism of his bravery, his foolish sparring with McGary had touched off that deeply troubled man.

In the years afterward, whenever Boone spoke of the Blue Licks defeat he was overcome with grief and wept openly. In the days before the battle Israel had been sick with a fever, and he was still suffering with a badly stiff neck when the fighting began. "His father and family tried all they could to persuade him not to go," said Nathan Boone. But Nathan's daughter Delinda Boone Craig told a different story that she said she heard from old Boone himself. When word comes to Boone's Station of the invasion of the Indian army, nearly all of the young men of Boone's Station sign up, but, confined to his bed, Israel does not. At dinner that day Boone reproves the boy, saying, "Israel, I did not hear your name when they were beating up for volunteers, and I had expected to have heard it among the first. I am sorry to think I have raised a timid son." Shamed by his father's remark, Israel leaves the cabin that very afternoon, rides to the station, and enrolls in the volunteer company. "Boone always blamed himself for the loss of his son," said Delinda. "Israel ought not to have gone, and would not but for his chiding."

For the Kentuckians, the Blue Licks battle marked the nadir of their struggle with the Indians. In the panic following the defeat, many settlers fled back over the mountains. One man offered to trade his farm for a horse and wagon to carry his family back to Virginia. It was no longer the land of bluegrass, another man remembered, because for him, after that day, the sky, the water, "everything looked red." The battle was commemorated in a ballad, sung for the next century in backwoods Kentucky:

> Then had the Indians their revenge,
> Their foes were rash and few;
> The waters gurgled red with blood
> Their mossy basin through;
> Scarce was a white man left to tell,
> What hand his clansmen slew.

For Boone, the Blue Licks defeat marked the lowest point in his own life. He could see his own instrumentality at work in the horrible defeat. "I cannot reflect upon this dreadful scene," he told Filson, "but sorrow fills my heart."

Boone now became the ranking officer of the Fayette militia, and in a series of letters to the governor he put on the record his own perspective on the defeat. Too much strength had been drained from north-central Kentucky to reinforce Clark's settlement at the Falls of the Ohio, he believed, leaving "our own Frontiers, open and unguarded," prey to Indian invasion. As a result, "sixty six of our Brave Kantetuckians fell, the Matchless Massecraed victoms of their Unprecedented Crueltie." Fayette required at least five hundred men from the eastern counties to garrison the crossings of the Ohio. "Our settlement, hitherto formed at the Expence of Treasure and much Blood seems to decline," he wrote, "and if something is not speedily done, no doubt will wholly be depopulated." "I have Encouraged the people here in this County all that I Could," he concluded, "but I Can no longer Encourage my Neighbours nor my Self to risque our Lives here at Such Extraordinary hazzards."

But no troops were forthcoming. Instead Clark mustered the Kentucky militia for yet another invasion of the Indian towns across the Ohio. During October, Boone was kept busy with details surrounding what he called, in his distinctive spelling, the "Shone [Shawnee] Expedistion." "I Exspet every exertion will be made by you to forward the Bisness," he wrote to one officer of the Fayette militia. At the end of the month eleven hundred Americans assembled at the mouth of the Licking, and with Clark in general command and Boone leading the men of Fayette, they crossed the Ohio on November 1, 1782. In nearly three weeks of campaigning the Americans plundered and burned six villages, as well as the British trading store at the head of the Great Miami River, and destroyed ten thousand bushels of corn, but they succeeded in killing only twenty warriors. The Indians certainly did not consider themselves beaten.

The United States and Great Britain signed preliminary articles of peace on November 3, 1782. When the Indians got word of the armistice in December they were "thunder struck," according to one British officer. The conclusion of the Revolution did not resolve the conflict between the Indians and the Americans over the control of the Ohio Valley, but as a result of the Kentucky invasion of

November 1782, the Shawnees and their allies relocated their towns farther north, making large-scale Indian invasions of Kentucky more difficult. In the aftermath of the invasion, wrote Peter Houston, "Boone was more hopeful than at any period since the establishment of Boonesborough."

It was in this frame of mind that Boone related his story of the Kentucky wars to John Filson in the spring of 1783. "My footsteps have often been marked with blood," he told Filson.

> Two darling sons, and a brother, have I lost by savage hands, which have also taken from me forty valuable horses, and abundance of cattle. Many dark and sleepless nights have I been a companion for owls, separated from the chearful society of men, scorched by the Summer's sun, and pinched by the Winter's cold . . . [But] I now live in peace and safety, enjoying the sweets of liberty, and the bounties of Providence with my once fellow-sufferers, in this delightful country, which I have seen purchased with a vast expence of blood and treasure.

On their return to Kentucky from the Ohio campaign in the fall of 1782, Boone, accompanied by his sons-in-law Will Hays and Flanders Callaway, and several others, spent a few days examining the land along the Ohio River at the mouth of Limestone Creek. This was the best landing on the Ohio for easy access to the Bluegrass, and settlers coming downriver were already disembarking here. Simon Kenton had founded a small settlement directly inland, and he encouraged his friend Boone to relocate on the river. The following spring Boone made final arrangements to establish himself as a merchant, trader, and innkeeper at the river port of Limestone. Anxious to connect the interior with this promising landing, the Fayette County Court appointed Boone and several of his associates "to view and mark the most convenient way from Lexington to Lower Blue Licks to mouth of Limestone." The Shawnees had twice forced him north along this path, and twice he had run its narrow trace south in desperate flights to freedom. He had watched his brother and his son die in its dust. But in 1783, as he entered his fiftieth year, he intended it to be a road pointing to a new period in his life.

Part Two

Daniel Boone dispatched his kinsman Lewis Bryan on October 5, 1809, with a letter for Judge John Coburn of the Superior Court of the Territory of Louisiana, sitting in St. Louis. "I am well in halth, But Deep in Markury," Boone wrote, "and Not able to Come Down." Actually he was feeling very poorly, medicating himself with liberal doses of calomel or mercurous chloride, a harsh purgative widely used as a cure-all. After years spent tramping through the woods in soggy moccasins, like most old backwoods hunters Boone now suffered from disabling rheumatic disorders that stiffened his joints and made movement agonizing, sometimes impossible. Setting out for a long hunt the previous winter, he had been stricken with a nearly fatal attack. Afterward his neck and shoulders became so painfully swollen that his children feared he might be afflicted with scrofula, lymphatic tuberculosis. His ruddy skin broke out in dry scales and the vision faltered in his red and inflamed eyes. There would be no long hunt this season. Boone would spend the fall with Rebecca under a doctor's care in St. Charles, twenty miles downstream from the settlement of his friends and relations on the Missouri River. Before departing, however, he forwarded to Judge Coburn a packet of documents and memoranda concerning his legal affairs. "I Shall Say Nothing about our petistion, but leve it all to your Self," he wrote. "If that Will not Do pleas Wright to me at St. Charles." In a rented house near the center of this French frontier village, Boone spent a discontented seventy-fifth birthday, polishing his rifle and wishing he were back in the woods.

Judge Coburn was assisting Boone in the preparation of an appeal to the United States Congress, praying for a grant of land on the Missouri in recognition of Boone's long service to the nation. The two men first met in the 1780s when Boone was a well-known Kentuckian and Coburn a young merchant trader recently arrived from Philadelphia. After Coburn's appointment in 1794 to the superior court they remained friends, despite legal difficulties that on several occasions placed Boone's name as a defendant on Coburn's civil docket. The judge was witness to Boone's mounting financial troubles during the transition from frontier to plantation in Kentucky. Resolving to improve his situation after the Revolution, Boone had parlayed his reputation into businesses in tavern keeping, trading, surveying, and land speculation, but he failed to succeed at these enterprises. Legal difficulties drained him of his energy, his money, and his land, and he grew increasingly bitter. Gradually he turned his attention back to the hunting life he knew and loved. In 1799, offered a large tract of land by the Spanish authorities west of the Mississippi, Boone finally led his extended circle of family and friends out of Kentucky and the United States to settle the wooded hill country on the north bank of the Missouri River in the district of St. Charles. But only four years later the American acquisition of Louisiana threw these Spanish grants into question. By the fall of 1809 a federal land commission that had been reviewing these claims was about to announce the results of its deliberations, and once more Boone was threatened with the loss of the land where he and his family had built their cabins and made their farms.

Coburn, who in the meantime had been appointed to the federal bench in Missouri, received inside information that the land commission was about to rule against Boone, and he let his old friend know. It was Boone's son Jesse, a county judge in Kentucky, who suggested the idea of an appeal to Congress, and Coburn kindly offered his assistance. The commission formally announced its rejection of Boone's claim in December. By then Coburn already had drawn up the petition and had placed it in the hands of his political friends in Washington. Early the next year House and Senate committees recommended a bill for Boone's relief, but without sponsors to guide it through the legislative process, the measure languished. Coburn had gone to Kentucky to accept a presidential appointment as collector of federal revenue there, and once again he used his political connections, this time to lay a "Memorial of Daniel Boone" before the Kentucky General Assembly. In 1812 the legislature passed a resolution requesting that the state congressional delegation sponsor Boone's case in Congress. In Missouri, meanwhile, Edward Hempstead, another of Boone's friends, had been elected territorial delegate to Washington, and he carried with him another version of the petition. Through these efforts, the House Committee on Public Lands favorably reported another bill in 1813. Boone's petition, read the committee's endorsement, went

> far in recommending to the consideration of the House the case of an aged, infirm, and worn-out man, whose best days have been usefully devoted to the settlement and prosperity of the Western Country, and whose only remaining earthly hope is that the benevolent interposition of the national Legislature in his behalf may, in his extreme old age, gladden his drooping heart, and raise him from poverty and distress.

Early in 1814 the Congress acted to provide Boone with land from the public domain.

The petition that succeeded in swaying Congress employed the formal rhetoric of an appeal to authority, voiced in the deferential third person. Coburn surely played a critical role in its composition, but it also expressed sentiments that Boone himself often repeated in his own words to family and friends. "Your petitioner has spent a long life in exploring the wilds of North America," the document begins. "Without pomp or parade" he led the settlement of the western country "at his own risque." Twice taken captive by the Shawnees, he escaped to organize the defense of the frontier, waging battle with the Indians on "the fatal fields, which were dyed with the blood of the early settlers, amongst whom some of his dearest connections are numbered." Kentucky was dear to his heart. He "assisted at her birth" and "watched over her infancy, when she was like to be strangled by the savage serpent." "Very different, indeed, is her appearance now from the time when your memorialist with his little band began first to fell the forest and construct their rude fortification at Boonsborough." Your petitioner dares to believe that "by his own personal exertions" he was "greatly instrumental in opening the road to civilization in the immense territories now attached to the United States." This rendition of Boone's accomplishments conformed to John Filson's account, portraying the conquest of Kentucky as a romantic struggle, with Boone cast in the role of the instrument of "an overrulling providence."

But with the victorious conclusion of the Revolution, the tone shifts. Filson's Boone deems the greatness of Kentucky itself sufficient reward for his sacrifices and is content with the virtuous satisfaction of a job well done; Coburn's Boone contrasts Kentucky's wealth and greatness with his own personal poverty. "He has to lament that he has not derived those personal advantages which his exertions would seem to have merited. He has secured but a scanty portion of that immeasurable territory over which his discoveries have extended, and his family have reason to regret that their interest had not been more the great object of his discoveries." His first object always had been the defense of the country, not the accumulation of wealth. Indeed, "He was ignorant how to acquire it, except from the chase or by the regular fruits of honest industry." He held to the sentimental ideal "not to monopolize, but to share in common with others," to claim only a reasonable portion of land "for the use of himself and his posterity." "Unacquainted with the niceties of law," however, he chose lands that "were through his ignorance generally swallowed up and lost by better claims." A novice in the ways of commercial civilization, Boone found himself bereft of all of his Kentucky land little more than a decade following the Revolution.

"Old age was fast advancing upon him, and he had scarcely [any]where to lay his head." It was under the press of these circumstances, says Coburn's Boone, that "he passed over to the Spanish province of Upper Louisiana under an assurance from the governor who resided at St. Louis that ample portions of land should be given to him and his family." To those who might question the decision to abandon the United States, he answers that "it was the country and not the government he had gone in pursuit of," and that he was among the first who "hailed the acquisition of Louisiana" by the United States. Once again he was in the vanguard of American occupation, but he was denied a modest personal reward. The "pittance of soil to which he conceived he had acquired a title under the Spanish Government has been wrested from him by a construction of the existing laws not in his contemplation, and beyond his foresight." "Unable to call a single acre his own," he remained "a wanderer in the world."

Coburn's Boone pressed this irony on the representatives in Congress. "The man who has opened the way to millions of his fellow men has not even a space to dispose the remains of a body, almost exhausted with age, exposure and exertion." What had been the virtuous hero of Filson's account becomes a victim. Coburn's Boone is cautious in blaming others, with only oblique references to the "niceties of the law" or the "strict instructions" to the land commission, arguing that the crucial factors were his own naivete and innocence. This self-depreciation was more than a little self-serving; the petition depended on the image of the innocent woodsman, unfamiliar with the ways of civilization. But while Boone had made plenty of mistakes during the preceding twenty-five years, there seems little doubt that he knew what he was doing. Boone lost his fortune not because he was a babe out of the woods but because he found himself unable to conform to the code of calculation and ruthlessness required by the world of finance and speculation. Coburn understood, of course, that the appeal of the victim was far more likely than the attack of the critic to gain Boone a sympathetic hearing from a legislative chamber filled with businessmen and lawyers.

The intended end of the petition thus determined something of its means, but it also reflected Boone's state of mind in his seventy-fifth year. Normally, as one Kentuckian put it, Boone was "quiet, of few words and to the point," and virtually everyone who knew him agreed on this description. "Boone was no chatterbox," a descendant remembered, "nor did he devote his time in repetition of extended details of many hairbreadth escapes and deadly encounters." According to his granddaughter Susan Callaway Howell, only rarely did he speak of himself at all, and what few details she learned of his life were the result of his offhanded references to past events. "This reminds me of when I was a captive," he might say, and to illustrate his point he would give a short rendition of some incident. But to provide Coburn material for the petition, in 1809 Boone dictated an autobiographical narrative to his grandson John Boone Callaway, a businessman in Saint Charles. As he reviewed his eventful life, his spirits lifted and his health gradually improved. Despite the hardship and disappointment of the previous twenty-five years, he still was able to end on an optimistic note.

"Your petitioner is not disposed to murmur or complain," Coburn's Boone assures Congress, although "he cannot but feel, so long as feeling remains, that he has a just claim upon his country for land to live on, and to transmit to his children after him." He asks not for a confirmation of his Spanish claim, expecting that problem to be resolved in the conventional manner. Rather, "he respectfully suggests that it might be deemed an act of grateful benevolence if his country, amidst their bounties, would so far gratify his last wish, as to grant him some reasonable portion of land within the territory of Louisiana." Encouraged by family and friends, and in the certainty of justice, Boone convinced himself that the world could still be put right, that the wrongs done to him would be overcome. The petition concludes "with a confidence inspired by that spirit which has led him so often to the deep recesses of the wilds of America" and relying on "that sense of right which governs your councils."

Although the manuscript narrative that Boone dictated to his grandson was later lost, the petitions themselves circulated widely. In 1813 the *Niles Weekly Register*, a national newspaper published in Baltimore, printed Boone's memorial to the Kentucky legislature and many other papers around the country copied it. The petition campaign led to a resurgence of national interest in Boone, but there was a significant shift in the interpretation of his life. Filson's triumphant tone gave way to a reading that included conflict and irresolution. "Possessing a different disposition" from the settlers and speculators who engrossed the land and thus "taking another view of things," wrote the Kentucky historian Humphrey Marshall in 1812, Boone "participated in a different fate." He "remained a hunter, and poor" and "from the country of his choice, and of his fondest predilection, he has been banished, *by difficulties he knew not how to surmount*." The petitions forced a rethinking of the optimistic premises of Filson's romantic interpretation of Boone's life. This was appropriate, perhaps, for a generation moving beyond the achievements of the Revolution and confronting the practical problems of national development. "The history of the settlement of the western country is the history of his life," Coburn's Boone declares. That history no longer told the expected tale of progress and improvement but rather a story that included failed hopes and bitter regrets.

Chapter Seven

Unable to Call a Single Acre His Own

1784 to 1789

After the Revolution thousands of Kentucky-bound settlers disembarked from their flatboats and barges at Limestone, making it one of the most important of the early American ports along the Ohio. "It is become a grate Landing place," Boone wrote to the governor of Virginia in 1785, and he proposed the construction of a garrison "for the purtiction and Recving [of] famylys when they arive." One woman from Pennsylvania thought "the Landing the Best on the River" but declared the town itself "very Indifferent." During the time the Boones lived there, from 1783 to 1789, Limestone consisted of no more than a dozen permanent households, ramshackle buildings, and wharves strung along the river. Boone owned a small warehouse and wharf for the loading and unloading of boats and the storage of goods, located a few hundred yards downriver from the mouth of Limestone Creek. Nearby was the Boone tavern, what Nathan Boone called a "house of entertainment." Boone was a leader of this small community from the time he directed the laying out of the road to Lexington in early 1783. When the Virginia assembly incorporated the town in 1786 under the name Maysville—rivermen and residents continued to call it Limestone for years more—it named Boone as one of the trustees.

He was also something of a celebrity among emigrants who had read his narrative. One arriving settler noted in his diary that he had been "introduced to Col. Boone, the first discoverer of the Kentucke country, who seems to be a very honest kind of Dutchman."

"Boone had a cabin built out of an old boat," one traveler remembered, set back from the river on what is now Front Street, and there he lived with his family. Rebecca, forty-six years old, with little Nathan underfoot, ran the tavern kitchen. Daniel Morgan, who looked increasingly like his father as he turned from adolescence to young manhood, now worked regularly with Boone, and it already was apparent that his younger brother Jesse Bryan would be powerfully built as well. The Boone boys were fair haired with blue eyes, the girls darker like their mother. Some of Rebecca's Bryan cousins still may have lived in the household, but Boone's two youngest daughters took husbands about the time the family moved to Limestone. Levina married Joseph Scholl before she was twenty, and they remained at Boone's Station with his family. Little sister Rebecca, just sixteen, lived in Limestone with her equally young husband, Philip Goe. Boone formed close personal connections with all of his sons-in-law, but he never liked Rebecca's husband. He complained to a granddaughter that over the years he had provided Goe with "enough for a comfortable start three or four times, but that he would drink and run it out." According to another relative, Goe was "a great drunkard, very dissipated," who "wasted all his property."

The Boone household also included a number of slaves. The Bourbon County tax roll for 1787 listed Boone with seven, although the names of only three survive in the records. In 1781 Boone's cousin John Grant sold him "one Negroe girl named Easter," who had come over the mountains with the Grant family during the great migration of 1779. Boone purchased a "garle Named Loos for the Sum of Ninty pounds current Money" in 1786, and the following year Will Hays sold him "one negro girl named Cote." These young women must have worked with Rebecca in the busy tavern. The other family slaves were probably children; a letter of Boone's from 1791 records the sale of a slave woman and her child. The slave owning of the Boone family has embarrassed Boone biographers, one of whom excused it with the assertion that "everyone in Kentucky kept a slave if he could afford it." But in fact, during this period slaves were present in fewer than four of ten Bluegrass households, and as the importance of slavery increased with the developing economy, thousands of antislavery Kentuckians departed in disgust for the Northwest Territory, where the institution was outlawed. Not only were the Boones among the minority who owned slaves, but they held about twice the number of the typical slave-owning household and carried their servants along when they emigrated from Kentucky to Missouri at the end of the century. There is another myth that Boone, in the words of William Bryan, regarded slavery "a permanent evil to be endured because it could not be put away," but in fact, the Boone family supported slavery until the end of the Civil War. Indeed, this kinsman had to admit that "slavery was a necessary feature" of the Boone family economy. Each of the Boone children held relatively large numbers of slaves, and grandson Albert Gallatin Boone was among the "pro-slavery men" who issued a call to arms against the "abolitionist" settlers of Kansas in 1856. Simply put, the Boones owned slaves because they wanted their labor and could afford them.

Boone did a brisk business in the lively market of Limestone. He fed travelers at Rebecca's table and provided sleeping facilities in the back room of the tavern. He supplied arriving emigrants with corn, flour, salt, beef, pork, dry goods, and housewares. He purchased country produce—skins or furs, ginseng root dug in the woods, corn whiskey distilled in backyard stills—collected it in his warehouse, and shipped it upriver to Pittsburgh on barges. His was mostly a barter business. In a typical receipt for goods Boone promised to pay a debt of £26.2.6 in "Beaf or Pork, at the market price of this town," and he used scrip, issued by a Louisville trader, backed by "beaver skins." His most valuable commodities were the horses raised on the rich limestone soils of the Bluegrass; much of his trading was aimed at the accumulation of herds that he sold in markets over the mountains. "I Leave it to your Self to sett your price," wrote an old friend who sent him a mare, "as I am but a poore Judge." Boone was always a great lover of horseflesh, and he became a good horse trader. "Tho Every Man Liked the horse," Boone wrote back to one client, "I could Not get a Single Bid for him," because "money is not to be had at any Rate. If I had Cash, I

Could by 20 horsis in a week of pepel who want to Lift there plots out of the ofis."

The "ofis" to which Boone referred was the land office of Fayette County, Kentucky, located in the boomtown of Lexington, where settlers made the payments necessary to conduct their land business, registering entries, arranging for official survey, obtaining certificates of plat and patents for their parcels of land. Boone's tavern keeping, merchandising, and horse trading were all but means to raise the stake he required to play in Kentucky's biggest economic game—real estate. He took on yet another moneymaking venture in December of 1782 when he was sworn in as a deputy surveyor of Fayette County, adding this to the assortment of titles that included county sheriff and lieutenant colonel of militia. For years Boone had been locating land in preparation for survey, but this new appointment allowed him actually to lay out plats and register them at the land office, a potentially lucrative source of income. In 1783 the authorities of Lincoln County, south of the Kentucky River, granted him the right to survey in their county as well, after reporting him "able and Qualified to execute the said office."

His qualifications amounted to little more than political connections and the ability to read, write, and cipher. Deputy surveyors worked entirely on their own hook and hired their own crews, including a marker and two men to stretch the four-pole measuring chain along the survey line. The methods of the day were crude, and many surveyors even dispensed with the use of directional and sighting devices. Boone "did his surveying with the eye," said one disparaging Kentuckian, and even Boone's devoted son Nathan had to admit that his father's "knowledge of surveying was limited," that while he "could survey square or oblong bodies," he frequently got into trouble with anything much more complicated. A glance at the crazy quilt pattern formed by the property lines of rural Kentucky suggests Boone's inadequacy to the task at hand. A surveyor turned a general location into a specific set of boundaries, running against the lines of adjacent tracts while attempting to incorporate all of the most desirable natural features within the limitations of his client's acreage. This resulted in tracts of wildly varying shapes.

All survey was by "metes and bounds," without benefit of pre-established baselines or parallels, the boundaries of every parcel described using the features of land and flora. One of Boone's early surveys began at "two Hickories and a White Oak being Madison's SE Corner, Thence East 92 Poles to a White Oak, Thence S25 E 118 Poles to Two Ciders on Bogses Fork, Thence East 88 Poles . . .," and so on, back "to the Beginning." In cases like this, where the boundary was complicated, Boone's surveys frequently failed to close mathematically, and considering the number of hickories and oaks that stood in those woods, or the cedars growing along the many forks and streams, one begins to grasp the problem of retracing these lines on the ground. "All Boone's entries were mighty vague," one surveyor remembered, but his were not the worst of the plats coming from the hundred or more deputy surveyors working in Kentucky's booming land market. Asked to read his plat aloud, one surveyor held the document upside down as he repeated its contents from memory, and another notorious character wrote out his field notes on the leg of his buckskin breeches. Some surveyors skipped the outdoor work altogether and made what were called "chimney-corner surveys," creating their notes and writing up their plats while comfortably seated before their fireplaces, naming corner trees and distances from memory or merely making them up. After a number of Boone's surveys proved faulty, some aggrieved persons accused him of precisely this practice, but after a careful examination of his plats, one historian concluded that while some of his competitors excelled him in precision, Boone's work was about "as good as the average."

The average, unfortunately, wasn't much good. Without proper training or tools, surveyors "shingled" their plats one atop the other in a confusing maze that kept several generations of Kentucky attorneys well fed. The young lawyer and future national political figure Henry Clay litigated one Kentucky land case in which "the same identical tract" was "shingled over by a dozen claims." The Bluegrass, it was said, had been surveyed with tracts enough to cover it four times over. The real blame, however, lay not with the surveyors but with the men who created the land system. Virginia issued certificates and warrants for far more acreage than there was available land in Kentucky, established cart-before-horse procedures that allowed for the entry of vague locations before official survey, and failed to provide an accurate means of cross-checking surveys. In other words, the state did just about everything it could to ensure that there would be an enormous mess. This tangle provided a powerful incentive for the development of the comprehensive system of prior survey and systematic location in the Land Ordinance of 1785, which became the basic land law of western settlement. It came too late, however, to save Boone from enormous difficulties.

But during the height of the land boom Boone's surveying business netted him a nice income. Competing for clients and charging what the market would bear, Boone had all the work he could handle. He was in great demand because he knew how to find the fresh springs, salt licks, and meadows. He was willing to go where others would not dare, despite continuing Indian raids and ambushes, although on occasion even Boone noted that certain locations were "to much Exsposed to Danger to Survay at this time." Most important, Boone was able to trade on his reputation as a hero of the Revolution. He brought to the business the same frank and open manner that had made him a popular leader. "Sorry to here of the Dath of your brother," he wrote to one of his clients, "as I make No Doubt it puts you to many Disadvantages. However We must submit to providence, and provide for the Living, and talk of our Lands." He maintained an active business correspondence, producing more writing during his Limestone years than in any other period of his life. "No Dout you are Desireous your Land bisness Should be Dunn," he wrote to one Jacob Cohen, "but that is a thing imposible without money." For surveying two tracts of land totaling five thousand acres on the Licking River, Boone required the "smart sum" of £22.10.8 be delivered to his nephew Samuel Grant, who carried the letter. "I will Bee accountable for any money put into his hands," Boone assured, "inless kild by the Indians." If Cohen doubted the justice of this price, Boone suggested he consult other surveyors "and See if I am Right or Not, and Send the money by the first opertunety." After paying the registration fees, wages, and other expenses on this job, Boone was left with a profit of ten or twelve pounds. On another occasion in 1786 he charged £26.17.8 for eleven days of surveying, again leaving about ten pounds for himself after his costs. At this rate Boone would have realized fifty to seventy-five pounds a year in Virginia money from his surveying work, in addition to the earnings on his Limestone enterprises, a comfortable if not fabulous income at a time when typical Pennsylvania farmers earned about twenty-five pounds a year, established storekeepers perhaps one hundred, and wealthy merchants upward of five hundred.

He also continued to offer his services as a land hunter, for which he usually received a portion of the land. After he located and surveyed some thirty thousand acres of land on the Licking River for Thomas Logwood in April of 1785, for example, Logwood assigned Boone tracts totaling five thousand acres. For friends and associates Boone might waive his charge. To Thomas Hart, who had forgiven Boone's obligations to him after the robbery in Virginia, for example, Boone wrote in 1785 that "for good Reasons of past favors and good friendship the Exspencies of Locating your Land is payd to my Satisfaction." But dozens of other men turned to him for advice on the placement of their claims and the work reaped Boone a rich return in land claims. Boone's endorsement alone was sufficient to increase the value of land entries. "I know the within land," Boone scrawled on the back of a land warrant. "The one fifth part of the within Tract of Land is rich Bottom, and I think the High Land will produce Sixty bushels of Corn to the Acre."

In his land business Boone relied on the assistance of his son-in-law Will Hays. "We have undertaken the location of lands in the Kentucky district for a number of Gentlemen," Boone and Hays announced in an April 1783 issue of the *Virginia Gazette*, and requested that their clients "send us a sufficiency of money without loss of time, to defray the expences of their land." Never much good at record keeping, Boone relied on Hays to keep the complicated schedule of locations and surveys straight and his accounts balanced. "He is Bater at the Bisness than my Self," Boone admitted to a friend. He employed other family members on his survey crews, sons-in-law Joseph Scholl and Flanders Callaway as markers, Daniel Morgan and Jesse as chainmen. Boone also engaged his boys to carry his letters and collect his debts. "Sir, if you will Send me Six ginnes [guineas] by my Litel Sun," he wrote to one client who owed him money, "it shall be Sateled."

He invested the profits of his various business activities in land speculation. It was an enterprise not a little like gambling, and because of the nature of the Kentucky land system, for Boone and other small investors it was a game in which the house enjoyed an extraordinary advantage. A man risked his capital not at the close of the round, when title was granted, but at the opening bid, when he procured land certificates or warrants. In December of 1781, for example, Boone purchased a number of Virginia treasury warrants. At prevailing prices his total investment in warrants, land certificates, and private rights purchased from individuals was in the range of seven to ten thousand pounds. These entitled Boone to make entries on thousands of acres of Kentucky land. An entry, however, was merely a claim on a particular tract and had to be defended through the frequently torturous process of official survey and grant of patent. Were other claimants to demonstrate prior rights or superior surveys shingling his tract, the entry was lost, and with it the entire investment.

By 1785 Boone already had begun to experience firsthand some of the risks of the land business, as an indirect but important party to one of the first and most complicated of the early Kentucky land disputes, the case of *Boofman v. Hickman*. This conflict went back to the early days of Boone's involvement in Kentucky. In 1774, during his trip with Michael Stoner to warn the Virginia surveyors of impending Indian attack, Boone spent some time locating a four thousand–acre tract for James Hickman on a stream feeding the Kentucky River from the north that thereafter was known as Hickman Creek. The following year, after the founding of Boonesborough, Boone encountered a surveyor on Hickman Creek who warned him to relocate the claim, since he previously had surveyed the lands along the creek for others. Boone located two new tracts of two thousand acres apiece on either side of the nearby stream known as Boone's Creek, where he was claiming land for himself. He engaged the surveyor John Floyd to run Hickman's boundaries and "make the entry agreeable to the survey."

Several months later, however, Floyd came to Boone with the news that the lines of Hickman's western tract had "run afoul" of another survey. "To be plain with you," Floyd told Boone, "I want that survey for Jacob Boofman. He has a fine spring on it and if you will give it up I will go with you and make the survey elsewhere on as good land as that." Floyd had promised Boofman, one of his chainmen, the land in lieu of wages. But Boone stuck by his obligations to Hickman, saying to Floyd that he "would do no such thing until I saw another tract surveyed." The ensuing Indian conflicts, however, kept the men from locating another tract for Hickman. The way Boone saw it, "We never made the other, nor was the former give up," and absent any word to the contrary, after Floyd departed for Virginia in the fall of 1776, Boone notified Hickman that his two tracts had been surveyed and entered.

Here the matter rested while Boone, Floyd, and Hickman were caught up in the Revolution. It was not until 1779, when Hickman was on his way to Kentucky, that a check at the land office of Fincastle County surveyor William Preston revealed that Floyd had entered only the plat for the two thousand–acre tract on the east side of the creek. Greatly alarmed that he might have lost half of his valuable warrant, Hickman sought out both Boone and Floyd when he arrived in Kentucky, and a confrontation of the principals took place at the land office at Harrodsburg in May of 1780. "Hickman, Floyd and myself was face to face," remembered Boone, and "I rehearsed over the circumstances from first to last." Hickman and Floyd got into a shouting match, with Hickman demanding the plat to the second tract and Floyd swearing "he would be damned" first. Finally Hickman threatened to go to the law, and although he continued to refuse to make out a plat, Floyd agreed to hand over a copy of his survey notes. After Hickman left with this document, Boone remarked that surely now he would get his patent. But Floyd believed that Colonel Preston, his father-in-law, was "not such a damned fool as to do any such thing without having a plat made out and signed by me."

Boone had a personal interest in the dispute not only because he felt an obligation to Hickman but because his own claims to the Boone's Station lands were sandwiched between these two tracts. In December of 1779 the land commission had granted a certificate entitling his eldest son, Israel, to a settlement and preemption claim "lying on Boone's Creek between and joining Hickmans two surveys on the said Creek." This entry required official survey, and during the summer of 1780 Boone asked Floyd to run those lines for him. By the way, Boone inquired, "hath Hickman or you ever entered that survey?" "No," Floyd replied, "Hickman never will get it." Since Hickman's claim was now out of the way, he was in fact about to make the survey for Boofman, his former chainman. "God Bless me," exclaimed Boone, "be as sparing as you can in running towards Boggs [Fork]," where Israel's claim lay. "I will save as much for Israel as possible," Floyd assured him. In short, with the assurance of Floyd, who was Preston's protégé and son-in-law, Boone agreed to the shingling of Israel's tract over the one he originally had located for Hickman. "If Hickman must loose the land," he thought, "I would have 400 acres off the south end."

But unbeknownst to Boone or Floyd, Hickman had *not* lost the land. Armed with Floyd's document, and threatening to sue William Preston if not satisfied, he obtained a patent for the tract. Floyd's survey for the Boone's Station lands would be in conflict with this grant, and that would invalidate the claim. But before this became evident, Boone embarked into a whirlwind of land speculations, entering twelve claims totaling more than six thousand acres in the vicinity of Boone's Creek. In order to raise money for other speculations, he sold off rights to some of that land, including a parcel that fell within the bounds of the tract to which Hickman now held the title. Boone does not seem to have become aware of the problem until early 1783, for it was then that he reported it to Floyd, who wrote an alarmed letter to Preston. It was not until 1785, however, that Hickman finally came to Limestone and showed Boone his deed to the property. The man was understandably angry and accused Boone of conspiring with Floyd against his interests. Boone proclaimed his innocence of any cunning in the affair, arguing that he himself "had been grossly imposed on by Floyd." Sadly, Floyd was unable to state his own side of the dispute, having died in an Indian fight in 1783. "If it was done according to law," Boone said to Hickman, "I have no more to say." Boone proposed to give Hickman "two acres for one on the waters of Licking in lieu of what he had sold," but Hickman refused this offer, demanding the return of the sold portion or an equivalent tract on Boone's Creek. "The land should be given up," Boone agreed.

Problems like these, of multiple claims, faulty surveys, and shingled tracts, were typical. Jacob Boofman had already died, but his heirs took possession of the disputed tract and Hickman was forced to sue in 1785. It required an incredible twenty-three years of litigation before this complicated case finally was settled in his favor. But long before the Hickman family established their rights at law to the Boone's Creek tract, Boone had made good on his promise. Of his claims in the vicinity of Boone's Station he and his sons eventually received patents to four parcels containing a total of 2,279 acres. In 1794 he sold Hickman six hundred acres of his land "along the waters of Boone's Creek" for the symbolic exchange of "ten pounds good and lawful money of Kentucky." It was a characteristic gesture for a man who believed, as he frequently stated, "it is Never to Late to Do good."

A great deal of nonsense has been written on Boone's brief period in business, some of it originating with Boone himself. His record of purchasing warrants, entering claims, surveying, and selling land, documented for instance in the case of *Boofman v. Hickman*, does not jibe with the characterization in his congressional petition that he had been "inattentive to the means of acquiring property" and "ignorant of how to acquire it." When his father settled at Limestone, Nathan Boone said, "he thought himself worth a fortune in the wild lands of the country." Public records indicate that Boone filed at least twenty-nine claims to nearly thirty-nine thousand acres, and there may have been other entries, the records of which have not survived, for Nathan believed that all of his father's claims amounted "to well nigh one hundred thousand acres." In either case, his entries of the mid-1780s qualified Boone as one of the largest resident land speculators in Kentucky. His strategy was to enter all the claims he could afford, reasoning that this offered him the best insurance against caveats, challenges, and failures. In fact, although many of the claims failed to prove up, his entries resulted in the eventual grant to him of more than twelve thousand acres. This was certainly not the record of a man ignorant of the means of acquiring property. Boone knew what he was doing, although, as his speculations in the vicinity of Boone's Station demonstrated, things did not turn out the way he planned.

"Little by little," said Nathan, "his wealth melted away." This was the result of a number of factors. In the first place, he provided land for each of his sons and sons-in-law. Nathan remembered that when he married in 1799, his father "grieved" because "he had nothing to give him and [his] wife with which to commence the world." One of Boone's first priorities was the provision for his children, and while this cost him resources, it certainly cannot be counted a loss. But Boone was as trusting as he was generous, and he often suffered as a result. He said, for instance, that he had "intrusted to Col. Floyd all his lands, contracts, and rights, to perfect," and when Floyd died, all of these papers were lost, resulting in the failure of a large number of entries. He also had a reputation for lending money to friends and associates. "Boone just loaned my father," one man remembered, "without ever having seen him before." "So confiding" was his father, said Nathan, that he stood as security for the five hundred–pound debt of one Ebenezer Plat, a man with whom he did business in Limestone, and then thought nothing of lending him a horse, saddle and bridle, and his only male slave, never considering that the man might use them to abscond. Plat rode off for New Orleans, never to be seen again in Kentucky, and Boone not only lost his property but had to pay off the obligation.

Boone was cheated by others, among them Gilbert Imlay, a smooth-talking emigrant, lately retired from the officer corps of the New Jersey Line, who appeared in Limestone during the late winter of 1783. Like so many men, Imlay had come to Kentucky to speculate in land, and Boone had land, or rather entries on land, to sell. Imlay signed an obligation to purchase Boone's entry to what Nathan Boone described as "a splendid tract" of ten thousand acres several miles outside Limestone on the road to Lexington. "The Condition of the above Obligation," read their agreement, was that Imlay would purchase the land in installments at the price of ten pounds per hundred or, failing that, pay a bond of two thousand pounds. When Boone filed the survey in August of 1785 he had yet to receive the promised first payment, but he nevertheless endorsed the plat: "I do hereby assign my right and title of the within survey to Gilbert Imlay and his heirs and assigns."

Soon thereafter Imlay fled the state one step ahead of a hoard of creditors, without having paid Boone a farthing on this contract. In December of 1786 he wrote Boone from Virginia to say he was "sincerely sorry it is not in my power to pay, for Such is the embarrassing State of affairs in this Country that I have not been able to recover a pound from all the engagements that have been made me." He suggested that Boone look for another buyer for the tract, but upon checking at the land office it turned out that for an undisclosed sum, Imlay already had assigned the tract to James Wilkinson, and Boone lost the entire value of the property. Wilkinson, who about the same time was accepting secret payments from Spanish authorities in New Orleans, was connected with Imlay in a number of intrigues. One of the most galling things about the whole affair came when Wilkinson promoted the sale of this property with the imprimatur of its having been "located and surveyed by Col. Dan Boone." Imlay swindled a number of others, who had warrants issued for his arrest and announcements published in several major newspapers around the country. But he was already in England, where he published *A Topographical Description of the Western Territory of North America*, including in later editions Filson's Boone narrative as an appendix. Perhaps it was his way of repaying his debt, for with no property to attach, Imlay's bond proved as worthless as his word.

Boone lacked the ruthless instincts that speculation demanded. As the cases of Hickman and Imlay suggest, for him business obligations were personal matters, and doing the right thing frequently meant taking a financial loss. When he sold entries he often bonded them against challenges to the claim, pledging to "forever Defend the land and premises hereby bargained." Unfortunately, many of these entries failed, and as his nephew Daniel Boone Bryan put it, "Boone's honour compel'd him to pay up his bond while he owned one acre of land." This was certainly not the behavior of the typical land speculator. One Kentuckian complained of men who would "swear any Thing that is required" to make their profits, condemning them as "the most unprincipled Men living." Boone straddled the gap between two worlds, attempting to participate in a speculative economy that operated on the principle of no holds barred, while holding to standards of honor and personal obligation.

All of these factors really were incidental, however, to the failure of Boone's investment strategy itself. In the overheated speculative environment that existed in early Kentucky, in the mid-1780s the state of Virginia decided to assess not merely lands held under title but land claims as well, and thus Boone's property taxes reflected a valuation of tens of thousands of acres even though he never held clear title to more than several hundred. In order to hold on to what he considered to be his most important entries, he began to sell perfected titles to other tracts, often, according to Nathan, "for a trifle." The surviving records indeed document an average selling price of only forty-three pounds per hundred, a rate considerably below the prevailing market value of one hundred pounds. In this manner Boone disposed of 11,279 acres of the 12,179 granted to him.

He even began to sell entries, as he had done with Gilbert Imlay. Before he received the patent in 1787 to the five thousand acres assigned to him by Thomas Logwood, for example, Boone already had borrowed three hundred pounds against it, with the obligation that once he took possession he would convey four hundred acres "lying on the Waters of Licking about Twelve Miles from Limestone." In some cases, where his entries were threatened by other shingled claims, he sold his interest at deep discount to speculators endeavoring to buy up all of the competing claims. In all, Boone sold his rights to entries for at least twelve thousand acres. The failure of many of these claims meant that he frequently had to make good the losses, which in turn increased his requirement for more cash. Thus the speculative structure Boone had built collapsed of its own weight.

His entrance into the speculative world of business, Boone said, "plunged him into difficulty" with the law, and soon legal matters began to consume his time, driving him to distraction. Boone found himself in court so frequently that in the fall of 1785 he retained a Lexington attorney who agreed "to appear for him the sd Boone in all actions at Law brought by all against him." "I am to pay a Large sum of money at Cort on tusday Next," Boone wrote one of his clients, "I hope you will Come Down and satel on Monday Next at my house as I am very on well myself." When it came to court appearances he pled illness more than once. "I am so unwill it Is out of [my] power to Com to Cort," he wrote on another occasion. "My Sute I would Wish it put of[f] till Next Cort, in Less Capt Hayes Should be at Cort and then the tryel may Com on." From 1786 to 1789 he was a party to at least ten lawsuits. Men sued him for faulty surveys, failed claims, and breach of contract, for the debts of his own and the debts of others for whom he had posted bond. He lost most of these cases.

Authorities called on him to testify in numerous other suits, usually asking him, as the surveyor, to identify corner trees or landmarks. The record books of Kentucky counties are filled with Boone depositions, and reading the numerous times in which the man was taken through the same round of questions, it is easy to understand how his patience was tried. At the end of his testimony the lawyer for the opposing side often asked whether or not Boone stood to benefit by the outcome of the case. It was one of those pro forma legal questions, but Boone always seemed to take it as an insinuation about his character. Was it not the case that the defendant Leonard Hall had paid him a certain sum of money for his testimony? one lawyer inquired. "[I have] not received one shilling," Boone shot back angrily, "nor was never offered any sum," although he said he "intended to charge the said Hall for his trouble." Will you gain if the land claimed in this entry is saved? another lawyer asked him in a different deposition. "Not a farthing!" Boone replied. "Sensitive as he was," Nathan Boone explained, "these things greatly annoyed him." His testimony inevitably enraged those who lost their claims as a result, and Boone again began to worry about the resentment of his neighbors. He told his children that his life had been threatened a number of times, and, fearing assassination, he hesitated to travel alone through the country. "Even in time of peace," he said sadly, "his own Kentucky was as dangerous to him as in time of Indian dangers."

Actually, even in these years of formal peace the Indian danger continued unabated. Writing to apologize for the delay in surveying a tract upon the Licking River, Boone explained to one of his clients that "Times are a Litel Difegult at pres[ent] about Indians. 2 or 3 Companys have Lately been Droveen from that Qurter." Along the Ohio, the end of the Revolution simply commenced a new phase of the struggle between American and Indian villagers for control of the Ohio country. Fed by the flood of settlers coming down the Ohio—more than twelve thousand landed in Limestone from 1786 to 1788 alone—Americans pushed across the river in violation of both law and treaty, forcing Congress to call out the undermanned U.S. Army to remove them. But according to a commission sent by Congress to investigate, the Americans were "daily going over and rebuilding their houses and clearing the fields for spring crops." The British continued to occupy their northwest posts, despite peace terms that specified their evacuation, and they supplied the Indian resistance to settler expansion. "The Indians seem determined to defend themselves," wrote the governor general of Canada, "and make the Americans feel the difference of a war carried on in their own manner." It was bloody guerrilla war, with angry raiding back and forth across the river by both Indians and Kentuckians. "We have reason to believe," wrote the members of the congressional commission, "that too great a number of our own citizens on the frontier of our country are as little disposed to peace with the Indians as our neighbours [the British] are anxiously endeavoring to prevent it." According to official estimates, Indians killed three hundred Americans and stole twenty thousand horses along the Ohio from 1783 to 1787. There is no comparable count of Indians killed or horses stolen by Americans, but according to Arthur St. Clair, governor of the Northwest Territory, "Though we hear much of the Injuries and depredations that are committed by the Indians upon the Whites, there is too much reason to believe that at least equal if not greater Injuries are done to the Indians by the frontier settlers of which we hear very little."

At the port of Limestone, "ye indians was continually amoungst us," in the words of one resident. As commander of the local militia Boone was kept busy with defensive operations. "Sir," he instructed one of his subordinates in 1783, "you are amedetly to Call on Duty one thurd of our melitia, as will mounted on horse as poseble," and "if Sine [sign] be found the Commander to act as he thinks most prudent as you will be the Best Judge when on the Spot." It was, however, impossible to stay on top of the escalating violence. Disturbed by "a Deale of Sine Seen in Different places, in purtickuler Limston," he wrote Governor Patrick Henry in 1785 to say that "an Inden Warr is Exspcted" and beg for reinforcements. In the meantime, he worked to calm the situation as best he could, attempting to restrain the worst of the hotheads among the Americans while Congress negotiated with the Indians. Representatives of the Wyandots, Delawares, Chippewas, and Ottawas signed a peace agreement in January of 1785 at Fort McIntosh on the Upper Ohio, and a year later discussions began with peacefully inclined Shawnees at Fort Finney, at the mouth of the Great Miami, downriver from Limestone. The chief delegate for the Indians was Moluntha, whom Boone had fought at Boonesborough and knew well from his days at Chillicothe. While these negotiations were going on, a group of Kentuckians crossed the Ohio, stole into the Indian encampment, and "plundered them of their horses." When the renegades returned to the American settlements, bragging of their coup, Boone ordered the militia to round them up and take back the stock. "Some few horses have been returned by the vigilance of Col. Boone," wrote General Richard Butler, "but so great was the opposition to his measures amongst the people that he was obliged to desist." The typical Kentuckian "thinks robbing the Indians of their horses justifiable," Butler noted, but Boone believed it was wrong. His attempts at evenhandedness may have been unpopular, but the settlers nonetheless continued to rely on his leadership. One of Boone's grandsons remembered that whenever the Indian alarm was raised in Limestone, people came dashing into the tavern, shouting, "Where's Colonel Boone?" "Why de debil don't dey go to doing something," complained one old slave, "and not be asking all the time for Colonel Boone!"

The 1780s were difficult years for the Indians of Ohio. Chief Moluntha counseled accommodation with the Americans, but after he signed the Treaty of Great Miami most of his villagers rejected him for ceding lands in southern Ohio. Famine had struck in 1782 and 1784, and the resulting hard times encouraged an intensification of raids against the American settlements. During the first six months of 1786 attacks along the river took a greater toll than any comparable period of the Revolution, Col. Levi Todd of Fayette County wrote to Governor Henry, and he appealed that something "be done to secure the Lives and property of the Frontier Inhabitants." A number of Kentucky voices were raised in favor of separation from Virginia, or even secession from the confederation and alliance with Britain or Spain. Writing to the governor, Boone hoped that such calls "Will Bee No Baryer aganst any asistence government might gave us, as it is intirely against the voce of the peepel at Large." Todd agreed with Boone's assessment of popular sentiment but urged that attention "to the welfare of Kentucky might not be in any respect withdrawn until we are in a Situation to plan and execute for Ourselves." It was imperative that Virginia make a demonstration of its concern and its power by acting now to "retaliate at pleasure" against the Indians.

With no approval forthcoming, the Kentuckians planned an unauthorized and illegal invasion of their own, as much to mollify those calling for action as to win strategic advantage. For Boone it turned out to be an occasion for settling an old and bitter debt. General Clark placed Col. Benjamin Logan at the head of a militia force that would strike the Shawnee village complex on the headwaters of the Mad River, while he prepared to move north from the falls toward the Wabash towns. Clark's attack never materialized, but his preparations so alarmed the Indians that the Shawnees sent four hundred of their warriors to defend the Wabash towns, thus leaving their Ohio villages vulnerable to attack. On the night of September 29, 1786, eight hundred Kentuckians began to ferry across the river at Limestone, an operation that took until late the next afternoon. Boone was in command of one of the companies.

The slow-moving Kentuckians reached the outskirts of the Shawnee villages at about noon on October 6. The British agent Simon Girty, who was staying in Moluntha's town, reported that when the Indians heard the attack begin they "rose their Yankee colours" to announce their peaceful intentions, but it made no difference. There was some resistance but mostly wild panic as women and children fled before the rangers, raising the cry of war as they charged into the village. Col. Thomas Kennedy dashed in among a group of terrified women, wounding several with his slashing sword, including one captive American girl whom he mistook for an Indian. So shocked were some of the men by this unmanly conduct that they ridiculed Kennedy during the battle by calling out anonymously: "Who hacked the squaws? Who hacked the squaws?" Some of the men were so famished after days of marching that they headed directly for the steaming kettles of food left hanging over the fires outside the cabins. Quickly reaching the bottom of a kettle of hominy, one group found a large turtle thrown in whole, ungutted. While one man tore ravenously into the flesh, the others choked up their meals in disgust.

Riding at the head of his company, Boone saw no Indians, only dogs running ahead. Follow the dogs, he shouted, and they would soon find Indians. Galloping through the village with a small group that included Simon Kenton, he soon spied several warriors retreating across a grassy meadow. As he bore down, one of the sprinting men looked back over his shoulder and Boone shuddered in recognition of the unmistakable face. "Mind that fellow!" he called out to the others. "I know him. Big Jim, who killed my son in Powell's valley!" This Cherokee had a reputation as one of the most notorious murderers among the Indians. With a Cherokee war party he had brought two captured American women to the Shawnee towns and tortured them to death. Hearing Boone shout his name, Big Jim wheeled and fired his rifle at his pursuers, killing one of the mounted Kentuckians, and at almost the same moment he himself took a ball and crashed down into the tall grass. Boone and his men quickly dismounted and gathered around their fallen comrade, which gave Big Jim the opportunity to reload. He fired again, wounding another American. "God damn, you, don't shoot me!" the ranger cried as he staggered backward and collapsed. Seizing the moment, Kenton charged forward through the grass to Big Jim, loading for a third shot, and plunged his hunting knife into the wounded man's chest. Boone stood watching numbly as the rangers scalped Big Jim and mutilated his body.

"The Indians were obliged to give way," read the official British report of the battle, "being overpower'd by numbers." Deaths on both sides were relatively low—a score of Americans and perhaps ten Shawnees—but a number of accommodationist chiefs were among them. Most of the Indian villagers escaped into the woods to the north, but the Kentuckians succeeded in rounding up several dozen prisoners, mostly women and children but also a few warriors. One of the principal objects of the campaign was to take hostages who later could be exchanged for American captives who remained among the Indians. Among the prisoners was Chief Moluntha himself. He "would not fly," said one report of the engagement, "but displayed the thirteen stripes, and held out the articles of the Miami treaty," surrendering himself peacefully with the women of his family. Among them was Nohelema, the sister of Cornstalk and a female chief—what the Americans called a "queen"—a longtime friend of the United States whom the Americans called "the Grenadier Squaw" because of her commanding height and pride. Because they were wearing their robes of office and were adorned with sparkling silver jewelry, there was no mistaking the station of Moluntha and Nohelema. These were precisely the kind of prisoners that Logan most wanted to take.

The prisoners were corralled, and in the late afternoon, after the battle had wound down, Boone and some of the other officers struck up friendly conversations with old Moluntha and Nohelema. Someone lighted a pipe and it began to circulate. It was one of those incongruous moments conducted according to the woodland code of honor, but this scene was shattered by the sudden appearance of Hugh McGary, the hothead from the Battle of the Blue Licks, who was in command of a company from Lincoln County. Angrily he strode up to Moluntha, who smiled and extended his hand. Taking it, McGary inquired, "Was you in the Battle of the Blue Licks?" In fact, Moluntha had not been there; few Shawnees were. He may have misunderstood the question or simply was attempting to be friendly, but he nodded as if answering in the affirmative. "Then God damn you," McGary screamed, drawing a tomahawk from his belt, "I'll give you Blue Lick play," and in one powerful blow he cleaved open the old man's skull, killing him instantly. There was sudden chaos. Indian women and children screamed and ran, fearing that another massacre like the one of the Christian Delawares at Gnadenhutten was beginning. Some Kentucky officers recoiled in horror, others jumped on McGary to restrain him from attacking Nohelema. Simon Kenton, his son remembered, was so enraged that he came near to killing McGary and had to be restrained himself. This time McGary's rashness would result in a court-martial that busted him from rank, but otherwise he suffered no criminal punishment for his crime. His was not the only barbarous act in the aftermath of the battle. In the evening Tom Kennedy, the officer ridiculed for hacking squaws, attempted to vindicate his manhood by breaking into one of the cabins where the prisoners were being housed and tomahawking an unarmed man Boone described as "a fine looking young warrior." One man remembered that he "went and peeped in through a crack and saw the Indian sitting up with his scalp off." McGary and Kennedy "was not much censured," said Boone, and this outraged him.

Before the Americans returned to Kentucky, read the British report of the battle, "they laid in ashes the four Towns, destroyed all their Corn, and other produce and every thing else they had." The Shawnees harassed their rear as they withdrew down the banks of the Great Miami River but did not press a counterattack for fear of injuring the captive women and children being driven along with the army. The rangers took home considerable booty and horses, but after dividing the spoils it amounted to less than one pound of Virginia money per man. The Shawnees again abandoned their destroyed towns and relocated on the Maumee and Auglaze rivers in northern Ohio. There would be two disastrous American expeditions under Josiah Harmar and Arthur St. Clair in 1790 and 1791 before Anthony Wayne finally dislodged them from this stronghold at the Battle of Fallen Timbers in 1794, but the Logan campaign would be Boone's last major battle.

Back in Limestone, Boone drew the assignment of housing the Indian prisoners and provisioning them from his tavern and warehouse. "State of virgania Dr 19 galons of Whiskey Delivered to the Indins priserers on there first arrivel at Limeston, £3/0/0," he noted in his accounts for October 15. This was the first of numerous items he entered in a special account he labeled "Daniel Boones Indan Book," documenting the provisions he supplied for the six to ten months that the prisoners remained at Limestone. These included 900 pounds of flour, 15 bushels of corn, 350 pounds of bacon and dried beef, 48 quarts of salt, 70 pounds of tobacco, and 82 gallons of whiskey and brandy. The state of Virginia eventually settled this account, paying Boone the full amount he charged: £101.1.6.

Boone's land business demanded his attendance at the land office and the court, but he seems to have quit surveying, possibly because his affairs in Limestone required so much of his time. As commander of the local militia and the man acknowledged to be the most expert in Indian affairs, the arrangements for the exchange of prisoners for captives fell to him. His accounts document his activities. Nothing occurred during the winter, but with the first thaws in early February, Boone supplied two of the prisoners, a French Canadian trader and his Indian wife, with horse and saddle, rifle and provisions, and sent them home to the Shawnee towns with an offer of exchange. On March 4, Noamohouoh, a Shawnee chief, came in with a small delegation. Captain Johnny, a chief of the whole Shawnee nation, proposed to "collect the whole of the prisoners, which he will do, and be at Limestone within one month of the date hereof." "We mean to be at peace," Noamohouoh declared. He had brought three captive children to show the goodwill of his people, but he required the immediate release of Queen Nohelema, who was being kept under guard at the interior town of Danville, south of Harrodsburg. The chief proposed that he remain in Limestone to await Nohelema's release.

They would then return to the Shawnee towns together, and that would be the signal for the gathering of the American captives to begin. Boone invited Noamohouoh to stay at his tavern; knowing how important it was that the reciprocal exchanges continue, he agreed to Noamohouoh's terms.

But he found his fellow militia officers resistant. He sent a message to Logan, but it required all Boone's persuasion to talk the colonel into the proposition that he should authorize the exchange of such a valuable prisoner as Nohelema for mere children. It was several days before Boone obtained permission and sent a rider to Danville with the instructions for her release. But the rider returned with word from Col. Robert Patterson, who was in charge there, that he refused to agree. Such conflicts of authority were typical within the militia. With his Shawnee guest growing impatient, Boone dispatched an outraged letter. Although you and the other officers might disapprove of the terms, he wrote Patterson, he was the man on the spot. "I am hire With my hands full of Bisness and No athoraty," Boone wrote angrily, "and if I am Not indulged in What I Do for the best it Is Not worth my While to put my Self to all this trubel." Boone may well have sighed to himself that it was too much to expect these men, unschooled in the culture of the woodlands, to understand the code of honor. Be that as it may, Boone had offered himself as "Spisel [special] Security for the Complyance" and the question now was simply how "to Clear me of my obligation that I Come under to the Chief." "I flater my Self," he concluded with a characteristic rhetorical flourish, that Patterson would "Send the Indian Woman with the bearer." Finally it was done, and late in March Noamohouoh and Nohelema returned to the Shawnee towns. On his Virginia account Boone entered the terse notation, "Shanee Chief 20 days diet, £1/16/0."

Late in April a Shawnee by the name of Captain Wolf brought in nine more captive Americans and Boone and Patterson arranged for another release of Shawnee prisoners, but it was not until mid-August that an Indian runner appeared at the nearby town of Washington with word that Captain Johnny, leader of the Shawnee peace faction since the death of Moluntha, would soon arrive. A few days later about seventy-five Shawnee warriors, accompanied by a group of American captives, appeared on the far side of the Ohio, and as a sign of trust Boone sent two young Indian prisoners to their camp, escorted by his seventeen-year-old son, Daniel Morgan. The Indians signaled the Kentuckians to come over and Boone ferried across, accompanied by Logan and a number of husbands and fathers anxious to locate their missing kin. "Our people is scattered so far apart that it took me a great deal of trouble to get all the prisoners," Captain Johnny explained in his formal speech to the Kentuckians. "I was two moons out on the Wabash towns" where a number of captives were living, but the warriors there "would not give them up to their brothers the Big Knife." Those "wild young fellows" were still for war, and although "we cannot do any thing with them," he said, many towns in Ohio were for peace. "Our women have talked to us to take pity on them, and to make peace that we may live in peace and plenty." So he did not have all the captives, "but we hope through time we will be able to redeem them all; then we will live in peace and plenty like brothers." The previous December the most militant tribesmen of the region, including the Wabash Shawnees, had conferred in formal council near Detroit and afterward announced that they considered the Ohio country the collective territory of all of the Indian inhabitants, that none of it could be alienated without the consent of all, and that they intended to maintain the Ohio River boundary with the Americans. For all his talk of peace, nothing that Captain Johnny suggested violated these principles.

As senior officer, Logan responded, saying he was happy to talk of peace, for if the fighting long continued, "your country will lie waste, then the Americans will sell it, but if you will live at peace and keep possession of it, I expect the people of the United States in America will not take it from you." He was glad to see that they had brought captives, whose families were awaiting them, but until all of the Americans returned, some of the Indian prisoners must remain in custody, otherwise "I think the Great Man above will not think it justice." He was not authorized, he said, to treat on any other matters beside the exchange of prisoners. "I have no more to say to you," he concluded, "only advise you to go home and live at peace, and I will assure you, no army shall march against you from Kentucke." Actually, less than a month later the Kentucky militia attacked the last remaining Shawnee town in southern Ohio, and Logan surely knew of these plans even as he made his pacific pronouncements. Thus, having made these rather empty mutual avowals of peace, Logan, Boone, and several other Kentuckians, Captain Johnny and two other Shawnees, signed their names or marks to the English transcriptions of the two speeches and the formal exchange of prisoners began.

The return of captives was always a heart-rending scene. Among the group one husband found his wife, a prisoner for two years, dressed in leggings and woolen stroud. "She seemed broken in spirit," said one witness, "and paid but little attention to the whites, though she recognized her husband, who was deeply moved." He gave her soap and clean clothes and she went to the willows by the river, where she washed herself and changed her clothes, then rode off with him without ever having made a sound. Another man found his daughter, who had been captured several years earlier as the family crossed into Kentucky over the Wilderness Road. During her captivity she had married a Shawnee man, and though she now intended to return with her father, she and her husband parted with great weeping and affectionate embracing. Many white children clung to their Indian mothers, crying hysterically and refusing to be parted, while their anguished fathers attempted to pull them away.

One little girl of seven caught Boone's eye. He learned from the Indians that she had arrived only within the past few months and had not yet grown attached to her Indian family. There was no one to claim her, so Boone took her home to Rebecca. She was old enough to remember her name, Chloe Flinn, and over the next few months Boone made inquiries about her along the river. It took some months, but eventually Boone located Chloe's relatives and returned her to them. Indian raiders had attacked the Flinn farm in western Virginia, killed her father, and marched her mother, brother, and sister into captivity. After her mother's death the Indians separated the siblings, sending them to different towns. Her sister and brother remained with the Indians; she grew up to marry a Shawnee man and raise an Indian family, he became an interpreter and frontier trader. Chloe told her children that all she remembered of her captivity was playing with other children on a bearskin when up came a friendly man who called to her to jump up on his horse "and he would take her home," and he carried her across the river and out of the Indian life forever. She named one of her sons Boone, and another son, a representative in the Virginia assembly, introduced the motion that created a new county in the western part of the state with the name of her rescuer.

That evening, after the exchange of prisoners, Boone invited the Shawnees to come across the river for a celebration at Limestone. He provided them with a couple of beeves, which they slaughtered and barbecued, and he opened several kegs of whiskey, dutifully noting it all in his accounts. That night there was a party on the banks of the Ohio by the Boone tavern. One man remembered "an Indian beating music with a stick on a pair of old saddle-bags" while the others danced about the fire, "hideously painted in their grandest war style." Plenty of Kentuckians were there enjoying the free "peck and booze," and everything went well until one man claimed to have seen one of the Indians in possession of a mare stolen from a local widow and began drunkenly boasting that he would reclaim the horse even if he had to scalp every Indian there. "Boone and Kenton saw trouble brewing," said one witness, "and bought the mare of its Indian claimant for a keg of whiskey, returned her to the needy widow, and thus allayed the rising storm."

Boone made a number of friends among the Shawnees, including a young chief named Blue Jacket. This warrior was in fact an adopted American named Marmaduke Van Sweringen, captured during the Revolution when he was seventeen, who had taken his name from the blue linsey shirt he was wearing at the time. Blue Jacket quickly rose to be one of the most admired of warriors and became a war chief in his twenties. During the fall of 1787 Daniel Morgan Boone accompanied him on several hunts north of the Ohio River. Although he was associated with the young hotheads, Blue Jacket told the Boones that he would see to it that Limestone people were not taken captive, and according to one witness he kept his word by releasing at least one local resident from the hands of raiding Shawnee warriors. Boone soon had a chance to return the favor. In 1788 several Kentuckians pursuing horse thieves captured Blue Jacket, pummeling him and raising a welt on his forehead the size of a man's fist. "Boone! Boone!" he cried, and told them in broken English he was Boone's friend. Thinking that this was something they should check before they did something rash, the men took their prisoner to Limestone, and Boone locked him up in a cabin that he assured them was "hog tight." He invited the men to enjoy the hospitality of his tavern, and soon they were all drunk. They awoke the next morning to find that Blue Jacket had escaped. "A knife happened to be sticking in the logs near him," Boone explained, and "he worked around till he got it, cut the rope with which he was bound, and cleared out just about day [break]." Blue Jacket later became a commander of the Indian forces that defeated American expeditions led by generals Harmar and St. Clair and was a counselor to Tecumseh, but he remained Boone's friend.

Over the next two years Boone spent relatively little time in Limestone. In 1787 the voters of Bourbon County elected him to be their representative in the state assembly, and soon after the prisoner exchange he caught a keelboat upriver for the trip to the state capital with Rebecca and little Nathan, leaving the tavern under the management of his daughter Rebecca and her husband, Philip Goe, and his land business in the hands of Will Hays. In Richmond Boone sat in the assembly from October to January, offering a bill to establish ferries in Kentucky and speaking in support of a resolution that demanded Great Britain's surrender of the western posts, but once again proving himself to be a rather quiescent delegate. At the close of the session he returned to Kentucky. "I heartily wish you and your good Lady and little son Safe on the Banks of Limestone," a friend wrote to him at his departure.

Boone was no sooner home, however, than with his boys as polemen and Rebecca as cook he piloted a keelboat back upstream loaded with fifteen tons of ginseng root. "Sang," as everyone on the frontier called it, fetched a good price from American apothecaries and shippers who sent it to China. Daniel Morgan and Jesse had been working all winter to assemble this cargo. On the Ohio, as they attempted to cross a strong current at the head of an island just above Point Pleasant, the boat careened on a drifting log and began to fill with water. No one was injured but the cargo was nearly ruined, and Boone steered the awkward vessel into port in a dour mood. But here the Boones spent several delightful days with the family of an old friend, John Vanbibber, a man Boone had once rescued in a Kentucky snowstorm and who was happy to return the favor. After several days the Boones set out again, passing Pittsburgh and reaching Redstone on the Monongahela "in cherry blossom season," as Nathan remembered. Then it was overland along what later would become the Cumberland Road to Hagerstown, Maryland, where Boone sold the ginseng to Thomas Hart, who had established a trading operation there. Because of the condition of the goods, he did not receive half the price he originally had expected.

Daniel Morgan and Jesse seem to have turned back for Kentucky, but Boone, Rebecca, and Nathan went on to the old Boone neighborhood in Pennsylvania for an extended visit. "He and his wife came from Kentucky on horseback," an Exeter resident remembered, "and their little son rode behind his father the whole journey." In the nineteenth century people from the old neighborhood still repeated stories that they claimed Boone had told during this visit. One old woman had a distinct recollection of both Boone and Rebecca, who lived for several months in a little cottage near her own. Rebecca "was very pleasant and sociable, and spoke very freely of their affairs," but Boone she found "stern looking, very taciturn and gloomy."

People generally emphasized his friendly and open demeanor, but Boone was in the midst of a personal crisis. According to Nathan, it was during this stay in Exeter that Boone decided to leave Kentucky and relocate with the Vanbibbers on the Kanawha River at Point Pleasant. Although land remained one of his preoccupations for the rest of his life, circumstantial evidence suggests that he now stopped speculating in real estate. He had already quit making entries, probably having reached the limits of his resources, his credit, and perhaps his emotional energy as well. Once he returned to Kentucky he made a last series of sales, but thereafter he seems to have put the whole project out of his mind. He would engage in some surveying during his years on the Kanawha, but his career as a speculator was over except for the continuing legal and financial mess. Having to face his personal failings was enough to make any man in his mid-fifties gloomy.

It was another year before Boone finally relocated at Point Pleasant. When he returned to Limestone at the end of the summer with his three boys, including seven-year-old Nathan, he spent the fall and early winter camped out in the Kentucky hills, mostly digging and collecting ginseng in anticipation of a late-winter shipment. He also circulated through the Bluegrass buying up horses, and in December sent Daniel Morgan and Jesse with them by way of the newly opened Sandy River route to Thomas Hart's in Hagerstown. That month Boone arranged for the sale of his river lots in Limestone, and after the new year he, Rebecca, and Nathan left on a keelboat upriver, transporting his ginseng to market. This cargo came through safely, but at the rendezvous with his sons in Redstone he learned that they had lost a large number of horses along the rough route and that Hart reported that the market for sang had collapsed. Boone failed to meet even his costs in this enterprise.

By now Boone was a familiar figure along the river, and shipping would remain his principal occupation over the next few years. "Col. Boone left this garrison this evening in a Kentucky boat for Limestone," noted the Fort Harmar record on May 13, 1789, and two days later Boone was at Point Pleasant, where a young emigrant arranged to take passage for his sister and himself on Boone's boat. "I took breakfast with Col. Boon and his family," wrote Joel Watkins in his journal, "the best I had eaten for days." The winds and currents were so strong that the boat tossed badly and took on so much water that Watkins feared it would sink, but Boone seemed confident and tied up along the bank to sit out the storm. Embarking once again in the calm of the evening, after two more days of pleasant sailing they arrived in Limestone, but Boone was only in town long enough to load up for the return upriver. By the summer of 1789 the return address on his correspondence was "Grate Conhowway."

Like all of Boone's removes, this one became the subject of folklore. As he prepares for his final departure Boone goes to a young friend to say good-bye. "Well," says he, "I have concluded to leave Kentucky." "Where in the world are you going and what for?" comes the shocked reply. "To some point beyond the bounds of civilization and spend the remnant of my days in the woods," answers Boone. "For all my privations and toils I thought I was entitled to a home for my family," but "another bought the land over my head." Boone offers these parting words of wisdom: "I have lived to learn that your boasted civilization is nothing more than improved ways to overreach your neighbor." Knowing that Boone is without funds, the young man presses two pounds sterling on him, and Boone throws his arms about his friend's neck and weeps like a child. Then he departs, leading Rebecca and little Nathan on horseback, an image resembling the flight of Joseph and Mary into the wilderness.

Aside from such tales, there is little in the evidence to suggest that Boone left Limestone in utter despair and none to suggest such impoverishment. His deepening failure in real estate, which must have been painfully obvious to him, was not yet publicly evident, and he certainly was not about to announce it. By no means did he abandon his pursuit of profit, but continued for several more years to work as a small merchant, militia sutler, and shipper. He enjoyed a great deal of respect from his contemporaries, which his recent military and diplomatic leadership at Limestone had done much to heighten.

But the folklore struck at an essential truth. Boone was one of many who had reason to complain about the course of development. Kentucky was on the fast track, and the initiative in affairs was passing from men like Boone to planters, merchants, and lawyers. The image of the poor pioneer "unable to call a single acre his own" may not have fit Boone's case, but it applied full well to many of his contemporaries. Of the Kentucky pioneers who received warrants, nearly half failed to prove their claims, and by 1790 more than half of all households in the Bluegrass owned no land at all.

Boone's troubles were taken to stand for the experience of his contemporaries. During the 1780s Boone had attempted to make the transition from frontier to plantation, moving away from his past as a woodsman and hunter, but he did not have the temperament. So he left for a country where there was no speculative fever, where the hills and forests prevented the transplantation of a Tidewater aristocracy. His remove to the Kanawha took him back to a world in which he felt far more comfortable and marked a sharp change in the direction of his life. In the 1790s, as he passed into his sixties, he began moving back to the life of the woods.

CHAPTER EIGHT

A Wanderer in the World

1789 to 1811

The mouth of the Kanawha River was one of the best-known spots on the Upper Ohio, in Algonquian called *Tuenda-wie*, "the meeting of waters." The river valley led southeast through the mountains to the New and Greenbriar rivers and was an ancient Indian thoroughfare. In 1774 a Virginian army came up this valley, camped at the river mouth, and christened it Point Pleasant. There they defeated the Shawnees led by Chief Cornstalk, and there, three years later, they murdered Cornstalk and his son as they lay in the dungeon of Fort Randolph. After the Revolution a small frontier settlement grew up around the fort, although some residents whispered that it was cursed, haunted by Cornstalk's ghost, and eventually the community atoned by constructing a monument to the chief on the courthouse lawn. The town lay on the point of land formed by the intersection of the rivers, offering a commanding view of the Ohio and its extending shore. This became a regular stop on the trip downriver from Pittsburgh, and travelers agreed that the location was well named. "Point Pleasant is a most beautiful place and very rich land," wrote one emigrant of 1789, with "very few inhabitants and but indifferent buildings." The Boones moved to a cabin here with their three boys. A century later old residents pointed to an old log structure still standing on the bank of Crooked Creek said to have been their house.

At the Point, Boone continued to operate a little store, although considerably more of his trade here was in skins and furs. Hunters and trappers from the Lower Kanawha brought their catch and bargained for supplies. The floor of the Boone place was piled high with packs and the rafters hung with meat. A friend who lodged with them during the summer of 1792 recalled that the bear bacon "dripped grease in my face that night as I lay there." Periodically Boone sent his collected produce upriver with Daniel Morgan or Jesse. Matthew Vanlear, a Maryland merchant, wrote to Boone in early 1790 to inform him that one of his sons had delivered at Hagerstown a shipment including 2 barrels of ginseng, 1,790 deerskins, 129 bearskins, and a number of fine fox and otter furs, which at current prices must have been valued at nearly three hundred pounds. These Boone exchanged for a supply of trade goods. "We have sent you such of the goods as we had on hands which you Ordered," Vanlear noted, and "the amount of Sales shall be duly passed to your Creditt after deducting Commission and other charges." At the conclusion of these transactions Boone continued to owe a balance on his account. "We have no Objection to Crediting 6 mo. but cannot want our Money longer," wrote Vanlear, reporting that "your son has given us Assurances that he will be in with us in June or July, with what furrs, Bever, &c he can Collect." Two years later Vanlear was writing again to "request your Assistance as early as possible." "If you can discharge the Ballance due us this Spring we shall be exceedingly oblidgd." It was the same old story. Boone never seemed to be able to dig himself out of debt.

He also worked some as a surveyor. Soon after arriving at the Point he assisted in stretching the chain at a site across the river called Gallipolis, in anticipation of the arrival of a group of French emigrants in October of 1790. At the Point he "laide off for Willeam Allin ten acres of Land Situate on the South Este Side of Crucked Crick." He did not qualify as a deputy county surveyor, although his name appeared numerous times in the records of the surveyor's office as a marker or guide. These various enterprises produced a modest income. On the county list of tithables for 1792 Boone's valuation was two horses, one slave, and five hundred acres of land.

But there was local fame if not fortune. In 1789 the state of Virginia created the county of Kanawha, covering the settlements scattered along the river from the head of navigation on the river at Kelly's Creek to the Point, and at the first meeting of the county court in October the justices recommended Boone for the post of lieutenant colonel in the militia. This made him the third-ranking officer in the county, serving under Sheriff Thomas Lewis and Col. George Clendenin, the largest local landowners.

Desperate guerrilla fighting characterized these final years before the defeat of the Ohio Indians at the Battle of Fallen Timbers in 1795, and at every alarm people at the Point fled to the fort where Boone led the defense. In 1789 Indians attacked Tackett's Fort, about forty miles upriver, and the next year stormed Fort Lee, but far more dangerous were the small raids on isolated cabins or small parties of hunters. Boone's friends the Vanbibbers were hit hard. While John Vanbibber was working in a sugar grove on the Indian shore, a canoe of Shawnees intercepted his son and daughter coming across in a canoe, killing and scalping Rachel and taking Joseph captive. Another group attacked the cabin of John's sister Brigetta only a mile or two away from the Point, killing her husband and children and dragging her into captivity. Indians waylaid two sons of Peter Vanbibber, capturing Jacob and wounding Matthias (known as "Tice"), who fell into a ravine and hid. Eventually these three kidnapped Vanbibbers returned, either escaped or redeemed, but their fate and the fate of others like them preoccupied this frontier community.

Daniel Morgan Boone said that with his hunting companion Tice Vanbibber he "had several narrow escapes from the Indians who chased them." Once, out hunting with his father across the river, young Daniel heard rifle fire and the whiz of a ball by his ear, and, looking around, saw three Indians bearing down on him. He raced desperately back to camp by the river, and as he burst through the trees he saw his father readying their canoe; they quickly passed over the river to safety. When Colonel Clendenin of the Kanawha militia received a report in December of 1789 that the Indians "have killed young Daniel Boone and took his father old Col. Boone prisoner," it was all too credible. "I fear this news is true," Clendenin wrote. Fortunately, it was not. "I shall be in Philadelphia this winter," Boone had promised some associates, and after he and his son had finished their business they tarried along the route home to hunt and trap, returning safe and sound in the early months of 1790. Three years later there was even greater concern over Boone's long delay in returning from his winter hunt, and even Rebecca, whom her children considered a tower of strength, began to worry. He finally came in, though, reporting that considerable movement among the Indians had forced him to lie low for several weeks. But the worry spreading through the settlements gave rise to a report from the Kanawha country, printed in April in the *United States Gazette*, that Boone had been "killed or taken." It would not be the last premature notice of his death.

In April of 1791, at the polling place of Fort Lee, which later grew into the city of Charleston, now capital of West Virginia, Boone participated in an election for two county representatives to the Virginia assembly. A man had to be extremely interested in voting to travel the many miles from his station or settlement, and not more than a few dozen citizens troubled to show up to take their turn announcing their choice to the county sheriff viva voce. "At an open and fair election," Sheriff Lewis certified, "George Clendenin and Daniel Boone were Chosen." Pairing him with Colonel Clendenin, being returned for the second of many consecutive terms, indicated the high regard in which the Kanawha settlers held Boone. During the assembly session that lasted from October through December, Boone sat quietly for his third term, voting with the majority most of the time and serving on two committees. He was there for the debates on the pending separation of Kentucky from Virginia and its admission as a sovereign state under the newly approved federal constitution.

Boone took Rebecca and Nathan with him to Richmond. A boy of ten at the time, Nathan later recalled this trip with nostalgic clarity. He remembered going to the sergeant at arms of the assembly to say he had an urgent message for his father, and Boone hurrying up with a worried look that changed to smiles when the boy told him he simply needed pocket money in order to buy some trinkets in town. He remembered a family picnic by the river, where his father bought oysters from a vendor and his mother roasted them over an open fire. The autumn evening growing cold, Nathan began to shiver, and Boone sat hugging him as they watched the flames together. On their way over the Midland Trail, which connected the Kanawha with the Shenandoah Valley, they stopped to visit Boone's old boyhood friend Henry Miller. One morning as they were walking through the fields, they spied a group of deer grazing by the wood's edge. "Name the one you want," Boone said to his friend. "Give me the large Buck." He fired and the buck dropped. "I have killed him, you stick him," Boone cracked. Later, admiring one of Miller's large bulls, Boone remarked what a good powder horn it would make. Miller had the animal killed, then presented the horn to Boone. In his evenings Boone worked it, engraving upon it his name and the year, and gave it to Nathan as a reminder of this wonderful trip.

But in standing for the assembly Boone had something more on his mind than a vacation with his wife and son. He believed in public service, never hesitated to claim the honor of office, and was not shy about using the perquisites of position. While he was in Richmond he presented the governor with a request. "Sum purson Must Carry out the armantstion [ammunition] to Red Stone" on the Monongahela River, he wrote. "I would undertake it, on condition I have the apintment to vitel the company at Kanhowway." Supply of the frontier counties was a constant problem, and absent the delivery of arms and ammunition from the state, county commanders such as Clendenin were required to purchase supplies with their own funds at high market prices. Boone proposed to supply the northwestern counties from the state's storehouse at cost, "without change or barter, solely in the service of the Commonwealth," if granted the exclusive right to supply rations. It was a business that promised a regular, if modest, income, and as an experienced militia commander and a frontier trader Boone seemed a logical candidate for the position. In December the state of Virginia contracted with him for his services.

At the close of the legislative session Boone hastened to the state armory on the Potomac, where on December 22 he was issued four hundred pounds of powder, sixteen hundred pounds of lead, and a keg of flints with instructions to transport them to militia companies along his route, from Moorfield in the Shenandoah Mountains to Morgantown on the Monongahela and Wheeling on the Ohio. It was a slow process, transporting the ammunition over the mountains and down the rivers, and it was April before Boone made the last of his deliveries. Supplying the Kanawha militia with rations, however, proved to be more problematic. Boone found that his outstanding debts made it impossible for him to purchase flour and bacon on credit, and when he landed at Point Pleasant in May he did not have sufficient supplies.

He found Hugh Caperton, captain of the Kanawha rangers, impatiently waiting, not only for rations but for ammunition as well. Colonel Clendenin had assumed incorrectly that Boone would be carrying powder and ball for his men, which he was not. There was an angry confrontation between Caperton and Boone that degenerated into shouting. Boone himself had recommended the appointment of young Caperton as "a fitt and proper person to command," but now he found that the man was a martinet. Caperton accused him of incompetence, and, fuming, Boone picked up his rifle and stomped off into the woods. He was gone for several days. "In consequence of the default of the contractor, Colonel Boon," Caperton reported to Clendenin, "it had not been in his power to bring forward his company, as no provision had been or was about to be made for them." Once again the colonel had to supply the militia from his own pocket, and he hurried down to the Point with Sheriff Lewis to investigate, but they were forced to cool their heels by Boone's absence. Lewis went off in pursuit, and finally came back with the news that, finding Boone in a woods camp, he had asked for an explanation, but Boone simply had declared that "Captain Caperton did not do to his liken." In his written report to the governor, Clendenin accused Boone of "total non-compliance" with his contractual obligations. He stood at risk of a court-martial, but in deference to his reputation Clendenin merely appointed another supplier in his place.

With this incident Boone's patience for business finally seems to have snapped. Sometime the next year he closed his store at the Point and relocated with Rebecca to a squatter's cabin sixty miles upriver near Fort Lee, commanding an expansive view of a celebrated salt lick at the mouth of Campbell's Creek on the Kanawha, where he often went to hunt. To his nephew John Grant in Kentucky, Boone granted his power of attorney, with instructions to handle his legal affairs but "never to contest these claims," for even if successful it "would cost more time, money, and vexation than they would be worth." He told his children that "he would rather be poor than retain an acre of land or a farthing in money, so long as claims and debts hung over him." He continued to keep in contact with old associates but became increasingly inattentive to their demands. "I have ever been friendly to you and wished you better success in life than you have experienced," wrote Charles Yancey, but he had to complain that "a number of the locations you charged me for are not surveyed or returned and may possibly be lost to us forever." He looked for a communication from Boone and hoped "that we shall be yet friendly and ready to render each other that service that common justice requires." But with his move up the Kanawha, Boone turned away from business, devoting himself completely to hunting and trapping, as he had as a young man.

Boone, however, was no longer young. During one hunting trip he appeared at the cabin of a family asking for lodging. To the young son of the householder he appeared to be a tired old man who badly needed a rest. "Come young man, get your trap and go with me," Boone invited the boy after a good night's sleep in a bed, "and I will show you how to catch beaver." He spent far more of his time trapping beaver now, for it required less exertion. He was afflicted with periodic spells of rheumatism, and during his winter hunt in 1793–94 he suffered so severely that he took to attending the traps while his comrades hunted for larger game, a task Boone had always reserved for himself. It got so bad that winter that one of the men had to carry Boone on his back across the creeks to his trap line, then back again at night. At such times, one of his relatives remembered, he could not lift his foot without difficulty. But even then, he said, old Boone "could kill more deer than his neighbors, he knew their haunts and habits so well."

One winter in the mid-1790s a Kentuckian found Boone in a hunter's camp on the Levisa Fork of the Big Sandy River in the mountains of eastern Kentucky, living with Rebecca and two of their daughters and their husbands. Boone had discovered this site while hunting with Jesse about 1790, and for most of this decade he and the family returned here each winter to hunt. "They had some half-faced camps," the man remembered, and "ate their meals from a common rough tray, very much like a sap trough, placed on a bench instead of a table, each using as needed a butcher-knife to cut the meat." Bear bacon and cured skins hung from the trees all around the camp. Boone boasted that he recently had killed "the master bear of all the Western country," a monster weighing five or six hundred pounds and measuring two feet across the hip bones. Boone told another friend that he had taken 155 bears near this camp during a single three-week period and one morning had "killed eleven by late breakfast time." This was commercial hunting. One fall the family rendered the meat into bear grease, which they brought downriver in vessels made of buffalo hide, and sold several dozen barrels at a dollar a gallon. This abundance was reflected in Boone's name for the nearby branch, Greasy Creek. (Today the hamlet of Boon's Camp, near Paintsville, Kentucky, stands on this site.)

While Boone's rheumatism continued, Rebecca became a regular companion on his hunts, keeping camp and carrying his gun when he was unable to do so himself. For the first time since they married nearly forty years before, they found themselves without children at home. Soon after their arrival at the Point, Jesse had begun courting Chloe Vanbibber, John Vanbibber's daughter, and by 1792 he was married and listed as an independent head of household on the county roll of tithables. Daniel Morgan, a man in his early twenties, seemed possessed of his father's wanderlust and was always out hunting and scouting for land. And in 1792 the Boones sent Nathan to Kentucky to attend a Baptist school.

Nathan returned to the Kanawha in 1794 when he was thirteen, his formal schooling at an end. That fall, when the air was frosty and the leaves falling, he and his father went on a hunting trip on the Indian shore across the river from the Point. Leaving the boy to tend the fire, Boone went into the woods the first morning, and as Nathan was picking up the camp he looked up to see a large buck standing not more than twenty steps away. He grabbed his rifle and fired as the buck darted into the forest. Boone reappeared instantly, and, relieved to find there was no trouble, took a look around and motioned the boy to follow him. Some eighty yards into the woods they found the dead buck. It was the first deer he had killed, Nathan remembered, and since he passed this test, his father now took him into the woods and began to teach him the tricks of his woodcraft. After several days of hunting, as they bedded down by the river, Boone heard the sound of chopping from the other side. The Indians had discovered their fire, he whispered, and were building a raft to cross; load the canoe and lie flat in the bow. The boy did as he was told and Boone silently pushed off from the stern into the dense fog covering the river. Bending his head low to the water, he soon caught a glimpse of the raft coming across. Turning the canoe into the current, he silently guided them downriver to safety.

This incident struck Nathan for the first time with the great dangers of his father's way of life. After several years in Kentucky, he said, he had grown accustomed to the "quietness and safety of the interior," and he appealed to his parents to move back to the Bluegrass, away from the river. Daniel Morgan owned a tract of unimproved land on Brushy Fork of Hinkston Creek, along the Maysville Road about twelve miles from the Blue Licks, and he offered it to his parents. The Indian danger was greater than ever, and this may have helped persuade the Boones to return. Moreover, the homes of their four daughters and their growing families were near the Bushy Creek land, and perhaps the Boones looked forward to spending more time with their grandchildren. During the summer of 1795 the Boones came down the river with their possessions and settled at Brushy Fork, where Boone and Nathan erected a one-room cabin and broke the land for several acres of crops.

Boone, Rebecca, and Nathan lived for three years in the little cabin on Brushy Fork, chopping in a crop of corn in the spring and hunting on Big Sandy for bears in the fall. But practically no game remained in the region of the Bluegrass. Boone later spoke wistfully of the depletion of game in Kentucky. "At the time when I was caught by the Indians," he sighed, "you would not have walked out in any direction for more than a mile without shooting a buck or a bear. There were then thousands of Buffaloes on the hills in Kentucky; the land looked as if it never would become poor; and to hunt in those days was a pleasure indeed." But by the 1790s all of this had changed. Sometime early in the decade an unknown hunter shot the last buffalo in the state. Reflecting back, Boone later remembered that "a few signs only of a deer were to be seen, and, as to a deer itself, I saw none." Tradition says that during their winters on Brushy Fork the Boones were reduced to living on mutton.

Few things went well for him during these years. In 1796 he applied to Governor Isaac Shelby, an acquaintance from pioneer days, for an appointment as a commissioner to oversee the upgrading of the Wilderness Road into a good wagon route, a position that paid a stipend of two thousand pounds. To Boone's way of thinking he was the obvious man for the job. "I think my Self intitled to the ofer of the Bisness, as I first Marked out that Rode in March 1775 and Never rec'd anything for my trubel," he wrote. "I am no Statesman," he declared, "I am a Woodsman, and think My Self as Capable of marking and Cutting that Rode as any other man." He asked the governor "to wright me a Line by the post the first oportuneaty," but he never heard back, and the position went to another. This letter is the only record of Boone's involvement in politics during these years. Boone's disillusionment with business extended to public service as well.

In fact, he had developed a reputation for unreliability, and that certainly did not help his case with Shelby. "Boone I believe has acted like a scoundral," Nathaniel Hart, Jr., declared to his uncle Thomas Hart concerning lands that Boone had surveyed for them. "Col. Shelby and myself went up last fall to Survey yours" and found that "Boone had Surveyed his Preemption on Uncle David Harts and my Fathers." "I expect I shall have to stand a Lawsuit," he wrote. A few years later young Henry Clay, who had married into the Hart family, filed a lawsuit to recover this land, with Boone one of the codefendants. Clay lost this case, with the court declaring that there was no evidence "to convict Boone of fraud," but Boone's reputation had already suffered badly. John Grant was kept busy with other suits such as these filed against his uncle Daniel and in September 1796 had to post bond in order to prevent being jailed for a £150 debt of Boone's that he had assumed. During these years several thousand acres of Boone's remaining lands in Kentucky were sold for nonpayment of taxes, and finally he deeded over to Grant his last remaining tract of ten thousand acres. Grant later wrote to say that "money is so scarce that it scarcely will be got for yr land enough to pay yr Expense of law." Boone "never troubled himself to enquire" how his nephew disposed of this tract, said Nathan. Finally, in November of 1798, the Fayette court directed the sheriff of Mason County to take Boone into custody after he had ignored a summons on a suit for six thousand pounds. The warrant still exists, with the sheriff's notation "Not Found" scratched on the reverse side. The Boones had left Brushy Fork only a few weeks before and were living in a cabin at the mouth of the Little Sandy River on the Ohio where, after the defeat of the Indians at Fallen Timbers, Nathan and his cousin Jonathan Bryan had gone to break land. As Fayette attempted to hunt Boone down, the Kentucky assembly carved out a new county along the Ohio from former Fayette territory and named it in his honor.

This move to the Little Sandy was only temporary, for Boone and his extended family were already planning a major emigration, one that would take them not only out of Kentucky but out of the United States entirely and into the Spanish territory of Upper Louisiana on the Missouri. After the Treaty of San Lorenzo of 1795, which settled the outstanding differences between the United States and Spain, the Spanish authorities in Louisiana began to focus on the danger of a British attack from Canada. Indeed, Britain and Spain went to war in the fall of 1796, and the Spanish worried about how they might defend their underpopulated territory. "I see no other means than that of the United States," wrote Lieutenant Governor Zenon Trudeau to the governor general in New Orleans, "who alone can supply a great number of families." Beginning in 1796 the Spanish circulated handbills throughout the American West, promoting a program of liberal land grants and no property taxes. Unable to find cheap land in Kentucky, it appeared to one member of the Kentucky gentry that "the poorer Class of people" were all headed for Spanish territory. "There seems at present to be a great rage for new and frontier places," another wrote, now that "the range and game are totally gone, which all the first settlers consider as invaluable." In Missouri, Trudeau jubilantly reported that "American families are coming to us daily," and a Spanish commandant on the Missouri wrote that "if there were about two hundred Families more permitted to emigrate to this district it would be one of the most Flourishing settlements in Louisiana."

Other Spaniards were not so sure. In 1798 a new governor general halted American emigration briefly while he reviewed the requirement that all settlers profess Roman Catholicism; although the requirement remained, the lieutenant governor in Saint Louis winked at violations. Another official argued that if the territory were to remain in Spanish hands, the Americans must be held at the Mississippi, especially "a person named Boone, who is the same one who first penetrated the wildernesses of Kentuqui." Boone himself later declared that he never would have thought to settle outside the United States "had he not firmly believed it would become a portion of the American republic." There was, to be sure, considerable hindsight in this observation. But Boone might well have held the same opinion as Thomas Jefferson, who upon hearing of the Spanish invitation to Americans declared, "I wish a hundred thousand of our inhabitants would accept," for "it may be the means of delivering to us peaceably what may otherwise cost a war." Indeed, by the time Jefferson acquired Louisiana in 1804, Americans constituted 60 percent of the ten thousand residents of the upper portion of the territory.

Boone's plan to emigrate to the Missouri country received encouragement from his brother Squire, back in Kentucky after nearly a decade of failed attempts to settle at a number of locations. Like Boone, Squire had emerged from the Revolution a hero, served a term in the Virginia assembly, and entered claims to thousands of acres of Bluegrass, but also like his brother, he soon was besieged by creditors and lawyers. Squire once compressed the story of his life into a short statement. While serving in the legislature, he said, he had been invited to dine with the governor, and "that is as high a grade of honour as I ever Rose to." Only a few years later he was so poor that he had to steal hominy from a slave, and "that is as low a grade as I ever have been Reduced to." And "every place between these two extremes I have experienced." In desperation Squire left Kentucky and with his family tried settling at the mouth of the Yazoo River on the Mississippi (near what would become Vicksburg), but was driven off by the Indians. He ended up spending three years in New Orleans, where he found the Spanish friendly and accommodating, but, uncomfortable with urban life, he made another unsuccessful attempt to settle in Spanish Florida, then took his family to Pennsylvania, where they lived with relatives for several years. Ever the optimist, Squire was now anxious to give Missouri a try.

Since 1795 Daniel Morgan Boone had been visiting various locations in the Old Southwest, looking for the right place to make his fortune. In 1797 he crossed the Mississippi to scout the Missouri country for his family, just as Boone's father had helped reconnoiter Pennsylvania for the clan back in England. Exploring the hill country on the northern bank of the Missouri, he located a beautiful valley along a creek called Femme Osage, with abundant game, rich bottom land, and easy access to the broad river. Representing his father, he paid a call on Lieutenant Governor Trudeau with two principal concerns: what compensation could the governor offer if Boone were to lead a large emigrant company to the territory, and would they be required "to embrace the Catholic religion." Delighted that a man of Boone's reputation would think of removing to his country, Trudeau wrote to Boone expressing his pleasure. Although Spanish regulations restricted individual grants to eight hundred arpents (a little more than a square mile), this would be waived in Boone's case, and as the leader of the company he would be granted one thousand arpents of land for himself, with six hundred for each family settling under his auspices. The religious requirement, he assured Boone, would not be enforced.

With four slaves, Daniel Morgan built a solid cabin and commenced breaking land near the mouth of Femme Osage Creek. Applying for his own grant, he found Trudeau ever so willing to bend the rules. Normal procedures required applicants for concessions to have settled on the land for at least a year, said Trudeau, but this would be no barrier. "Daniel Morgan Boone, owner of four slaves, and of numerous cattle," read the French text dated September 1, 1797, "has the honor of representing to you that with your agreement he has settled for more than a year on a tract located in the area of the Femme Ozage River." This was stretching the truth, but below the appeal Trudeau indicated his approval in Spanish.

Daniel Morgan was back with his father at the mouth of the Little Sandy in the fall of 1798, leaving his slaves behind to tend the farm at Femme Osage. Trudeau's letter and his son's firsthand report convinced old Boone that the time was right to try the Missouri country. As had been the case when he moved across the mountains to Kentucky, Boone was being both pushed and pulled. In most accounts it is the push that gets the emphasis. "He was harrasd and pestered," said Daniel Boone Bryan, and it was "the bad treatment of those for whom he had located lands" that "was the cause of his leaving his beloved Kentucky and moving into the Spanish Government." In the words of a family friend, Boone "was soured against Kentucky." These comments and others like them tell only half the story. The souring had begun at least a decade before, yet it had not prevented the Boones from returning from the Kanawha and moving into the cabin along Brushy Creek. Boone surely was pulled by Missouri as much as he was pushed by Kentucky.

He gave expression to his motives in a 1797 conversation with Francis Bailey, an English adventurer whom Boone encountered canoeing alone on the Ohio River with his dog and traps. Bailey called to come aboard his flatboat, and Boone was delighted when the traveler, learning his identity, produced a copy of Filson's narrative and began to read aloud from it. It must give you a good deal of satisfaction, declared Bailey, practically quoting from Filson's conclusion, to have witnessed the mighty state of Kentucky arising from the wilderness you discovered. But old Boone shook his head in disagreement. Kentuckians "were got too proud," said he, and pronounced himself "unwilling to live among men who were shackled in habits." He wished only "to hunt for beavers in some unfrequented corner of the woods," to live a life undisturbed by the troubles of civilization. "I easily conceived his meaning," wrote Bailey. "He was one of that class of men who, from nature and habit, was nearly allied in disposition and manners to an Indian, and may be ranked under those who form the first class of settlers in a country." Bailey got it right. Boone's happiness was the life of the frontier. The prospect of a new start in a fresh land, his family and friends gathered about him, lifted his spirits. He might yet succeed in constructing a little backwoods community where he would be honored as a founder, a patriarch. Jemima put it well when she later told her daughter that in Kentucky her father "became somewhat disheartened." But then the Spanish governor wrote, "promising him ample Portions of Land for himself and family," and so "he pilled up Stakes, hearing of the Game and Indians in Misoura."

The family began making preparations for moving in the spring of 1799. Boone and Nathan cut down a huge poplar they had found about a half mile from their cabin and began constructing a large pirogue measuring fifty or sixty feet long and five feet across. It was September before the dugout was finished, the household goods, supplies, and tools packed and loaded, and the family ready to depart. Nathan and Daniel Morgan were responsible for manning the great boat on which their mother was a passenger. Squire Boone and several of his grown sons occupied another dugout; Jane Van Cleve Boone, his wife, exhausted after their many moves, refused to accompany the party, but Squire was hopeful that he could persuade her to follow him once he had built a house for her in Missouri. There must have been several more boats to accommodate the others who joined the emigration, both families and single men, including a number of Daniel Morgan's friends who, like him, were headed west to begin their adult lives. Boone, with a hired man and several slaves, drove the cattle, horses, and hogs along the river trail. The two contingents came together briefly at Limestone, where Susannah, Jemima, and their families joined the party, Boone's daughters and seventeen grandchildren finding places in the pirogues while Will Hays and Flanders Callaway helped to drive the stock. Three Boone children—Jesse, Levina, and Rebecca—remained with their families in Kentucky. A Limestone resident remembered the commotion of the Boone camp, the children playing and crying, women unpacking and repacking tin cups, cooking utensils, and blankets, and the tearful farewells.

Through these first days of the journey Nathan grew increasingly troubled, for each mile took him further from young Olive Vanbibber, the girl he had been courting, who lived fifteen or twenty miles upriver from the mouth of Little Sandy. People said she was "the handsomest young lady north of the Ohio." By the time the party stopped at Limestone he had decided to return and marry the girl, but he did not know if he could convince her to make the move to Missouri. His brother Jesse was married to Olive's cousin Chloe, and although they would remain behind, another of her cousins, Isaac Vanbibber, had recently married sister Susannah's eldest child, Elizabeth, and already was en route. It was the old Boone pattern of family alliance through a series of marriages. Obtaining his parent's blessing and a marriage license in Limestone, Nathan turned back. A week later, on September 26, 1799, the couple was wed. A child of westering folk, Olive agreed without hesitation to make the move. "On the first of October, without any company but my husband," she would remember many years later, "I started out to Missouri," her trousseau packed on a horse. The couple survived on parched corn and the wild game Nathan took along the way, sleeping at night on the ground by an open fire. At Vincennes they were laid up with a crippled horse for a week or more, and it was the end of the month before they entered Spanish territory. "My husband rowed and I steered and held the horses by the bridle," she remembered. "It was rather a perilous trip for so young a couple. I was just sixteen, my husband eighteen."

The main party crossed the Mississippi in the first week of October. Young Henry Dodge remembered Boone leading his family into Saint Louis. "He rode a sad looking horse [with] saddle bags, rifle on his shoulder, leather hunting shirt, and a couple of hunting knives in his belt, accompanied by three or four hunting dogs." But he was greeted with pomp and ceremony. Trudeau had passed the duties of the lieutenant governor's office on to Don Charles Dehault Delassus, a French aristocrat in the Spanish service, but both men were present to welcome the Americans. The small Spanish garrison paraded, with flags unfurled, drums rolling, sabres flashing in an impressive display. It would be the only time in his life that Boone received military honors. In a private meeting Boone presented Delassus with a list of fifteen Americans, heads of household emigrating under his authority. The governor told Boone that not only was he prepared to honor all of Trudeau's commitments but he would lay off the country of the Femme Osage as a separate administrative district with Boone himself "syndic," or chief administrative officer, an office vested on local land barons, combining the functions of justice of the peace and militia commandant. Boone's official appointment came through on June 11, 1800.

Using Boone's list, Delassus issued concessions for each "associate of M. Daniel Boone" who had "received the agreement of Monsieur le Lieutenant-General of the Illinois Territory, to obtain there for himself and his men tracts of land." The applicant, read each petition, "having no other aim than that of living as a peaceful farmer and subject of the laws of the Government, will at all times provide an example of faithfulness and obedience." As syndic Boone would decide about the specific allocations of land. To strengthen the land claims of the emigrants, Trudeau helpfully signed each concession in advance, antedating them to correspond with the date of his original offer. In order to receive final title these tracts had to be surveyed and a plat filed, the land improved with a dwelling house, fences, and cultivated fields, and a deed procured from the office of the governor general in New Orleans. But with a wave of his hand Delassus assured Boone that these conditions did not apply to a syndic. A strong advocate of emigration to the territory, he even suggested that if Boone was able to encourage another one hundred American families to take up residence in the Femme Osage, the government would increase the size of his concession from one thousand to ten thousand arpents. After Boone's experiences in Kentucky the cooperative attitude of the Spanish governor must have seemed like a dream, but again he was too trusting, for he did not bother to have these understandings committed to paper.

Within a few days the emigrants were passing through Saint Charles, a frontier village situated on the first high ground upriver from the mouth of the Missouri. "The ordinary occupations are hunting and trading with the Indians," wrote a French visitor to Saint Charles about this time, "and it would be difficult to find a collection of individuals more ignorant, stupid, ugly and miserable." Allowing for the familiar prejudice against hunters and trappers, it must have been the kind of place familiar to Boone, although the people here spoke French rather than English. The party followed the north bank of the Missouri west about twenty-five miles to the head of the valley where Daniel Morgan had built his large double log cabin on a bluff overlooking the river bottom. The slaves had raised crops on ten or fifteen acres, and the family settled in for the winter.

They spent their first few weeks locating their lands. So many of Daniel Morgan's unmarried friends claimed land on the alluvial Missouri bottom near the mouth of Femme Osage that for a time it was known as Bachelor's Bottom. Old Boone also located his concession there, on land lying between Daniel Morgan's place and the Missouri, acreage that in the nearly two centuries since has largely disappeared with the shifting course of the river. Because Nathan had not been present for the enumeration of settlers in Saint Louis, he missed getting a concession (although within a year the governor granted him one for land farther upriver), so he bargained with Robert Hall, a man who already had decided to move on, exchanging the horse that had carried Olive's goods overland for a claim near a flowing spring in the valley of the Femme Osage. Jemima and Flanders found a site lower on Femme

Osage, near a branch known ever since as Callaway Fork. The Boone's oldest daughter, Susannah, never got the chance to help locate the home for the Hays family. Only a few days after the party arrived she died of what was called "bilious fever." She was the mother of ten, in only her fortieth year. Over the next decade many other friends and relations joined the Boones in the area, Bryans (including most of the cousins who had been raised in the Boone household), Vanbibbers, Scholls, and Callaways. This community was first consecrated when Susannah's bones were laid in the burying ground along the Femme Osage.

"On his arrival in Louisiana," read the summary of Boone's testimony before the land commission in 1806, "he took up his residence, with his lady, at his son Daniel M. Boone's, in the said district of Femme Osage, and adjoining the lands he now claims, [and] they remained there until about two years ago." A few months after the arrival of the Boones, Daniel Morgan married Sara Lewis, the daughter of an American from the Bon Homme settlement on the south side of the Missouri. At fourteen years she was only half his age but apparently was "Amazonian" in stature. The newlyweds occupied one side of the double log cabin on the bluff overlooking the river, Daniel and Rebecca the other. Boone later claimed that these years were among the happiest of his life.

During his first winter in Missouri Boone hunted the Femme Osage, familiarizing himself with the country. Experiencing a resurgence of his health, he determined to resume his lifelong pattern of annual long hunts. The winter of 1800–01, with Nathan and Daniel Morgan, he hunted and trapped the Pomme de Terre and Niangua rivers, headwaters of the Grand Osage. It was like stepping back three or four decades to his first trans-Appalachian hunts, and the experience lifted Boone's spirits. The harvest of beaver was especially rich, and over the next decade the Boone men earned their income primarily from the sale of furs and pelts. In other ways, too, Boone found the country much like early Kentucky. One day in Osage country they rounded a grove of timber and saw a party of forty or fifty men of the Osage nation not more than a few hundred yards ahead. It was their first encounter with these Siouan-speaking Indians who would be the cause of a good deal of trouble for them over the next few years. There could be no

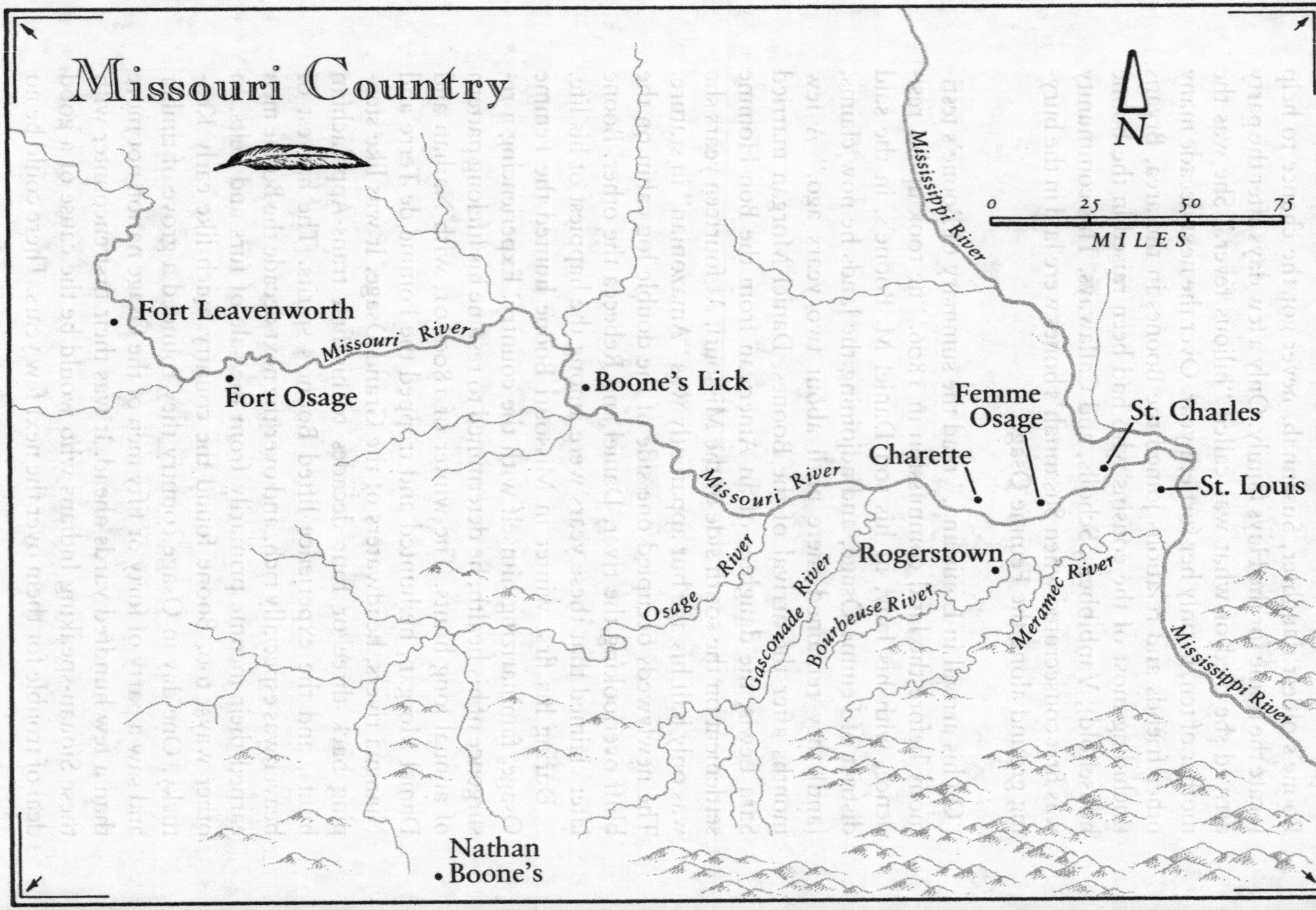
Missouri Country
N
0 25 50 75
MILES
Fort Leavenworth
Missouri River
Fort Osage
Boone's Lick
Missouri River
Mississippi River
Femme Osage
Charette
St. Charles
St. Louis
Rogerstown
Osage River
Gasconade River
Bourbeuse River
Meramec River
Mississippi River
Nathan Boone's

thought of escape, so the three went forward with smiles and howdy-dos. As they attempted to converse in trade jargon and signs, one of the young warriors stepped forward and tried to take Daniel Morgan's fine new rifle out of his pack. Boone told his son to hand it over with a smile. After admiring it for some time, the Indian handed back a rusty and worthless old musket, turned, and abruptly walked away. As Boone recalled the incident, "The others raised a grate laugh and all moved off." Daniel Morgan was fit to be tied. He was "not about to loose this fine rifle without a fight," he declared, and reached across for his father's gun. "Best to let them go," Boone said softly, laying his hand on his son's shoulder, for they "had come off well," lucky to keep their furs, not to mention their scalps. Late that winter Boone delivered his share of his first Missouri catch to a French merchant in Saint Louis, the value of sixty-two beaver pelts, two otter, six wildcat, and forty-one deerskins, credited against his outstanding balance ("l'obligation de plus"). *Plus ça change, plus c'est la meme chose.*

Daniel Morgan and Nathan returned to the Osage country the following season but, fearing further confrontations with the Indians, insisted on leaving their father behind. They would have been happiest if old Boone had remained quietly at home, but he could not, he objected, since he had just purchased a new wagon on credit and must trap to pay his account. "He had no earthly use for it," complained Nathan, who believed that his father had bought it simply to provide himself with "an excuse to go out hunting to procure the means to pay for it." His sons finally agreed that Boone might trap "the neutral ground" south of the Missouri and nearer to home. On this expedition Boone was joined by one of Daniel Morgan's slaves, an excellent young woodsman by the name of Derry Coburn. While Boone set and watched the traps, Derry kept camp, cooked, and prepared the pelts. The two men came to greatly enjoy each other's company, and for the remainder of Boone's life Derry was his regular companion in the woods and probably his closest friend. Derry, according to a member of the Boone clan who knew them both well, "was a man of that same peculiar disposition which characterized Daniel Boone, non-communicative." The two of them might sit for hours without exchanging a word, yet know precisely what the other was thinking. Intuitive communication was an essential part of Boone's social makeup, and in Derry he found the perfect companion. Derry had a wife and several children, all of them owned by members of the extended Boone family, and when he died in 1851 he was buried with the other kith and kin in the community burying ground.

On their first long hunt together Boone and Derry brought in a profitable haul of beaver, and during the winter of 1802–03 they ventured farther west. One day Boone observed Indian sign as he patrolled his line, and, taking cover, he soon spied an Osage hunter pulling their traps. He and Derry were especially careful for the next few days and avoided using their rifles until the store of meat was nearly depleted. Finally, when he felt it was safe, Boone shot a deer and hoppused it into camp, and Derry set to preparing it in his own special way, roasted in a kettle with a great deal of spicy red pepper. As the two men sat at the fire hungrily awaiting their meal, eight or ten Osages suddenly came running into camp, yelling and firing their guns in the air. Derry was petrified but Boone was his typically cool self, knowing immediately that if the Indians had meant to do more than simply take his pelts and goods they would have fired from the cover of the woods. As the warriors began to gather up their plunder, one of them lifted the lid of the steaming kettle, cut himself a hunk of venison, and thrust it into his mouth. But Derry's pepper so shocked his palate that he spit it out in a great burst and angrily kicked the kettle, spilling the meat and sauce into the fire. "He never was so mad in his life," said Derry, "to lose all his venison in that way after doing without."

Leave this country, demanded the Osages as they retired, but, true to his history, Boone simply moved their camp and continued to trap, though watchful for sign. On the Grand River, on the north side of the Missouri, they laid in a supply of meat and established themselves in a cozy cave, hidden among the river bluffs. But arising one morning, they found that a large hunting party of Osage or Sacs had made camp nearby. Luck was with them, however, for a deep snow fell that same day, covering Boone's traps and secreting the entrance to the cave. There was nothing for them to do but sit it out, daring to light only the smallest of fires at night to provide some warmth and allow them to roast small bits of meat. It was twenty days before the Indians departed and Boone concluded it was safe to leave. He later confessed that he had never felt so much anxiety over such a long period. But his troubles were not yet over.

As he collected his steel traps, one of them sprung on him, smashing and holding his hand tight in its grip. He tried forcing it open using his one good hand and his foot, but, failing in this, had to drag himself back to camp. Before Derry was able to pry it open his mangled hand was nearly frozen. The two men returned with a good catch, but it had been a rough winter.

During these years Boone played his part as "Saindic de la Femme Ozage," acting as intermediary with the Spanish authorities in Saint Louis, supervising the survey of tracts in the Femme Osage, and continuing to recommend applicants for land concessions. In 1802, for instance, he granted "permistion to Benjamin Gardner to satle on a pies of land cald Little Purrary, on the Missury." One of the few literate men in the district, he frequently witnessed documents or executed agreements and contracts. Boone heard the kind of petty criminal cases that typically came before a frontier justice. According to tradition, he held his court under the shade of an elm, known to a later generation as the Judgment Tree, which must have been located near Daniel Morgan's cabin on the bluffs. In 1804 one Berry Vincent complained that he and James Meek "had some differance Which Came to blows and in the scuffle the said James Meek bit off a piece of Bery Vinzants Left Ear." According to one of Boone's nephews, in such cases he frequently gave the offender the choice of being taken to Saint Charles for trial in justice court or being whipped on the spot and set free. Most chose the lash.

One folktale of this period told the story of a man, accused of stealing a hog, who is summoned to appear before Boone under the Judgment Tree. Later the same day he returns home. Well, how did it turn out? his neighbor inquires. "Whipped and cleared," comes the curt reply. In another, a desperado is tied to the whipping post, and he curses Boone. Why, if you weren't so old, he cries, I'd kick your. . . "Let not my gray hairs stand in the way," Boone shouts, "for old as I am, I am young enough to whip the likes of you," and he administers the punishment himself. For a man who considered himself the victim of legal procedure, it must have been a delight to be making it up as he went along. In one story a miser, to satisfy a debt, seizes the only cow of a poor widow. "The widow owes you," Boone declares, "take it and go. But never look an honest man in the face again." Then, turning to the widow, he says, "I'll give you a better one," and he does that very afternoon. There is no real evidence that Boone conducted his court in such a manner, although Nathan later said that he "governed more by *equity* than *law*." When the Americans assumed authority in 1804 Governor Delassus provided his successor with a personal assessment of the territorial officials working under him, including the syndic of Femme Osage. "Mr. Boone," he wrote, is "a respectable old man, just and impartial. He has already since I appointed him offered his resignation owing to his infirmities. Believing I know his probity, I have induced him to remain, in view of my confidence in him for the public good."

Boone continued to perform the duties of his office during the first year of the American period. One of his last official acts was surely the most difficult he was required to perform. In December, 1804, Will Hays, Boone's partner in business affairs for thirty years, the widower of Boone's daughter Susannah, and the father of ten of Boone's grandchildren, was killed by his son-in-law James Davis. Boone ordered Davis taken into custody and after a preliminary hearing remanded him to Saint Charles to stand trial for murder. "One James Davis," read the indictment, "not having the fear of God before his eyes, but being moved and seduced by the instigation of the Devil," had shot his wife's father "with a certain rifle gun, four feet long."

Boone had known Will Hays better than anyone else—had depended on him, trusted him, loved him—but he also knew that Hays, as Nathan put it, was "a bad tempered, drinking man," and the more he drank, the more bad tempered he became. During a playful scuffle with a friend at a tavern, Hays got his dander up, pulled a knife, and drew blood before others could pull him off. Within the family he had a reputation for battering Susannah, a strong-willed woman with a mind of her own. He "used to whip aunt fearfully," one daughter heard Jemima Boone bitterly complain, "and grandpa used to go when he herd it." But "for fear they would see the Bloody Stripes," Hays would keep his wife covered up. "Don't let the wind blow on you, my dear," he would say, "it will give you cold." "Hays whipped her badly," said Jonathan Bryan, and he repeated a family tale that old Boone had "whipped Hays as badly" when he found out. A Vanbibber descendant reported that Boone's son-in-law "became dissapated and trifling, treating his wife very badly, and Boone to cure him caused his two oldest sons Daniel and Jesse to tie him to a tree and flog him severely." These tales are implausible, but they suggest the level of concern in the family about Hays and the consensus that he deserved a comeuppance from the family patriarch.

After Susannah's premature death Hays sank into despair, drinking heavily and raging frequently. It was in the midst of "a drunken spree" that he got into the argument with Davis, who was married to his daughter Jemima. The two had gone at it previously, with Hays warning Davis never again to show his face around the place, but his son-in-law was on his way to Saint Charles for supplies and had come to borrow a horse. Hays stormed inside his cabin to get his rifle and Davis sought safety behind a tree. "Ah, you needn't run," cried Hays as he emerged with his cocked gun, "all the trees in the woods shan't save you." He leveled his piece, "still cursing Davis, and daring him to shoot." Faced with no alternative but to defend himself, the young man finally jumped into the open and fired, hitting Hays in the chest. He suffered terribly for several hours before he died. Old Boone learned these details from his grandson, Daniel Boone Hays, the only eyewitness to his father's shooting. The syndic escorted Davis into Saint Charles himself, where he posted a personal bond of $3,000 for his release, and he provided testimony at the trial concerning Hays's character. Eventually the young man was acquitted.

By the time this tragedy occurred, a period of troubles had begun in Boone's life. Following his accident with the trap he suffered an agonizing attack of rheumatism in the spring of 1803, and his physical ailments were aggravated by a series of personal blows. About this time he learned of the death of his daughter Levina in Kentucky. Only thirty-six years old, she expired from some unrecorded cause, and soon thereafter her husband, Joseph Scholl, brought their eight children to live in Missouri. Youngest daughter Rebecca continued to live with her husband and seven children in the one-room cabin on Brushy Fork, which they had purchased from Daniel Morgan. There was considerable concern about her in the family for she was "weakly," suffering it was said from "consumption." Two years later, in 1805, she too died prematurely at the age of thirty-seven, and soon thereafter her husband, Philip

Goe, in the words of several Boones, "drank himself to death." Among the four Boone daughters, only Jemima survived her child-bearing years, and although the complications of pregnancy and childbirth may not have been the direct cause of her sisters' deaths, the strain placed on their systems by the burden of having so many children certainly did not help. "The men and dogs have a fine time, but the poor women have to suffer," a woman in the Boone neighborhood wrote to her sister in Kentucky. "I don't want to have any more children." Daniel Morgan returned to Kentucky and brought five of the seven Goe children back to his cabin on the bluff. His wife, Sara, went on to have twelve of her own.

Olive Vanbibber Boone, Nathan's wife, followed in this tradition. She was an amazingly resourceful woman, making do in her husband's frequent absences with very few resources. When the couple first settled on the Femme Osage, Nathan erected a small cabin with a dirt floor, which flooded during the first spring rains. Her husband was away on a hunt, but, not one to be disheartened, the fifteen-year-old bride and an equally young slave girl cut down poles and laid them for joists, and spread peeled elm bark for flooring. With a cross-cut saw they cut through several courses of logs in one wall, laid a stone fireplace, and built a chimney of sticks and mud. When Nathan returned he could not believe what she had accomplished, in addition to tending the cattle, putting in the crops, chopping wood for fuel, hauling water, and doing the cooking. That summer he built her a large and solid cabin, and she converted the old cabin into her loom house. But Olive's fireplace "proved to have the best draft of any chimney on the farm," Nathan would recall proudly. All the more remarkable, at the time she was pregnant with their first child, born in July of 1800. Olive had a total of fourteen children, two of whom died in infancy.

Sometime after his accident, Boone and Rebecca moved from Daniel Morgan's some miles up the Femme Osage to a cabin of their own on Nathan and Olive's land. There they spent their last years together, hard by a boiling spring in a beautiful valley where game came to water. Boone was forced to forgo long hunting, but according to Elijah Bryan, he "could sit in the door of his cabin, and lay in a winter's supply of meat for his family without the trouble of hunting." Old Boone himself presented his situation somewhat differently. "Here are turkies and deer," he admitted to a visitor in

1805, "but whare is the elk and buffalow? Oh, they have left for the west." Jemima and Flanders recently had moved to a larger farm on rich bottom near the mouth of Charette Creek, twenty miles up the Missouri, and each spring Boone and Rebecca joined them there to make sugar at a camp in the Callaways' sugar bush. Such substitutes would have to suffice until his health recovered.

His sons continued to hunt and trap commercially, but the Osages became more troublesome as increasing numbers of American woodsmen penetrated their country. In early December of 1804 Nathan and Tice Vanbibber were surprised in their winter camp on the Kansas River by a party of Osages, who took their horses and furs and told them forcefully to "Clear out!" Kansa tribesmen were hot on their trail, the Osage chief warned them, and they would regret it if they were caught. Not more than a few minutes later the Kansa overtook them, in an angry mood, probably because they had been beaten to the punch by their Osage cousins. The two Americans were left stripped of everything they owned, including their blanket coats, although the Indians thoughtfully allowed them to keep a single gun. Some two hundred miles from home, the men followed the Missouri River eastward on foot through bitter storms, fighting off hunger and frostbite, pushing each other to keep going. Nathan finally succeeded in shooting a panther, and they devoured the steaming flesh raw and wrapped themselves in the bloody skin to try to find some relief from the cold. Finally, with more than a hundred miles to go and about to give up hope, they were rescued by a party of Americans that included one of Jemima's boys and were brought home to the Femme Osage on Christmas Eve, suffering the effects of extreme exposure. Vanbibber's body and spirits were broken, and although he was yet a young man, he remained bedridden until his death two years later. Nathan recovered, but he dated the origin of many of the ailments that later plagued him from the trauma his body suffered at that time. Years later Olive was able to be ironic when she recalled the horrible sight of her husband being brought in on a litter. "It was the first Christmas he had spent at home since our marriage," she said with a wink, "and I had to thank the Indians for that." While Nathan lay recovering, Boone was in the midst of the Will Hays murder trial. Troubles always seemed to come in a run for him.

On their return trek down the Missouri River, Nathan and Tice had come upon a series of salt springs in a narrow valley in what is today Howard County. These would later become famous as Boone's Lick, the destination of many hundreds of emigrants drawn by little more than the promise of the Boone name. Contrary to popular impression, however, old Boone had nothing to do with their discovery, and he never lived at the licks. In the spring of 1805, after he had recovered his strength, Nathan returned to test the salinity of the waters. It was relatively weak, but salt was selling at such high prices that he and his brother decided to invest in a commercial works at the site. Through that summer and fall they employed six or eight men to operate forty kettles, manufacturing about twenty-five bushels per day, which Nathan transported downriver in keelboats and sold in Saint Louis for $250 per hundred. Isolated from the settlements, however, Boone's Lick was a vulnerable target for Indian raids. "I am informed that the salt works of a son of old Dan Boone, about one hundred and fifty miles up the Missouri have been broken up," the territorial governor wrote in December 1805; raiders had "killed or carried away the cattle and destroyed the salt works." The next year Nathan and Daniel Morgan rebuilt and enlarged the facility, employing up to twenty men who turned out more than a hundred bushels per day, but with continued Indian troubles the high wages required to make the risky work attractive, and the low level of salinity and productivity, the operation failed to become financially successful. The Boones sold their interest in about 1810 and the works continued in other hands until it finally closed in the 1830s. Old Boone never approved of the venture. "He seemed opposed to Boone's Lick," said a man who spoke with him about it in 1808, "with its toils and exposures, for all which the remuneration was so uncertain." Perhaps his own experience as a salt maker had something to do with his feelings.

By the late fall of 1805, ill health and anxiety had Boone's spirits at low ebb. Perhaps it was in an attempt to cheer him that his sons took him out to hunt on the waters of the Gasconade, about seventy miles southwest of the Femme Osage. All went well until their return just before Christmas. By the time they arrived at the Missouri, the ice was running thick on the river and there was no possibility of crossing. Knowing how much their wives wanted them home for the holiday, they made a disappointed camp on the riverbank. That night was bitterly cold and, awakening to find the river frozen hard, they decided to risk crossing on the ice, using poles to test the way ahead of each step. In the lead to mark the path, Nathan and Daniel Morgan had just reached the northern shore when they heard their father crash through the ice. He was in shallow water up to his armpits but could not find ice about him able to support his weight. Daniel Morgan headed back out but Boone waved him off; the ice was too weak. In Boone's weakened condition, the freezing water might kill him within minutes. Nathan set to building a bonfire while Daniel Morgan shouted encouragement as Boone squirmed out and across the thin cover to the riverbank. His sons stripped him to the skin and dried him before the fire, then carried him home.

The crisis over Boone's Spanish land grant came in this context of troubled times. The United States had pledged that the inhabitants of Louisiana would be protected in the "free enjoyment of their liberty [and] property." In 1805 Congress passed a land law for the territory and created a land commission that began taking testimony in December. Each claimant was to state the specifics of his claim and produce his documentation for the commissioners, who were to call witnesses and take testimony before making their decision. The law promised to honor all grants for claimants who were "actual settlers on the land." But Boone had never lived on his claim nor improved it, and this provision clearly concerned him. When he appeared before the commissioners on February 13, 1806, producing the offering letter from Don Zenon Trudeau, his concession, and his certificate of survey, he also was ready with his explanation. He had asked Governor Delassus "as to the propriety of improving and settling his land within a year and a day from the date of the concession, as directed by the Spanish laws," he said, but the governor had told him that "being commandant of the said district, he need not trouble himself about the cultivating," since "by the commission he held of commandant of said district, he was not considered as coming within the meaning of said laws." He produced his syndic's commission but could offer no documents regarding the governor's assurances.

Initially the commissioners were inclined to be liberal. In the case of Nathan's claim to the concession purchased from Robert Hall, they issued a preliminary favorable decision. But forces were at work that soon compelled them to rethink their assumptions. American land speculators arrived and began buying up private claims in an attempt to engross large tracts of land. Discrepancies began to appear in the Spanish records as the result of the fudging of dates, and the concern arose that a fraud was being perpetrated against the government and that if the commissioners were not careful, the people would be hoodwinked out of a vast proportion of the public domain. In mid-1806 the Jefferson administration instructed the commissioners to adhere strictly to the letter of the law, forcing them to withdraw their preliminary decisions. It required another two years before final decisions began to be announced. Many of the Boones fared quite well. The commission approved Daniel Morgan's original concession in December of 1808 and confirmed the claims of Flanders Callaway, Isaac Vanbibber, and the Hays estate. But Boone soon heard from his friend Judge John Coburn that he could expect a negative decision. There would be no exception to the rule of occupancy and improvement.

Boone's health had by then reached a point of crisis. During the winter of 1808–09, after two years languishing at home, he had attempted another long hunt with Derry. The family argued strenuously against it, but the old man stubbornly refused to listen. "They thought he was too old for such exposures," a friend of the family remembered, "but he was unhappy to remain at home and would go." His nephew Daniel Boone Bryan warned him that "it was too late," and he was "too old to be going any more a trapping, and ought now to be staying with his family." But Boone replied, "Dan'l, you know I have never been a farmer, and I cannot make anything by cultivating the soil. My wife is getting old and needs some little coffee and other refreshments, and I have no other way of paying for them but by trapping." Soon after he and Derry departed, however, Boone was stricken by an attack that left him completely disabled. As one of Boone's cousins told the tale, "The weather was stormy and disagreeable, which had a depressing effect both upon the old colonel and his servant boy," and Boone finally concluded that his time was up. When the sky cleared, he asked Derry to help him walk to the crest of a nearby hill. Here, he declared, is where he wants to be buried, with the woods spread out below him, and "he marked out the ground in the shape and size of a grave." This attack subsided sufficiently for Derry to get Boone back home, but in the worst condition of his life. In 1809 he finally placed himself under the care of a doctor in Saint Charles.

This was the Boone who helped to write the petitions to Congress, "an aged, infirm, and worn-out man" whose best days were behind him. But Boone somehow recovered from this crisis. Without discounting the positive benefits that may have resulted from his medical treatment, there seems to have been something therapeutic about his work on the congressional petitions. Not only did he dictate a narrative of his life to his grandson for Coburn's use, but he spent many hours in uncharacteristic conversation about his life with Stephen Hempstead, his Saint Charles neighbor. Hempstead had not been in Saint Louis more than a week after his arrival from the East, he said, when his brother Edward, a prominent attorney aspiring to become Missouri's first territorial representative in Congress, "sent me to St. Charles county to visit Col. Boone." Boone "gave me many anecdotes of his life," and Hempstead passed them along to his brother, who later used them to support Boone's case in Congress.

Out of this process of reflection Boone emerged with a renewed conviction of the importance of his life and a strengthened sense of his self-worth. He was always at his weakest and most vulnerable when he felt public suspicion and doubt, when he felt deserted, but he was able to withstand ferocious attack so long as he had allies and supporters. In 1809, with his family gathering about him, with the help of Coburn and the Hempsteads, and with the assurance of a favorable reception by political leaders, he mustered his strength. John Shaw, who met Boone at this time, was impressed with the look of defiance in his eyes, despite the illness that had laid him low. "Boone considered himself an emissary," he wrote, "chosen to open the American wilderness." Another visitor, Joseph McCormick, found Boone "feeble," but still "energetic and indomitable." "After all his early discoveries, trials and dangers," Boone complained to him, he "owned not a foot of soil." He "seemed to feel his poverty quite keenly," McCormick remembered, and "wished for more, for hospitality's sake." Boone told his nephew John Scholl that all his life had been a struggle, and now he fought against the lawyers who, "by altering the laws," were destroying the dreams of men like himself. By the time word of the commissioners' decision reached him in December 1809—"It is the opinion of the Board that this claim ought not to be confirmed"—Boone had prepared himself.

In these years Boone drew closer to friends who shared his perspective. In 1809, hearing of Boone's difficulties, Simon Kenton came to Missouri to visit his old comrade in arms. According to a story told by Kenton's children, he arrives at the Boone place one evening and asks Rebecca for lodging, but, failing to recognize her old friend, she answers that they have no room. "You would if you knew who I am," he laughs, and, stepping closer, she peers through the twilight at him. In a flash of recognition she tosses aside her old clay pipe and kisses him. "Daniel," she calls out to Boone, chopping firewood, "there's a gentleman here wishes to see you." There is no reply, and Boone keeps on with his chopping. She calls several more times, but it is not until Boone has finished that he ambles into the house. Seeing Kenton, he bursts into tears. Why did you not tell me who it was? he scolds her. He "supposed it was some neighbor." Kenton remained for several weeks, the three of them "rehearsing the story of the olden time and the varied fortunes of their ancient companions in the early settlement of Kentucky." Kenton had lost all his lands, served time in debtor's prison, and now was dependent on his son and daughter. The famous case of *Kenton v. McConnell*, in which the Kentucky Court of Appeals ruled in 1794 against Kenton's claim under the 1779 land law, was a key piece of evidence in the growing resentment of pioneers against lawyers, judges, courts, and all aspects of the legal system. There were scores of stories of other men who had lost all. Boone's brother Squire had finally returned to Louisville after failing to convince his wife to join him in Missouri, and in 1804 he was thrown into debtor's prison and not released until friends could raise his bond. Old William Brooks, one of the salt makers, died so poor, it was said, that his creditors attached his body in order to extort payment from his children.

The next year two of Boone's old Kentucky associates, Michael Stoner and James Bridges, came to hunt and explore the Upper Missouri, stopping first at the Boone cabin to visit. Boone, in the midst of one of his temporary recoveries from rheumatism, could not resist their offer to join them. They set out in the early fall—Stoner, Bridges, Boone, and Flanders Callaway. Callaway brought along his slave Mose, "to chew my venison for me," he said. Derry and Will Hays, Jr., who now frequently assumed the place his father had filled at Boone's side, assisted this party of older men. They "went high up the Missouri trapping," said Stoner's son, and according to Hays they made it all the way to the Yellowstone. That would have been quite an accomplishment, but men were doing such things in 1810, and Boone was gone for a full six months. Unfortunately, there are no further details about this long hunt, except that the party returned with loads of valuable furs packed in mackanaw boats.

Stephen Hempstead recalled seeing these boats descending the river in the early months of 1811, "with housing over the cargo, a sure sign of fur coming from the upper Missouri," and he went down to the Saint Charles landing to see who was aboard. Derry was rowing one of them, with Boone at the rudder. They were on their way to Saint Louis, the old man shouted, where they could get a decent price for their beaver. After Boone had returned again to the Femme Osage, he met John Bradbury, who was traveling with John Jacob Astor's fur traders headed for the Columbia. Bradbury recorded in his journal that Boone "had lately returned from his spring hunt, with nearly sixty beaver skins." Washington Irving later wrote a history of these "Astorians" in which he provided a memorable account of this meeting with Boone. "The old man was still erect in form, strong in limb, and unflinching in spirit," he wrote. "And as he stood on the river bank, watching the departure of an expedition destined to traverse the wilderness to the very shores of the Pacific, very probably felt a throb of his old pioneer spirit, impelling him to shoulder his rifle and join the adventurous band." But Boone at last had enjoyed a successful hunt of his own.

Part Three

In the late months of 1818, newspapers around the country printed a report of Boone's death. "We are informed by a gentleman direct from Boone's Settlement on the Missouri," read the account, that the old man "breathed out his last" while sitting in a hunter's blind, his face pressed to the breech of his cocked rifle, his eye lined up on the bead. "As he lived so he died, with his gun in his hand." It was true that about that time Boone had fallen seriously ill on a hunt, but the report of his death was premature. One of his sons stormed into the office of the local paper where the story had originated and compelled the editor to print an apology and a retraction. But the story had the effect of sparking considerable interest in seeing the old pioneer before he died, and over the next two years a steady stream of Americans beat a path to Boone's door, "induced by curiosity to visit this extraordinary person," in the words of one anonymous traveler.

The visitors found Boone, now in his mid-eighties, shifting restlessly between the homes of Jemima, Daniel Morgan, Nathan, and Jesse, who finally had left Kentucky and moved his family to the Femme Osage about 1816. Boone had ceased to maintain a household of his own after Rebecca's death in 1813 but spent most of his time with Jemima and Flanders so he could be near his wife's grave in the Boone-Bryan burying ground on Tuque Creek, in the settlement of Charette. It sometimes took persistence to track him down, but quite a number succeeded. "Seeing strangers approaching," Nathan remembered, "and anticipating their prying curiosity and inquisitiveness," Boone would "take his cane and walk off to avoid them." But he "retained his mild disposition to the last," and if cornered, he usually agreed to talk. "Though at first reserved and barely answering questions," said one visitor, "he soon became communicative, warmed up, and became animated in narrating his early adventures in the West." Asked about the false obituary, Boone was inclined to laugh it off. "I would not believe that tale if I told it myself," he said. "I have not watched the deer's lick for ten years. My eyesight is too far gone to hunt." Although he still went exploring in the woods around the settlement with his grandchildren, Boone's hunting days were over.

Mortality was much on his mind in the years following Rebecca's death. "How we Live in this World and what Chance we Shall have in the next we know Not," he wrote to his sister-in-law in 1816, but "I beleve god never made a man of my prisipel to be Lost." He ordered his own coffin built and often inspected it. "Well, Sucky," he told his granddaughter Susanna Callaway, "I am tired of living," and he wondered aloud why they could not dispatch old men like old horses when they were no longer fit for work. "It made her shudder," Susanna remembered, "to see him thump around his coffin, whistling so happy and content."

His rheumatic disorders continued to incapacitate him and by his last two years he was nearly blind, but his spirits never failed him. "An irritable expression was never heard," wrote the Baptist minister John Mason Peck, who interviewed Boone at the Callaways' in December 1818. Peck expected that this "celebrated hunter and Indian-fighter" would be "a rough, fierce-looking, uncouth specimen of humanity," and when he first saw the gentle old man coming forward in his homespun hunting shirt and soft deerskin moccasins, he was greatly surprised. "His high, bold forehead was slightly bald, and his silvered locks were combed smooth; his countenance was ruddy and fair, and exhibited the simplicity of a child. His voice was soft and melodious." Boone's weight was now down to a mere 155 pounds, and his frailty worried his children. Peck watched as the "affectionate daughter" Jemima helped him find a place by the fire, his grandchildren scurrying to fetch the little things he needed to be comfortable. "Every member of the household appeared to delight in administering to his comforts."

"He was sociable, communicative in replying to questions," wrote Peck. What had prompted him to cross the mountains and lead Americans to Kentucky so many years before? Surely Boone had rehearsed the answer a hundred times or more. Well, he muses, he reckons he was just "naturally romantic." But then people shouldn't put such an emphasis on his own accomplishments. "It is true that I have suffered many hardships and miraculously escaped many perils," says he, "but others of my companions have experienced the same." It was a time worth remembering, a time of bravery and glory. "Our fort was continually surrounded by the red men, and their continued cries in the vicinity threw a gloom over the most courageous. Pressed by hunger within the fort, hundreds of miles from a white settlement, and threatened with instant death if we left our residence, we were certainly in a perilous situation." Family and friends perished, Boone himself was severely wounded, then captured by the Indians. But "after many struggles we subdued the country and the Indians, and our fields were waving with corn and our friends settling around us. We then expected to pass together many happy days.

"But alas!" he continues. "It was then my misery began." He was one of those who wrested the country from the Indians, but "new claimants successfully contested our land titles, and once again we were thrown into poverty and despair." "He had settled in that country to end his Days," reported a grandson, "but they got up so many squabbles over land, that it annoyed him, and he Did not want to Die among them." When the dream died in Kentucky, Boone said, "I determined to quit my native land." According to Joseph Bryan, Boone "formed a determination when he left Kentucky that he never would again put his foot upon its soil" because the state "had treated him badly." He removed to Missouri, where the Spanish awarded him a generous grant, but "here his misfortune did not end." Once again the lawyers and speculators followed him, and eventually his Spanish grants were declared "null and void." The lands he had secured, says Boone, always "proved an injury rather than a benefit." It all served to make him "indifferent in the affairs of the world."

The fires of old Boone's anger had finally flickered out, leaving behind the ashes of bitter bemusement. Through all of these trials, he asks his visitors, who do you suppose turned out to be his most constant friends? Why, those very people he had helped to dispossess—the Indians. Never an Indian hater, he had always "respected the rights of the preemptor of the soil" and "fought the Indians fairly, on terms that made him respected among the tribes." Throughout his life he had followed a simple code, learned during his Quaker youth in the Pennsylvania woods:

> Always meet them frankly and fearlessly, showing not the slightest sign of fear or trepidation. By kind acts and just treatment, keep on the friendly side of them. Bestow upon the squaws small presents, however short you may be of them, which will conciliate them and secure their good will of friendship against any hostile designs, and command their aid and sympathies in case of sickness while among them.

As a result, when he had been forced to "seek refuge with my deadliest foes and trust to their magnaminity," the Indians "were kind and generous in their intercourse with me, [and] pitied my helpless and wretched situation." He joked that "while he could never with safety repose confidence in a Yankee, he had never been deceived by an Indian," and if he was forced to choose, "he should certainly prefer a state of nature to a state of civilization."

His Shawnee captors had become his second family. Years afterward, following his remove to Missouri, he reestablished his relations with the Indians who also emigrated westward, and during the last two decades of his life they paid frequent visits to each other's homes and camps, hunting together and talking over old times. Although others might portray him as a fierce border warrior, Boone declared in fact he had "never delighted in shedding human blood" and had "avoided it whenever he could." He knew he had taken Indian lives, but "I am very sorry to say that I ever killed any, for they have always been kinder to me than the whites."

This version of his autobiography took shape in Boone's mind during his final years. If his congressional petitions had first introduced an element of contradiction into Filson's romantic story of his life, this final rendition overlaid it with deep irony. While Boone continued to believe in the justice of colonization, ambiguity now replaced righteousness. I explored "from the love of Nature," says he. "I've opened the way for others to make fortunes, but a fortune for myself was not what I was after." All he ever wanted, he claims, was a country where a man could "tickle the soil with a hoe, and she would laugh you a bountiful harvest," where he might "hunt and live at ease." It might be true that he was "an *instrument* ordained to settle the wilderness," to use the words of Filson's Boone. But old Boone reminds his visitors that to the Indians he was "the *instrument* by which they lost their hunting grounds." The ironies did not end there. "The love and gratitude of my country-men," which Filson's Boone had suggested would be sufficient reward, had been short-lived. Just as his enemies had become friends, so his countrymen had proved unreliable. In his new telling, Boone even turned Filson's narrative devices to new uses. For Filson's Boone, it was the Shawnees who threatened elysian Kentucky; "the time of our sorrow was now arrived," says he, in anticipation of his first Indian captivity. But for old Boone, the threat to his happiness issued not from the Indians but from the arrival of the lawyers and politicans—the "Yankees." "It was then," says he, that "my misery began."

Through these interviews, Boone helped shape the final form of his public image. Versions of his life with a sardonic edge began to appear in print even before his death in 1820. But although Boone had told his own story, he could not determine that others would retell it exactly as he pleased. Some interpreted his biography in the tradition of refined Enlightenment protest. After speaking with the old pioneer on the Femme Osage, for example, a traveler wrote that Boone and his family had "retired through choice" from civilization, "placing themselves at a distance from the deceit and turbulence of the world," far enough so that "they are truly free." He converted Boone into a Jeffersonian version of the "natural man." Other accounts were less enthusiastic about westering. "This singular man could not live in Kentucky when it became settled," one writer noted in 1816. "He might have accumulated riches as readily as any man in Kentucky," but he "prefers the woods, where you see him in the dress of the roughest, poorest hunter." Such interpretations emphasized the antisocial tendencies that had led Boone to the happy discovery of Kentucky but ultimately resulted in a lonely and unhappy life. Filson's original narrative created the archetype of the primary American myth, later to be known as the "Western," which since has appeared countless times in literature, art, and film. Old Boone's emendations to Filson's text suggested a paradoxical ending. Subsequent interpreters worked through these implications in hundreds of works that left Boone the most famous as well as the most ambiguous of all American pioneers. It was perhaps an appropriate fate for Boone the hunter, the man who could skillfully blend into his habitat, the man with the mysterious capacity to make quite different groups regard him as one of their own.

But the distortions of his own perspective frustrated and sometimes angered Boone. "Nothing embitters my old age," he complained to visitors, like "the circulation of absurd stories that I retire as civilization advances, that I shun the white men and seek the Indians, and that now even when old, I wish to retire beyond the second Alleganies." Old Boone remained a man of few words, but they often went straight to their target. "Many heroic actions and chivalrous adventures are related of me which exist only in the regions of fancy," he concluded. "With me the world has taken great liberties, and yet I have been but a common man."

Chapter Nine

God Never Made a Man of My Prisipel to Be Lost

1811 to 1820

The fighting men of the Charette settlement, fifteen miles west of Femme Osage, were out on defensive maneuvers and Boone was in charge of the fortified cabin of Jemima and Flanders known as Callaway Post when a messenger arrived on the morning of May 20, 1815, with news of an Indian attack on the cabin of the Robert Ramsay family several miles north. Boone shouldered his rifle and followed the man back along the wooded trail. Sauk warriors had struck early that morning, cutting down Mrs. Ramsay while she milked the cow and tomahawking three of her children before her peg-legged husband could hobble to his gun and fight back. Boone and others had warned Ramsay about living on the fringe of the settlement and implored him to bring his family into the community fort at Jemima and Flanders's place. Now Boone found the Ramsay children lying in pools of blood, their lives draining away with every wheezing breath, while their mother groaned in agony from the adjoining room, where neighbor women assisted in the premature delivery of another child. Mr. Ramsay had taken a ball in his groin, and Boone could see that he was the only one who stood a chance of survival. Boone's "lips were compressed and a fire gleamed from his eyes," as William Bryan told the tale, but calmly and surely he extracted the bullet and dressed the wound. When Mrs. Ramsay, the mangled children, and the baby died soon after, eighty-year-old Boone had already left to follow the Indian trail through the woods. He concluded that warriors were still in the area.

The next day a small war party attacked the cabin of Jonathan Bryan, Boone's cousin, who lived near Nathan's place on Femme Osage. The men of the family were all out in pursuit of the party that had attacked the Ramsays and only women and young slaves were about. Mary Bryan heard a scream and, looking out, saw an Indian with an upraised tomahawk chasing one of the slaves. As the boy scrambled into the cabin, she slammed the door, catching the warrior half inside, and as she pressed her body against the door one of the slave women wrenched the tomahawk from his hand and smashed his skull. Grabbing a rifle resting nearby, Mary jerked open the door and brought down a second warrior only a few feet away, and the rest of them retreated into the woods. Three days later the Missouri militia, Boone's sons and their units from the Boone settlement among them, engaged a large Sauk force at the bloody Battle of Sink Hole near the mouth of the Cuivre River on the Mississippi. The Treaty of Ghent, ending the war between Britain and the United States, was already three months old. These were the final engagements of the War of 1812.

The first two years of the war along the Missouri consisted of defensive actions. In early 1812, after a band of Kickapoos or Potawatomies murdered a settler family on the Salt River, fifty miles north of Femme Osage, Governor Benjamin Howard organized a company of mounted riflemen with Capt. Nathan Boone in command. Nathan had proved his mettle in 1808 when he enlisted under Gen. William Clark and led a company of mounted dragoons westward to the site of Fort Osage, securing the area while Clark's men built this far-western fortification on the Missouri. Now he supervised the construction of Fort Mason on the Mississippi, near the site of present-day Hannibal, and maintained a patrol southwest to Fort Clemson at the mouth of Loutre Creek on the Missouri, in charge of the protection of the entire Saint Charles district, nearly two thousand square miles of territory wedged between the rivers. Capt. Daniel Morgan Boone commanded a local militia company known as "Howard's Rangers." His responsibilities included the construction of fortified posts along the river. The wall he threw up around his cabin on the Missouri bluff made it the strongest of the pioneer stations along the river.

Boone himself was too old for militia duty. In one tale, the local rangers mount for a foray and Boone prepares to join them. Go back home, Grandfather, they tell him, and he turns away in disgust. But from most of the stories of this period he appears as the wise old war leader, cautious and steady. In one he is at Nathan's with the women of the family when a hired man rushes into the cabin with a frantic report that he has seen an Indian warrior down the road. The women immediately are infected with panic, but Boone remains "perfectly cool and collected," having seen no Indian sign during his local patrol of the woods. What was the warrior doing when you saw him? he inquires skeptically. "He seemed to be stopping in the middle of the road, picking off ticks," replies the hired man. Boone boils over. "It is a lie. No Indian ever would stop in a public road, in an enemy's settlement, in time of war, to pick off wood ticks!" Olive remains frightened for her children and still wishes to fly to the fort on the river. "Derry and I alone can defend our house," Boone assures her, and, tossing Derry a gun, the two men sit down with their backs against the cabin door, their guns across their laps, keeping watch all night.

There were numerous Indian scares. On one occasion, when Boone was with Jemima and her family, there came a midnight warning of a massive assault on all of the settlements of the Saint Charles district. It proved a false report, but, fearing that they were too isolated to take the risk of remaining, Boone counseled an evacuation to Daniel Morgan's fort, and the people of the settlement went overland while the slaves put all of their goods in pirogues, lashed them together, and floated them downriver. Boone's party arrived at the fort in the early morning but the slaves were delayed in coming in, and there was much fretting before they finally arrived in the afternoon. The boats had run against a sawyer in the river and capsized, and the slaves had clung to the wrecks for several hours before being rescued. No one was injured but the family goods were lost, including nearly all of Boone's papers and books, among them the manuscript autobiography he had dictated to John Boone Callaway. Jemima had dictated her story as well, declaring that "she would have all the events of her life written," and this manuscript too was lost that night in the dark river. A few years later Boone dictated another version of his autobiography to Dr. John Jones of Charette, the husband of his granddaughter Minerva Callaway, but it disappeared after Jones died in 1842.

The last months of the war brought personal disaster for the Boone family. Although the Indian resistance in the East had been broken and the British had signed an armistice, Sauks and Mesquakies systematically raided the American settlements along the Missouri from the summer of 1814 through early 1815. In March, Jemima's son, Capt. James Callaway, a man in his early thirties, was in command of a local company led by Shawnee scouts who had left Fort Clemson in pursuit of Indians who had stoken a number of horses. In a brief engagement they retook the stock and were on their return when Callaway's lieutenant warned that the scouts feared a counterattack. Callaway "flew into a passion," calling coward anyone who wished to hold up and ordering that the march continue. As they forded Prairie Fork of Loutre Creek the Sauks sprang their ambush, killing Callaway with a single shot through the back of his head. Nine other local men died in the attack, their bodies mutilated and hung on bushes, but Callaway's sank unnoticed to the bottom of the creek, where it was recovered by the burial party several days later. His wife, Nancy Howell Callaway, the mother of three children, received the news of his death without reaction, walked the several miles to her home in absolute silence, and collapsed as she entered the door.

But for Boone, the worst calamity of the war years had nothing to do with the fighting. Following what had become their common practice, in the late winter of 1813 he and Rebecca went upriver to camp at the Callaway sugar grove. Sugar-making time was a joyous season. The work was relatively easy and in the best years the days were warm and sunny, the nights clear and cold, encouraging the sap to run and the spirits to rise after winter's confinement. He and Rebecca had lived together in their own cabin on Nathan's place for seven years, probably spending more time together than ever before during their marriage. They had been working at the grove for nearly a month when Rebecca complained of feeling poorly. She had rarely been sick a day in her life but always had played the role of family doctor and community midwife. Once when she lived on the Kanawha and her husband was away at the legislature, her granddaughter remembered, "tidings came that Col. Boone was very ill and she was sent for to go to Richmond to attend him, and got ready and started in fifteen minutes." Now it was Boone's turn to attend to her. He placed her in a litter and got her to Jemima's, but she grew worse, and after suffering for a week she died quietly on March 18, 1813, in her seventy-fourth year. Her family laid her in the burying ground on David Bryan's property, a grassy knoll along Tuque Creek, looking out over the bottom, with the rolling Missouri visible through the still-bare trees. Boone fell into a depression that lasted for weeks. It was "the Saddest affliction of his life," said his granddaughter Susanna Callaway. "He oftimes said it was an inexpressible loss."

"After Grandmother Boone died," one descendant recalled, "he never was Contented." Following her death there was an aspect of summary or conclusion to Boone's behavior. In 1814 Congress had finally acted on his petition, but, refusing to act on his request for a new and larger grant from the public domain, it merely confirmed his original Spanish grant of Missouri bottomland. Boone fumed that "he was no beggar" and declared to his children that he would refuse the grant. Gradually his anger subsided, and over the next few years he sold this land off in parcels. According to one set of tales, using the proceeds from these sales he returned to Kentucky to settle up his affairs. According to John Mason Peck, Boone "had kept no book account, and knew not how much he owed, nor to whom he was indebted, but in the honest simplicity of his nature, he went to all with whom he had dealings and paid whatever was demanded." In one story Boone suddenly appears before a Kentuckian to pay a debt he owes to the man's father. He died long ago, the man explains, and he advises Boone to forget it, for his father certainly had. "I have come here to pay my debts," declares Boone, "and will not leave here indebted to any man," and he forces the young man to take his money. In another version Boone visits the couple who many years before had given him traveling money when he left Kentucky. "Well," says Boone, "I have settled with all but you," and he takes out three pounds to pay the debt with interest. "Oh, Uncle Boone," cries the wife, "do not insist." "I must insist, and I will take no denial," says Boone, for "if you do not, I shall leave you believing you have lost all respect for me." When he returns to Missouri he has only four bits left in his pocket. "Now I am ready and willing to die," he says to his family. "I have paid all my debts, and no one will say when I am gone, 'Boone was a dishonest man.' "

Some people remembered seeing Boone in Kentucky after the War. John James Audubon claimed to have gone shooting with him in the Kentucky woods. "My companion, a stout, hale, and athletic man, dressed in a homespun hunting-shirt, bare-legged and moccasined, carried a long and heavy rifle," Audubon wrote. Boone points to a squirrel on the branch of a tree about fifty paces distant, gradually raises his piece to his eye, and hits the bark directly beneath the animal, killing it with the concussion, an operation known as "barking." Later, retiring to their shared room, Boone arranges his blankets on the floor and takes off his shirt. "The stature and general appearance of this wanderer of the western forests approached the gigantic," Audubon observed. "His chest was broad and prominent; his muscular powers displayed themselves in every limb." This description does not give Audubon's account much credibility. A man who saw Boone take off his hunting shirt at about this same time described him as only "medium sized," and another visitor thought that although the old man was still "capable of endurance," he was "not very strong." At this point Boone was eating nothing more than a little mush and milk, and he had grown so "feeble" that his family was worried. Audubon later painted a portrait of Boone from memory that was as inaccurate as his pen picture.

Another tradition said that Boone visited Limestone about that time, staying with his cousin Jacob Boone, a prominent merchant in that town. Boone had supposedly come downriver after visiting his son Jesse at Greenupsburg and was honored at a gala dinner that included all of the distinguished local citizenry. After the meal one of the men asks Boone for a story, and he begins a tale but is interrupted by a man who claims that his story is "impossible." With this remark Boone shuts up, and despite urgings that he continue, he refuses to speak further. Later that evening, when he has retired to the room he shares with the son of the tavern keeper, the boy asks him about his silence. "I dislike to be in a crowd," Boone explains, and "would not have opened my lips had that man remained." Well, we are alone now, says the boy, and he presses the old man to tell the story. "You shall have it, honey," says Boone, who has taken a fancy to him, and proceeds to tell of killing a ten-foot, hairy giant he called a "Yahoo." The Yahoos were giant beasts in human shape from Boone's favorite book, *Gulliver's Travels.* It was a tall tale that Boone repeated to a number of people during his last year, one such as he would have told in a winter camp.

Unlike Audubon's account, this story is laced with convincing detail, including authentic insight into his character and habits, but it runs against the assertion of nearly all members of his family that Boone never returned to Kentucky after his removal in 1799. His Kentucky kin frequently wrote, asking him to visit, but the old man firmly declined each invitation because, as his niece Sarah Hunter put it, "he was greatly insulted with the Kentuckians." Boone told a visiting grandson in 1815 that he had never been back to Kentucky, and five years later, just a few weeks before his death, he told a nephew that he had kept his vow to never again set foot in the state that had treated him so badly. "I remember his remark," Joseph Bryan wrote years later, for "although a boy, I felt ashamed for my state. I have felt it ever since." The daughter of the merchant Jacob Boone, who lived her whole life in Limestone, declared that old Boone never once visited her family there. Despite "the romance" of the stories of Peck, Audubon, and the others, said Nathan, the truth was that his father had never gone back to Kentucky.

Nevertheless, family traditions all agree that one of Boone's principal concerns during these years was to clear all of his accounts. According to Nathan, after the announcement of Boone's congressional confirmation in the papers, several Kentuckians with claims against Boone hastened to Missouri to press their demands, and he paid them all. The tale was told that after all of these men are satisfied, and Boone thinks he is finally clear, yet another Kentuckian arrives with a claim. He is the husband of a woman to whom years before Boone had given a generous gift of land after her parents were killed by Indians. But like many Kentucky tracts, her land proves to be shingled over with other claims, and she eventually loses it in a lawsuit. I insist you make good the loss, her husband demands. Stunned, Boone replies that he gave it purely out of charity, not obligation, that it cost her nothing. But the fellow continues to press for his pound of flesh, and Boone finally gives him the verbal heave-ho, in his characteristically droll way. You have "come a great distance to suck a bull," says he, and I reckon you will "have to go home dry."

Within the space of a few months in 1815 and 1816, three of Boone's siblings died, including Squire, the brother to whom he had been the closest. Excepting brothers Israel, who died of tuberculosis at an early age, and Edward, killed by Indians when he was only forty, most of Boone's other brothers and sisters survived into their eighties and nineties. Squire, however, died at the age of seventy-one, worn down by invalidism, the result of his many wounds suffered during the Indian wars. "Disgusted and disheartened owing to land disputes and losses," in the words of his son, in 1806 Squire had finally convinced his wife to leave Kentucky, moving across the Ohio River to Indiana. On the public road about twenty-five miles west of Louisville he and his sons built and operated a small gristmill that remained a successful family business until the 1870s. He lived in a nearby stone house, like those of his Pennsylvania birthplace, which he named "Traveler's Rest." On the large foundation stones of his mill he carved religious images and verses, still visible today.

My God my life hath much befriended
I'll praise him till my days are ended.

Squire had long been a Baptist lay preacher and had helped organize several churches in Virginia and Kentucky. He also had entertained an enthusiasm for spiritualism that flourished during his last years, and as he approached his death he instructed his sons to bury him in an underground cavern near the mill, camping nearby to await his communication from the other side. After several days of honoring their father's last whim, the Boone boys finally packed up and returned to their homes, placing a heavy stone over the mouth of the cave.

Boone told Nathan that he once had shared his brother's interest in spiritualism. During their conversations one winter, the Boone brothers and one of their hunting companions made an agreement that the first of them to die would make every attempt to contact the others. His friend perished soon afterward, old Boone said, and despite the fact that he listened attentively, "he never received the promised intelligence from the spirit land" and thereafter refused to believe in such things. This was characteristic. During Boone's last years, religious revivalism made a dramatic appearance on the Femme Osage. At camp meetings there were outbreaks of the "jerks," in which people would shake and writhe about uncontrollably, speaking in tongues and sometimes cursing and swearing, all considered manifestations of the holy spirit. Many of the Boones and Bryans were affected by this revival. Flanders and Jemima were founding members of the Friendship Baptist Church in Charette and Nathan's daughter Delinda married James Craig, a "hard-shell" Baptist preacher. One of Jonathan Bryan's daughters frequently got the jerks "and was rather fond of exhibiting her proficiency," went a family story, until one day, sitting on the fence before her father's house, she suffered an actual epileptic seizure, which cured her of her spirituality. Boone remained aloof from the enthusiasm. Had there never been a time "when you experienced a change in your feelings toward the Saviour?" one hopeful Baptist preacher inquired of him. "No, sir," Boone answered sharply, "I always loved God ever since I could recollect."

During these episodes, Boone excused himself by expressing a preference for Presbyterianism. It was undoubtedly his way of avoiding conflict, for he had been unchurched from the time his mother and father emigrated to North Carolina. His spiritual condition was typical of many frontier Americans. "Very few of the pioneers made any pretensions to religion," wrote William Bryan. In Kentucky and Missouri not more than one in five adults were members of the various Protestant denominations and sects. Moreover, every community included people who actively opposed organized religion. While Boone lived at the Forks of the Yadkin, for example, one old farmer eagerly played the role of local skeptic, challenging preachers at local prayer meetings and services. When one itinerant declared that God's love would save everyone, the skeptic, seated on the front bench, called out to one of his slaves in the loft, "Moses, ain't that God damned good news?"

But Boone was never one of those hostile to religion. While he and Rebecca did not affiliate with a church, they had all of their children baptized. After Rebecca's death, facing his own mortality, he became an avid Bible reader, frequently attending services at

Jemima's. And according to Nathan, his father "well remembered what he heard and read." Boone himself left the clearest statement of his religious beliefs in a letter to Sarah Day Boone, his Quaker sister-in-law, the woman who had taught him to read and write. In 1816, soon after he received the news of the death of her husband, his older brother Samuel, he wrote,

> You can gass at my feilings by your own as we are So Near one age. . . . how we Leve in this World and what Chance we Shall have in the next we know Not. for my part I am as ignerant as a Child[.] all the Relegan I have [is] to Love and fear god, beleve in Jeses Christ, Dow all the good to my Nighbour and my Self that I Can, and Do as Little harm as I Can help, and trust on gods marcy for the Rest and I beleve god never made a man of my prisipel to be Lost.

"I cannot think that God will damn any man for the errors of his judgement," William Penn once said, and Boone's restatement of the Golden Rule echoed this first principle of his Quaker upbringing.

There may have been another influence as well. According to Timothy Flint, one of the missionaries who visited Boone during his last years, "He worshipped, as he often said, the Great Spirit—for the woods were his books and his temple, and the creed of the red men naturally became his." To be sure, Boone's religious beliefs had little in common with the complex spirituality characteristic of indigenous woodland cultures, but he shared in Indian beliefs that one early nineteenth-century observer described as a "mixture of their own opinions and creed with those taught by the whites." Many Indians incorporated simple versions of Christianity taught by Quakers and Moravians, and in turn, Americans like Boone adopted them along with other Indian ways. Such movement from both sides of the frontier toward a common ground helps to explain some of the mutual attraction of men like Boone and his Shawnee friends. Thomas Wildcat Alford, a nineteenth-century Shawnee, said that the "first principle" of the ethical code of his people was: "Do not kill or injure your neighbor, for it is not him that you injure, you injure yourself. But do good to him, therefore add to his days of happiness, as you do to your own." It sounds a great deal like Boone's.

When Boone removed to Missouri there was a small village of Indians across the river from Saint Charles, where the western Saint Louis suburb of Bridgeton now lies. There he encountered a number of friends from his days as a captive, Delawares and Shawnees from the town of Chillicothe on the Little Miami who had emigrated during the 1780s, including a number of former American captives who had chosen to remain and had raised Indian families, like Joseph Jackson, a former salt maker, Charles "Indian" Phillips, and Jimmy Rogers, now the village chief. In the area surrounding Sainte Genevieve to the south there were larger concentrations of "Absentee" Shawnees. There appeared to be little difference between the village of Rogerstown and that of Charette, where Boone spent most of his time after 1813. Both were settled by farming people who loved horses and hunting. The Rogerstown people were determined to get along with the Americans. They served as guides for local militia companies during the war, and Jimmy Rogers's two sons, Lewis and Jim, scouted with Nathan's cavalry company. After the American acquisition of the Missouri the Rogerstown community moved westward to the ford of the Bourbeuse River, near the present town of Union, about twenty miles south of Boone's settlement on the Femme Osage. They had a good deal of trouble with American claim jumpers who invaded their lands, eventually relocating further west to Kansas and finally to Oklahoma. William Clark called them "a peaceable and well disposed people, of great service to our frontier settlements."

Boone was a frequent visitor at the Shawnee village, and in the years before he gave up hunting entirely, he often joined his Indian friends for short hunts in the woods. On several occasions the Shawnees came to see Boone at Femme Osage. One day, before the war, one of Boone's granddaughters, seeing strange horses tied up before the house, asked Rebecca who had come. "Your grandfather has got some visitors, old friends," she said, "some of the identical old Shawanoes with whom he was a prisoner." Together they did some local hunting, then sat up late around a fire built outside the cabin. One of Boone's grandsons remembered listening to the Shawnee men "talk over their old narotives," stories that reflected their own distinctive point of view. "Dan, you remember when we had you prisoner," one tale began, "and our chief adopted you as his son, and you and he made an agreement that we would all go to Boonsburow, and you would make them all surrinder, and, all bury the Tomahack & all live like Brothers & Sisters." And the tale ended, "Then you rember we were all glad." There is no mention of Boone dissenting from this version.

The winter following the conclusion of the war in Missouri, Boone and Derry went trapping once again, accompanied this time by Indian Phillips, a Shawnee who lived with his Osage wife in Charette, one of a number of mixed families there. "All the grandchildren were afraid of him," one of Nathan's daughters remembered, for there were rumors that he was a murderer, and he played up this sense of menace by adopting a ferocious demeanor. Nathan and Jemima opposed Boone's going out with Derry, but with Phillips along they worried all the more. He was "pretty much a savage in feelings and appearance," one man remembered, and thought Boone took him along only because "his services, such as they were could be easily obtained." But Phillips had a reputation as a man who knew how to hunt deer better than anyone else in Missouri, someone who could bring them in even when no one else could find them. He was precisely the kind of man Boone understood.

At the end of 1815 Boone and his companions began working their way upriver from Charette. By April 1816 they were reported at Fort Osage, near the great bend of the Missouri, some 250 miles west. "We have been honored by a visit from Col. Boone," read a letter published in the *Columbian Centinel* of Massachusetts. "He has taken part in all the wars of America, from Braddock's war to the present hour. He has held respectable State appointments, both civil and military; has been a colonel, a legislator, and a magistrate." But "he prefers the woods, where you see him in the dress of the roughest, poorest hunter." When asked about his plans, Boone said, "I intend, by next season, if I can obtain permission, to take two or three whites and a party of Osage Indians, and visit the Salt Mountains, lakes and ponds, and see the natural curiosities of the country along the mountains. The Salt Mountain is but five or six hundred miles west of this place." In his eighty-second year Boone's ambition for exploration remained boundless, but soon afterward he fell sick and was forced to take to a bed at the fort until strong enough to return. The next year he confined his trapping nearer to home, but again he fell sick and was carried home to Jemima's in February 1817.

The following November, still feeling weak, he attempted a short hunt with his seventeen-year-old grandson James Boone, Nathan's oldest boy. Boone's children knew it was impossible to dissuade him from going. He was "as naturally inclined each fall to go trapping," Boone said, "as the farmer in spring to set about putting in his crops." The first evening it began to snow, and, building a campfire, the old man and the boy sat down to warm themselves. Suddenly a wild duck flew down into their clearing, landing within a few feet of the fire. James grabbed it and wrung its neck with his bare hands. It "came to them as the quails came to the children of Israel," Boone declared. In all his years in the woods he had never seen anything like this before. The woods were still a wonderment to him, and he felt elated to be out in them again, sitting by the fire with James as he had with his own boy, his grandson's namesake. For two days they hunted while Boone recounted his life and adventures to the boy, but the old man found that his frail frame was discomfited by the deepening cold, and finally, shivering uncontrollably as his son James had fifty years before, he was forced to give it up. His grandson took him to the cabin of Isaac Vanbibber, who lived near Loutre Lick, then hastened to Nathan's with the news that old Boone was "alarmingly ill, and was thought to be dying."

The news was not unexpected. Before Nathan departed for his cousin's place he ordered a coffin made so that the funeral might be held immediately on his return, before the ground froze. Arriving at the Vanbibbers, however, he found that the tough old man had made yet another recovery. But this would be Boone's last camping trip into the woods. "His fondness for his gun and trap and scouring the woods for discovery continued till the last," said a friend, and he continued to make plans for his next hunt. But weak and nearly blind, he was simply "too debilitated" to leave home. The next year a visitor saw him at the home of a granddaughter, sitting in the corner by the fireplace, scraping a cow's horn with a piece of glass. "Making a powder-horn," Boone said when asked what he was doing; "he intended to go out and hunt in the fall."

Boone objected to the coffin Nathan had ordered. It was "too rough and uncouth," he said. When Rebecca died, Boone had a coffin made of hand-picked black walnut, and he insisted on an identical copy for himself. Fearful that his wish might be dismissed as the "idle whim of an old man," he hired the same craftsman and kept his coffin stored at Nathan's house. "He would get it down from the garret, where it was kept, and examine it frequently," his granddaughter Delinda remembered, "rub and polish it up, and cooly whistle while doing so." He terrified a young neighbor girl by lying down inside, "to show how well it fit him," and told one of his nephews that he had "taken many a nice nap" in it. The story of old Boone's coffin spread over the countryside. "He had fallen into a second childhood," his friends sighed. Perhaps he *was* "as ignerant as a Child."

It was the eccentric whim of a man preparing to die, but all the while Boone's mind remained clear and vigorous. "He appeared quite smart and pert," said one of his nephews, "wishing to know all about every matter brought to his attention." Although his short-term memory failed frequently—he would forget on Tuesday what he had done on Monday—he could tell vivid anecdotes of his life in Pennsylvania eighty years before. This was the first time that his children had heard the stories of Boone's childhood. The man who had spent so little time with his own offspring now took special delight in his grandchildren and great-grandchildren, playing with them, telling stories, and singing songs.

Possum up a green stump,
Raccoon in the hollow,
Pretty girls at our house,
As fat as they can wallow.

They long remembered his little mottos: "Better mend a fault than find a fault." "If we can't say good, we should say no harm." "A man needs only three things to be happy: a good gun, a good horse, and a good wife."

And so Boone passed the last years of his life. When not among the children, in warm weather he would take a deerskin or a fur rug and recline on the grass under the shade of a nearby tree, whistling or singing to himself, enjoying the solitude of nature he had craved for most of his life. In the summer of 1820 the aspiring young painter Chester Harding sought Boone out to do a portrait. "I found the object of my search engaged in cooking his dinner," he wrote, "lying in his bunk, near the fire," alone in a little cabin behind Jemima's house. He had "a long strip of venison wound around his ramrod, and was busy turning it before a brisk blaze, and using salt and pepper to season his meat." At first Boone refused to sit for a portrait, according to William Bryan, "being governed by feelings of modesty and a strong dislike to anything approaching display or public attention." But Jemima prevailed upon him and he finally agreed. So frail had he become that a friend had to stand nearby to steady his head as he sat. In Harding's oil sketch Boone looks gaunt, with pitted skin, red-rimmed eyes, and drooping lids, but Harding caught the dignity of Boone's direct gaze, the determination of his hard-set mouth. "He was much astonished at seeing the likeness," Harding recalled. When the family gathered around, said Nathan, "they all thought it good, except that it did not exhibit the plump cheer, and hence the broad face he used to exhibit in his robust days." In the fully painted copies Harding produced from this sketch, he filled Boone out a bit and dressed him in a splendid fur-collared coat.

While at Jemima's during the late summer of 1820, Boone suffered recurrent bouts of fever. Anxious to see his family on the Femme Osage, he wanted to go back to Nathan's, but Dr. Jones warned him that even so short a journey could be fatal. After a few weeks of recovery he finally made the trip over the hills in a light carriage. Nathan had completed the construction of an impressive stone house on his land near the creek, patterned after the homes he had admired as a boy when he visited Pennsylvania with his parents, and here Boone arrived about noon on September 21. There was a good deal of anticipation that this might be his last visit, and family, friends, and neighbors all gathered to greet him. One man remembered "the deep feeling" that pervaded the crowd, the people jostling one another, craning their necks, and leaning forward to see him. Old Boone was in the process of becoming a legend.

Olive had prepared a special meal, including plenty of sweet potatoes, one of his favorite dishes, and a family tradition says that he overindulged. He spent that afternoon and evening among the children, sampling their little gifts of cakes and nuts.

The next morning Boone arose cheerful and happy and went riding with some grandchildren to see the fall crops, but at the noon meal he complained of still feeling full from the day before and took only a little warm milk in a favorite china bowl. Afterward he seemed feverish, and Olive put him to bed in the small front room of the house. Boone's son Jesse was in Saint Louis serving a term in the Missouri legislature, and Daniel Morgan had recently moved upriver, so neither was present, but on the evening of the twenty-fifth Jemima arrived with her family, including Dr. Jones, who prescribed medication. No, said Boone, he would take nothing, for this would be his last sickness: "He was about worn out." The death watch began, with everyone playing a part in a family ritual that is now practically unknown.

Boone asked for his coffin, and after they brought it down and placed it beside his bed, he thumped at it with his cane to test its soundness. He discussed the arrangements for his funeral, making sure that all understood his wish to be buried next to Rebecca on the hill by Tuque Creek. Then he asked that they prepare him. A family slave shaved him and Jemima cut his hair, preserving his locks. His granddaughter Delinda brushed his teeth for him; he was proud that he had not lost them. "My teeth would yet serve anybody a lifetime," he boasted. Why, he would use them awhile longer, she told him. No, he said once again, "I am worn out." He passed the night quietly with his family. "I have not heard you sing in a long time," he said to Olive. "Please sing to me." And she sang some of his favorite tunes. Death held no fear for him, he said. In his life he had tried to do right, had struggled to pay his debts, been charitable to the poor, and now he trusted in the mercy of God. When morning came he asked for his bowl of warm milk, finished it with relish, then requested that all of his relatives and slaves come to his bedside, that he might bid them good-bye. He had a kind word for everyone, asking them not to grieve, for he had lived to a good old age and was going to a world of happiness. Nathan and Jemima then took their places by the bedside, each holding one of his hands. He spoke to them until almost the last moment. "I am going," he said finally, "my time has come." They were his last words. He died "when the sun was half an hour high" on September 26, 1820.

The family laid Boone in his coffin and carried him back to Jemima's. Word of his death spread rapidly and the crowd at his funeral two days later was too large for the house, so they held the services in the barn around back. Delinda's husband, the Baptist minister James Craig, spoke about the things Boone had done for the country, his exploration of the great West, and his defense of the settlements. Craig was "only an ordinary preacher," Abner Bryan remembered, "yet did pretty well." The procession then began along the road to the burying ground on the knoll a mile north, young Jimmie Bryan mounted on a horse in the lead, an American flag in his hands. They buried Boone next to Rebecca on September 28, a month shy of his eighty-sixth birthday.

CHAPTER TEN

Left Until I'm Put in the Ground

Myth and Memory

Two years before Boone's death a young visitor asked him for his reaction to *The Mountain Muse*, a 250-page epic poem about his life published in 1813 by Daniel Bryan, a distant cousin of Rebecca's from Rockingham County, Virginia. Boone knew the work; his granddaughter Harriet, Jesse's girl, who with her family emigrated to Missouri from Kentucky in about 1816, had brought him a copy. She was fond of poetry and was listed in the back of Bryan's book as one of the subscribers to the volume. A young man who met this "handsome, educated young lady" on an Ohio River keelboat put up with her reading aloud from *The Wild Irish Rose* by Lady Morgan, a work he described as an "extravagant specimen of unrestrained imagination." Boone might well have used the same description after Harriet read Bryan's poem to him. *The Mountain Muse* "contained a historical basis," he thought, but was filled with inaccuracies. Bryan depicted him as "a wonderful man who had killed a host of Indians," yet in truth, he protested to his young visitor, "I never killed but three." As for Bryan's melodramatic description of the rescue of Jemima and the Callaway girls, "hardly one word of it is correct." Outfitted with heavenly choirs and long-winded orations, the poem was simply "too highly colored and exaggerated" for the old man's taste. It was too bad, Boone concluded, that he could not sue his kinsman for slander, and added with droll humor that "such productions ought to be left until the person was put in the ground."

Bryan's American epic was an early contribution to the shifting popular image of Daniel Boone. There would be scores of books, including one of the best-selling biographies of the nineteenth century. He would become the subject of paintings and engravings, great literature and dime novels, poems inspired and insipid. His story would encourage fakery as well as serious historical investigation. Men would use his legacy to promote militant national expansionism as well as criticize commercial civilization. Carvings, rifles, homes, and other relics would become the objects of well-meaning preservationists and jealous collectors. And even Boone's resting place, his final piece of ground, would become the contested object of promoters and boosters.

John Filson's Boone was both fighting frontiersman and forest philosopher. Even in the abridged text, which sacrificed the most reflective passages for an emphasis on action, Boone comes across as a man who loves the wilderness for its own sake. But the vision of Boone in *The Mountain Muse* is thoroughly civil. He is the divinely appointed pathfinder and precursor of civilization. Bryan begins with an assembly of angels appointing Boone to "open in the regions of the West / A sanctuary from the foes of VICE." Boone's glory, the heavenly messenger tells him, will be the "Republic, which thy patriot hand / Implanted in the direful Wilderness." When the hero gazes for the first time on the mighty Mississippi he does not rhapsodize on nature's wonder but rather

His thoughts prospectively he also cast,
And through Imagination's optics viewed;
With brilliant diadems of COMMERCE crown'd,
And with the products of a thousand farms,
And riches of Mercantile Kingdoms fraught
With Freedom's Cities and REPUBLICS lined
And Happiness and Heavenly Virtues cheer'd.

It was understandable if Boone was impatient with this "highly colored" verse. The poem, a contemporary reviewer noted, "needs nothing but a little exaggeration to be heightened into broad caricature," and Bryan himself later admitted that it was "the wild offspring of a rude undisciplined fancy."

In his last years Boone grew uneasy with the conception of him as the harbinger of progress. Originating with Filson and elaborated in John Coburn's petitions, this idea enjoyed great popular appeal, for it threw a sanctimonious mantle over what in truth was a bloody business. "Few men have excelled Col. Boone," Judge Coburn eulogized in 1820, for he "has been the instrument of opening the road to millions of the human family from the pressure of sterility and want, to a Land flowing with milk and honey." But before his death Boone himself declared that he had never entertained any ideas about "empire, or rule, or profit." Even John Mason Peck, who wrote a biography in which he attempted to make his subject over into a proponent of Manifest Destiny, said that Boone's own statement was that he had "entered into the wilderness with no comprehensive views or extensive plans of future improvement" and "had only followed the pathway of duty in the course he had pursued." Yet it was as providential pathfinder for civilization that Boone was most celebrated by his contemporaries.

This was the interpretation of Boone's first biographer, Timothy Flint, who used Boone's life to illustrate God's progressive plan for America. Thanks to the efforts of this pioneer, Flint wrote, "the rich and boundless valleys of the great west—the garden of the earth—had been won from the domination of the savage tribes, and opened as an asylum for the oppressed, the enterprising, the free of every land." Flint's prose echoed Bryan's poetry. He was, in fact, one of the few who praised *The Mountain Muse*, complaining that it had been "consigned very unjustly to oblivion." In Flint's words, Boone "caught some glimmerings of the future, and saw with the prophetic eye of a patriot that this great valley must soon become the abode of millions of freemen." As Boone played out the divine script, "his heart swelled with joy." "Wonderfully was he endowed by Providence for the part which he was called to act."

Flint came from a Puritan New England background. After a

boyhood in rural Massachusetts he trained for the clergy at Harvard, but, feeling constrained in the pulpit of a small Massachusetts church, he went west in 1815 as a missionary and not long after left the ministry entirely to pursue a literary career. He achieved fame and fortune in the 1820s by writing travel accounts and "border romances" with titles like *George Mason, the Young Backwoodsman* (1829) and *Shoshonee Valley* (1830), and by then Flint was at work on his Boone biography. He had paid several visits to the Callaway home, where he talked with old Boone before his death. He gathered stories from family and friends and collected folk legends and tales. Flint imagined himself fashioning a founding epic for young America. "Although much has been said in prose and sung in verse about Daniel Boone," he wrote, "this Achilles of the West wants a Homer, worthily to celebrate his exploits." The book that resulted from his labors was indeed like myth in the absence of much verifiable detail. Fellow Western writer James Hall declared it "little better than a caricature," and Kentucky historian Mann Butler reproached Flint for writing a work so bereft of fact, to which the author jocularly replied that the book "was made not for use, but to sell."

Sell it did. *Biographical Memoir of Daniel Boone, the First Settler of Kentucky*, published in 1833, went through fourteen editions before 1868, making it the most widely read biography of antebellum America, second only to Filson's narrative in creating the image of Boone in the popular imagination. His goal, Flint wrote, was "not to bury the memory of our pioneer in that most revolting of all sepulchers, a dull biography." In an age of garrulous writing, his prose stirred with action. Boone nearly kills his lady love in the firehunt story here made famous. He defends himself in ferocious hand-to-hand combat with an Indian warrior, his foot planted on the body of another savage whom he has already dispatched. He escapes from the murderers of his brother Ned by swinging Tarzan-like through the forest on a vine. He grapples with a huge bear that falls "harmless to the ground" after he plunges his hunting knife "directly to the heart of the animal."

Since Flint had collected much of his evidence during conversations with westerners, the biography spread the folkloric image of the pioneer, but most Boone descendants scorned the book because of its numerous errors of fact and fancy. Boone's grandson Septimus Scholl penned a rebuttal for the benefit of his children. "The account in Flint's Life of Boone, of Boone's being taken when in pursuit of the girls is false. Also, his jumping a long stride by means of a grape vine to avoid being trailed. Also, his conflict with a bear." Boone's nephew Daniel Boone Bryan was livid. "Could any man of reason," he wrote to Lyman Draper in 1843, "believe that a man running for life—not for money or property, but for his life—his pursuers close to his heels, their dog in close bay—I ask, could any man suppose or believe he would stop to cut loose a grapevine to swing?" Bryan's anger came through loud and clear. "I suppose it was on this vine," he concluded, "that Mr. Flint swong so often from the truth." But what did it matter to Flint's readers, mostly boys by the thousands, who devoured his pages? His Boone was godfather to the dozens who fought their way through the pages of sensational dime novels. As the historian Marshall Fishwick once observed, "Flint was Boone's Parson Weems," and the story of his bear fight and the tree carving that commemorated it were the equivalent of Washington's cherry tree. When asked what they know about Daniel Boone, many an American will respond with the phrase "D. Boon cilled a bear."

Many also imbibed Flint's moral lesson. "There is a kind of moral sublimity in the contemplation of the adventures and daring of such men," he wrote, for they "re-inspire something of that simplicity of manners, manly hardihood, and Spartan energy and force of character which formed so conspicuous a part of the nature of the settlers of the western wilderness." Flint used the West of his imagination to reinforce the standards of a more vigorous place and time when a man was a man. Boone and the frontiersmen, he declared, "read a lesson to shrinking and effeminate spirits, the men of soft hands and fashionable life, whose frames the winds of heaven are not allowed to visit too roughly." He also urged the example of selfless frontier women on "modern wives, who refuse to follow their husbands abroad, alleging the danger of the voyage or journey, or the unhealthiness of the proposed residence, or because the removal will separate them from the pleasures of fashion and society." Pioneering was already becoming an important metaphor in a campaign to forestall a sense of decaying masculine potency and combat a fear of rising feminine power in American culture. Flint would not be the last easterner to interpret the frontier experience in the light of nostalgia. In the late nineteenth century Theodore Roosevelt and other idealogues of the West organized "Boone and Crockett Clubs" to encourage "energy, resolution, manliness, self-reliance, and a capacity for self-help" among wealthy sportsmen. This concept was extended to boys of all backgrounds when Daniel C. Beard, with President Roosevelt's backing, founded the Boy Scouts of America in the early twentieth century. He originally thought of calling the organization "The Sons of Daniel Boone."

Flint's Boone offered a model of masculine vigor, but in Flint's vision of history the pioneer himself was required to step aside for the onward march of progress. Boone's life confronted the pathfinder school of interpretation with a problem, for his removal from developing Kentucky to primitive Missouri and his return to hunting and trapping in old age indicated his failure to adapt to the commercial civilization he had been destined to establish. In the hands of other writers such a contradiction might be worked into the stuff of moral dilemma, but for Flint, moral choices always had to be clear and simple. "The restless spirit of immigration, and of civil and physical improvement," he wrote, eventually "swept by the dwelling of Daniel Boone, driving off the game and monopolizing the rich hunting grounds." But Flint's Boone manfully accepts the providential design.

> He saw that it was in vain to contend with fate; that go where he would, American enterprize seemed doomed to follow him, and to thwart all his schemes of backwoods retirement. He found himself once more surrounded by the rapid march of improvement, and he accommodated himself, as well as he might, to a state of things which he could not prevent.

Shouldering his misfortune, and sighing for new adventures, Flint's Boone moved farther west.

One of Flint's anecdotes provided the archetypal expression of Boone's wanderlust. As he moves down the Ohio River toward Missouri in 1799, someone asks what induced him to leave "so rich and flourishing a country as his dear Kentucky, which he had discovered and had helped to win from the Indians, for the wilds of Missouri?" "Too crowded," Boone exclaims, "too crowded—I want more elbow room!" In the context of Flint's conception of his hero, Boone's declaration carries a certain irony, since his move was not determined by choice but by historical necessity or "fate." But in folklore Boone is always held personally responsible for his decision to remove. The tales of his restlessness are double-sided, for while they celebrate migration, the very essence of American pioneering, they also question Boone's social commitments. Boone "did not stay [in] one plase long [enough] to get acquainted," said one old man who lived near him in Kentucky. He "always lived in a world of his own." The pioneers depended on mutual assistance for survival and despised men who refused to be neighborly. In one folktale a man asks old Boone why he left settled Kentucky for the wilds of the West. "They crowded me too much," he says. "I could not stand it. I wanted to go where I would not be around so much by neabors." But despite his move to the frontier, he complains, "I am too much crowded now where I live in Missouri." Well, how close *are* your nearest neighbors? the man inquires, and he is incredulous at Boone's reply. They are only twenty miles away!

A variant of this tale found its way into print soon after Boone's death. In Kentucky, Boone declares, "I fought and repelled the savages, and hoped for repose," but "was molested by interlopers from every quarter. Again I retreated to the region of the Mississippi, but again these speculators and settlers followed me. Once more I withdrew to the licks of Missouri, and here at length I hoped to find rest. But I was still pursued, for I had not been two years at the licks before a damned Yankee came and settled down within a hundred miles of me!" In a small volume of Boone material published in 1823, an unnamed "near relation" declared that "the great object of the Colonel appears to have been to live as remote as possible from every white inhabitant, except those of his own family." In what was perhaps the apogee of such commentary, a piece published in 1827, Boone abandons even his family for the isolation of the wilderness. At the end of his life he sits "silent and dejected" in a rude hut, finally realizing the cost of his social disaffection. "Alone! Alone!—how drear it is / Always to be alone!" he laments.

The red deer like the breezes fly
To meet the bounding roe,
But I have not a human sigh
To cheer me as I go!
I've hated men—I hate them now—
But since they are not here,
I thirst for the familiar brow,
Thirst for the stealing tear.

The poem was accompanied by an engraving of Thomas Cole's 1826 painting *Daniel Boone at His Cabin at Great Osage Lake*, which featured an isolated, scowling Boone in the midst of an inaccessible and overpowering wilderness. Cole's surviving studies for the work reveal that he overlaid the body of Boone on a drawing of an Indian, suggesting the extent to which the artist believed that the old pioneer had abandoned civilization to take up Indian ways.

There were others, however, who celebrated Boone as a "natural man" who fled not from society itself but from its corruption. "As civilization advanced, so he, from time to time, retreated," wrote the editor of a New York paper in 1823, "not as a misanthrope, but as a philosopher." This was a revival of Filson's notion of Boone as forest philosopher, and indeed, by 1821 the interest in this notion was sufficient to warrant the reprinting of Filson's full and unexpurgated narrative for the first time in thirty years. An important source of this idea was the published work of Gilbert Imlay, the scoundrel who had cheated Boone out of his property. In his *Topographical Description of the Western Territory of North America*, Imlay celebrated Boone and other backwoods Americans as "people in a state of innocence," living in striking contrast with the "distorted and unnatural habits of the Europeans." Perhaps he wrote this tongue in cheek, for Imlay certainly had played confidence man to Boone's country bumpkin, but of course his readers knew nothing of this personal history. In 1793 Imlay added Filson's narrative as an appendix to the second edition of the book. That same year, assisted by his lover Mary Wollstonecraft, the feminist writer, Imlay published an implausible novel entitled *The Emigrants* (1793), the story of a group of English settlers who construct a utopian settlement in the Ohio country, attempting to escape the fate of "the bulk of mankind [who] have been the mere machines of states." In both of these works Imlay impressed his readers with the possibilities of a virtuous and natural life in the American wilderness.

A similar philosophy of refined protest against civilized convention is evident in the description of Boone in Henry Marie Brackenridge's account of his travels in western America published in 1814. He found old Boone living on the Femme Osage amid a community of some forty families that, he wrote, "respect him as a father, and who live under a kind of patriarchal government, ruled by his advice and example." "They retired through choice," Brackenridge declared, "placing themselves at a distance from the deceit and turbulence of the world. They enjoy an uninterrupted quiet, and a real comfort in their little society, beyond the sphere of that larger society where government is necessary." And here, he concluded, "they are truly free, neither assailed by the madness of ambition, nor tortured by the poison of party spirit. Is not this one of the most powerful incentives which impels the Anglo-American to bury himself in the midst of the wilderness?"

Boone's most famous incarnation as "natural man" came in the lines written by the British poet Lord Byron. Byron read Brackenridge's description of Boone and undoubtedly was familiar with the American pioneer through Imlay's work as well, for his circle included Mary Goodwin, daughter of Mary Wollstonecraft and half-sister of Fanny Imlay. After reading about Boone and discussing him with a number of American visitors, Byron wrote seven stanzas on him, which he included in the eighth canto of his epic masterpiece *Don Juan*. In the midst of an extended description of European warfare, Byron suddenly digresses:

> Of the great names which in our faces stare,
>   The General Boon, back-woodsman of Kentucky,
> Was happiest amongst mortals any where;
>   For killing nothing but a bear or buck, he
> Enjoyed the lonely vigorous, harmless days
> Of his old age in wilds of deepest maze.

Americans could have read these lines in late 1822, and they were reprinted scores of times throughout the century. In them the poet celebrated Boone's life on the fringe of civilization.

Crime came not near him—she is not the child
  Of Solitude; health shrank not from him—for
Her home is in the rarely-trodden wild,
  Where if men seek her not, and death be more
Their choice than life, forgive them, as beguiled
  By habit to what their own hearts abhor—
In cities caged. The present case in point I
Cite is, that Boone lived hunting up to ninety;

And what's still stranger, left behind a name
  For which men vainly decimate the throng,
Not only famous, but of that good fame,
  Without which Glory's but a tavern song—
Simple, serene, the antipodes of shame,
  Which hate nor envy e'er could tinge with wrong;
An active hermit, even in age the child
Of Nature, or the Man of Ross run wild.

'Tis true he shrank from men even of his nation,
  When they built up into his darling trees,—
He moved some hundred miles off, for a station
  Where there were fewer houses and more ease;
The inconvenience of civilization
  Is, that you neither can be pleased nor please;
But where he met the individual man
He shewed himself as kind as mortal can.

He was not all alone: around him grew
  A sylvan tribe of children of the chace,
Whose young, unwakened world was ever new,
  Nor sword nor sorrow yet had left a trace
On her unwrinkled brow, nor could you view
  A frown on Nature's or on human face;—
The free-born forest found and kept them free,
And fresh as is a torrent or a tree.

And tall and strong and swift of foot were they,
  Beyond the dwarfing city's pale abortions,
Because their thoughts had never been the prey
  Of care or gain: the green woods were their portions;
No stinking Spirits told them they grew grey,

No Fashion made them apes of her distortions;
Simple they were, not savage; and their rifles,
Though very true, were not yet used for trifles.

Motion was in their days, Rest in their slumbers,
And Cheerfulness the handmaid of their toil;
Nor yet too many nor too few their numbers;
Corruption could not make their hearts her soil;
The Lust which stings, the Splendor which encumbers,
With the free foresters divide not spoil;
Serene, not sullen, were the solitudes
Of this unsighing people of the woods.

His epic, Byron said, was "a Satire on abuses of the present state of Society," and as such he had little interest in understanding Boone himself or the North American frontier from which he came. Byron employs Boone for contrast with the bloody heroes found elsewhere in his detailed description of warfare. Boone's "unsighing people of the woods" use their rifles too, but not for the "trifles" that pit civilized states against one another. It hardly requires saying that this idyllic portrait of Boone's world was in most respects pure fantasy, considering the disease and death, the hate and envy, the "sword and sorrow" of Boone's life. Byron notwithstanding, the Boone of flesh and blood gained his fame in warfare, bargained in real estate, and kept the accounts of a grocery store.

But there is enormous appeal in Byron's lines, the elegiac tone countered by witty rhyme, the meter and syntax in beautiful balance, the memorable phrasing. Their appeal to several generations of Americans suggests that there was something more at work here than poetic brilliance or the attractions of a philosophy of primitivism. Byron's Boone, "even in age the child of Nature," was the man who "lived hunting up to ninety." There was great popular interest in Boone's pursuit of his livelihood past three score and ten, and in the nineteenth century writers most frequently portrayed him as an aged yet active frontiersman. Byron helped to fix this image of an energetic old Boone in the public mind.

When Byron's poem first appeared, James Fenimore Cooper was engaged in writing his own version of Boone. Published in early

1823, *The Pioneers* was an enormous success, selling thirty-five hundred copies on the first morning of its publication and establishing Cooper as one of the first American authors able to support himself solely by the practice of his craft. The similarity between Boone and Leatherstocking, Cooper's fictional backwoods hero, was lost on few. There was the deliberate echo in their names—Daniel Boone and Nathaniel Bumppo. Both were ancient backwoodsmen, forced to give way to civilization and move farther west. One of the novel's first reviewers suggested that Cooper's character "has been modeled from the effigies of old Daniel Boone, who abandoned the society of his kindred and built a hut among the Indians, and persisted in removing further into the interior as the path of civilization invaded his wild domains." Most Cooper criticism remained within the conventions of Boone discourse, something evident, for example, in the remark of one critic that Leatherstocking, "though averse to the modes of life 'down in the settlements,' was neither a savage nor a misanthrope." As the historian Francis Parkman later noted, Leatherstocking's real-life counterpart was "the character of Daniel Boone."

Cooper followed his first backwoods novel with *The Last of the Mohicans* (1826), the most popular of what became known as the Leatherstocking Tales. Its central episode of captivity was loosely based on accounts of Boone's rescue of Jemima and the Callaway girls. As if to strengthen the association of this character with Boone, in the opening pages of his next tale, *The Prairie* (1827), Cooper explicitly called the reader's attention to "Colonel Boone, the patriarch of Kentucky," reminding them that this "hardy pioneer of civilization" removed west of the Mississippi "because he found a population of ten to the square mile inconveniently crowded." Like Boone after his last remove, old Leatherstocking is reduced to trapping. He prefers the company of Indians to white men and calls them "the rightful owners of the country." He finally dies, his gaze fastened on the sun setting on the western horizon. Cooper brought him back as a youth in the last two novels in the series, *The Pathfinder* (1840) and *The Deerslayer* (1841).

Cooper suffered his share of criticism for his inadequately drawn feminine characters, for his implausible dialogue, and for the sympathy with which he portrayed "good" Indians, infuriating Indian haters. But Cooper's Boone/Bumppo rose from the blows to become what the *Cambridge History of American Literature* calls "the most memorable character American fiction has given to the world." What was most striking about Leatherstocking was Cooper's conception of him as "philosopher of the wilderness" and critic of civilization. "Our ways doesn't agree," old Bumppo declares to Judge Temple, the representative of civil order in *The Pioneers*. "I love the woods, and ye relish the face of man; I eat when hungry and drink when a-dry, and ye keep the stated hours and rules." When the men of the settlement participate in a massive slaughter of passenger pigeons (a species that Americans hunted to extinction during the nineteenth century), Leatherstocking turns away in disgust, growling that "this comes of settling a country." The irony is bitter when he is tried and jailed for hunting deer out of season. "What has a man who lives in the wilderness to do with the ways of the law?" he wonders, evoking Boone's plea of legal naivete. He rejects the law of the "clearings" and condemns the settlers, who "scourge the very 'arth with their axes." "I tarried till the mouths of my hounds were deafened by the blows of the chopper," he echoes Boone in *The Prairie*, "and then I came west in search of quiet." In *The Deerslayer* he declares that "when the colony's laws, or even the king's laws, run a'gin the laws of God, they get to be onlawful, and ought not to be obeyed."

Cooper's saga is permeated by the conflict between natural freedom and civilized restraint. But unlike Byron—who declares "the great joys of civilization" to be "War, Pestilence, the despot's desolation / The kingly scourge, the Lust of Notoriety, / The millions slain by soldiers for their ration"—Cooper was no cynic, believing wholeheartedly in the development of the country and the progressive nature of history. Judge Temple in *The Pioneers* is a visionary leader patterned on Cooper's own father, the founder of Cooperstown, New York. "Where others saw nothing but a wilderness," Temple sees "towns, manufactories, bridges, canals, mines, and all the other resources of an old country." Yet Cooper's views also contrasted with those of simpleminded progressives like Flint, whose Boone shrugs his shoulders and moves aside for change. Cooper allows Leatherstocking to make a powerful case against civilization. "The garden of the Lord was the forest," says he, and was not patterned "after the miserable fashions of our times, thereby giving the lie to what the world calls its civilizing."

Indeed, Flint was disgusted by the Leatherstocking Tales, lambasting them for what he thought to be their moral equivocation. While Cooper presents a defense for "the march of our nation across the continent," his sentimental attachments remain with "forest freedom," forcing his readers to dwell on the price of progress. Parkman summarized Cooper's message: "Civilization has a destroying as well as a creating power," and "must eventually sweep before it a class of men, its own precursors and pioneers, so remarkable both in their virtues and their faults that few will see their extinction without regret. Of these men Leatherstocking is the representative." Cooper created a Boone/Bumppo who was potentially tragic, invoking his own destruction by his pursuit of virtuous and noble ends.

Unfortunately, as the critic John William Ward observes, Cooper's theme was greater than his art. His civilized characters are so lifeless and our sympathies are so entirely captivated by Leatherstocking that his destruction seems completely unjust, and thus the work fails to achieve a tragic dimension. Nevertheless, to Americans laboring intently to construct a commercial and mechanical civilization, Cooper's ambivalence about progress spoke to a deeply felt regret about the loss of the wilderness as an imagined place of unbound freedom. Leatherstocking personified these contradictory feelings. It was not long before Boone biographers were appealing to their readers' knowledge of Cooper for an understanding of their own subject, as did Cecil Hartley in 1860 when he wrote that "a reader of Mr. Cooper's *Last of the Mohicans* may comprehend, in some measure, the arts by which [Boone] was preserved." Thus did fiction transmutate into history.

An alternative to the primitivist or pathfinder image was the bragging, fighting, Indian-hating frontiersman. This character rose into the spotlight of national popular culture from sources in western folklore during the 1820s, and in the figure of Davy Crockett and other similar semifictional frontiersmen came to symbolize national expansion during the era of Andrew Jackson. Although the popular image of Boone was in stark contrast with that of Crockett, the Jacksonian backwoodsman developed out of the context of Boone image making.

Shortly after Boone's death, an advertisement in the *Missouri*

Gazette announced the publication of "an engraving of the venerable Col. DANIEL BOON," a "means of rescuing from oblivion the features of one who took the most active part in sustaining the early settlements of the Western Country." The work of the self-taught artist James Otto Lewis of Saint Louis, the print was said to be "a good copy of the painted likeness" of Boone completed by Chester Harding during the summer of 1820. This was a full-length, life-size painting, one of at least three portraits that Harding produced from the oil sketch he made at the Callaway home. Harding offered this work to the state of Kentucky and for more than two decades it hung in the capitol in Frankfort. But because he had done the work on an ordinary table oilcloth it began to crack and peel, and officials eventually replaced it with another romantic, if inauthentic, portrait of Boone by William C. Allen. Harding went on to become a fashionable portrait painter in Boston, and many years later, after retrieving the full-length painting from a Kentucky attic, he cut out the head, pasted it on a new canvas, and repainted the "drapery."

The Harding paintings of Boone, particularly the original oil sketch, provide a haunting likeness of the old man's face, but after the mutilation of the full-length portrait, only Lewis's engraving remained to suggest his figure and costume. A woman who met Boone in his old age described him as looking just as she saw him depicted in this "old woodcut," although another contemporary thought it "made him look too tall." The print features a gaunt Boone leaning against his long rifle, dressed in fringed hunting shirt, leggings, and moccasins, with his beaver hat in hand and hunting knife tucked in his belt. It was among the earliest of published prints to feature the authentic costume of an American frontiersman. In the depressed economy of the early 1820s, however, the prints did not sell well, and to increase their appeal Lewis hired Noah Ludlow, an unemployed musician and actor, to gild frames for them. Apparently all of the copies eventually were sold, although they seem to have been little appreciated, since only three are known to have survived into the twentieth century.

Yet the engraving had a reverberating influence in helping to establish the standard costume for the American backwoodsman of popular culture. Two years after assisting Lewis with the sale of the prints, Noah Ludlow was performing in New Orleans, where he sought to incorporate into his minstrel act a newly published song called "The Hunters of Kentucky," commemorating the victory of frontiersmen over the British at the Battle of New Orleans. Familiar with the costume of *the* Kentucky hunter from the engraving, Ludlow donned a set of fringed buckskins and moccasins, but, unable to locate a hat in Boone's preferred style, he wore a coonskin cap. That night he took the stage, long rifle in hand.

> We are a hardy freeborn race,
> Each man to fear a stranger,
> Whate'er the game, we join in chase,
> Despising toil and danger;
> And if a daring foe annoys,
> Whate'er his strength and forces,
> We'll show him that Kentucky boys
> Are "alligator horses."
> O Kentucky, the hunters of Kentucky.
> O Kentucky, the hunters of Kentucky.

At the chorus Ludlow threw his cap to the boards and lowered his rifle at the audience, and, as he remembered it, the boatmen and backwoodsmen let out a "prolonged whoop or howl, such as Indians give when they are especially pleased." "The Hunters of Kentucky" was an instant hit and became the unofficial campaign song of Andrew Jackson's presidential runs in 1824 and 1828. Through a long career as a minstrel performer, Ludlow toured the nation as "The Old Kentucky Hunter," a characterization that shaped all subsequent stage portrayals of the backwoodsman, one of the most important of which was Nimrod Wildfire, a Kentuckian come to New York in James Kirke Paulding's hit melodrama of the 1830s, *The Lion of the West*. Davy Crockett adopted the look and the humor of Wildfire for his public image, and after Crockett the image came full circle. Timothy Flint's biography, for example, included a series of charming woodcuts with Boone dressed in his authentic costume, but with Ludlow's coonskin cap replacing his own beaver hat.

The Davy Crockett of the 1830s may have owed his look to Boone, but the Jacksonian backwoodsman was a different character altogether, a "half horse, half alligator," a hater and killer rather than a civilizer or a philosopher. An important text in establishing this new image was John A. McClung's *Sketches of Western Adventure*, a chronicle of legendary Indian fighters published in 1832. Reviewing the story of Boone's capture and captivity by the Shawnees, of the Boonesborough defense and the aborted treaty negotiations, McClung found the pioneer hero lacking in the ferocity requisite for the times and with a touch of sadness concluded that "we look here in vain for the prudence and sagacity which usually distinguished Boone." In the Jacksonian age of Indian removal the idea of negotiating on equal terms with native peoples had become heresy, and rather than allowing the historical evidence to suggest a revision of his ideas about Boone's character, McClung chose to interpret the whole complicated episode as a curious lapse of heroic standards. McClung's Boone, come to his senses, afterward longs for the "thrilling excitement of savage warfare."

A starker tone of imperial destiny and racial superiority was evident in many of the "border romances" published to fill the demand first created by Cooper. Robert Montgomery Bird loosely patterned the hero of his *Nick of the Woods* (1837) on Boone. Old Nick disguises himself as a gentle Quaker, for example, but is actually a vicious Indian hater and murderer. Bird condemned Cooper for his "poetical illusions" about Indians, and in the novel he had one ugly character declare, "I'm a white Injun, and there's nothing more despicable." Another popular novelist, William Gilmore Simms, also took care to establish his distance from Cooper, declaring in *The Yemasee* (1835) that it was "utterly impossible that the whites and Indians should ever live together and agree," undercutting the very bedrock of Leatherstocking's way of life. In one of his literary essays Simms suggested a redefinition of Boone himself. Quoting Byron's first stanza on the "backwoodsman of Kentucky," he declared that in at least one instance the poet had "sacrificed the truth to the rhyme," for "Boone's rifle occasionally made free with much nobler victims than bear and buck. He was a hunter of men too, upon occasion." Boone may not have inclined to war, said Simms, yet "he smote the savage man" and "could take a scalp with the rest." This new Boone was a dime novel character, like the one in Emerson Bennett's *Ella Barnwell* (1853) who declares, "Why, thar's more real satisfaction in sarcumventing and scalping one o' them red heathen, than in all the amusement you could scare up in a thick-peopled peaceable settlement in a life time." While Filson's language may have sounded silly coming from Boone's lips, it at least had a plausible relationship to Boone concerns. This dialogue slandered the truth of Boone's life.

Filson had written of the Shawnee affection for Boone, and in the nineteenth century a few other biographers, mostly Yankees like the Congregational minister John Abbott, continued to comment on his "real sympathy for the savages." But after McClung most biographers lent Boone the characteristics of the Indian hater. One suggested that in his old age Boone had been overcome with a kind of senile sentimentality that prevented him from acknowledging "having killed an enemy in battle or elsewhere" and kept him from wanting "the blood of many redskins on his hunting shirt." Reports of Boone's regard for the Shawnees should be allowed to "quietly sleep," he thought, because they were "not much to his credit." The biography of Boone ghost-written for "Buffalo Bill" Cody was typical. In the aftermath of the siege of Boonesborough Cody's Boone criticized his own attempt to negotiate with the Shawnees, admitting that "he didn't know how it happened, but he had played the great fool."

The image of Boone as the exemplar of the fighting frontiersman was most hideously represented in the colossal marble statuary group known as *The Rescue*, executed by the American sculptor Horatio Greenough and installed in 1851 at the Capitol in Washington, D.C. A gigantic pioneer, clad ridiculously in classical drapery and helmet, restrains a naked savage from bludgeoning a cowering mother and child. Greenough wanted to show, he said, "the peril of the American wilderness, the ferocity of our Indians, the superiority of the white-man, and why and how civilization crowded the Indian from his soil." Although the artist intended his work as a general statement, it was commonly taken to represent Boone, an association made explicit in a popular lithograph of 1874 in which the figures were copied and retitled *Daniel Boone Protects His Family*. The statue itself stood on the east front steps of the Capitol portico for over a century, but after World War II officials found its imagery embarrassing. During renovations in 1958 it was damaged while being removed and stored at the Capitol power plant.

The most famous of all nineteenth-century Boone paintings, George Caleb Bingham's magnificent *Daniel Boone Escorting Settlers through the Cumberland Gap*, deliberately countered this image of the Indian-hating and violent pioneer. "I am now painting the Emigration of Boone and his family to Kentucky," Bingham wrote a friend in 1851. "The subject is a popular one in the West, and one which has never been painted." Bingham was at the height of his powers and popularity, a genre painter widely celebrated for his scenes of everyday life in the Mississippi Valley frontier. His Boone strides directly forward at the head of a long column of settlers that stretch back through the dark and forbidding pass in the mountains. A brilliant light, however, illuminates the Boone family group that immediately follows. Boone leads a white horse that carries Rebecca, who, covered in a dark shawl, evokes the Christian images of the Madonna and the flight into Egypt. One of the Boone girls, Susannah perhaps, rides a little behind her mother, and a man identified as Flanders Callaway, later to become Jemima's husband, walks at Boone's left, his rifle at the ready. The young man on the right, who has laid his gun aside to adjust his mocassin, may be meant to represent Boone's son James, who was killed in the ambush near the gap. Bingham depicted a noble Boone, a patriarch who rises above the Indian fighters, adventurers, and alligator horses prominent in the nation's perception of the West. His hero shares the dignity of the original Harding portrait. In fact, in one of Bingham's earliest boyhood memories, he watched Harding work on the Boone portraits, and in one of his first commercial assignments, Bingham attempted to reproduce Harding's full-length Boone as a tavern sign. The Boone of Bingham's masterpiece is a considerably younger and heavier man, and though his cleft chin seems an alien element, he shares the eyes and nose of the Harding. Perhaps most significant, Bingham dresses Boone in exactly the costume found in the Lewis engraving. Like Boone himself, Bingham disdains the uncouth coonskin cap, choosing instead the Quaker-style beaver.

Conflicting images continued into the twentieth century. The dime novel hero found a place in new forms of mass media. The fighting Boone was featured in comic strips and was a frequent character in radio programs. "I started in to listen to a series of Boone adventures," Boone descendant William Bryan wrote to a friend following the national radio broadcast of Katherine Clugston's *Wilderness Road*, "but they turned out so badly that I broke the machine and kicked it out the back door. They were about as much like Boone as my old shoe is like a potato." The people who produced such things, he thought, "know but little about the subject and just write to fill the space, thinking to themselves, 'Oh well, everybody's dead, and there's nobody left to kick me—so here goes!' "

Much the same thing could be said of the dozen or so Boone films, matinee shoot-em-ups each and every one. The Edison Company released a two-reel *Daniel Boone* in 1907, and before the end of the 1920s this cardboard characterization reappeared in four more silents. Cowboy star George O'Brien played a beefy Boone in a 1936 film that was most memorable for the villainous performance of John Carradine as Simon Girty, a role he reprised to great effect in John Ford's *Drums Along the Mohawk* (1939). The otherwise forgettable *Daniel Boone, Trail Blazer* (1956) caused a brief stir when a Kentucky congressman attempted to organize a boycott of the picture because it had been shot in Mexico rather than on location in the Bluegrass State. Finally, the popular television series that ran from 1964 to 1970 portrayed Boone as "the rippin'est, roarin'est, fightin'est man, the frontier ever knew." If this seems more evocative of Davy Crockett than Boone, it was in large part because actor Fess Parker simply was replaying the character he had ridden to fame and fortune in the Crockett craze of the 1950s. Parker's Crockett/Boone, in fact, is largely responsible for the persistent popular confusion that exists today between these two frontier heroes. Is it true, people ask, what they say about Daniel Boone's death at the Alamo?

But a number of modern novelists have portrayed Boone as a sympathetic man of flesh and blood and contradiction. In Caroline Gordon's *Green Centuries* (1941) Boone returns home from across the mountains with Rebecca on his mind, "crazy about that woman now as if she was a young girl." His children crowd about him excitedly, and after fond greetings he sends them out to see what he's brought, but one lingers at his father's side. "Can't you find something to do outdoors, boy?" Boone says irritably, and his companion, understanding his friend's desire, laughs and takes the boy out. It is the sharp voice of Rebecca that is front and center in

Never No More (1964), by Shirley Seifert. "Two months!" she scolds her husband after his long-delayed return from a long hunt, "me not knowing what to think from day to day. Teetering from one foot to the other." But uncertainty is the price she decides to pay for the love of a "traipsing man." Boone's role in *The Great Meadow* (1930), a haunting work by Elizabeth Madox Roberts, is "messenger to the chaotic part, a herald, an envoy there, to prepare it for civil men." He inspires the young emigrant woman Diony Hall to face the hard tests of frontier life, to be "a Boone kind of woman." Interestingly, in the years since Cooper, women have written the best of the Boone fiction.

Meanwhile, the debate about Boone's cultural legacy continued. In an essay on Leatherstocking that applies equally well to Boone, D. H. Lawrence revived concerns about pioneer misanthropy. "Men are free when they are in a living homeland," he argued, "not when they are escaping to some wild west." What sort of a man "gets his deepest thrill of gratification," he wondered, "when he puts a bullet through the heart of a beautiful buck, as it stoops to drink at the lake"? "Why, he is a man with a gun," Lawrence declared in a justly famous passage, "he is a killer, a slayer. Patient and gentle as he is, he is a slayer. Self-effacing, self-forgetting, still he is a killer." For Lawrence, Boone/Bumppo was an avatar of the national character: "The essential American soul is hard, isolate, stoic, and a killer."

For William Carlos Williams, however, Boone was an American hero who "lived to enjoy ecstasy through his single devotion to the wilderness with which he was surrounded." Unlike the Puritan, who "keeps his frightened grip upon the throat of the world," or the conquistador, who destroys the very object of his desire, Boone "sought only with primal lust to grow close to it, to understand it and to be part of its mysterious movements—like an Indian." Boone the existential man. "He wants to have the feet of his understanding on the ground, his ground, *the* ground, the only ground that he knows, that which *is* under his feet." Boone thus represents that part of the American character unafraid of new territory to explore, new connections to make. "Not that he settled Kentucky or made a path to the west, not that he defended, suffered, hated and fled, but because of a descent to the ground of his desire was Boone's life important and does it remain still loaded with power." Even Lawrence found Williams's conception compelling. "There are two ways of being American," he wrote after reading Williams's essay on Boone,

> by recoiling into individual smallness and insentience, and gutting the great continent in frenzies of mean fear. It is the Puritan way. The other way is by *touch*; touch America as she is; dare to touch her! And this is the heroic way. And this, this sensitive touch upon the unseen America, is to be the really great adventure in the New World.

This notion of Boone as the embodiment of American possibility remains his most powerful cultural legacy. "Did you know that Daniel Boone was eighty-four years old when he crossed the Rockies?" Cathy O'Donnell asks Jimmy Stewart in the Western movie classic *The Man From Laramie*. "Oh yes, everyone knows that," Stewart replies. The breadth of Boone's explorations, his wanderlust, strikes a vein running deep in the American character. Flint called Boone the Achilles of the West, but he was more like the frontier Odysseus, the man who "always finds a way." The western American poet William Stafford conjures up an image of Boone the searcher.

> He traced ahead a deepening home,
> and better, with goldenrod:
> Leaving the snakeskin of place after place
> going on—after the trees
> the grass, a bird flying after a song.

For Americans, the loss of community is far less worrisome than the confinement of possibilities.

> Children, we live in a barbwire time
> but like to follow the old hands back—
> the ring in the light, the knuckle, the palm,
> all the way to Daniel Boone,
> hunting our own kind of deepening home.

Another recent poet, Susan Mitchell, confronts this vision of Boone while camping on the midwestern prairie.

> I felt the grass growing westward
> starting to pick up speed
> like an animal running for the sheer
> joy of running,
> and I thought of Boone following his traps,
> each trap biting deeper
> into the green absence of prairie.
> I understood
> his wanting to keep it for himself,
> the space that lay down with him each night,
> breathing into his face.

Folklore and fabrication thus contributed more to the popular image of Boone than did historical research. Rebecca Boone Lamond complained that she had taken the trouble to "read Imlay's and Bryant's, McClung and Flint" in the 1850s and found that "they have none of them taken much pains to obtain particulars, and find in them all inaccuracies." The many "discrepancies and conflictions" among these versions also troubled young Lyman Copeland Draper when he was a student at Granville Literary and Theological Institution in Ohio during the 1830s. Draper devoured American history and by 1838, when only twenty-three years old, he had decided to devote his life to researching and writing the history of the American frontier. "I am a small bit of a fellow but five feet one," he wrote, "yet small as I am, and as 'good for nothing' as I often think myself, I yet feel that I have something to do." He might not be able to live a life of daring like the men he so admired, but he would be able to tell their tales. "Very much precious historical incident must still be treasured up in the memory of aged Western Pioneers, which would perish with them if not quickly rescued." He sketched out plans for a series of volumes on "The Lives of the Pioneers" and decided to begin with a biography of Boone, who, he wrote to a friend, "is generally acknowledged the pioneer of the West."

Supported by a wealthy relative until the early 1850s, and serving thereafter as secretary of the State Historical Society of Wisconsin, in his day Draper was foremost among collectors of frontier historiana. Though his archival standards—liberally editing and expurgating the testimony he recorded, clipping and selling autographs from original manuscripts, annotating them with red ink and even correcting their spelling—would drive today's librarians to distraction, such practices were not unusual then. "The above is written in a poor hand and Verry disconnected," Edward Boone Scholl concluded an account of Boone written for Draper in 1854. "You will put the incidents together, and correct my bad Spelling, and Do the best you can with the Same."

Draper's collection constitutes the most important archive for the history of the Mississippi Valley frontier. Over more than fifty years Draper traveled at least fifty thousand miles on research trips through the American backcountry, usually alone and on horseback, collecting materials and interviewing hundreds of people. He sought out old documents and correspondence and copied or purchased historical records. Although he became infamous among archivists in Kentucky and Tennessee as "the man who stole all our documents and carried them off to Wisconsin," Draper's efforts probably preserved those materials from almost certain destruction during the Civil War, and no one has ever proved that he kept anything without permission. His papers, which he bound into nearly 500 volumes and now run to more than 120 reels of microfilm, form the heart of the manuscript collection at Wisconsin, the granddaddy of state historical libraries.

During several long research trips in the 1840s Draper familiarized himself with Boone sites, took notes, and made sketches. In 1843 he made his first important contact with the Boone family when he began to correspond with Daniel Boone Bryan of Lexington. Bryan, desperate to set his uncle's record straight before he died, sat down for a long conversation with Draper in 1844. Soon afterward Draper acquired important additional material in interviews with the three surviving sons of Squire Boone, Jr. These men introduced him into the considerable family network in Kentucky and Missouri.

Of the four Boone children who survived their father, three were dead by the time Draper began his research. Jesse Bryan Boone died just a few weeks after his father at the age of forty-seven while serving a term in the Missouri legislature. In 1824

Jemima's husband, Flanders Callaway, died, leaving her an estate of several hundred acres and a dozen slaves, and she lived for five years more on the Missouri bottom near Charette. During her last years she would sit on her front step and talk about old times while she smoked her old stone pipe and, growing melancholy, would cry for her son James Callaway, killed by Indians in 1815, and "grieve about always being on the frontier." Daniel Morgan Boone, who looked the most like his father, in 1825 became the first American to settle near the mouth of the Kansas River on the Missouri, the future site of Kansas City. He died of cholera in 1839 at the age of seventy.

In 1842 Draper established a correspondence with Nathan, Boone's last surviving child. He and his wife, Olive Vanbibber Boone, had continued to live in the large stone house in the Femme Osage Valley with their many children during the 1820s, one of the wealthiest families in the county. The family had memories of high times in that house, dancing on the waxed hardwood floors in white kid slippers. "They were affectionate kind hearted, gay people," one great-granddaughter remembered, "great fiddlers and dancers." In the 1830s, however, at about the age of fifty, Nathan began a long period of wanderlust, working first as a federal surveyor in Iowa, then in 1832 joining the regular army. He served as captain of mounted rangers during the Black Hawk War, then received an appointment as captain in the United States Dragoons, the first organized cavalry regiment in American military history. During twenty years of service in the West, he patrolled and protected the route of the Santa Fe Trail, led exploring expeditions through the western plains, laid out several important military roads, negotiated treaties with Indian tribes, and fought in the Mexican War, eventually rising to the rank of lieutenant colonel. One of his contemporaries remembered him as "a remarkable woodsman who could climb like a bear and swim like a duck." In the early 1850s, nearing seventy, Nathan finally retired from active duty.

The family had fallen on hard times during the depression of the late 1830s. Nathan sold the house in Saint Charles County in 1837 to pay off a large debt, according to some accounts, but he also wanted to move his family nearer his postings on the frontier. He and his sons built a dog-trot cabin in the Ozark foothills of southwest Missouri. It was a far cry from the fine stone house—as daughter Delinda Boone Craig told her grandchildren, "she knew what it was to be rich and what it was to be poor"—but during his days as a trapper Nathan had fallen in love with this isolated country on the headwaters of the Osage River, and there he retired. Draper now had the opportunity for an interview, and he spent three weeks with Nathan and Olive at their home in October and November of 1851.

Nathan had a good memory, and with Olive supplying details of her own, Draper accumulated more than three hundred pages of interview notes, the most important source for reconstructing the personal side of Daniel Boone's life. As Draper prepared to depart at the conclusion of this very successful visit, Nathan handed him a small bundle containing the few surviving papers of his father, "carefully rolled up in the pieces of deer skin in which he left them," including account books, survey and land records, and letters from friends and family. Draper placed his notes along with these papers in a small trunk and boarded a stage for home. Somewhere along the way the trunk fell off and it took Draper three agonizing days of backtracking before he finally relocated it, unopened, in the possession of "an honest Negro man."

This was Draper's only opportunity to talk with Nathan and Olive, for Boone's son died in 1856 and his wife followed him two years later, but the couple had helped Draper piece together a Boone genealogy, and this guided him to other descendants. Most of the several dozen surviving Boone grandchildren still lived in Missouri, although some of the family had moved farther west. Jesse's daughter Panthea Boone Boggs and his son Alphonso Boone emigrated overland in 1846, her family taking the southern fork to California, his the northern route to Oregon. Their brother Albert Gallatin Boone was a pioneer in Colorado, an associate of Kit Carson, who was himself related to the Boones by marriage. Over the next forty years Draper interviewed scores of direct descendants and solicited testimonials from nearly four dozen Boone kin, who in effect appointed him to write the authorized biography.

But Draper never published his projected life of Boone. "Why don't you publish," a friend once wrote him, "tell me when (Oh When!) will it appear?" "You have already dispatched the laborious part and have got nothing but pleasure before you," Francis Parkman wrote, "while I, for my part, have the greater part of delving and rummaging still to look forward to." Draper didn't say that he loved the "delving and rummaging," but writing petrified him. During his long career Draper succeeded in producing only one substantial work, a credible account of the battle of King's Mountain, fought by backcountry militiamen during the Revolution. He labored for years on his biography of Boone but never completed it, leaving at his death a hand-written manuscript of several hundred pages that took the story through the siege of Boonesborough. "I have wasted my life in puttering," he wrote in despair toward the end. "I can write nothing so long as I fear there is a fact, no matter how small, as yet ungarnered." It is tempting to see Draper as making his own contribution to the Boone legacy of failure.

Draper's frustration with his inability to publish is understandable, but his life's work was far from a waste, for his research was considerably more powerful than his writing and provided the abundant evidence that made it possible to disentangle the real Boone from the legend. "When you are gone the Historical Society of Wisconsin will be your monument," a friend wrote to him, "more enduring than brass or marble."

Draper at first allowed other scholars and writers liberal access to his collection. For his Boone biography of 1847 John Mason Peck used the firsthand information he had gathered in his interview with Boone in 1818, but he had to admit that he had been so overcome with "veneration" for the old pioneer that he came away with "no more than a few brief notes." For most of Peck's evidence he relied on the collection assembled by Draper, "to whose kindness the author acknowledges his indebtedness." Critics praised the biography for its detail and apparent reliability, characteristics that reflected Draper's scholarship. Facing increasing difficulties completing his own manuscript, Draper grew concerned about the use of his material by others for whom writing came more easily. He toyed with the idea of collaborating with professional writers, but these projects fell through because of the jealous guard he threw up around his papers. Eventually he closed his collection to all but his closest colleagues.

One of those few, Reuben Gold Thwaites, inaugurated the modern era of Boone biography. Thwaites was a former journalist whom

Draper trained to be his successor at the State Historical Society of Wisconsin, and following his mentor's death in 1891, he added the Draper manuscripts to the library's public archive. Thwaites was one of the founding generation of modern history. He transformed the society into a research center that complemented one of the nation's most distinguished history programs at the University of Wisconsin, and he supervised the publication of collections of historical documents, which set the scholarly standard for modern historical editing. Among several original works of history, Thwaites's biography of Boone, published in 1902, employed a similarly modern sensibility.

But his approach created problems that Thwaites found himself unable to resolve. He began the book with a series of disclaimers. "Poets, historians, and orators have for a hundred years sung the praises of Daniel Boone," he wrote, but "despite popular belief, he was not really the founder of Kentucky." Others had preceded him in exploration and bested him at Indian fighting. He possessed but "small capacity for the economic and political sides of commonwealth-building." Although previous writers had made these points before, Thwaites was the first to suggest that placing Boone in realistic perspective required abandoning romantic interpretations. But if Boone was not the man he had been made out to be, why the need for a new biography? Once the real man standing behind the fog of myth had been exposed as a character of relatively minor stature, where was the sustaining interest in his story? "Boone's picturesque career," he suggested, "possesses a romantic and even pathetic interest that can never fail to charm the student of history." If this were true, however, it was because of Boone's role as a heroic symbol of the American imagination, a subject that Thwaites, for the most part, ignored.

The perils of realism are best illustrated in the career of Boone scholar Archibald Henderson. Although Henderson was a professor of mathematics at the University of North Carolina, he became fascinated with western history at a young age and early in the twentieth century sketched out plans for a Boone biography "of the most elaborate sort." He authored an influential series of articles on Boone, and within the historical profession there would have been widespread agreement with the comment of a mistress of ceremonies introducing him at a public lecture in 1914: "Since the death of Dr. Reuben Gold Thwaites, Dr. Henderson enjoys the distinction of being the greatest living authority on Daniel Boone." His was the contribution of the debunker.

Henderson stated his basic argument most clearly in the title of a piece published in 1910, "Daniel Boone Only the Agent." For all their outfitting of Boone with "countless disguises," he argued, historians had missed the essential truth about him. "Boone may have been the instrument of Providence, as he so piously imagined, but it is indubitable that he was the agent of commercial enterprise and colonial promotion." Here was an argument refreshingly modern, one in bold contrast with the hero worship of the romantic school. Although Boone had been a remarkable scout and a great hunter, he lacked what Henderson called, using the language of Main Street, "executive ability" and "civic talent." He argued that Boone had been merely the employee of Richard Henderson, the North Carolina real estate magnate. His evidence was entirely circumstantial, actually rather flimsy. In the words of a local historian who knew the record as well as anyone living, "Aside from Dr. Henderson's unsupported statements, there is no satisfactory evidence that Boone owed Richard Henderson one cent [or] that he was employed by Henderson to go to Kentucky in 1769." Not incidentally, Archibald Henderson the historian was a lineal descendant of Richard Henderson the land speculator, and while he found it easy to be iconoclastic about Boone, he tended toward grandiloquence when it came to his ancestor, who, he wrote, "rolled back the tide of aboriginal predatory conquest and first established in the heart of the West a solid and enduring bulwark." It was not so much Henderson's evidence that made his case but his logic, which fit so beautifully with the cynical mood of the day.

Far more popular than Henderson's work was an irreverent Boone essay written by Clarence Alvord, professor of history at the University of Illinois, that appeared in H. L. Mencken's *American Mercury* in 1926. "Legend affirms that Boone was the agent who called the people across the mountains," said Alvord, but in fact, "Boone was among the conjured, not the conjuror." Truth be told, all he was really after was a fast buck, and not the four-footed variety. "A fortune in realty has been the magnet which has drawn the millions across the continent," he declared, "even as their descendants are doing today in Florida." That his conclusions would be rejected by many, Alvord was sure. "Without doubt the unlearned will continue to exalt the name of the simple soul whose fictitious career exemplifies so fully their idea of historical causation and typifies so fittingly their conception of the common man in history." The honest historian must "extract what pleasure he can from the contemplation of truth. A lonely occupation indeed!" His reward must lie in the certainty "that he has freed himself from the hallowed tradition of the multitude, and that he belongs to the small group of the elect who understand."

Archibald Henderson must have sought similar solace more than once, for over the years he became involved in a number of confrontations with Alvord's "unlearned multitude." Although his research on the Boone biography continued, he had trouble making progress on the manuscript. After making the case that Boone was of little importance, he had little of interest to say about either the man's life or his legend. Henderson's passion for the truth about Boone was devoted entirely to debunking. It was one thing, however, to condemn American myths in the pages of the *American Mercury*, its readers eager for evidence of American Babbittry, but quite a different matter to raise these points at Henderson's favorite venues—Fourth of July picnics or chapter meetings of the Daughters of the American Revolution. To a public conditioned to thinking of Boone as forest philosopher, Indian fighter, and pathfinder, Henderson came across as a cranky intellectual.

The most notable incident on record occurred when he delivered his set speech at the dedication ceremonies for a new monument at Boonesborough in 1936. He asserted that "in the antiquated and out-of-date histories of this region are embalmed innumerable errors of fact," referred to Boone's "delusions of grandeur," and put forward once again his claim that Richard Henderson was the "real empire builder." As he finished, angry murmurings arose from the crowd and one of the numerous Boone descendants invited to attend the ceremony, a woman who had come all the way from Oregon, fled the platform in tears. Tom Wallace, editor of the *Louisville Times*, strode to the podium, tossed aside his prepared remarks, and proceeded to denounce what he said was Henderson's attempt to build up his own ancestor at Boone's expense. The best that might be said of Boone's employer, Wallace declared to the growing delight of the crowd, was that "when capitalists hire brains they ought to be congratulated." Henderson's desire "to take the shirt from Daniel Boone would only leave him hanging on the coattails of the great pathfinder who always will be the romantic figure in the pioneer history of Kentucky."

This confrontation between debunkers and true believers has been replayed many times in the years since. In a public talk at Old Fort Harrodsburg in 1962 the Louisville writer Robert McDowell declared that Boone was an "irresponsible hunter, who through a freak of fate was elevated to the role of folk hero in his own lifetime." The real Boone, said McDowell, wasn't much of an Indian fighter, he was always straying off and getting himself captured, and his legal difficulties were his own fault. He joked that his comments might get him lynched by Boone's numerous descendants and admirers, but no one could have anticipated the reaction of outrage that extended from the man in the street to the governor of the state. "It took a lot of courage for Boone to do all the things he did," said one Kentuckian who thought McDowell had slurred Boone's good name. "We forget we have police protection and Daniel Boone didn't." This was a controversy that produced much heat but little light. "I'm neither a defender nor a detractor of Boone," the distinguished Kentucky historian Thomas D. Clark replied to an inquiring reporter. "I don't know why we get into these things."

The Boone debunkers reared up once again in 1982 when the National Park Service rejected plans to mark the Daniel Boone Trail, a series of roadways that led across the Cumberland Gap. In the 1910s the Daughters of the American Revolution had marked the route all the way to Missouri with a series of picturesque inscribed tablets manufactured of metal salvaged from the wreck of the battleship *Maine*, but after seventy-five years of road improvement only a few of them remained. The proposal for federal designation was actually rejected as a way of trimming several million dollars from the budget, but the park service constructed its intellectual case with the arguments of the Boone debunkers. Boone had not been first to explore Kentucky; the settlement of Boonesborough had come after the founding of Harrodsburg; a majority of Kentucky settlers came down the Ohio rather than following Boone's route over the mountains—for such reasons the Daniel Boone Trail was not of "sufficient historical importance" to warrant federal designation. It was a pedantic reading of the facts, and the park service found itself under heavy attack by Boone partisans. Were the bureaucrats arguing that Boone's reputation was all a great mistake? Actually, before the end of the eighteenth century more than two hundred thousand people, most of them poor and many of them slaves, had come to Kentucky over the Wilderness Road, the route first explored, marked, and laid out by Boone. On the floor of the U.S. Senate the Honorable Wendell H. Ford rose to declare sensibly that "there are those of us in Kentucky who feel that Daniel Boone had a pretty large impact on our heritage."

Senator Ford was closer to the historical truth than the park service. As Kentucky state historian Hambelton Tapp suggested, the debunkers consistently failed to ask the right questions. "Boone was as much a figurehead, as much a personification of the westward movement as he was an actual man on the ground," said Tapp. What makes Boone significant and worthy of historical attention, even commemoration, is that he stands for some of the things that Americans feel are most important about themselves—the central significance of the frontier in their history, a fantasy of wanderlust yet a commitment to family, a love and admiration of nature coupled with an almost desperate desire for development and material advancement. Beginning with sensible corrections about Boone's accomplishments, the debunkers ultimately fail to connect with the central importance of Boone's story. By considering Daniel Boone's life and legend, Americans have always sought to learn something of themselves.

The monuments and the reconstructions at Boonesborough and Harrodsburg, the picturesque DAR markers along the Daniel Boone Trail—all testified to the continuing importance of the Boone legend so despised by the debunkers. Tall tales are easy to expose, but the wellsprings of myth are more difficult to plumb. The essence of the Boone mystique has proven resilient, for it thrives on the qualities of its hero as Everyman. The plainer and more ordinary Boone is made out to seem, the more compelling is the fame attached to "but a common man." The nineteenth-century fascination with Boone was one of the first signals of the emergence of a new kind of democratic history, a vernacular past contrasting with the formal commemoration of grand statues and monuments. To fill the demand for everyday objects, enterprising farmers throughout the upper South cut down scores of beech trees decorated with appropriate initials and dates, and many of them ended up in glass display cases. Shot pouches, powder horns, and salt kettles went on exhibit in museums scattered from Pennsylvania to Missouri. The popular "Boone Relics" display at the Kentucky Historical Society featured Boone's gun, powder horn, hunting knife, and other memorabilia. The Filson Club, a distinguished private historical society in Louisville, Kentucky, acquired Boone's "hunting shirt," a fringed and embroidered buckskin blouse, and displayed it with his rifle, powder horn, and tomahawk.

The flimflam generated by this proliferating flood of Boone artifacts was not the responsibility of Alvord's "unlearned multitude" but of professionally trained and sophisticated collectors and curators who abandoned good sense in their eagerness for a piece of the true cross. A good example is the Boone rifle in the Kentucky Historical Society, carved on the stock with the inscription "BOoNs bESt FREN" and fifteen notches that would appear to be a tally of his human target practice. The state of Kentucky purchased this relic in 1903 from "Professor" Gilbert Walden, a notable faker who on his letterhead listed his qualifications as "Cow-boy Orator, Rough Rider, Scholar and Rifle Shot." Gradually other prominent relics were similarly exposed as fakery. Someone finally had the good sense to point out that the hunting shirt at the Filson Club was about the right size for a boy of ten, not a man of Boone's heft. In 1926 another level-headed Boone researcher cautioned an archivist preparing to mount an exhibit at the Missouri Historical Society that "if all the so called relicts of Boone were collected together it would take several rooms to hold them. Whereas, bear in mind, that Boone lived in a one room cabin."

There was equal public interest in his one-room cabins and home sites. A log house at the junction of the Dix and Kentucky rivers advertised as "built by Boone with his own hands" was a favorite subject of tinted picture postcards, but the claim lacked any supporting evidence. Most of the actual Boone log homes had crumbled long before, although at some locations old foundation stones and cellar holes remained visible in the early twentieth century. Salvagers discovered Boone's last Kentucky residence, the log cabin on Brushy Creek, when they removed the clapboard siding from an abandoned house in the 1930s. Workers later dismantled and reconstructed it on private land in Nicholas County, east of U.S. 68, near where a state historical marker stands today. The National Register of Historic Places certified the authenticity of the Flanders and Jemima Boone Callaway house, which Boone may have helped to construct and where he lived for most of his last years. The house suffered regular flooding from the Missouri and its residents eventually abandoned it. Dismantled and later reconstructed without the original clapboard siding or the beautiful interior woodwork, it must now resemble its original condition when built as a blockhouse during the War of 1812.

The stone house on Femme Osage Creek, where Boone died, survived in excellent condition. The house had a long string of owners before the first attempts to preserve it as a historic site in 1925, when the Boone Home Memorial Association drew up plans to convert the property into a hunting and fishing preserve, what the group called "a huntsman's paradise such as would have been approved by Boone himself." This group proved unable to raise sufficient funds, however, and a wealthy Saint Louis attorney purchased the house and had it extensively redecorated and modernized. After the house served for thirty years as a private residence, in 1956 the owner allowed another civic group, the Daniel Boone Shrine Association, to open the site to the public while attempting to raise the funds necessary to buy it. The group planned to develop the surrounding property into a historic museum on the model of Old Sturbridge Village in Massachusetts. They solicited the state for support, but, pleading poverty, Missouri refused assistance, and after some years this effort failed as well. A local businessman who had backed the project with his own capital ended up purchasing the property to protect his investment.

Now a privately operated house museum listed on the National Register of Historic Places, the stone house draws thousands of tourists each year but has difficulty making ends meet. The state of Missouri's neglect of this historic treasure must be held responsible for a state of affairs that has resulted in a concern over finances that contributes to the exaggerated claims that the museum makes. It is billed inaccurately as the "Daniel Boone Home." There is no evidence that Boone assisted in its construction or possessed the expertise required to carve the fine walnut mantelpieces, nor can the museum offer provenance for the furniture and personal possessions in the house attributed to the Boones. William Boone Douglass, who served in the 1920s as president of the Boone Family Association, put it best when he wrote that "the old Nathan Boone house is beautiful, and well deserving of preservation. Let us be content to accept it as the house in which Daniel Boone died. I sincerely hope it will be preserved, but let us oppose the cheapening of both the house and Daniel Boone as well by persons making for it unwarranted claims." The house is a remarkably interesting building, evoking the stone dwellings of Boone's Pennsylvania birthplace while possessing the powerful emotional resonance as the place where Boone died.

The "Daniel Boone Homestead," the farm on Owatin Run, near Reading, where Boone was born, offers a model of what can be accomplished on a similar historic site. The Pennsylvania Historical and Museum Commission acquired the farm in 1937 and dedicated it to "the American boy." The state convinced the federal government to support the project by setting unemployed young people to work clearing the property and erecting a "wayside shelter" to be used as a youth hostel, and the commission drafted a long-range program for the site's development as a historical museum interpreting the life and times of the Boones. Rather than attempt to freeze the site as a disjointed piece of the past, the museum interprets it as a genuine historical remnant, preserving the many historical strands that come together on the property. After the Boones moved to North Carolina in 1750, the new owners tore down the old log structure and replaced it with a handsome stone dwelling. The historical commission moved other contemporary structures to various parts of the farm, allowing a visitor's interest in Daniel Boone to move easily from mere relic gawking to a thoughtful consideration of the ways in which "Daniel's boyhood home changed to reflect the growth, prosperity and cultural diversity" of America. The basement springhouse of the Boone family remains, and a visitor may still sip the indoor supply of drinking water that supplied the household from the cool cellar, where Daniel's mother, Sarah Morgan, once stored her milk and butter.

The greatest relic of them all was Boone's remains, and the controversy over them has been ongoing since the 1840s. By that time, according to one observer, the Bryan graveyard on Tuque Creek was "grown over with a thicket of briars several feet high and almost impenetrable. The traveller passes by the spot, and never knows that there lies buried one of the most wonderful men that has existed in our country." It was a typical early American burying ground, a small, unkempt, and unfrequented space into which the deceased members of the Boone settlement were crowded. Most graves went unmarked. "In those days," said descendant Elijah Bryan, who lived nearby, "there was no such thing as regular grave stones." There were no markers on the Boone graves until the mid-1830s, when several Bryans arranged to set in place two small stones, inscribed with the names of Daniel and Rebecca in the rough hand of the local blacksmith. Meanwhile, other members of the Boone and Bryan families, including Flanders and Jemima Callaway, as well as numerous family slaves, found their places in the small yard.

But it was an age of commemoration. Private citizens established the Washington National Monument Society, and Congress voted to construct a crypt for President Washington's bones under the Capitol rotunda, although his heirs eventually refused to grant consent for the removal of the remains from Mount Vernon. Throughout the country local movements sprang up to dedicate monuments to the memory of Revolutionary War heroes. At a celebration at Boonesborough in 1840 the governor of Kentucky delivered an oration on Boone and his legacy, and some prominent Kentuckians proposed raising a statue to Boone and the pioneers there. Saint Louis newspapers discussed the possibility of a monument at the site of Boone's grave in Charette. Before the Missourians could act, however, in April 1845 the Kentucky legislature passed a resolution authorizing the reinterment of Boone's remains at the state capital in Frankfort. This plan originated with the proprietors of the new capital cemetery company, who were improving a site high on a hill overlooking the city. Cemeteries were different from graveyards, painstakingly landscaped to be comfortable places for the living to visit and contemplate the departed. They were also business enterprises; Boone's grave, the proprietors reasoned, would provide them with a central attraction and offer a wonderful opportunity to promote the venture. Their reverence came mixed with a liberal dash of boosterism.

Soliciting the assistance of a number of Kentucky luminaries, the proprietors appealed to Nathan Boone for permission to remove his father's remains. "It is understood," wrote the state treasurer, "that his remains were deposited in a remote village in Missouri. This should not be." "Kentucky (and none other) is the place to contain the remains," declared a former governor of the state, adding that he was certain that if "from the other world" the Boones could speak, "they would prefer being buried in Kentucky to any part of the globe." Boone, of course, had left explicit instructions regarding his burial, and they did not include Kentucky, in which he had disdained to set foot after 1799. In Missouri, officials attempted to fend off the Kentuckians by appropriating five hundred dollars to erect a monument over Boone's grave. Suddenly fearing they might be outmaneuvered, the Frankfort cemetery proprietors responded by rushing off a second set of appeals to Boone's surviving son. "$10,000 will be expended on the grounds and improvements," they promised, "and it will be the most beautiful cemetery in the West." They retained Boone's elderly nephew, William Linville Boone of Kentucky, and sent him to Missouri to handle the delicate negotiations with Boone descendants.

Unable to reach Major Nathan Boone, who was campaigning with his dragoons, William Boone conferred with the descendants whom he reasoned would carry the most influence, among them Harriet Boone Baber and Panthea Boone Boggs, both daughters of Boone's son Jesse, the first married to a Missouri state legislator, the other to Lilburn W. Boggs, the former governor. Apparently obtaining their consent, on the morning of July 17, 1845, Boone and fellow Kentuckians Thomas L. Crittenden and Jacob Swigert called at the house of Harvey Griswold, who several years before had purchased the Bryan farm on Tuque Creek, and announced their intentions. Griswold, Crittenden wrote in his legalistic report of the episode, told them he was "opposed to a removal of said remains from the place selected by said Boone in his life time, and to any act which may deprive Missouri of the credit of doing appropriate honours." Crittenden claimed that in response to Griswold's concerns, William Boone produced "satisfactory evidence that the immediate relations of Col. Boone had been consulted and had given their written consent." After being assured on this point, Griswold turned to other concerns. He "had paid an extravagant price for the farm on which said remains were interred, mainly because those relicts were deposited on it, and because the removal of them would greatly lessen the value of the property." The Kentuckians assured him that the Frankfort cemetery would gladly compensate for any loss of value. Griswold's son later claimed that they led his father to believe that the cemetery company would pay to "erect a monument to Boone" at the Bryan farm graveyard, but nothing was heard afterward from the cemetery company and the Griswolds nursed their bitterness for years.

The Kentuckians had hired three local black men to excavate the graves for them, and through them, word of what was about to happen spread through the neighborhood. By the time the Kentuckians concluded their negotiations with Griswold, a crowd of Boones, Bryans, and other curious onlookers had gathered at the graveyard. There were "still numerous descendants of Col. Boone in the neighborhood of his grave who had not been consulted," Griswold told the Kentuckians, and their "consent must be obtained before the disinterment could be permitted." That afternoon, before a "large concourse of ladies and gentlemen consisting of family relations and neighbors," Crittenden laid out the case for Boone's final remove. There were certainly many who were against it. "If Col. Boone's bones could but speak the real feelings the old man cherished in his life-time," a family friend declared just three years later, "they would have protested indignantly against their removal to Kentucky." But this does not seem to have been the attitude of the family members present at the graveyard. According to a news report printed in a Saint Louis paper only a few days after the event, the assembled members of the Boone family declared to the Kentuckians that the bones "were freely given up" with the expectation that Kentucky would "faithfully carry out their object of doing suitable honors to the remains of their illustrious ancestor."

"There were 30 or 40 persons standing around," said Swigert, "who identified the grave of Boone." The plots in the burying ground were placed hither and yon, but guided by the stones of Boone and Rebecca, the diggers were soon turning up pieces of bone, shroud, and coffin. "The coffins were entirely rotten and gone," the newspaper reported, "except the bottom plank, which remained in a very imperfect state." Many of the bones crumbled in the attempt to lift them, but the men transferred what they could to pine boxes. A number of local people picked up teeth and bits of bone scattered about the site and kept them as relics. No one bothered to backfill the graves and the stones eventually fell over and cracked. Many years later one of Boone's grandchildren retrieved these markers and gave them to a little museum at Central Methodist College in Fayette, Missouri, where they are on display today.

Meanwhile, the Frankfort cemetery proprietors made plans for a grand ceremony of reburial "under as imposing auspices as the occasion should demand." The night before the great day a number of prominent Kentuckians gathered at the capitol to witness the transfer of the remains into new coffins. "The skull of Boone was handled by the persons present and its peculiarities commented upon," remembered John Mason Brown, who, although only a boy of eight, was there with his father. "My father placed it in my hands that I might say that I had lifted it." One of the men made a plaster cast of Boone's skull so that a phrenologist might make the measurements necessary to analyze his character. Performed with the knowledge that this was a model of Boone's skull, his reading provided a convenient summary of contemporary views of Boone. This was the head of a man with great physical powers, who "could jump farther and higher and run faster than almost anyone else." He was a man of "unconquerable perserverence," always on the alert and never taken by surprise, and with commanding patience under trying circumstances. He was passionately fond of traveling and "could not be lost in the woods." The measurements for all of these traits were exaggerated, the phrenologist reported, while those for "social sentiments" were undersize, indicating that Boone was a man of "no local and but few personal attachments" with "no affinity for society—he fled from it."

On Saturday, September 13, 1845, several thousand people assembled in the streets of Frankfort to witness marching bands, state dignitaries, military companies, and fraternal organizations that proceeded from the capitol building, across the river, and up the hill to the cemetery, led by four white horses drawing the hearse carrying the Boone coffins. At the gravesite, high on the bluffs overlooking the Kentucky River valley, John J. Crittenden offered a florid tribute to Boone. Less than a month later the Frankfort cemetery announced the first public sale of lots and did a brisk business. But the proprietors failed to erect the promised monument, just as they failed to keep the promise made to Harvey Griswold in Missouri. A few years later a group of prominent Kentuckians tried to get up a private fund to pay for one, but soon after they were forced to admit that there "has not been a single response." Not until 1860, when the state legislature appropriated two thousand dollars for the purpose, did the state finally erect a Boone monument.

The completed fifteen-foot monolith included panels with scenes of Boone's life: Filson's philosopher reclining in the forest; Flint's pathfinder struggling with savage Indians; Peck's civilizer instructing his slave; a fourth showed Rebecca milking the family cow. During the monument's construction, workers again opened the graves, and one observer watched as they shoveled up remains "as carelessly as if they had belonged to any ordinary mortal." Anxious for a relic, he fled with a fragment in his pocket of what he believed was Boone's vertebrae. Over the next fifty years other souvenir seekers picked and chipped away at the monument until it was practically mutilated. The neglect disgusted many of the people who came to pay homage. "It is simply scandalous," complained a visiting Missouri state official. "Why the names of Boone and wife are scarcely discernible from the ruthless manner in which the raised letters have been chipped off by relic hunters." "If you Kentuckians don't protect this monument better," he remarked to his companion, a descendant of the Crittendens, "you may expect to hear a demand that the ashes of Daniel Boone and wife be returned to Missouri soil." Pressured by the Rebecca Bryan Boone chapter of the Daughters of the American Revolution in Frankfort, the Kentucky legislature finally appropriated restoration funds in 1910, and cemetery officials surrounded the monument with a substantial fence to protect it from Boone's adoring public.

Unfulfilled promises and neglect fueled resentment. Boone's grave had been "desecrated to gratify a spasm of Kentucky pride," declared the Saint Louis *Globe Democrat* in 1888 and concluded that the removal of the remains was something "for which Missouri should never forgive." Among some of the residents near the Bryan farm graveyard, memories of the disinterment grew bitter. The Griswolds told the tale that the Kentucky delegation "came quietly and went to digging" without asking permission, and would not stop until threatened by a large crowd of neighbors. By promising to erect a monument to Boone's memory at the graveyard, the smooth-talking Kentuckians persuaded the Boone descendants to allow the removal to continue. There were even descendants who began to whisper rumors that the Kentuckians "didn't get Boone." According to this tale, when Boone had been buried in 1820, the grave diggers discover that another coffin already occupies his chosen spot by Rebecca's side, so they lay him instead at her feet. When the Bryans later set the stones in place, however, they mistakenly place them side by side, but with the lackadaisical attitudes about graveyards, the mistake is never corrected. At the disinterment the Boone descendants, angry with the arrogant Kentuckians, allow them to uncover the wrong grave. Despite the fact that the two coffins were identical, and Rebecca's moldering longer, hers is found intact while "Boone's" is entirely rotted away. The family, the tale ends, "considered it a smart deception and justifiable."

This notion that the Kentuckians "didn't get Boone" has long created mischief and it is time to lay it to rest. While the smooth-talking Kentuckians surely made false promises and used guile to get their way, the contemporary accounts all indicate that the family's consent was "freely given." Obviously there could have been a mistake in the crowded graveyard; for a quarter century and more after the original burials, the bones of the Boones were intermingled with those of the community. But the record clearly indicates that the Boone family actively participated in pointing out the graves. A conspiracy among those present to violate the grave of another member of the community out of spite is scarcely credible. The surviving "bottom plank" in one of the graves was transformed by years of rumor into Rebecca's intact coffin, ignoring the contemporary report that the contents of both graves "were entirely rotten and gone."

Some members of the Boone family objected to these rumors when they first circulated. In October of 1915, at dedication ceremonies for a DAR monument to Boone at the Tuque Creek graveyard before an assembled crowd of two thousand, including nearly everyone from the neighborhood, one Boone kinsman publicly denounced the tale. "For shame!" George Chester Bryan cried at the very thought that the family might participate in such a deception. "There was not a single body buried here," he said, pointing to the graves about him, "that was not [connected to] some one living near to whom the memory was dear." The community "would have prohibited the desecration of the graves for such a purpose as deception." Perhaps the rumors, he suggested, had been spread by those "who in the last few years have started two fake movements to raise funds from the Boone and Bryan relatives," one of which, he had been told, "raised a little over $500 and never gave any accounting of it."

There is no way to know if Bryan's conjecture was correct, but it is obvious that the continuing controversy over Boone's remains in the years since has had everything to do with filthy lucre. With tongue in cheek, officials in Missouri several times have requested the return of *Rebecca's* remains from Kentucky, in order that they be reinterred in their rightful place by her husband's side. In 1987 the government of Warren County, where the Bryan farm graveyard is located, requested that the governor of Missouri issue a proclamation declaring that Boone's bones had never left the state. This was not simply an issue of historical interest, according to one local official, but of tourist dollars. "It's amazing the number of people who stop in here and inquire about Daniel Boone." For the most part, Kentuckians chose to ignore these demands, although for a time they considered an idea of their own to move the Boone remains to a "location more accessible to the public," at Boonesborough State Park. "We think it would be a natural," declared a local official, and "it would definitely help our tourism," but the proposal finally was rejected by the state legislature.

Kentuckians received a shock in 1983 when Dr. David Wolf, the state's forensic anthropologist, examined the plaster cast of the Boone skull at the Kentucky Historical Society and announced that the round forehead and long, narrow head suggested to him that this was not Boone's. "Boy, this really could be the skull of a Negro," he exclaimed. It was a poor cast, he admitted, and it gave him very little to go on, but this did not prevent Wolf from broadcasting his provocative speculations, which were picked up by the wire services and reprinted in newspapers throughout the country. An examination of the rest of Boone's remains, he argued, would resolve the question of identity. But considering the conditions of the original Missouri burying ground, the evidence of disintegrated coffins and crumbling bones, and the disinterment of the graves at least once again in Kentucky during the restoration of the monument, it seems highly unlikely that the remaining mortal traces could prove anything at all.

"We say his remains are here," declares the record keeper at the cemetery, but who can say what lies beneath the Boone monument in Frankfort, or for that matter in the graves at Tuque Creek? Visits to both sites picked up dramatically following Wolf's announcement, confirming the first principle of advertising: there is no such thing as bad publicity. Boone may not be buried in Kentucky. Nor was he the first man across the mountains, nor the greatest of the Indian fighters, nor the founder of the commonwealth.

I was a woodsman, says Boone, a man who loved nature and sought a place to hunt and live at ease, but who opened the way for thousands to follow and crowd me out. I was a husband and father devoted to my family, but who craved solitude. I was a man who loved the Indians and hated violence, but who rose to fame as the leader of a war of dispossession. I was a man of contradictions. There was an inherently elusive quality about Daniel Boone that allowed him to appear in many guises. Perhaps it was fated that we may not be sure of where he is buried, but the views from both graves are worthy of consideration. The monument in Frankfort, with its commanding vista of the wooded hills, the river gorge, and the capitol dome below, brings to mind not only Boone's first sight of Kentucky but the contest over his legacy and his legend. The lonely hillside in Missouri, overlooking land farmed by his children and slaves and the little mixed community of Indians, French, and Americans under the bluffs on the river bottom, evokes thoughts of Daniel Boone's beginning and end among the common men and women of the American frontier.

Abbreviations

AHC: Daniel Boone Papers, Archibald Henderson Collection, University of North Carolina

BBF: Boone Biographical File, Kentucky Historical Society (KHS), Frankfort

DB: Daniel Boone

DBB: Daniel Boone Bryan

DBC: Lyman Copeland Draper (LCD) interview with Delinda Boone Craig, 1866

DC: Durrett Collection, University of Chicago

DHDW: *Documentary History of Dunmore's War, 1774*, ed. Reuben Gold Thwaites (RGT) and Louise Phelps Kellogg (Madison: State Historical Society of Wisconsin, 1905)

DM: Draper Manuscripts, State Historical Society of Wisconsin, Madison

DT: *Westward into Kentucky: The Narrative of Daniel Trabue*, ed. Chester Raymond Young (Lexington: University Press of Kentucky, 1981)

ELC: Elizabeth L. Cushow

FAUO: *Frontier Advance on the Upper Ohio, 1778–1779*, ed.

	Louise Phelps Kellogg (Madison: State Historical Society of Wisconsin, 1916)
FC:	Filson Club, Louisville, Ky.
FCHQ:	*Filson Club History Quarterly*
FW:	Felix Walker, "Narrative of His Trip with Boone from Long Island to Boonesborough in March, 1775" [written in 1824], in George W. Ranck, *Boonesborough* (Louisville, Ky.: Filson Club, 1901)
IB:	LCD interview with Isaiah Boone, 1846
JC:	John Dabney Shane (JDS) interview with Josiah Collins, c. 1840s
JDS:	John Dabney Shane
JG:	JDS interview with John Gass, c. 1840s
JJ:	LCD interview with Joseph Jackson, 1844
JW:	John Walton, *John Filson of Kentucke* (Lexington: University of Kentucky Press, 1956)
KHS:	Kentucky Historical Society, Frankfort
LCD:	Lyman Copeland Draper
LIFE:	LCD, "The Life of Boone," MS
MB:	LCD interview with Moses Boone, 1846
MHS:	Missouri Historical Society, St. Louis
NH:	JDS interview with Nathaniel Hart, Jr., c. 1843–44
NOB:	LCD interview with Nathan and Olive Boone, 1851
PH:	Narrative of Peter Houston, MS, c. 1830s
RBL:	Rebecca Boone Lamond
RCD:	Randolph C. Downes, *Council Fires on the Upper Ohio: A Narrative of Indian Affairs in the Upper Ohio Valley Until 1795* (Pittsburg: University of Pittsburgh Press, 1940)
RGT:	Reuben Gold Thwaites
RH:	Richard Henderson, "Journal, 1775," in Ranck, *Boonesborough*
RKHS:	*Register of the Kentucky Historical Society*
SH:	Stephen Hempstead
ST:	*Shawnese Traditions:* C. C. *Trowbridge's Account*, ed. Vernon Kinietz and Erminie W. Voegelin (Ann Arbor: University of Michigan Press, 1939)

Sources of Quoted Material

Introduction

"He acted with wisdom": LCD interview with John and Sarah Kenton McCord, 1851, DM 5S150.

Part One

"When I visited Kentucke": John Filson, *The Discovery, Settlement and Present State of Kentucke* (Wilmington, Del.: James Adams, 1784). Available in numerous modern editions; further quotations are uncited throughout the book.

"Exaggerated and sophomorical": Timothy Flint, *Indian Wars of the West* (1833), quoted in James K. Folson's intro. to Flint, *Biographical Memoir of Daniel Boone* (New Haven: College and University Press, 1967), 14–16.

"Minor value": RGT, *Daniel Boone* (New York: D. Appleton, 1902), 199.

"The silly phrases": William Carlos Williams, *In The American Grain* (Norfolk, Conn.: New Directions, 1925), 133.

"None of Boone's": NOB, DM 6S128–29.

"Adulterated and tangled": DBB to LCD, October 24, 1843, DM 22C9[6].

"The old man's face": Francis Baily, *Journal of a Tour in Unsettled Parts of North America in 1796 & 1797*, ed. Jack D. L. Holmes (Carbondale: Southern Illinois University Press, 1969), 115–17.

"All true!": John A. McClung, *Sketches of Western Adventure* (1832; Dayton, Ohio: Ellis, Claffin, 1847), 79–80.

Chapter One. Curiosity Is Natural: 1734 to 1755

"A ferocious panther": Elijah Bryan, quoted in William S. Bryan and Robert Rose, *A History of the Pioneer Families of Missouri* (St. Louis: Bryan, Brand and Company, 1876), 4.

"Joined themselves": Gwynedd minutes, DM 1C19. The best source for Boone genealogical data is Ella Hazel Atterbury Spraker, *The Boone Family* (Rutland, Vt.: Tuttle Company, 1922).

"Cleanness from Other Women": Gwynedd minutes, DM 1C19.

"Greatly pet him": NOB, DM 6S281–82.

"Belligerence": Rachel D. Griscom to LCD, December 3, 1888, DM 1C24.

"To take the smallpox": NOB, DM 6S42–43.

"Above all her children": PH, DM 20C84[3].

"They are not girls": IB, DM 2B28; NOB, DM 6S43–44; DBC, DM 30C42.

"Wishing to gain his point": N. L. Clarke to LCD, May 13, 1886, DM 19C232.

"I give up": LCD interview with Enoch Boone, 1858, DM 19C122.

"Best nag": IB, DM 19C60–61.

"Love for the wilderness": NOB, DM 6S21–23.

"Dan would learn to spell": Elijah Bryan, quoted in Bryan and Rose, *Pioneer Families of Missouri*, 4–5.

"Let the girls do the spelling": quoted in William Boone Douglass, "The Ancestry and Boyhood of Daniel Boone," *Kentucky School Journal* 13 (1934) :14.

"In Oley sind die Schulen": quoted in John Bakeless, *Daniel Boone: Master of the Wilderness* (New York: Morrow, 1939), 10.

"A common farmer's hand": NOB, DM 6S5, 6S23, 6S90, 6S281;

statement of William Sudduth, 1840, DM 12CC96; DBC, DM 30C77.

"She can not read": diary of George Soelle, Moravian missionary, September 14, 1771, trans. Adelaide Fries, AHC; for Sarah Morgan Boone, see indenture of sale of farm in Pennsylvania, 1750, DM 25C3; for Jemima Boone Callaway, see the testimony in Morgan Bryan to LCD, May 27, 1855, DM 23C93.

"The full and free privileges": quoted in Francis Jennings, *The Ambiguous Iroquois Empire: The Covenant Chain Confederation of Indian Tribes with English Colonies from its Beginnings to the Lancaster Treaty of 1744* (New York: Norton, 1984), 358.

"Pen-and-Ink work": quoted in Jennings, *Ambiguous Iroquois Empire*, 358.

"To defend our fronteers": George Boone, Sr., to Governor of Pennsylvania, March 12, 1728, in *Pennsylvania Archives*, 1st series (Philadelphia: Joseph Severns, 1852), 1:217–18.

"Even more particular": quoted in Stephen Aron, "The Hunters of Kentucky: Backcountry, Frontier, and Transition Questions" (unpublished MS, 1991) :25.

"Proud of his Indian-like dress": Joseph Doddridge, *Notes on the Settlement and Indian Wars of the Western Parts of Virginia and Pennsylvania* (1824), in Samuel Kercheval, *A History of the Valley of Virginia*, 4th ed. (Strasburg, Va: Shenandoah Publishing, 1925), 251.

"Hybrid-Caucasian culture": Alfred Kroeber, quoted in Bruce G. Trigger, ed., *Handbook of North American Indians: Northeast* (Washington, D.C.: Smithsonian Institution, 1978), 623.

"Half-Indian appearance": quoted in Terry G. Jordan and Matti Kaups, *The American Backwoods Frontier: An Ethnic and Ecological Interpretation* (Baltimore: Johns Hopkins University Press, 1989), 92.

"Generally white Savages": missionary David McClure, quoted in Richard White, *The Middleground: Indians, Empires, and Republics in the Great Lakes Region, 1650–1815* (Cambridge: Cambridge University Press, 1991), 341.

"He was no ways Countenancing" and subsequent Exeter minutes: DM 1C24, 1C55–56.

"My transgressions and sins": quoted in John James Van Noppen and Ina Woestemeyer Van Noppen, *Daniel Boone, Backwoodsman* (Boone, N.C.: Appalachian Press, 1966), 36.

"Forwardness": Gwynedd minutes, DM 1C19.

"A man of great bodily strength": Joseph Foulks to LCD, June 14, 1853, DM 1C31.

"Brought up with those Religious views": MS of Nathan Boone, September 1851, DM 6S5.

"I never knew any good": PH, DM 20C84[46–47].

"Some hay from a Swiss": Moravian diarist, quoted in Constance Lindsay Skinner, *Pioneers of the Old Southwest* (New Haven, Conn.: Yale University Press, 1919), 20.

"Went on a general jamboree": George Boone Moffitt to LCD, September 13, 1883, DM 2C11.

"Boone was very profligate": H. H. McDowell to LCD, August 10, 1887, DM 20C39.

"Upon Grants Creek": James W. Wall, Flossie Martin, and Howell Boone, eds., *The Squire, Daniel and John Boone Families in Davie County, North Carolina* (Mocksville, N.C.: Davie Printing Company, 1982); George H. Maurice, *Daniel Boone in North Carolina* (Eagle Springs, N.C.: privately printed, 1959); "The Daniel Boone Homeplace, Davidson County, NC: A Report from the Department of Archives and History to the Historic Sites Advisory Committee, April 25, 1966," in North Carolina Collection, Wilson Library, University of North Carolina.

"On the E. Side": Wall, Martin, and Boone, ed., *Boone Families in Davie County*.

"Inhabitants flock in here daily": Governor Gabriel Johnston to British Board of Trade, February 15, 1751, quoted in Archibald Henderson, "The Creative Forces in Westward Expansion: Henderson and Boone," *American Historical Review* 20 (1914) :93.

"The back of the colony": August Gottlieb Spangenburg, quoted in Adelaide L. Fries, ed., *Records of the Moravians in North Carolina* (Raleigh, N.C.: State Printers, 1922), 1:33.

"Pony-built man": LCD interview with Peter Smith, 1863, DM 18S113.

"Never took any delight": DBB to LCD, February 27, 1843, DM 22C5.

"Ever unpracticed": JDS interview with DBB, c. 1844, DM 22C14[14].

"He was so fond of gunning": NOB, DM 6S28–30.
"They couldn't shoot up to Boone": Thomas L. Bouchelle to LCD, May 12, 1885, DM 9C73.
"I'll kill first": W. P. Boone to LCD, April 27, 1846, DM 19C1; IB, DM 19C61.
"They must starve": Shawnees to the Pennsylvania Council, August 10, 1737, quoted in RCD, 34.
"You have cheated us": quoted in ST, 10.
"This very ground": quoted in Francis Jennings, *Empire of Fortune: Crowns, Colonies & Tribes in the Seven Years War in America* (New York: Norton, 1988), 279.
"Interfere much more": quoted in RCD, 14.
"Be Permitted to Live": quoted in Jennings, *Empire of Fortune*, 154–55.
"Like Leaves in Autumn": quoted in Paul E. Kopperman, *Braddock at the Monongahela* (Pittsburg: University of Pittsburg Press, 1977), 73.
"The yell of the Indians": quoted in Kopperman, *Braddock at the Monongahela*, 204.
"Until that he saw": quoted in LIFE, DM 2B48.
"He drew his knife": Ralph Clayton to the *St. Louis Christian Advocate*, May 30, 1877, DM 7C43[1–3].
"Boone had very little of the *war spirit*": John Floyd, quoted in Louise Phelps Kellogg, "The Fame of Daniel Boone," in *The Daniel Boone Bicentennial* (n.p.: n.p., n.d. [1936]), 51.

Chapter Two. My Domestic Happiness: 1755 to 1769

"Publick House": Wall, Martin, and Boone, *Boone Families in Davie County*, 4.
"One of the handsomest persons": G. Hedrick to LCD, June 26, 1866, DM 28C67.
"A buxom daughter": J. D. Imboden to LCD, May 17, 1883, DM 6C76[2–3].
"A rather over common sized woman": DBB to LCD, October 24, 1843, DM 22C9.
"One of the neatest": L. W. Boggs to LCD, January 18, 1857, DM 23C27.
"Keep their things": DBC, DM 30C75.

"My little girl": RBL to LCD, August 23, 1845, DM 22C35[1].
"Firehunt": J. D. Imboden to LCD, May 17, 1883, DM 6C76; Thomas L. Bouchelle to LCD, May 12, 1885, DM 9C74; Flint, *Biographical Memoir of Daniel Boone*, 38–40.
"Without foundation": IB, DM 19C60.
"As fabulous as it is absurd": RBL to LCD, August 23, 1845, DM 22C35.
"Shining of eyes": NOB, DM 6S40–41, 6S71.
"*To try her temper*": NOB, DM 6S40–41; R. G. Prunty to LCD, January 26, 1883, DM 16C57.
"Much of this world's goods": George Soelle, June 1772, in Fries, ed., *Records of the Moravians*, 1:790.
"Many a good washing": R. G. Prunty to LCD, January 26, 1883, DM 16C57.
"Needed kind subduing": LCD interview with Samuel Mosby Grant, 1868, DM 22S234.
"Where is Black Betty?" quoted in Doddridge, *Notes*, 262.
"Small hope of his recovery": Fries, ed., *Records of the Moravians*, 1:136–37; Wall, Martin, and Boone, *Boone Families in Davie County*, 6.
"Snuff the autumnal winds": Doddridge, *Notes*, 257.
"A woman is ill": Bishop August Gottlieb Spangenberg, November 11, 1752, in Fries, ed., *Records of the Moravians*, 1:48–49.
"A severe flogging": NOB, DM 6S84.
"Fired a gun": C. A. Coleman to LCD, January 25, 1887, DM 2C66.
"The people about here": Fries, ed., *Records of the Moravians* 1:40–41, 58, 134, 161, 243, 251–52.
"We have now the pleasure": *Colonial Records of North Carolina* (Raleigh, N.C.: Josephus Daniels, 1890), 1:827.
"A great hunter": quoted in Aron, "Hunters of Kentucky," 24.
"At once recognizing the place": W. W. Lenon to LCD, October 20, 1883, DM 9C216[2–3].
"Strait to them all": John C. Barkley to LCD, January 22, 1887, DM 9C230[2].
"Knew how to cook": PH, DM 20C84[47–48].
"Tate, you boast so much": IB, DM 19C113.
"Habit of contemplation": John Mason Peck, *Life of Daniel*

Boone, the Pioneer of Kentucky (Boston: Charles C. Little and James Brown, 1847), 18.

"His wanderings": RBL to LCD, August 23, 1845, DM 22C35[1].

"Ah! Wide mouth": LCD interview with George Smith, 1844, DM 32S481; LCD interview with Elijah Callaway, DM 2C101.

"Tawber no make so!": Wellborn Coffey to LCD, September 28, 1884, DM 19C240.

"D. Boon CillED A. BAr" and other carvings: photos in DM 17C17, 17C20; J. H. Duff, Scott County, Va., to LCD, September 15, 1883, DM 6C80; Joe Nickell and John F. Fischer, "Daniel Boone Fakelore," *FCHQ* 62 (1988) :464–65.

"The child was born": Silas W. Parris writing for Thomas Norman to LCD, October 15 and November 3, 1884, DM 2C53, 2C77.

"The race will be continued": NH, DM 17CC195.

"His wife quite lusty": SH to LCD, February 15 and March 6, 1863, DM 16C75–77.

"It may be a damned lie": *Denver Tribune*, copied in Louisville *Courier-Journal*, April 4, 1883, clipping in DM 3C75.

"The main fact is not new to me": LCD to SH, February 24, 1863, DM 16C77. For other versions not otherwise cited in the notes below, see JC, DM 12CC97; M. B. Woods to LCD, April 9 and April 23, 1883, DM 4C26–27; David Meriwether to the Louisville *Courier-Journal*, April 15, 1883, clipping at DM 3C61; David Meriwether to LCD, December 5, 1883, DM 3C78; Samuel Alley to LCD, April 28, 1884, DM 6C70–70[1]; Adam Rader to LCD, May 19, 1885, DM 6C22[2–3], 23–23[1]; J. T. Alderman, "Notes on Davie County," in AHC.

"As a ruse": NOB, DM 6S85.

"His wife into favor": "Incidents in the Life of Henry Skaggs," MS DM 5C76.

"A much younger": JDS interview with Jacob Stevens, ca. 1840s, DM 12CC136.

"Didn't live happily": JDS interview with Robert Wickliffe, Sr., 1859, DM 15CC84.

"Live with less labor": William Byrd, *History of the Dividing Line Betwixt Virginia and North Carolina*, ed. William K. Boyd (New York: Dover, 1967), 90, 92.

"Little of the work": Fries, ed., *Records of the Moravians* 1:39–40, 50, 105.

"New made Indians": Michel-Guillaume Jean de Crevecoeur, *Letters from an American Farmer*, ed. Warren Barton Blake (New York: E. P. Dutton, 1912), 47, 49.

"Boone was not unfeeling": Peck, *Life of Daniel Boone*, 22.

"Cries for shame": JC, DM 12CC97.

"Wonderfully mortified": A. L. Pridemore to LCD, April 18, 1884, DM 6C69–69[1].

"Falls upon her knees": John Rader, Sr., to LCD, April 28, 1885, DM 6C22–23.

"A whisper to the disadvantage": SH to LCD, February 15, 1863, DM 16C75.

"Put her child away": John Rader, Sr., to LCD, April 28, 1885, DM 6C22–23.

"You had better": LCD interview with Stephen Cooper, 1889, DM 11C101.

"I could not well use it": LCD to SH, February 23, 1862, DM 16C77.

"Carefully and guardedly": LCD to Sarah Hunter, May 22, 1854, DM 22C62.

"Hushed her up": JC, DM 12CC97.

"Gathered up the family": *Denver Tribune*, copied in Louisville *Courier-Journal*, April 4, 1883, clipping in DM 3C75.

"Slow pay": J. Rumple to LCD, August 30, 1883, DM 8C190[2].

"So I trust": J. M. Storah to LCD, July 30, 1884, DM 8C191.

"Squire Boone departed this life": tombstone in Joppa cemetery, Mocksville, N.C.

"Cabin in the Blue Ridge": Silas W. Parris to LCD, October 15, 1884, DM 2C77; NOB, DM 6S152.

"Old and sick": diary of George Soelle, AHC.

"One watsh plade away": DB account book, MS, c. 1765, DM 4C75[8].

"I can't say": DB quoted in Chester Harding, *My Egotistography* (Cambridge, Mass.: J. Wilson and Company, 1866), copied at DM 16C56.

"Not well satisfied with the country": NOB, DM 6S34–35.

"Very poor": diary of George Soelle, AHC.

"Boone used to say": J. W. Wiseman to LCD, May 20, 1885, DM 8C125.

"Daniel's own boast": Thomas S. Bouchelle to LCD, July 28, 1884, DM 9C68[3].
"Too thickly settled": J. Rumple to LCD, c. 1885, DM 8C182[2].
"Game began to be scarce": DBB to LCD, February 27, 1843, DM 22C5.
"Hugging the little fellow": NOB, DM 6S41–42.
"She is by nature": diary of George Soelle, AHC.

Chapter Three. In Quest of the Country of Kentucke: 1769 to 1773

"The Blue Lick Town": quoted in Charles A. Hanna, *The Wilderness Trail* (New York: G. P. Putnam's Sons, 1911), 2:255; George R. Steward, *American Place Names* (New York: Oxford, 1970).
Skipaki-thiki: William Albert Galloway, *Old Chillicothe* (Xenia, Ohio: Buckeye Press, 1934), 19; Lucien Beckner, "Eskippakithiki: The Last Indian Town in Kentucky," *FCHQ* 6 (1932): 355–82.
"People of the south": Trigger, *Handbook of North American Indians: Northeast*, 589, 634.
"The center of this Island": *ST*, 5n.
"Skipakicipi ou la Riviere bleue": Hanna, *Wilderness Trail*, 1:124, 2:94.
"No, stranger": quoted in Arthur K. Moore, *The Frontier Mind* (New York: McGraw-Hill, 1957), 24.
"What a Buzzel": Rev. John Brown to William Preston, May 5, 1775, in *Revolution on the Upper Ohio, 1775–1777*, edited by RGT and Louise Phelps Kellogg (Madison: State Historical Society of Wisconsin, 1908), 10.
"O my dear honeys": *The Christian Traveler* (1828), quoted in Moore, *The Frontier Mind*, 24.
"Charming a description": LCD interview with Edward Coles, 1848, DM 6S309.
"They are ketched": Statement of Nathan Boone, September 1851, DM 6S7.
"Work upon their feelings": MB, DM 19C2–3.
"I thought of Kentucky": William Hickman, "Account of Life and Travels": MS, c. 1800, Codex 94, DC.

"The prospect of seeing": Levi Todd to J. McColloh, February 15, 1784, reprinted in *RKHS* 76 (1978) :219–20.

"Damned lawyers": Herman Husband, quoted in James A. Henretta and Gregory H. Nobles, *Evolution and Revolution: American Society, 1600–1820* (Lexington, Mass.: D. C. Heath, 1987), 121.

"The best branch of business in America": Silas Deane, quoted in Jack M. Sosin, *The Revolutionary Frontier, 1763–1783* (New York: Holt, Rinehart and Winston, 1967), 24.

"Under the guize of hunting" and following quote: Henderson, "Creative Forces in Westward Expansion," 100, 101.

"Conditions performed": photocopies of Rowan County Court dockets, 1768–1770, and arrest warrant, September 5, 1772, in AHC.

"He wasn't just bird counting": quoted in Frankfort *State Journal*, January 11, 1976, clipping in BBF.

"Gave a description": Nathaniel Hart [Jr.] to Mann Butler, Springhill [N.C.], October 10, 1833, DM 2CC25; NH, DM 17CC204.

"Boone was the only woodsman": JDS interview with DBB, c. 1844, DM 22C14[2].

"All the confidence in him": NOB, DM 6S57–58.

"Stand at Cumberland Gap": Frederick Jackson Turner, *The Significance of the Frontier in American History* (1893; New York: Ungar, 1963), 35.

Ah-wah-nee: Robert M. Rennick, *Kentucky Place Names* (Lexington: University Press of Kentucky, 1984), 283.

"As rich as Boaz": statement of Septimus Schull, c. 1833, DM 11CC51.

"Show me your camps!": NOB, DM 6S46–52.

"In the most friendly manner": JDS interview with DBB, c. 1844, DM 22C14.

"Go home and stay there": quoted in LIFE, DM 2B188.

"Steal horse, ha?" NOB, DM 6S46–52.

"In Search of the Western world": Squire Boone, Jr., Memorial to U.S. Congress, MS, c. 1812, Squire Boone Collection, FC.

"Never went west again": JDS interview with DBB, c. 1844, DM 22C10[2]; Beckner, "John Findley," 111–12.

"As there are no plum trees": deposition of DB, September 6, 1796, DM 4C91–92.

"We had with us": deposition of DB, September 16, 1796, DM 2C80.
"Alive with maggots": Hugh H. Bell to LCD, n.d., LIFE, DM 3B65–67, 67n.
"Incommoded Squire": SH to LCD, February 15, 1862, DM 16C76; LCD interview with SH, 1868, DM 226182–83.
"Imbued more with wanderlust": Thomas D. Clark, *A History of Kentucky* (New York: Prentice-Hall, 1937), 45.
"He never enjoyed himself": quoted in *Illinois Magazine* 2 (June 1832) :401, DM 6S323.
"The pleasure of hearing": LCD interview with Lewis Bryan, 1863, DM 18S279–80.
"Flat upon his back": LCD interview with George Smith, 1844, DM 32S481, 31C1[60].
"Forced to make a leap": LCD interview with "Mr. Wolf," n.d., DM 31C1[44], 3B37; refuted by Isaiah Boone, DM 19C98.
"While I was looking": NOB, DM 6S65–66; other family versions of this tale: DBC, DM 30C44; LCD interview with Abner Boone, 1890, DM 4C45.
"All the proceeds": statement of Isaac Shelby, n.d., DM 4C73.
"You need not refuse": John B. Roark to LCD, March 30, 1885, DM 16C81.
"Finding that grants": quoted in Henderson, "Creative Forces in Westward Expansion," 89.
"Conceals himself": copy of Rowan County records in BBF; see also Julia Goode Eagan, "Daniel Boone's Father Owned Much N.C. Land," *The Uplift* 24 (November 7, 1936) :12–13, North Carolina Collection, Wilson Library, University of North Carolina.
"DB. 1773": deposition of David Hall, September 1, 1810, DM 4C126–28; Samuel Duncan to LCD, February 21, 1852, DM 4C131.
"Present opportunity": quoted in W. W. Abbot, "George Washington, the West, and the Union," *Indiana Magazine of History* 84 (1988) :6.
"As soon as a man's back": quoted in RCD, 153, 156.
"Young Indian Warriors": quoted in Archibald Henderson, *The Conquest of the Old Southwest* (New York: Century Company, 1920), 204–5.
"Captain William Russell": Arthur Campbell to Lord Dunmore,

December 14, 1773, quoted in James William Hagy, "The First Attempt to Settle Kentucky: Boone in Virginia," *FCHQ* 44 (1970) :228.

"The company going": deposition of Thomas Sharp, February 20, 1774, quoted in Hagy, "First Attempt to Settle Kentucky," 231.

"A gentleman of some distinction": Lord Dunmore to Lord Dartmouth, December 24, 1774, DM 6C16.

"Best Hands": William Russell to Col. William Preston, June 26, 1774, in *DHDW*, 50–51.

"When a halt was called": PH, DM 20C84[3].

"Baskets made of fine hickory": Thomas W. Carter, in M. B. Woods to LCD, April 9, 1883, DM 4C26.

"You may assure them": Lord Dunmore to John Stuart, December 20, 1773, DM 6C15; *South Carolina Gazette*, December 14, 1773, DM 6C5–6.

"Illiteral and obscure": Tabaitha Moore to LCD, February 7, 1842; Arthur Campbell to William Preston, June 20, 1774, in *DHDW*, 38–39.

"Easier to find 200 Men": Lord Dunmore to Lord Dartmouth, December 24, 1774, DM 6C16.

"Murder of Russel": Campbell to Preston, June 20, 1774, in DHDW, 38–39.

"My father's intention": Chloe Saunders to LCD, February 17, 1848, DM 6C20–21.

"Scarcely refrain": NOB, cited in LIFE, DM 3B110.

"Dressed in deer-skin": George Christian to LCD, August 25, 1853, LIFE, DM 3B106–7.

"The melancholy of his feelings": NOB, DM 6S82–83.

Chapter Four. On the Banks of Kentucke River: 1773 to 1776

"Deprive us of the hunting": Cornstalk to Thomas Bullitt, June 7, 1773, quoted in Henderson, *Conquest of the Old Southwest*, 204–5.

"In such haste": Daniel Smith to William Preston, March 22, 1774, DM 3B115.

"Tho' we are apprehensive": William Russell, instructions to rangers, April 15, 1774, DM 3B118–19.

"Prevailed on the foolish People": quoted in RCD, 174.
"Hopes of a pacification": quoted in Robert M. Addington, *History of Scott County, Virginia* (Kingsport, Tenn.: privately printed, 1932), 31.
"We shall begin instantly": Russell to William Preston, June 26, 1774, in *DHDW*, 50–51.
"Well, Mike": LCD interview with George W. Stoner, 1868, DM 24C55[1–2]; deposition of DB, April 22, 1794, and October 6, 1817, DM 6C103, 6C105[1–2].
"His nature was sutch": John M. Stoner to LCD, November 1, 1853, DM 24C53.
"An awkward Dutchman": NOB, DM 6S85.
"I was employed": deposition of DB, April 24, 1794, quoted in Neal O. Hammon, "John Filson's Error," *FCHQ* 59 (1985): 463.
"Schoot her, gabtain!": NOB, DM 3B127–28.
"Alarmed by finding": quoted in William Preston to Governor Dunmore, August 13, 1774, in *American Archives*, ed. Peter Force (Washington, D.C.: M. St. Clair Clarke and Peter Force, 1837–53), 4th ser., 1:707.
"An Express from Mr. Boone": William Russell to William Preston, August 28, 1774, in *DHDW*, 172.
"For which reason": John Floyd to William Preston, August 28, 1774, in *DHDW*, 168.
"A very popular Officer": Arthur Campbell to William Preston, August 28, 1774, in *DHDW*, 171.
"Great desire": William Russell to William Preston, August 28, 1774, in *DHDW*, 172; NOB, DM 3B133.
"Would all go out": JDS interview with Mrs. Samuel Scott, ca. 1840s, DM 11CC225–26.
"The plunder of the Country": William Preston, quoted in RCD, 175.
"But when you killed": quoted in Addington, *History of Scott County*, 50.
"It was a skittish time": unidentified "eyewitness," quoted in LIFE, 3B139; Samuel Alley to LCD, April 28, 1884, DM 6C70.
"Well, Kate": Catherine Porter, quoted in Addington, *History of Scott County*, 55.
"Difirent from that left at Blackmores": Arthur Campbell to William Preston, October 1, 1774, in *DHDW*, 220–21.

"Murder, murder!": quoted in Addington, *History of Scott County*, 35; Arthur Campbell to William Preston, October 12, 1774, and Daniel Smith to William Preston, October 13, 1774, in *DHDW*, 245, 248–49.

"Mr. Boone is very diligent": Arthur Campbell to William Preston, September 29, 1774, in *DHDW*, 218.

"I believe it contains": Daniel Smith to William Preston, October 13, 1774, in *DHDW*, 248–49.

"They are mowst in need of": Arthur Campbell to William Preston, October 13, 1774, in *DHDW*, 250.

"Semi-civil": Addington, *History of Scott County*, 73.

"I do hereby certify": DB, discharge of William Poage, November 27, 1774, MS, Arthur Campbell Papers, FC; DB, account book, 1774–75, MS, DM 4C75[1].

"Settling the country": Articles of the Louisa Company [Henderson and Company], August 27, 1774, DM 1CC2–9.

"Proposals for the Encouragement": advertisements of December 25, 1774, and February 22, 1775, reprinted in *Colonial Records of North Carolina*, 2:1129–31.

"Henderson talks with great freedom": William Preston to George Washington, January 31, 1775, DM 15S100.

"Contrary to Law and Justice": Proclamation of Governor Martin, February 10, 1775, in George W. Ranck, *Boonesborough* (Louisville, Ky.: Filson Club, 1901), 149–50.

"Out of his head?": Archibald Neilson to Andrew Miller, January 28, 1775, quoted in Archibald Henderson, "Richard Henderson and the Occupation of Kentucky, 1775," *Mississippi Valley Historical Review* 1 (1914) :351.

"Mikel Stoner Entered": DB, account book, 1774–75, MS, DM 4C75[3].

"Pretty good looking": LCD interview with Abner Bryan, 1890, DM 4C51.

"Trot father": JC, DM 12CC97.

"Notorious prostitute": NH, DM 17CC195.

"Indian Half-Breeds": deposition of Charles Robertson, October 3, 1777, in *Calendar of Virginia State Papers* (1874; reprint, New York: Kraus, 1968), 1:291–92.

"Cheap goods": deposition of Samuel Wilson, n.d., DM 1CC161.

"You, Carolina Dick": deposition of Samuel Wilson, n.d., DM 1CC161.

"Encroaching spirit": Dragging Canoe paraphrased in John Haywood, *The Civil and Political History of the State of Tennessee* (Knoxville: Heiskell and Brosn, 1803), 58–59.

"He did not love": deposition of Charles Robertson, October 3, 1777, *Calendar of Virginia State Papers*, 1:291–92.

"We give you from this place": deposition of Charles Robertson, October 3, 1777, *Calendar of Virginia State Papers*, 1:291–92.

"Active and enterprising": FW, 161–63.

"Buffaloes made the road": deposition of Archibald Wood, August 27, 1814, quoted in Neal O. Hammon, "The First Trip to Boonesborough," *FCHQ* 45 (1971):259.

"Pretty difficult to follow": deposition of Samuel Estill, circa 1810, quoted in Hammon, "First Trip to Boonesborough," 257.

"Crost about 50 times": "Journal of William Calk," in *The Opening of the West*, ed. Jack M. Sosin (Columbia: University of South Carolina Press, 1969), 43.

"No part of the road": Richard Henderson to Transylvania Company, June 12, 1775, DM 3B193.

"Pleasing and rapturous appearance": FW, 163–64.

"A letter from Daniel Boone": RH, 171.

"Dear Colonel": DB to Richardson Henderson, April 1, 1775, printed in Lewis Collins and Richard H. Collins, *History of Kentucky* (Covington, Ky.: Collins and Company, 1878), 2:498; see also DM 17CC166–67.

"Col. Boon, and a few others, appeared": FW, 163–67.

"Instantly caught his rifle": FW, 165.

"Such a sight": FW, 166.

"The absolute necessity" and following quotes in this paragraph: Henderson to partners, April 8, 1775, quoted in LIFE, DM 3B185–86; RH, 171.

"Depended on Boone's": Henderson to partners, June 12, 1775, quoted in LIFE, DM 3B187–88.

"I proposed": statement of William Cocke, DM 7C76; deposition of William Cocke, c. 1799, DM 2CC1.

"Welcome us in": "Journal of William Calk," 43.

"Dropped off my shoulders": Henderson to partners, June 12, 1775, quoted in LIFE, DM 3B187, 193.

"Expressing himself": deposition of William Cocke, c. 1799, DM 2CC1.

"We was at work": deposition of DB, October 6, 1817, DM 66105[1–2].

"Should any successful attack": Henderson to partners, June 12, 1775, DM 4B16.

"There was only": LCD interview with Mrs. Elizabeth Poage Thomas, 1844, DM 12C27[15].

"Without care" and following quotes in this paragraph: Henderson to partners, June 12, 1775, DM 4B16.

"You could not discover": J. F. D. Smyth, *A Tour in the United States of America* (Dublin, 1784), quoted in William Stewart Lester, *The Transylvania Colony* (Spencer, Ind.: Samuel R. Guard, 1935), 111.

"The Indians should do us the favor": Henderson to partners, June 12, 1775, DM 4B16.

"Advise, but not command": Doddridge, *Notes*, 266–67.

"A set of scoundrels": RH, 176–77.

"I feel pleased": DB to Charles Telfridge, May 19, 1775, Boone Bicentennial Commission Records, 61W11, Special Collections, University of Kentucky, Lexington.

"Every body seemed well satisfied": RH, 173.

"Many a man": JDS interview with Joshua McQueen, c. 1845, DM 13CC121.

"This day we Begin": "Journal of William Calk," 44.

"All power": quoted in Ranck, *Boonesborough*, 200–201.

"Roused the attention": John Williams to Proprietors of the Transylvania Company, January 3, 1776, *Colonial Records of North Carolina*, 10:382–87.

"Work their own Ruin": "George Rogers Clark Papers, 1771–1781," ed. J. A. Hill, *Collections of the Illinois State Historical Library*, 8:36–37.

"An infamous Company": Governor Josiah Martin, March 23, 1775, in *Colonial Records of North Carolina*, 9:1175–76.

"Quit-rents": quoted in James Hogg to Richard Henderson, January 1776, in Ranck, *Boonesborough*, 229.

"Within the limits of Virginia": quoted in Archibald Henderson,

"The Transylvania Company Study in Personnel: James Hogg," *FCHQ* 21 (1947) :13.
"For the signal services": Transylvania Company minutes, September 25, 1775, in Ranck, *Boonesborough*, 214.
"Troubled himself": NOB, DM 6S88.
"Boone set off": RH, 178.
"The devil himself": Henderson to partners, July 18, 1775, DM 4B36–37.
"A headstrong man": DB, DM 22C11.
"Could manage McGary": JDS interview with Sarah Graham, c. 1840s, DM 12CC45.
"Just enough for two": JDS interview with "Mrs. Shaulkin," c. 1840s, DM 11CC219.
"4 peecs of Linin": DB, account book, 1774–75, MS, DM 4C75[6].
"Every Kentuckian": NH, DM 17CC195.
"Getting land for taking it up": Doddridge, *Notes*, 85.
"A Kind of Right": Hermon Husband, "An Impartial Relation of the First Rise and Cause of the Present Differences in Publick Affairs in the Province of North Carolina," in *Some Eighteenth-Century Tracts Concerning North Carolina*, ed. William K. Boyd (Raleigh, N.C.: n.p., 1927), 309.
"The people in general": John Floyd to William Preston, April 21, 1775, DM 33S267–70.
"Many have come": John Floyd to William Preston, May 19 and May 27, 1776, DM 33S293–297.
"I am afraid": John Todd, June 22, 1776, quoted in LIFE, DM 12C26[1].
"In the time Bucks were rutting" and following quotes in this paragraph: deposition of DB, July 27, 1795, Shelby County Deed Book B1, 272–73.
"Sporting, dancing": William Hickman, "Account of Life and Travels," MSS, Codex 94, DC.
"Imagination had painted Indians": Benjamin Sharp to LCD, April 10, 1845, DM 7C23[2].
"A row or two of Smoky cabins": William Hickman, "Account of Life and Travels."
"Dirty, lousy": JC, DM 12CC74.
"Tired of the confinement": Nathan Reid, MS, n.d., DM 31C[24–25].

"Was so fond": JDS interview with DBB, c. 1844, DM 22C14[10].
"Perhaps she was more": SH to LCD, December 23, 1862, DM 16C75.
"Mother was an expert hand": Eudocia Estill to LCD, February 8, 1852, DM 24C31.
"Law! Simon": NH, DM 17CC192.
"Grandmother said": ELC to LCD, March 31, 1885, DM 21C28.
"When I was a small boy": Alfred Henderson to LCD, February 12, 1853, DM 24C38.
"How well I remember": ELC to LCD, March 31, 1885, DM 21C28.
"Giving free rein": Nathan Reid to Nathan Reid Jr, n.d., LIFE, DM 4B67–68.
"The savages have the girls": ELC to LCD, March 31, 1885, DM 21C28.
"Boone directed us": statement of Nathan Reid, n.d., DM 31C2[25].
"Held a little chat" and following quote: ELC to LCD, March 31, 1885, DM 21C28.
"We have done pretty well": NOB, DM 6S96.
"Laugh and halloo": ELC to LCD, May 2, 1885, DM 21C37.
"Were making tracks" and following quotes in this paragraph: statement of Nathan Reid, n.d., DM 31C2[25–26].
"Here Boone paused a moment" and following quote: statement of Nathan Reid, n.d., DM 31C2 [25–26].
"Stop to cook": NOB, DM 6S96–101.
"To get the prisoners": John Floyd to William Preston, July 21, 1776, DM 33S300–305.
"No man to touch a trigger": statement of Nathan Reid, n.d., DM 31C2[26–27].
"A fine young squaw": LCD interview with William Phelps, 1868, DM 24C57[1].
"Gave herself up": SH to LCD, February 15, 1863, DM 16C76.
"She unconsciously was opening their hair": SH to LCD, February 15, 1863, DM 16C76.
"Creeping upon his breast": LCD interview with Jacob Boone, 1890, DM 14C84.
"She saw blood burst": JC, DM 12CC75.
"That's daddy," NOB, DM 6S101.

"She sensibly felt it touch her head": Richard Holder to LCD, October 8, 1850, DM 24C29[1–2].
"Almost naked": John Floyd to William Preston, July 21, 1776, DM 33S300–305.
"For God's sake": Samuel H. Dixon to LCD, February 3, 1852, DM 24C30[5].
"Thank Almighty Providence" and following quote: ELC to LCD, March 31, 1885, DM 21C28–29.
"She both laughed and cried": ELC to LCD, May 2, 1885, DM 21C37.
"And not the white people": William Wilson, report of September 26, 1776, in *American Archives*, 5th ser., 2:514–15.
"A man distinguished": *New York Magazine*, May 1796, 280, DM 6S337.
"Ten at least": John Floyd to William Preston, July 21, 1776, DM 33S300–305.
"Smitten with them": William Bailey Smith, LIFE, DM 4B251[1]n.
"The Indians should violate": JDS interview with Robert Wickliffe, Sr., 1859, DM 15CC84.
"Make love to the girls": DBC, DM 30C48–49.
"Not characteristic": MB, DM 19C49.
"Pretty squaw": statement of David Henry, n.d., DM 31C2[40].
"Real handsome": ELC to LCD, March 14, 1885, DM 21C24.
"A fine woman": LCD interview with Abner Bryan, 1890, DM 4C51.
"I wouldn't have done it": DBC, DM 30C48–49.
"As large as her thumb": DBC, DM 30C48–49.
"Care and counsel": ELC to LCD, June 12, 1885, DM 21C48[1].

Chapter Five. Prisoners to Old Chillicothe: 1776 to 1778

"Remote from the Seat of Government": Harrodsburg Memorial to the Virginia Convention, June 20, 1776, DM 14S11–12.
"Conserning the American Cause": Minutes of the Eaton Church, Forks of the Yadkin, November 3, 1775, copy in AHC.
"This immense and fertile country": Harrodsburg Memorial to the Virginia Convention, June 20, 1776, DM 4S11–12.
"Bryans and other Tories": John Floyd to William Preston, May 19, 1776, DM 33S293.

"Erred gravely": RBL to LCD, March 22, 1853, DM 22C41.
"Loyal to the English": Mary C. Dalton to LCD, June 22, 1885, DM 8C83[1–2].
"Rather unpopular in this section": R. J. Fickle to LCD, September 12, 1884, DM 7C34[2].
"Always acted with the Whigs": Joseph Bryan, quoted in Robert B. McAfee, "Life and Times of Robert B. McAfee," MS, Codex 127B:197, DC.
"One of the most trying things": RBL to LCD, March 22, 1853, DM 22C41.
"A war of intrusion": Maria R. Audubon, ed., *Audubon and his Journals* (New York: Charles Scribner's Sons, 1897), 2:241.
"The inroads of the Savages": Harrodsburg Memorial to the Virginia Convention, June 20, 1776, DM 14S11–12.
"My Brothers!": *ST*, 17–23.
"Appear to him as a spectre": JDS interview with Sarah Graham, 1840s, DM 12CC45.
"Sell your lives": JDS interview with John Gass, c. 1840s, DM 11CC12.
"Made right at them": JDS interview with John Gass, c. 1840s, DM 11CC12.
"Tem gottam yellow rascals" and following quote: Willis A. Bush to LCD, October 10, 1853, DM 24C59[2].
"40 or 50 Indians attacked Boonesborough": "Diary of George Rogers Clark," in *George Rogers Clark Papers*, 3:21.
"You have behaved": LCD interview with John and Sarah Kenton McCord, 1851, DM 5S145.
"Boone was badly wounded": Isaac Shelby to Joseph Martin, June 20, 1777, LIFE, DM 4B132.
"To hunt Indians": "Diary of George Rogers Clark," 3:22.
"Boone, come up!": MB, DM 19C7.
"The best little Indian fight": MB, DM 19C8.
"Literally riddled": Thomas E. Lee to LCD, January 12, 1853, DM 1C37.
"Exciting an alarm": quoted in RCD, 195.
"Neither spoon": JDS interview with William Clinkinbeard, c. 1840s, DM 11CC55.
"Women could read": NH, 1844, DM 17CC207.
"If we was only": DT, 76.

"Boyle your Brimstone": DB account book, DM 27C35.
"And that had to do": JDS interview with William Clinkinbeard, c. 1840s, DM 11CC55.
"Allowed but one": deposition of Arabia Brown, September 13, 1832, DM 9C44[2].
"Many of the families": John Bowman to General Hand, December 12, 1777, LIFE, DM 4B140–41.
"Almost destitute": petition of Kentuckians concerning salt, November 25, 1777, DM 14S13–14.
"For curing the provisions": deposition of James Callaway, October 10, 1832, DM 21C75.
"Because they use so much salt": quoted in White, *Middleground*, 332.
"The Great Spirit above": quoted in RCD, 206–7.
"I was taken prisoner": deposition of DB, September 20, 1785, DM 29C108.
"Howdydo, Captain Will" and following quotes in this paragraph: NOB, DM 6S106–7.
"Used duplicity": NOB, DM 6S128.
"Don't fire!": JJ, DM 11C62[4–5].
"We were ordered": Ansel Goodman, petition for a Revolutionary War pension, October 29, 1832, DM 11C28–30.
"Brothers! What I have promised": JJ, DM 11C62[5–7].
"This is not for your men": NOB, DM 6S107–110.
"I'm a man": DBC, DM 20C52.
"I set out full speed": statement of Boone Hays, February 1846, DM 23C36[3–4].
"It was a heavy load": Ansel Goodman petition, October 29, 1832, DM 11C28–30.
"Here, strike!" JJ, DM 11C62[8–10].
"It was all habit": DBC, DM 30C51.
"He was compelled": Ansel Goodman petition, October 29, 1832, DM 11C28–30.
"All these Chillicothys": Josiah Harmar, October 30, 1790, quoted in Galloway, *Old Chillicothe*, 44.
"Ordered to dance": Ansel Goodman petition, October 29, 1832, DM 11C28–30.
"They could have defended themselves": LCD interview with Noble Callaway, 1868, DM 25S125.

"Regretted they had not fought": LCD interview with James Callaway, 1868, DM 25S258–59.
"Our own Flesh and Blood": Shawnees to British, May 10, 1765, quoted in RCD, 112.
"Shawnee women used to steal": LCD interview with Charles Tucker, 1868, DM 23S172–177.
"Was mad": DBC, DM 30C54.
"Many things happen": John Warth, quoted in J. P. Hale, "Daniel Boone, Some Facts and Incidents not Hitherto Published," *West Virginia School Journal* 2, no. 4 (February 1882):85–86.
"To replace that slain son": DB, quoted by D. Thompson, n.d., DM 11C81.
"Without Shedding one drop of blood": William Bailey Smith to George Rogers Clark, March 7, 1778, in *George Rogers Clark Papers*, 3:40.
"Much Dejected": DBB to LCD, October 24, 1843, DM 22C9[2].
"The whole dirt": William Fleming, "Journal," MS, February 6, 1780, Codex 67, DC.
"Half-starved people": JC, DM 12CC67.
"It was hard times" and quotes in the next paragraph: DT, 47.
"All of Boone's party": Patrick Henry to William Christian, March 15, 1778, DM 25S222.
"Captured at the Blue lick": DBB to LCD, February 27, 1843, DM 22C5[11].
"Supposing her husband dead": JC, DM 12CC64.
"She thought best": DBB to LCD, October 24, 1843, DM 22C9[2].
"They were glad": LCD interview with Sabina Ellis, 1858, DM 7S45–52.
"Much better treated": John Wade to LCD, December 28, 1859, DM 24C135.
"Conducted me to Detright": deposition of DB, September 20, 1785, DM 29C108.
"They had the good fortune": Henry Hamilton to Guy Carleton, April 25, 1778, in "Haldimand Papers," Michigan Pioneer and Historical Society, *Historical Collections* 9 (1886):435.
"The report of Burgoyne's disaster": NOB, DM 6S110–114.
"The true reason": Joseph Bryan, quoted in McAfee, "Life and Times" Codex 127B:196–97, DC.
"He had probably wandered off": DBC, DM 30C54.

"Boone was a Tory": JDS interview with DBB, 1844, DM 22C14[12].

"Whistling and contented": NOB, DM 6S122.

"Friendly and sociable": DBC, DM 30C53.

"Housewifery of his Indian mother": IB, DM 19C76–78.

"With the greatest kindness": Bettie T. Bryan to LCD, September 5, 1884, 22C28.

"I have been obliged": SH to LCD, December 23, 1862, DM 16C75.

"Said he had a squaw": ELC to LCD, May 3, 1887, DM 21C63[1–2].

"Would do Every thing": ELC to LCD, March 14 and April 23, 1885, DM 21C24[12–13] and 21C33[2].

"Never much on raising corn": LCD interview with Abner Bryan, 1890, 4C46.

"I'm a chief at home": DBC, DM 30C53.

"You haven't done much": John C. Boone to LCD, November 20, 1890, 16C132.

"The habits and customs": Bettie T. Bryan to LCD, September 5, 1884, DM 22C28.

"Boone ain't going away": Ephraim McLain to LCD, May 17, 1884, DM 16C7, 16C8.

"His simple-hearted people": DBC, DM 30C55.

"I felt it to be my duty": DBC, DM 30C54.

"Could have escaped": LCD interview with Joseph Scholl, 1868, DM 24S109–11.

"Huy! Huy!": JC, DM 12CC76.

"To go to there towns" and following quotes in this paragraph: William Whitley, "Narrative of a Kentucky Pioneer," MS, c. 1810, DM 9C26–28.

"The worst act": NOB, DM 6S122.

"As soon as he found out": Bettie T. Bryan to LCD, September 5, 1884, DM 22C28.

"Boone cut the tugs": JJ, DM 11C62[11–13].

"She tried to persuade him": Bettie T. Bryan to LCD, September 5, 1884, DM 22C28; Elijah Bryan, May 12, 1885, DM 4C33.

"Boone is lost": LCD interview with Joseph Scholl, 1868, DM 24S109–11.

"Straight as a leather String": John C. Boone to LCD, November 20, 1890, DM 16C132.

"On June 19, 1778": deposition of DB, September 28, 1795, DM 15C25[4].

"You may depend upon it": LCD interview with Henry Wilson, n.d., DM 31C2[72].

"Bless your soul": quoted in LIFE, DM 4B192–93.

Chapter Six. A Vast Expence of Blood and Treasure: 1778 to 1784

"Capt. Boone has runaway": John Todd to Patrick Lockhart, June 29, 1778, quoted in *FCHQ* 2 (1928) :160.

"He was now come home": DT, 57.

"Arms and amunition": deposition of William Buchanan, November 28, 1778, DM 14S18–19.

"Well-grown boy": Doddridge, *Notes*, 277.

"To batter down our fort" and following quotes in this paragraph: deposition of William Hancock, July 17, 1778, DM 4B205.

"Kill all the men": Robert Hancock to LCD, February 26, 1853, DM 24C17[1–3].

"Why you stole her": JC, DM 12CC105.

"Both French and Indians": DB to Arthur Campbell, July 18, 1778, DM 4B204.

"Too much engross'd": Arthur Campbell to William Fleming, July 31, 1778, in *FAUO*, 123.

"The Shawanese have drawn together": Henry Hamilton to Governor Haldimand, September 5, 1778, in "Haldimand Papers," Michigan Pioneer and Historical Society, *Historical Collections* 9 (1886) :465.

"Boone when a prisoner": LCD interview with Stephen Cooper, 1889, DM 11C97–99.

"Make a great speck" and following quotes in this paragraph: DB, quoted in DT, 57.

"The Indian Shore": quoted in Samuel M. Wilson, *The First Land Court of Kentucky, 1779–1780* (Lexington: Kentucky State Bar Association, 1923), 75.

"Painted their faces": William Bailey Smith, in *Hunt's Western Review* (January 1821) :362, clipping in DM 32C97.

"The famous partisan": clipping from a Williamsburg newspaper, October 9, 1778, in DM 31C2[78].

"As freely and readily" and subsequent quote: JG, DM 11CC12–14.
"Howdy": JC, DM 12CC75.
"Thought very strange": Willie A. Bush to LCD, October 10, 1853, DM 24C59[7].
"You killed my son": *John Bradford's Historical Notes on Kentucky*, ed. Douglas S. Watson (San Francisco: Grabhorn Press, 1932), 41.
"They would be put to death": JDS interview with DBB, 1844, DM 22C14[13].
"He had been gone so long": JG, DM 11CC12–14.
"Make a good peace": DT, 58.
"Free from blame": JG, DM 11CC12–14.
"Half of the men": JDS interview with Jesse Daniel, ca. 1843, DM 11CC94.
"Kill the first man": NH, DM 17CC198.
"Refuse the offer": Smith, in *Hunt's Western Review*, clipping in DM 31C2[87].
"He would never give up" and following quote: LCD interview with John Gass, 1844, DM 24C73[4].
"I have brought forty horses": *John Bradford's Historical Notes on Kentucky*, 41.
"They wouldn't be safe": JG, DM 11CC12–14.
"Fine squaws": MB, DM 19C11.
"They took out their Combs": ELC to LCD, March 14 and March 28, 1885, DM 21C24, 21C27.
"The people have determined": NOB, DM 6S129–33.
"To think the Indians were sincere": John Bowman to George Rogers Clark, October 14, 1778, DM 31C2[90].
"Placed no confidence": Smith, in *Hunt's Western Review*, clipping in DM 31C[87].
"Without one moment's delay": John N. James interview with Simon Kenton, c. 1835, DM 11C77–78.
"As Indians were more numerous": MB, 19C11–13.
"These are not chiefs": NOB, DM 6S133–36.
"By what right": JDS interview with DBB, 1844, DM 22C14[13].
"Allegiance to the King": Peck, *Life of Daniel Boone*, 89–90.
"It was deemed best": MB, DM 19C11–13.
"Give out the big talk": MB, DM 19C11–13.
"Calleway was the first" and quote in the next paragraph: DT, 58.

"Well ornamented": MB, DM 19C16.
"Fourteen bullet holes": JG, DM 11CC12–14.
"Utmost confusion": JDS interview with Richard French, c. 1840s, DM 12CC205.
"The women cried and screamed": MB, DM 19C15.
"I was not made for a fighter": JG, DM 11CC12–14.
"She was always his doctor": MB, DM 19C15–16.
"Habitual swearers": JDS interview with John Rankins, c. 1840s, DM 11CC81–83.
"It would be more becoming": JG, DM 11CC12–14.
"Fire your damned cannon": JDS interview with DBB, 1844, DM 22C10[9].
"So valuable a slave": petition of Nathaniel Henderson, November 21, 1778, DM 14S18–19.
"Come out and fight": MB, DM 19C20.
"It might hurt": DT, 58–59.
"What are you doing": NOB, DM 6S138, 6S143; JG, DM 24C73[3–4], 11CC12–14.
"Without these necessary ornaments": JDS interview with John Rankins, c. 1840s, DM 11CC81–83.
"Climbed a tree": Aley Yates to LCD, February 26, 1884, DM 9C77[2].
"The insulting part of his body": Thomas W. Carter, quoted in M. B. Woods to LCD, April 9, 1883, DM 4C22[11–12].
"At any considerable distance": John G. W. Dillin, *The Kentucky Rifle* (Washington, D.C.: National Rifle Association of America, 1924), 71.
"Leather Stocking never surpassed this": W. H. Bogart, *Daniel Boone, and the Hunters of Kentucky* (Auburn, N.Y.: Miller, Orton and Mulligan, 1854), 225.
"We've killed Boone": LCD interview with Susan Callaway Howell, 1868, DM 23S223.
"Dat de ball": quoted in LIFE, DM 4B237.
"Where's Pompey?" JG, DM 24C73[10]; MB, DM 19C18; JJ, DM 11C62[16].
"It was so light in the fort": MB, DM 19D21–22.
"Run up to the fort": DT, 59.
"They quit on this account": John N. James interview with Simon Kenton, c. 1833, DM 11C77–78.

"Damn you, come on!" DT, 60–62.
"God damn them": JDS interview with DBB, 1844, DM 22C14[12].
"Against their consent": DT, 63–64.
"It was Boons management": John Wade to LCD, December 28, 1859, and July 24, 1860, DM 24C135–36.
"His men thought very hard": Carter J. Kelley to LCD, April 15, 1852, DM 24C124.
"Always spoke well": LCD interview with Louisa Aldridge, 1866, DM 20S146.
"Complain of Boone surrendering": DBC, DM 30C51.
"Was not pleased about it": DT, 63–64.
"The worst barbecued": JG, DM 11CC16.
"A long and interesting account": Joseph Martin to William Martin, October 15, 1844, DM 24C41.
"Never bear an Indian's presence": JDS interview with Richard French, c. 1840s, DM 12CC205.
"Boone never deserved any thing": JDS interview with Jesse Daniel, c. 1843, DM 11CC94.
"Mr. Daniel Boone was here": quoted in Wall, Martin, and Boone, *Boone Families in Davie County*, 11.
"To prevail upon Mrs. Boone": NOB, DM 6S144.
"Had to run off": JDS interview with William Clinkinbeard, c. 1840s, DM 11CC55.
"It was like an army": JDS interview with George Bryan, c. 1844, DM 22C16[19].
"We began our journey" and following quote in this paragraph: PH, DM 20C84[13].
"A loud scream": PH, DM 20C84[13–15].
"A dirty place": William Fleming, journal, Codex 67, DC.
"Half-faced camps": statement of Mrs. Rachel Henton, n.d., DM 31C2[96].
"Severely cold": William Fleming, quoted in Wilson, *First Land Court of Kentucky*, 48.
"Weare too poore" and following quote: DT, 73–75.
"Like to have starved": JDS interview with William Clinkinbeard, c. 1840s, DM 11CC60.
"Divided even to his last pone" and following quotes in this paragraph: E. B. Scholl to LCD, January 5, 1856, DM 23C104.

"Old backwoods hunter": Christopher Mann to LCD, October 15, 1883, DM 15C26.
"Lying on the waters of Licking": quoted in J. R. Cooper, typescript of article of March 8, 1925, in the *Lexington Herald*, KHS.
"He doth bind him Self": contract between DB and Geddes Winston, December 17, 1781, DM 25C78.
"The 2000 acres of Land": DB to Geddes Winston, May 9, 1786, facsimile in Bakeless, *Daniel Boone*, 343.
"To be advanced on warrants": DB receipt, February 12, 1780, AHC.
"For to bring a warrant": DB receipt, February 10, 1780, AHC.
"I will freely grant": Thomas Hart to Nathaniel Hart, August 3, 1780, DM 33S324–25.
"It was a heavy loss": NOB, DM 6S145.
"Completely unmaned": PH, DM 20C84[10–11].
"I feel for the poor people": Thomas Hart to Nathaniel Hart, August 3, 1780, quoted in Bakeless, *Daniel Boone*, 245–46; another version in DM 33S324–25.
"Run to the council house": JJ, DM 11C62[17–23].
"Made a broken trip": DT, 68.
"I don't believe": Henry Bird to Arent De Peyster, July 1, 1780, in "Haldimand Papers," 19 (1892):538.
"Should the Enemy approach": Daniel Broadhead, September 23, 1780, quoted in RCD, 263.
"By ripping up her Belly": William Homan to Henry Bird, August 15, 1780, in "Haldimand Papers," 10 (1888):418–19.
"The Indians stood": JDS interview with Mrs. John Morrison, ca. 1840s, DM 11CC153.
"Silent and seemingly unheeding": James Handasyd Perkins, quoted in LIFE, DM 4B69–70.
"Old Monongahela": NOB, DM 6S211.
"There are Indians near": PH, DM 20C84[20–24].
"We must do something": H. C. Anderson, in *Brownsville Democrat*, January 3, 1884, clipping in DM 13C11–13.
"Now, Boone": unidentified granddaughter, retold in Peck, *Daniel Boone*, 141–44.
"Let's crack some of these walnuts": Joshua Pennington to LCD, June 18, 1856, DM 23C43[1].

"We've killed Daniel Boone": Thomas S. Bouchelle to LCD, July 28, 1884, DM 9C68[5].

"He looked so much": Silas W. Parris to LCD, November 3, 1884, DM 2C77.

"Wanted a dog to seize him": statement of DBB, DM 31C2[100].

"Choppings, blazings, and paintings": deposition of DB, June 20, 1817, DM 15C25[5–6].

"A *colonel*, ha?": LCD interview with Joseph Ficklin, 1846, DM 13C79[19].

"Boone, who was with Lord Corwallis": William Christian to William Preston, June 30, 1781, quoted in John Cook Wyllie, "Daniel Boone's Adventures in Charlottesville in 1781: Some Incidents Connected with Tarleton's Raid," *Magazine of Albermarle County History* 19 (1960–61) :15.

"Not to take up arms any more": NOB, DM 62151.

"Daniel Came to See us the first time": James Boone, family record, MS, n.d., DM 1C59.

"The Sergeant at Arms": quoted in J. P. Hale, "Daniel Boone," 92.

"Come on, by Jesus" and following quotes in this paragraph: JDS interview with John Rankins, c. 1840s, DM 11CC81–83.

"Fool-brave": JDS, n.d., DM 11CC53.

"Boyish conduct": LCD interview with George M. Bedinger, 1843, DM 1A17–18.

"Fouled his pantaloons": LCD interview with John Brady, 1860, 16S248.

"They wouldn't die": LCD interview with George M. Bedinger, 1843, DM 1A12–13.

"The most comely sight": Bogart, *Daniel Boone*, 125.

"The yellow militia": John Floyd to William Preston, August 12, 1782, DM 17CC142.

"Overrun your country": quoted in *John Bradford's Historical Notes on Kentucky*, 120.

"Shoot his damned gourd": JDS interview with Sarah Graham, c. 1840s, DM 12CC45.

"Concealing their numbers": DB, quoted in Robert Wickliffe, "The Life of Col. John Todd," MS, c. 1840s, DM 5C51[8–9].

"By counting the Indian's fires": deposition of Benjamin A. Cooper, November 9, 1836, quoted in Samuel M. Wilson, *Battle of the Blue Licks, August 19, 1782* (Lexington, Ky.: n.p., 1927), 55–56.

"They intend to fight us": DB, quoted in Wickliffe, "Life of Col. John Todd," DM 5C51[8–9].

"Run heedlessly": LCD interview with Joseph Scholl, 1868, DM 24S212–15.

"I say not follow": DBC, DM 30C61–63.

"We have force enough": PH, DM 20C84[30–33].

"By Godly": JDS interview with Jacob Stevens, c. 1840s, DM 12CC134–35.

"I never saw any signs": DBC, DM 30C61–63.

"No man before": RBL to LCD, August 23, 1845, DM 22C36.

"I can go as far": LCD interview with Joseph Scholl, 1868, DM 24S212–15.

"Them that ain't cowards": JDS interview with Jacob Stevens, c. 1840s, DM 12CC134–35.

"The contagion was irresistible": LCD interview with Samuel Boone, 1868, DM 22S264–65.

"Come on": RBL to LCD, August 23, 1845, DM 22C36.

"Kept near to Boone": PH, DM 20C84[34–35].

"Shot down like pigeons": RBL to LCD, August 23, 1845, DM 22C36.

"It fell to my lot": DB to Benjamin Harrison, August 30, 1782, in *Calendar of Virginia State Papers*, 3:275–76.

"He *believed* he had killed" and following quote: NOB, DM 6S157.

"The Enemy was immediately on our backs": DB to Benjamin Harrison, August 30, 1782, in *Calendar of Virginia State Papers*, 3:275–76.

"Damned if I didn't": JDS interview with Jacob Stevens, c. 1840s, DM 12CC134–35.

"Father, I won't leave you": NOB, DM 6S165–66.

"Bullets all the while showering round me": JDS interview with Jacob Stevens, c. 1840s, DM 12CC134–35.

"Stand and fire" and following quote: PH, DM 20C84[35–36].

"The smell of a human": JDS interview with Sarah Graham, c. 1840s, DM 12CC50.

"A want of proper authority": Arthur Campbell to William Davies, October 3, 1782, in *Calendar of Virginia State Papers*, 3:337.

"I am much sensured": Hugh McGary to Benjamin Logan, August 28, 1782, in Wilson, *Battle of the Blue Licks*, 66–67.
"Blamed himself in some degree": LCD interview with Joseph Scholl, 1868, DM 24S212–15.
"His father and family": NOB, DM 6S165–66.
"I did not hear your name": DBC, DM 30C62.
"Everything looked red": JDS interview with Sarah Graham, c. 1840s, DM 12CC50.
"Then had the Indians their revenge": DM 31C3[16].
"Our own Frontiers": DB and other Fayette County officers to Governor Benjamin Harrison, September 11, 1782, in *Calendar of Virginia State Papers*, 3:301–2.
"Our Brave Kantetuckians": DB to Benjamin Harrison, September 11, 1782, Huntington Library, San Marino, Calif., quoted in Michael A. Lofaro, "Tracking Daniel Boone: The Changing Frontier in American Life," *RKHS* 82 (1984) :332.
"I have Encouraged": DB to Benjamin Harrison, August 30, 1782, Virginia State Library, quoted in Bakeless, *Daniel Boone*, 308.
"Shone Expedistion": DB to Capt. Hazelrigg, January 6, 1783, DM 14C2.
"I Exspet every exertion": DB to Robert Patterson, October 25, 1782, DM 25C80.
"Boone was more hopeful": PH, DM 20C84[42].
"To view and mark": *Kentucky in Retrospect: Noteworthy Personages and Events in Kentucky History, 1792–1942*, ed. Louise P. Drake (n.p.: Sesquicentennial Commission, Commonwealth of Kentucky, 1942), 31; see also Boone's receipt for his expenses, March 1, 1783, DM 14C2[1].

Part Two

"I am well": DB to John Coburn, October 5, 1809, facsimile in William H. Cody (Buffalo Bill), *Story of the Wild West and Camp-Fire Chats* (Philadelphia: Historical Publishing Company, 1888), 137.
"Far in recommending": "Report of the Congressional Select Committee," January 29, 1813, DM 16S150–55.
"Your petitioner" and subsequent quotations from the several versions of the petitions: "To the Senate and Representatives of the Citizens of the United States in Congress Assembled" (1810),

in *American State Papers. Public Lands* (Washington, D.C.: Gales and Seaton, 1834), 2:10; *Report of the* [*Senate*] *Committee to whom was referred the Petition of Daniel Boon* (Washington, D.C.: Roger C. Weightman, 1810); *Report of the* [*House*] *Committee Appointed on the Petition of Daniel Boon* (Washington, D.C.: Roger C. Weightman, 1810); "Memorial of Daniel Boone, To the Honorable the Senate and House of Representatives of the General Assembly for the State of Kentucky," January 1812, DM 23C2, reprinted in *Niles Weekly Register* 4 (March 13, 1813) :33; "To the Honorable the Senators and Representatives of the Freemen of the United States," March 1812, DM 15C85; *Report of the* [*House*] *Committee to whom was referred The Petition of Daniel Boone, Together with the Resolutions of the Legislature of the State of Kentucky* (Washington, D.C.: Roger C. Weightman, 1813).

"Quiet, of few words": LCD interview with George Edwards, 1863, DM 19S83.

"Boone was no chatterbox": Dr. S. Paul Jones to LCD, May 13, 1887, DM 21C1.

"This reminds me": LCD interview with Susan Callaway Howell, 1868, DM 23S248.

"Possessing a different disposition": Humphrey Marshall, *The History of Kentucky* (1812; Frankfort, Ky.: Geo. S. Robinson, 1824), 1:10, 16–17.

Chapter Seven. Unable to Call a Single Acre His Own: 1784 to 1789

"A grate Landing place": DB to Gov. Patrick Henry of Virginia, August 16, 1785, DM 32C81A.

"The Landing the Best": Mary Colburn Dewees, MS, Codex 58, DC.

"Was introduced to Col. Boone": Erkries Beatty, diary entry for May 16, 1786, MS, Codex 11, DC.

"A cabin built": JDS interview with Daniel Deron, c. 1840s, DM 12CC243.

"Enough for a comfortable start": DBC, DM 30C73–74.

"A great drunkard": LCD interview with John Scholl, 1868, DM 22S273.

"One Negroe girl" and other records of slaves: see DB bills of sale, September 10, 1781, DM 25C76–77; March 7, 1786, DM 26C148; c. 1787, AHC; and DB to William Harris, March 3, 1791, DM 14C105[1].

"Everyone in Kentucky": Bakeless, *Daniel Boone*, 329.

"A permanent evil": William S. Bryan, "Daniel Boone's Western 'Palatinate,'" *Missouri Historical Review* 3 (1906–9) :198–99; for A. G. Boone, see broadsides, MHS.

"Beaf or Pork": DB promissory note, December 16, 1786, Miscellaneous Manuscripts, box 4, DC; see "beaver script" in AHC.

"I Leave it to your Self": Bartlet Searcy to DB, September 26, 1788, DM 27C2.

"Tho Every Man": DB to unidentified correspondent, August 28, 1784, facsimile in Dillin, *Kentucky Rifle*, plate 5.

"Able and Qualified": certificate of Willis Green, Lincoln County Clerk, August 19, 1783, DM 25C81.

"Did his surveying": JDS interview with William P. Hart, c. 1840s, DM 17CC158.

"Knowledge of surveying": NOB, DM 6S221.

"Two Hickories": DB, survey plat, November 15, 1784, manuscripts, KHS.

"All Boone's entries": JDS interview with William Rich, ca. 1840s, DM 11CC87.

"As good as the average": Willard Rouse Jillson, *With Compass and Chain: A Brief Narration of the Activities of Col. Daniel Boone as a Land Surveyor in Kentucky* (Frankfort, Ky.: Roberts Printing Company, 1954), 7–11.

"The same identical tract": quoted in Stephen A. Aron, "How the West was Lost: The Transformation of Kentucky from Daniel Boone to Henry Clay" (Ph.D. diss., University of California, Berkeley, 1990), 276–77.

"To much Exposed": DB to unidentified correspondent, August 28, 1784, in Dillin, *Kentucky Rifle*, plate 5.

"Sorry to here": DB to Charles Yancey, May 30, 1785, DM 14C14–14[1].

"No Dout": DB to Jacob Cohen, April 28, 1784, AHC.

"For good Reasons of past favors": DB to Thomas Hart, August 11, 1785, 52W84, Special Collections, University of Kentucky.

"I know the within land": DB inscription, manuscripts, FC.

"We have undertaken": *Virginia Gazette*, May 3, 1783.
"He is Bater": DB to Charles Yancey, May 30, 1785, DM 14C14–14[1].
"Sir, if you will Send": DB to Nathaniel Rochester, July 17, 1785, DM 14C7.
"Make the entry agreeable": deposition of DB, April 24, 1794, in Charles R. Staples, ed., "History in Circuit Court Records, Fayette County," *RKHS* 30 (1932) :353.
"To be plain with you" and following quotes in this paragraph: DB deposition, April 24, 1794; reprinted in J. R. Cooper, transcript of article of March 22, 1925, in the *Lexington Herald*, KHS.
"He would be damned": deposition of William Hays, May 15, 1790, in Staples, "History in Circuit Court Records," 352.
"Not such a damned fool": deposition of DB in Staples, "History in Circuit Court Records," 354.
"Lying on Boone's Creek": quoted in Neal O. Hammon, "Daniel Boone's Land Problems" (unpublished MS, 1991), 4.
"Hath Hickman or you": deposition of William Hays in Staples, "History in Circuit Court Records," 352.
"Grossly imposed on": deposition of Thomas McClanahan, May 17, 1790, in Staples, "History in Circuit Court Records," 351.
"Done according to law": deposition of William Jenkins, August 10, 1790, in Staples, "History in Circuit Court Records," 352.
"Two acres for one": deposition of Richard Hickman, May 25, 1790, in Staples, "History in Circuit Court Records," 348.
"Good and lawful money": quoted in J. R. Cooper, transcript of article of March 29, 1925, in the *Lexington Herald*, KHS.
"Never to Late": DB to unknown correspondent, August 28, 1784, in Dillin, *Kentucky Rifle*, plate 5.
"Inattentive to the means": DB, "To the Honorable the Senators and Representatives," March 1812, DM 15C85.
"Ignorant of how to acquire it": DB, "Memorial of Daniel Boone," January 1812, DM 23C2.
"Worth a fortune": NOB, DM 6S215–21.
"He had nothing": NOB, DM 6S252.
"Intrusted to Col. Floyd": David Todd to Mann Butler, March 17, 1834, DM 15CC126.
"Boone just loaned": JDS interview with David Thompson, c. 1840s, DM 12CC201.

"The Condition of the above": Gilbert Imlay, indenture, March 15, 1783, DM 25C83.
"I do hereby assign": quoted in J. R. Cooper, transcript of article of February 13, 1927, in the *Lexington Herald*, KHS.
"Sincerely sorry": Gilbert Imlay to DB, December 1786, DM 26C152.
"Located and surveyed": quoted in J. R. Cooper, transcript of article of February 13, 1927, in the *Lexington Herald*, KHS.
"Forever Defend the land": DB deed, July 20, 1786, Samuel Wilson Collection, University of Kentucky.
"Boone's honour": DBB to LCD, February 27, 1843, DM 22C7.
"Swear any Thing": John May to Samuel Beall, December 18, 1786, FC.
"For a trifle": NOB, DM 6S215–17.
"Lying on the Waters": DB promissory note, May 28, 1787, DM 26C177.
"Plunged him": DB, quoted in LCD interview with Edward Coles, October 5, 1848, DM 6S310.
"To appear": T. Perkins, receipt, October 26, 1785, DM 26C69.
"I am to pay": DB to Lawrence Thompson, August 6, 1784, DM 14C5.
"I am So unwill": DB to unknown correspondent, June 4, 1786, manuscripts, KHS.
"Not received one shilling": deposition of DB, September 8, 1795, DM 4C86–87.
"Not a farthing!": deposition of DB, September 15, 1796, DM 2C80.
"That even in time of peace": NOB, DM 6S215–21.
"Times are a Litel Difegult": DB to Nathaniel Rochester, July 17, 1785, DM 14C7.
"Daily going over": Richard Butler and Samuel H. Parsons to the President of Congress, February 1, 1786, DM 15S7–8.
"The Indians seem determined": quoted in RCD, 280.
"Though we hear much": Arthur St. Clair to Secretary of War, January 27, 1788, quoted in White, *Middleground*, 418.
"Ye indians": Isaac Ruddell, c. 1785, quoted in Bakeless, *Daniel Boone*, 315.
"You are amedetly": DB to unknown correspondent, February 15, 1783, DM 14C2–2[1].

"An Inden Warr": DB to Governor Patrick Henry, August 16, 1785, DM 32C81A.

"Plundered them": Richard Butler and Samuel H. Parsons to the President of Congress, February 1, 1786, DM 15S7–8.

"Robbing the Indians": diary of Gen. Richard Butler, quoted in White, *Middleground*, 411n.

"Why de debil?": LCD interview with Joseph Scholl, 1868, DM 24S217.

"Be done to secure": Col. Levi Todd to Governor Patrick Henry, June 22, 1786, in *Calendar of Virginia State Papers*, 4:151.

"Will Bee No Baryer": DB to Governor Patrick Henry, August 16, 1785, DM 32C81A.

"Rose their Yankee colours": Simon Girty to Alexander McKee, October 11, 1786, *Michigan Historical Collections* 24 (1895) :35.

"Who hacked the squaws?": LCD interview with Abner Bryan, 1890, DM 4C50.

"Mind that fellow!": NOB, DM 6S161.

"God damn, you": LCD interview with William Cassidy, 1866, DM 20S192.

"The Indians were obliged": W. Ancrum, October 20, 1786, *Michigan Historical Collections* 24 (1895) :37.

"Would not fly": Josiah Harmar, November 15, 1786, quoted in RCD, 298.

"Blue Lick play": JDS interview with Isaac Clinkenbeard, c. 1840s, DM 11CC3.

"Fine looking young warrior": NOB, DM 6S159.

"Went and peeped": JDS interview with Isaac Clinkenbeard, c. 1840s, DM 11CC3.

"They laid in ashes": W. Ancrum, October 20, 1786, *Michigan Historical Collections* 24 (1895) :37.

"19 galons": DB account books, reprinted in David I. Bushnell, Jr., "Daniel Boone at Limestone, 1786–1787," *Virginia Magazine of History and Biography* 25 (1917) :1–11.

"Collect the whole": *Virginia Gazette*, April 19, 1787, quoted in Bushnell, "Daniel Boone at Limestone," 1–2.

"I am hire with my hands full": DB to Robert Patterson, March 16, 1787, DM 26C176.

"Shanee Chief": DB account books, reprinted in Bushnell, "Daniel Boone at Limestone."

"Our people is scattered" and following speech by Logan: quoted in the *Kentucky Gazette*, August 25, 1787, clipping in DM 33S17–25.

"She seemed broken": LCD interview with Annah Boone Nicholson, 1858, DM 7S35–38.

"And he would take her home": Boone Ballard to LCD, December 6, 1882, DM 14C50[1].

"An Indian beating music" and following quotes in this paragraph: LCD interview with George Edwards, 1863, DM 19S82–83.

"Boone! Boone!": JDS interview with Thomas Jones, c. 1840s, DM 12CC233; JDS interview with John Hanks, c. 1840s, DM 12CC141.

"I heartily": Charles Yancey to DB, January 14, 1788, DM 27C1.

"In cherry blossom season": NOB, DM 6S167–72.

"Came from Kentucky": Thomas E. Lee to LCD, January 12, 1853, DM 1C37.

"Was very pleasant": John F. Watson to LCD, March 4, 1853, DM 1C19.

"Col. Boone left this garrison": Josiah Harmar, May 13, 1789, quoted in DM 14C97.

"I took breakfast": Joel Watkins, "Diary of 1789," MS, Codex 189, DC.

"Grate Conhowway": DB to Hart and Richardson, July 30, 1789, DM 14C92.

"I have concluded": PH, DM 20C84[52–61].

Chapter Eight. A Wanderer in the World: 1789 to 1811

"A most beautiful place": Joel Watkins, May 15, 1789, diary, Codex 198, DC.

"Dripped grease": JDS interview with James Lane, c. 1840s, DM 12CC56–57.

"We have sent you": M. W. Vanlear to DB, April 27, 1790, DM 27C6.

"Request your Assistance": M. W. Vanlear to DB, March 6, 1792, DM 27C10.

"Laide off for Willeam Allin": DB survey, June 14, 1791, DM 14C82.
"Had several narrow escapes": LCD interview with Daniel Boone (son of Daniel Morgan Boone), 1868, DM 23S163–64.
"Killed young Daniel Boone": George Clendenin to Governor of Virginia, December 22, 1789, DM 6S333.
"I shall be in Philadelphia": DB to John Philips and John Young, July 30, 1789, DM 14C93–93[1].
"Killed or taken": *United States Gazette*, April 27, 1793, clipping in DM 15C15.
"At an open and fair election": quoted in Roy Bird Cook, *The Annals of Fort Lee* (Charleston: West Virginia Review Press, 1935), 102.
"Name the one you want": John H. Crawford to LCD, September 10, 1884, DM 20C31.
"Sum purson": DB to Governor Henry Lee, December 13, 1791, DM 14C105.
"Without change or barter": DB receipt, December 22, 1791, *Calendar of Virginia State Papers*, 5:416.
"A fitt and proper person": DB to Governor Henry Lee, December 15, 1791, AHC.
"In consequence": George Clendenin to Governor Henry Lee, December 18, 1794, *Calendar of Virginia State Papers*, 7:405–6.
"Caperton did not do": quoted in W. S. Laidley, "Daniel Boone in the Kanawha Valley," *RKHS* 2 (1913):9–12.
"Total non-compliance": George Clendenin to Governor Henry Lee, September 21, 1792, *Calendar of Virginia State Papers*, 6:67.
"Never to contest" and following quote: NOB, DM 6S217–18.
"I have ever been friendly": Charles Yancey to DB, February 29, 1796, DM 15C32–35.
"Come young man": Paddy Huddleston, quoted in J. P. Hale, "Daniel Boone," 85.
"Could kill more deer": LCD interview with Edward Bryan, 1863, DM 19S170.
"Some half-faced camps": LCD interview with William Champ, 1863, DM 15C31.
"Killed eleven by late breakfast": Ralph Clayton to LCD, April 10, 1883, DM 16C44[4]–45.

"Quietness and safety": NOB, DM 6S205.
"At the time": DB, quoted by John James Audubon, *Delineations of American Scenery and Character* (New York: G. A. Baker, 1926), 115.
"I think my Self intitled": DB to Governor Isaac Shelby, February 11, 1796, quoted in Samuel M Wilson, "Daniel Boone, 1734–1934," in *The Daniel Boone Bicentennial* (n.p.: n.p., n.d. [1936]), 44.
"Boone I believe": Nathaniel Hart, [Jr.] to Thomas Hart, January 10, 1791, MS, FC.
"To convict Boone": quoted in J. R. Cooper, transcript of article of April 19, 1925, in the *Lexington Herald*, KHS.
"Money is so scarce": John Grant to DB, September 4, 1805, DM 27C79.
"Never troubled": NOB, DM 6S215–16.
"Not found": arrest warrant, November 29, 1798, Daniel Boone Collection, FC.
"I see no other means": Zenon Trudeau to Governor-General Francois Luis Hector Carondelet, January 15, 1798, in A. P. Nasatir, ed., *Before Lewis and Clark: Documents Illustrating the History of the Missouri, 1785–1804* (St. Louis: St. Louis Documents Foundation, 1952), 542–43.
"The poorer Class": John Breckinridge to James Breckinridge, May 9, 1797, quoted in Fredrika Johanna Teute, "Land, Liberty, and Labor in the Post-Revolutionary Era: Kentucky as the Promised Land" (Ph.D. thesis, Johns Hopkins University, 1988), 385.
"There seems at present": William Lytle to John Breckrenridge, March 11, 1797, quoted in Teute, "Land Liberty, and Labor," 385.
"American families": Zenon Trudeau to Governor-General Francois Luis Hector Carondelet, July 3, 1796, in Nasatir, *Before Lewis and Clark*, 442.
"About two hundred Families": James Mackay to Governor-General Gayoso de Lemos, November 28, 1798, in Nasatir, *Before Lewis and Clark*, 588.
"A person named Boone": Vincente Folch, "Reflections on Louisiana," 1803, in James Alexander Robertson, *Louisiana under the Rule of Spain, France, and the United States, 1785–1807* (Cleveland: Arthur H. Clark, 1911), 2:343.

"Had he not firmly believed": DB, quoted in Peck, *Life of Boone*, 167.

"I wish a hundred thousand": Jefferson, quoted in William E. Foley, *The Genesis of Missouri: From Wilderness Outpost to Statehood* (Columbia: University of Missouri Press, 1989), 61.

"As high a grade": DBB to LCD, February 27, 1843, DM 22C6[2].

"To embrace": NOB, DM 6S213–14.

"Owner of four slaves": concession of land to Daniel Morgan Boone, September 1, 1797, Boone Family Papers, MHS.

"Harrasd and pestered": DBB to LCD, February 27, 1843, DM 22C7.

"Was soured": LCD interview with Edward Coles, 1848, DM 6S310–11.

"Were got too proud": Baily, *Journal of a Tour*, 115–17.

"Became somewhat disheartened": ELC to LCD, March 14, 1885, DM 21C24[10].

"The handsomest young lady": *History of the Lower Scioto Valley*, quoted in DM 6S332.

"On the first of October": quoted in Spraker, *The Boone Family*, 126–27.

"A sad looking horse": John M. Krum to LCD, January 17, 1883, DM 16C54[1–2].

"Associate of M. Daniel Boone": Robert Hall, land concession [original in French], January 26, 1798 [sic], DM 27C68.

"The ordinary occupations": French visitor quoted in Folley, *Genesis of Missouri*, 87.

"On his arrival": DB, quoted in *American State Papers. Public Lands* (Washington, D.C.: Gales and Seaton, 1834), 2:473.

"Raised a grate laugh": Samuel Boone to LCD, July 5, 1854, DM 22C73[3].

"L'obligation de plus": Antoine Foulard, receipt [original in French], DM 27C70.

"No earthly use": DBC, DM 30C95–96.

"Was a man": Dr. S. Paul Jones to LCD, May 13, 1887, DM 21C1[5–6].

"He never was so mad": S. H. Jones to LCD, April 23, 1887, DM 21C15[1–2].

"Saindic de la Femme Ozage": Andre Foulard, receipt [original in French], March 14, 1801, DM 27C70.

"Permistion to Benjamin Gardner": DB, certificate, February 23, 1806, DM 6S326.
"Had some differance": DB document, June 30, 1804, DM 15C65.
"Whipped and cleared": Bryan and Rose, *Pioneer Families of Missouri*, 89.
"Let not my gray hairs" and subsequent story: Millard Fillmore Stipes, *Gleanings in Missouri History* (Jamesport, Mo.: Millard Fillmore Stipes, 1904), 196.
"Governed more by *equity*": NOB, DM 6S225.
"Mr. Boone, a respectable old man": Governor Carlos Dehault Delassus, MS, DM 15C64.
"One James Davis": indictment reprinted in *Missouri Historical Review* 3 (1908–9) :200.
"A bad tempered": NOB, DM 6S152.
"Used to whip": ELC to LCD, May 3, 1887, DM 21C63[3].
"Hays whipped her badly": LCD interview with Abner Bryan, 1890, DM 4C60.
"Became dissapated": G. Hedrick to LCD, June 26, 1866, DM 28C67.
"A drunken spree": JDS interview with Samuel Treble, c. 1840s, DM 12CC44.
"Still cursing Davis": LCD interview with Abner Bryan, 1890, DM 4C58.
"Weakly": DBC, DM 30C73–74.
"Drank himself to death": DBC, DM 30C73–74; LCD interview with John Scholl, 1868, DM 22S273.
"The men and dogs": unidentified correspondent, quoted in Bryan and Rose, *Pioneer Families of Missouri*, 77–78.
"The best draft": NOB, DM 6S243–44.
"Could sit": William S. Bryan, "Daniel Boone in Missouri," *Missouri Historical Review* 3 (1906–9) :92–93.
"Here are turkies": Samuel Millard to Rev. Thomas P. Hinds, October 14, 1844, DM 24C112.
"Clear out!" and following quote in this paragraph: NOB, DM 6S232.
"I am informed": James Wilkinson, quoted in Robert T. Bray, "Boone's Lick Salt Works, 1805–33," *Missouri Archaeologist* 48 (1987) :1–66.

"He seemed opposed": LCD interview with Joseph McCormick, 1871, DM 30C108–11.

"Free enjoyment of their liberty": Eugene Morrow Violette, "Spanish Land Claims in Missouri," *Washington University Studies* 8, no. 2 (1921) :167–200.

"As to the propriety": *American State Papers. Public Lands*, 2:473.

"He was too old": LCD interview with Stephen Hempstead, 1868, DM 22S188–89.

"It was too late": JDS interview with DBB, 1844, DM 22C14[14].

"The weather was stormy": Bryan and Rose, *Pioneer Families of Missouri*, 50–51.

"Worn-out man": "Report of the Congressional Select Committee," January 29, 1813, DM 16S150–55.

"Sent me to St. Charles": SH to LCD, December 23, 1862, DM 16C75.

"Boone considered himself": LCD interview with John Shaw, 1855, in *The Jess M. Thompson Pike County History* (n.p. [Pittsfield, Ill.]: n.p. [Pike County Historical Society] n.d. [1967]), 70.

"It is the opinion": *American State Papers. Public Lands*, 2:473.

"Feeble": LCD interview with Joseph McCormick, 1871, DM 30C111.

"By altering the laws": LCD interview with John Scholl, 1868, DM 22S273.

"You would if you knew": LCD interview with John and Sarah Kenton McCord, 1851, DM 5S172; LCD interview with William M. Kenton, 1851, DM 5S125.

"To chew my venison": LCD interview with Elijah Bryan, 1868, DM 23S243.

"High up the Missouri": LCD interview with George W. Stoner, 1868, DM 24C55[10–11].

"With housing over the cargo": SH to LCD, March 6, 1863, DM 16C78.

"Had lately returned": John Bradbury, *Travels in the Interior of America [1819]. Early Western Travels, 1748–1846*, ed. RGT (Cleveland: Arthur H. Clark Company, 1904), 5:44.

"The old man was still erect": Washington Irving, *Astoria, or,*

Anecdotes of an Enterprise beyond the Rocky Mountains, ed. William H. Goetzmann (1836; Philadelphia: J. B. Lippincott, 1961), 1:117.

Part Three

"We are informed": *Chillicothe Supporter*, copied in *Niles Weekly Register* 15 (September 19, 1818) :64.

"Induced by curiosity": "A Traveller," in the *New-York Statesman*, copied in the Cincinnati *National Republican*, August 19, 1823, DM 16C67.

"Seeing strangers approaching": NOB, DM 6S277.

"Though at first reserved": LCD interview with Edward Coles, 1848, DM 6S311.

"I would not believe": Peck, *Life of Daniel Boone*, 4.

"How we Live": DB to Sarah Boone, October 19, 1816, DM 27C88.

"Well, Sucky": ELC to LCD, May 25, 1885, DM 21C45[2–3].

"An irritable expression": Peck, *Life of Daniel Boone*, 186–89.

"Naturally romantic": "A Traveller," DM 16C67.

"He had settled": B. J. Goe to LCD, September 4, 1887, DM 16C94.

"Formed a determination": Joseph Bryan to LCD, December 14, 1866, DM 22C23[2–3].

"His misfortune did not end": DBB to LCD, April 14, 1843, DM 22C7.

"What lands he had secured": David Todd, quoted in Kellogg, "The Fame of Daniel Boone," 49.

"Respected the rights": LCD interview with John Shaw, 1855, in *Jess M. Thompson Pike County History*, 70.

"Always meet them frankly": LCD interview with Joseph McCormick, 1871, DM 30C110–13.

"Seek refuge": "A Traveller," DM 16C67.

"While he could never": *Life and Adventures of Colonel Daniel Boon, the First White Settler of the State of Kentucky* (1823; reprint, New York: Heartman's Historical Series, 1916) :33.

"Never delighted": Peck, *Life of Daniel Boone*, 186–89.

"From the love of Nature": DBC, DM 30C78.

"I am very sorry to say": Bettie T. Bryan to LCD, August 18, 1884, DM 22C25.

"The *instrument*": "A Traveller," DM 16C67.

"Retired through choice": Henry Marie Brackenridge, *Views of Louisiana Together with a Journal of a Voyage up the Missouri River* (1814; Chicago: Quadrangle Books, 1962), 116–19.

"This singular man": *Columbia Centinel*, copied in *Niles Weekly Register* 10 (June 15, 1816) :261 (misprinted 361).

"Nothing embitters"; and following quotes: "A Traveller"; DM 16C67.

Chapter Nine. God Never Made a Man of My Prisipel to Be Lost: 1811 to 1820

"Lips were compressed": Bryan, *Pioneer Families of Missouri*, 103–4.

"Perfectly cool": NOB, DM 6S269–70.

"He seemed to be stopping": DBC, DM 30C70.

"She would have": DBC, DM 30C67–69.

"Flew into a passion": Bryan, *Pioneer Families of Missouri*, 95–100.

"Tidings came": DBC, DM 30C75.

"The Saddest affliction": ELC to LCD, May 25, 1885, DM 21C45[2–3].

"After Grandmother Boone died": ELC to LCD, May 11, 1891, DM 21C70.

"He was no beggar": LCD interview with Edward Coles, 1848, DM 6S310–11.

"Had kept no book account": Peck, *Life of Daniel Boone*, 174.

"I have come here": Joseph Trotter, quoted in F. W. Houston to LCD, November 2, 1887, DM 20C88[4–5].

"I have settled": PH, DM 20C84[61–64].

"Now I am ready": Peck, *Life of Daniel Boone*, 174.

"My companion": Audubon, *Delineations of American Scenery and Character*, 61, 111; dated by Maria R. Audubon in *Audubon and his Journals*, 2:241.

"Medium sized": LCD interview with Mr. Gossett, c. 1841–43, DM 31S325.

"Capable of endurance": R. W. Wells to LCD, July 20, 1862, DM 28C53.
"Feeble": ELC to LCD, May 11, 1891, DM 21C70.
"I dislike to be in a crowd": Buckner Payne to LCD, November 6, December 8, and December 26, 1875, and January, 1876, DM 16C23–26.
"He was greatly insulted": Sarah Hunter to LCD, December 15, 1855, DM 22C65.
"I remember his remark": Joseph Bryan to LCD, December 14, 1866, DM 22C23[2–3].
"The romance": NOB, DM 6S231.
"Come a great distance": NOB, DM 6S251–52.
"Disgusted and disheartened": MB, DM 19C40–46.
"Traveler's Rest": Willard Rouse Jillson, "Squire Boone: A Sketch of His Life and an Appraisement of His Influence on the Early Settlement of Kentucky," *FCHQ* 16 (1942) :141–71.
"He never received": NOB, DM 6S39–40.
"And was rather fond": Bryan, *Pioneer Families of Missouri*, 83–84.
"When you experienced a change": James E. Welch, in the Louisville *Christian Repository*, March 1860, in DM 16C47.
"Very few of the pioneers": Bryan, *Pioneer Families of Missouri*, 81.
"Ain't that God damned good news?": J. T. Alderman, "Notes on Davie County," AHC.
"Well remembered": NOB, DM 6S280–81.
"You can gass at my feilings": DB to Sarah Day Boone, October 16, 1816, DM 27C88.
"I cannot think": quoted in Richard Hofstader, *America at 1750: A Social Portrait* (New York: Random House, 1971), 192.
"He worshipped": Flint, *Biographical Memoir of Daniel Boone*, 186.
"Mixture of their own opinions": *ST*, 40–41.
"First principle": Thomas Wildcat Alford, *Civilization* (Norman: University of Oklahoma Press, 1936), 19–20.
"Peaceable and well disposed": quoted in Foley, *Genesis of Missouri*, 217.
"Your grandfather": DBC, DM 30C66–67.

"Talk over their old narotives": John C. Boone to LCD, November 20, 1890, DM 16C132.

"All the grandchildren": DBC, DM 30C72.

"Pretty much a savage": LCD interview with John Givson, 1868, DM 15C107.

"We have been honored": *Columbian Centinel*, copied in *Niles Weekly Register* 10 (June 15, 1816) :261 (misprinted 361).

"As naturally inclined" and following quotes in this paragraph: NOB, DM 6S273–77.

"His fondness": David Todd, quoted in Kellogg, "Fame of Daniel Boone," 49.

"Making a powder-horn": Nathan Kouns to LCD, January 16, 1863, DM 16C36.

"Too rough and uncouth": NOB, DM 6S273–77.

"Idle whim": Elizabeth Corbin to M. D. Lewis, in the St. Louis *Daily Dispatch*, April 2, 1868, DM 16C97.

"He would get it down": DBC, DM 30C78.

"To show how well": A. J. Coshow, in the *Republic*, 1894, in Miscellaneous Clippings, MHS.

"Taken many a nice nap": LCD interview with Samuel Boone, 1868, DM 22S259–60.

"Fallen into a second childhood": Elizabeth Corbin to M. D. Lewis, in St. Louis *Daily Dispatch*, April 2, 1868, DM 16C97.

"He appeared quite smart": LCD interview with Samuel Boone, 1868, DM 22S259–60.

"Possum up a green stump": ELC to LCD, May 11, 1891, DM 21C70.

"Better mend a fault" and following quote: DBC, DM 30C78.

"A man needs": LCD interview with Joseph Scholl, 1868, DM 24S217.

"I found the object": Harding, *My Egotistography*, 35–36.

"Being governed by feelings": Bryan, *Pioneer Families of Missouri*, 2–3.

"They all thought it good": NOB, DM 6S278–79.

"The deep feeling": H. C. Dodge to LCD, January 25, 1883, DM 16C27.

"He was about worn out" and other deathbed quotes: DBC, DM 30C79–83.

"Only an ordinary preacher": LCD interview with Abner Bryan, 1890, DM 4C57.

Chapter Ten. Left Until I'm Put in the Ground: Myth and Memory

"Handsome, educated young lady": Clement L. Martzolff, ed., "The Autobiography of Thomas Ewing," *Ohio Archaeological and Historical Quarterly* 22 (1913) :155.

"Contained a historical basis": Ralph Clayton to *St. Louis Christian Advocate*, May 30, 1877, DM 7C43[1–5]; LCD interview with Joseph Scholl, 1868, DM 24S218.

"Open in the regions of the West" and subsequent quotes: Daniel Bryan, *The Mountain Muse: comprising the Adventures of Daniel Boone; and the power of virtuous and refined Beauty* (Harrisonburg, Va: Davidson and Bourne, 1813).

"Needs nothing": *Analectic Magazine* 6 (1815) :170, quoted in John P. McWilliams, Jr., *The American Epic: Transforming a Genre, 1770–1860* (Cambridge: Cambridge University Press, 1989), 101.

"Rude undisciplined fancy": Daniel Bryan, *The Appeal for Suffering Genius* (1826), quoted in McWilliams, *The American Epic*, 259n. (McWilliams mistakenly identifies the poet as Boone's nephew, Daniel Boone Bryan of Kentucky.)

"Few men have excelled": John Coburn, MS, in DM 16C85.

"Empire, or rule": DBC, DM 30C78.

"Entered into the wilderness": Peck, *Life of Daniel Boone*, 186–89.

"Rich and boundless": Flint, *Biographical Memoir of Daniel Boone*, 171.

"Consigned very unjustly": Timothy Flint, *Indian Wars of the West* (Cincinnati: E. H. Flint, 1833), 233.

"Achilles of the West": Timothy Flint, *Recollections of the Last Ten Years in the Valley of the Mississippi*, ed. George R. Brooks (1826; Carbondale: Southern Illinois University Press, 1968), 51.

"Little better" and following quote: James Hall, *Sketches of History, Life and Manners in the West* (Cincinnati: Hubbard and Edmands, 1834), 1:241.

"The account": "Statement of Septimus Schull [sic]," 1833, DM 11CC52.

"Could any man of reason": DBB to LCD, October 24, 1843, DM 22C9[3].

"Boone's Parson Weems": Marshall W. Fishwick, "Daniel Boone and the Pattern of the Western Hero," *FCHQ* 27 (1953) :127.

"Moral sublimity": Timothy Flint, preface to *Personal Narrative of James O. Pattie*, ed. Richard Batman (1831; Missoula, Mont.: Mountain Press, 1988), viii.

"Energy, resolution, manliness": Howard R. Lamar, ed., *The Reader's Encyclopedia of the American West* (New York: Thomas Y. Crowell, 1977), 114.

"A world of his own": Christopher Mann to LCD, October 15, 1883, DM 15C26.

"They crowded me": B. H. Payne to LCD, March 1, 1879, DM 15C54.

"A damned Yankee": *Niles Weekly Register* 24 (May 17, 1823): 166; *Western Sun*, June 14, 1823, quoted in Thomas D. Clark, *The Rampaging Frontier: Manners and Humors of Pioneer Days in the South and the Middle West* (Indianapolis: Bobbs-Merrill, 1939), 310; *Life and Adventures of Colonel Daniel Boon*, 31.

"The great object": *Life and Adventures of Colonel Daniel Boon*, 31, 33.

"Silent and dejected": Samuel Griswold Goodrich, ed., *The Token, a Christmas and New Year's Present* (Boston: n.p., 1828), 48f.; see J. Gray Sweeney, *The Columbus of the Woods: Daniel Boon and the Typology of Manifest Destiny* (St. Louis: Washington University Gallery of Art, 1992), 19–23.

"Not as a misanthrope": New York *American*, quoted in *Niles Weekly Register* 24 (May 17, 1823) :166.

"A state of innocence": Gilbert Imlay, *A Topographical Description of the Western Territory of North America* (London: J. Debrett, 1793).

"The bulk of mankind": Gilbert Imlay, *The Emigrants*, ed. Robert B. Hare (1793; Gainesville, Fla: Scholars' Facsimiles and Reprints, 1964).

"A kind of patriarchal government": Brackenridge, *Views of Louisiana*, 116–19.

"Of the great names": Truman Guy Steffan and Willis W. Pratt, eds., *Byron's Don Juan: A Variorum Edition*, 2d ed. (Austin: University of Texas Press, 1971), 3:142–46.

"Effigies of old Daniel Boone": *Port Folio* 15 (March 1823):232.

"Though adverse to the modes of life": W. H. Garnor in *North American Review* 23 (1826), reprinted in George Dekker and John P. McWilliams, eds., *Fenimore Cooper: The Critical Heritage* (London: Routledge & Kegan Paul, 1973), 114.

"The character of Daniel Boone": Francis Parkman, "The Works of James Fenimore Cooper," *North American Review* 74 (1852):151.

"The most memorable character": epigram to *The Leatherstocking Saga*, ed. Alan Nevins (New York: Pantheon, 1954).

"Philosopher of the wilderness": from the 1851 intro. to James Fenimore Cooper, *The Prairie: A Tale* (New York: Signet/New American Library, 1964), vii; quotes are otherwise taken from the modern standard texts in *The Leatherstocking Tales* (New York: Library of America, 1985).

"A reader of Mr. Cooper's": Cecil B. Hartley, *Life and Times of Col. Daniel Boone* (1860), quoted in Kent Steckmesser, *The Western Hero in History and Legend* (Norman: University of Oklahoma Press, 1965), 7, who makes the point about fiction and history.

"The venerable Col. DANIEL BOONE": *Missouri Gazette*, October 11, 1820, quoted in Clifford Amyz, "The Authentic Image of Daniel Boone," *Missouri Historical Review* 82 (1988):154–55.

"Good copy": quoted in Leah Lipton, "Chester Harding and the Life Portrait of Daniel Boone," *American Art Journal* 16 (1984):4–19.

"Old woodcut": Nancy Heath to William Riley Willsey, n.d., cited in *Jess M. Thompson Pike County History*, 258.

"Made him look too tall": JDS interview with Francis Flournoy Jackson, c. 1858, DM 15CC7–8.

"We are a hardy freeborn race": Benjamin A. Botkin, ed., *Treasury of American Folklore* (New York: Crown, 1944), 9–12.

"Prolonged whoop or howl": Noah M. Ludlow, *Dramatic Life As I Found It* (St. Louis: G. I. Jones, 1880), 238.

"We look here in vain": McClung, *Sketches of Western Adventure*, 54, 79.

"Poetical illusions": Robert Montgomery Bird, *Nick of the Woods; or, The Jibbenainosay: A Tale of Kentucky* (1837), quoted in Richard Drinnon, *Facing West: The Metaphysics of Indian Hating and Empire Building* (1980; New York: Schocken, 1990), 163.

"Sacrificed the truth": William Gilmore Simms, "Daniel Boon, the First Hunter of Kentucky," *Southern and Western Magazine and Review* 1 (1845) :225–26.

"More real satisfaction": Emerson Bennett, *Ella Barnwell: A Historical Romance of Border Life* (Cincinatti: U. P. James, 1853), 10.

"Real sympathy": John Stevens Cabot Abbott, *Daniel Boone, The Pioneer of Kentucky* (New York: Dodd and Mead, 1872), 198.

"Having killed an enemy": J. W. Cunningham to LCD, January 16, 1883, DM 16C31.

"Played the great fool": Cody, *Story of the Wild West*, 64.

"The peril": quoted in Drinnon, *Facing West*, 120.

"I am now painting": quoted in Elizabeth Johns, "The 'Missouri Artist' as Artist," in *George Caleb Bingham* (New York: St. Louis Art Museum in association with Harry N. Abrams, 1990), 136.

"I started in to listen": W. S. Bryan to Benjamin Emmons, December 6, 1937, William S. Bryan Papers, MHS.

"Crazy about that woman": Caroline Gordon, *Green Centuries* (New York: Charles Scribner's Sons, 1941), 35.

"Two months!": Shirley Seifert, *Never No More* (Philadelphia: J. B. Lippincott, 1964), 261.

"Messenger to the chaotic part": Elizabeth Madox Roberts, *The Great Meadow* (New York: Viking Press, 1930), 338.

"Men are free": D. H. Lawrence, *Studies in Classic American Literature* (New York: Thomas Seltzer, 1923), 9, 91, 86, 92.

"Lived to enjoy ecstasy": Williams, *In the American Grain*, 136–37, 213.

"There are two ways": D. H. Lawrence, "American Heroes," *The Nation* 112 (April 14, 1926) :413.

"He traced ahead": William Stafford, "For the Grave of Daniel Boone," in Alexander W. Allison, ed., *The Norton Anthology of Poetry* (New York: W. W. Norton, 1983).

"I felt the grass": Susan Mitchell, "Boone," in Jack Myers and Roger Weingarten, eds., *New American Poets of the 80s* (Green Harbor, Mass.: Wampeter Press, 1984).

"Read Imlay's": Mrs. W. W. Page to LCD, December 14, 1858, DM 22C42.

"Discrepancies and conflictions": LCD, quoted in William B. Hesseltine, *Pioneer's Mission: The Story of Lyman Copeland Draper* (Madison: State Historical Society of Wisconsin, 1954), 27, 41–42.

"I am a small bit of a fellow": quoted in Hesseltine, *Pioneer's Mission*, 41–42.

"The pioneer of the West": quoted in Kellogg, "The Fame of Daniel Boone," 60.

"Written in a poor hand": Edward Boone Scholl to LCD, August 23, 1854, DM 23C7[5].

"The man who stole": quoted in Hesseltine, *Pioneer's Mission*, vii.

"Grieve about": Harriet Boone Baber to LCD, May 8, 1861, DM 23C34[1–2].

"They were affectionate": ELC to LCD, March 14, 1885, DM 21C24[9].

"A remarkable woodsman": quoted in Foley, *The Genesis of Missouri*, 221.

"What it was to be rich": quoted in Lilian Hays Oliver, *Some Boone Descendants and Kindred of the St. Charles District* (Burlington, Vt.: Chedwato Service, 1964), 42.

"Carefully rolled up": LCD quoted in Hesseltine, *Pioneer's Mission*, 133.

"Why don't you publish": Charles Larrabee to LCD, quoted in Hesseltine, *Pioneer's Mission*, 71.

"You have already dispatched": quoted in Hesseltine, *Pioneer's Mission*, 64.

"I have wasted my life": quoted in RGT, "Lyman C. Draper: A Memoir," in *Wisconsin Historical Collections* 1 (1903) :xvii.

"When you are gone": Cyrus Woodman to LCD, January 8, 1869, quoted in Larry Gara, "Lyman Copeland Draper," *Keepers of the Past*, ed. Clifford L. Lord (Chapel Hill: University of North Carolina Press, 1965), 50.

"A few brief notes": Peck, *Life of Daniel Boone*, 10, 187.

"Poets, historians, and orators": RGT, *Daniel Boone* (New York: D. Appleton and Company, 1902), vii, 201.

"The greatest living authority": quoted in "The Winners of the West," *Sky-Land Magazine* (September 1914) :647.

"Daniel Boone Only the Agent": *North Carolina Review* 1 (October 1910); quotes are from the scholarly version of this essay, "The Creative Forces in Westward Expansion."

"Dr. Henderson's unsupported statements": John P. Arthur to Archibald Henderson, December 15, 1915, AHC.

"The conjured": Clarence Walworth Alvord, "Daniel Boone," *American Mercury* 8 (1926) :266–70.

"Antiquated and out-of-date" and following quotes of this incident: *Boone Bulletin* 2, nos. 10–11 (1934–39) :201; Louisville *Courier-Journal*, November 18, 1962, clipping in BBF.

"Irresponsible hunter" and following quotes in this paragraph: *Harrodsburg Herald*, May 25, 1962; Louisville *Courier-Journal*, November 18, 1962; Louisville *Courier-Journal Magazine*, December 2, 1962, and December 9, 1962, clippings in BBF.

"Sufficient historical importance" and following quotes in this paragraph: "Daniel Boone Draft Trail Study," National Parks Service, U.S. Department of the Interior (June 1982); *Senate Report 98–557, 98th Congress, 2d Session; House Report 98–719, 98th Congress, 2d Session.*

"Cow-boy Orator": Nickell and Fischer, "Daniel Boone Fakelore," 451.

"The so called relicts": Ben L. Emmons to Nettie Beauregard, May 13, 1926, Boone Family Papers, MHS.

"Built by Boone": handbill in DB file, Iconographic Collections, State Historical Society of Wisconsin, Madison.

"A huntsman's paradise": *Kansas City Times*, 1925, Miscellaneous Clippings, MHS.

"The old Nathan Boone house": William Boone Douglass to Bess L. Hawthorne, May 26, 1927, Boone Family Papers, MHS.

"Daniel's boyhood home": *Daniel Boone Homestead, Berks County, PA*, pamphlet, Pennsylvania Historical and Museum Commission, 1988.

"Thicket of briars": unidentified clipping copying the St. Louis

New Era, February 1845, DM 28CC57; cf. *Literary Journal*, February 1845, DM 16C33.

"In those days": Elijah Bryan to LCD, May 12, 1885, DM 4C33.

"This should not be": for this correspondence see "Removal of Boone Remains," Manuscript Collection, KHS, as well as "Daniel Boone and the Frankfort Cemetery," *RKHS* 50 (1952):217–18.

"Opposed to a removal": Thomas L. Crittenden and William Boone to proprietors, July 17, 1845, in "Removal of Boone Remains," KHS.

"Erect a monument": David Gardyne to Benjamin Emmons, September 23, 1915, enclosed in Benjamin Emmons to Archibald Henderson, September 20, 1915, in AHC.

"Still numerous descendants": St. Louis *New Era*, datelined Marthasville, July 17, 1845, copied in *Frankfort Commonwealth*, August 5, 1845, quoted in "Daniel Boone and the Frankfort Cemetery," 220–21.

"Col. Boone's bones": LCD interview with Edward Coles, 1848, DM 6S310–311.

"30 or 40 persons": JDS interview with Jacob Swigert, 1846, DM 11CC289.

"Imposing auspices": *Maysville Eagle*, August 6, 1845, clipping in DM 28CC72.

"The skull of Boone": John Mason Brown, Louisville, to LCD, October 4, 1882, DM 16C82.

"Could jump farther": *Frankfort Commonwealth*, February 9, 1846, quoted in "Daniel Boone and the Frankfort Cemetery," 231–32.

"Has not been a single response": Frankfort *Kentucky Yeoman*, copied in the *Weekly Journal*, September 8, 1848, clipping in DM 29CC125.

"Any ordinary mortal": unidentified Kentucky newspaper, copied in the Chicago *Times*, August 12, 1870, clipping in DM 32C91.

"It is simply scandalous": unidentified clipping, c. 1890s, in "W. B. Stevens Scrapbook," 159, MHS.

"A spasm of Kentucky pride": St. Louis *Globe Democrat*, September 1, 1888, clipping in DM 16C98–99.

"Came quietly": Sylvanus Griswold, quoted in *Missouri Historical Review* 4 (1909–10):44.

"Didn't get Boone": unidentified newspaper clipping, reprinted in Rolla P. Andrae, *A True, Brief History of Daniel Boone* (Defiance, Mo.: Daniel Boone Home, 1985), 90.

"For shame!": statement of George Chester Bryan, October 29, 1915, enclosed in George Chester Bryan to Archibald Henderson, January 25, 1916, AHC.

"It's amazing" and other quotes in this paragraph: St. Louis *Post Dispatch*, September 13, 1987, clipping in MHS; Louisville *Courier-Journal*, December 19, 1977, clipping in BBF.

"The skull of a Negro": Frankfort *State Journal*, June 24, 1983, clipping in BBF.

"We say his remains are here": Lexington *Herald Leader*, July 5, 1985, clipping in BBF.

Index